AF710511

R. KENNETH WALTER

INTRODUCTION TO DATA MANAGEMENT AND FILE DESIGN

A Reston Book
Prentice-Hall
Englewood Cliffs, New Jersey

Library of Congress Cataloging in Publication Data

Walter, R. Kenneth.
Introduction to data management and file design.

Includes bibliographies and index.
1. Data structures (Computer science) 2. File organization (Computer science) 3. Data base management. I. Title.
QA76.9.D35W35 1986 001.64'42 85-10815
ISBN 0-8359-3245-1

A Reston Book
Published by Prentice-Hall
A Division of Simon & Schuster, Inc.
Englewood Cliffs, New Jersey 07632

Copyright © 1986 by Prentice-Hall, Englewood Cliffs, New Jersey 07632

All rights reserved. No part of this book may be reproduced in any way, or by any means, without written permission from the publisher.

10 9 8 7 6 5 4 3 2 1

Printed in The United States of America.

CONTENTS

Chapter 6 Introduction to Linear and Nonlinear Data Structures 141

Chapter 7 Sequential Files and Searching 151

Chapter 8 Linked Lists, Queues, Stacks, and Trees 169

Chapter 9 Sorting 203

Chapter 10 Random Access Files 223

Chapter 11 Partitioned and Indexed Organizations 269

Chapter 12 Developing a Data Base 307

To my wife, Zora

PREFACE

This book discusses data organization, storage media, file design, and data management techniques. It is intended to introduce computer users, professionals, and computer science students who wish to be information systems specialists to computer data storage systems, data representations, and methods of organizing, accessing, sorting, and searching data effectively. The file management techniques that are addressed here arc critical for efficient data handling, whether you use a mainframe with extensive auxiliary storage capability or a microcomputer with a single flexible disk.

Those who use this book should already have an introductory background in the concepts of computer hardware and software and be acquainted with a programming language or be learning computer programming concurrently. Specifically, the data organization and accessing methods that are developed have been recommended for a second course in computing by the ACM Curriculum Committee on Information Systems*. These provide a foundation for a study of advanced computer programming and data base techniques.

A logical progression from storage media, to file design concepts, and finally to actual data handling algorithms is represented by the three major divisions of the book. However, most of the chapters are independent; they may be studied in a different order, if desired. Individual chapters and sections, especially those on Data Representations, Sequential Files, Linked Lists, Stacks, Queues, Sorting, Searching, Random Access Files, Indexed Organizations, Multilists, and Inverted Files, may be used for reference purposes as needed.

Within each chapter are numerous examples, and at the end of each chapter are questions. You will find that the examples and questions are designed not only for review but also to teach, to stretch your understanding, and to help you tie the material together. You are encouraged to study the examples and questions conscientiously. A few answers are provided in the Appendix so that you may check your comprehension. Although a limited number of the questions assume some sophistication in mathematics, the reader who understands elementary algebra should find the text readable and the material easy to master. We urge you to use the algorithms in the final two chapters to actually begin *doing* some file handling on whatever equipment is available to you.

*Nunamaker, J. F., et al. (Eds.). "Infomation Systems Curriculum Recommendations for the '80s: Undergraduate and Graduate Programs," *Communications of the ACM*, 1982, *25*(11), pp. 781-805.

PART I

DATA MANAGEMENT

PROLOGUE

HERMAN HOLLERITH

Herman Hollerith (*Courtesy of International Business Machines Corporation*)

One of the earliest and most lasting data management techniques was invented in 1887 by Herman Hollerith. Hollerith was born in Buffalo, New York, in 1860 and graduated at age 19 from Columbia University. Within a few years, after holding positions with the U.S. Census, at MIT, with the U.S. Patent Office, and as a statistician with the Army Surgeon General, he had developed the tabulating machines which were used for the 1890 Census in the United States, Austria, Canada, Italy, Norway, and Russia. In 1890, Columbia University awarded him a Ph.D. for his achievements.

The familiar punched cards, on which Dr. Hollerith recorded the statistics to be counted by his machines, are still in use in some computing facilities today. They were made the size of the large U. S. dollar bill of the 1890's because it was easy to obtain ready-made cabinets and drawers in which to store them. In 1896 Hollerith formed the Tabulating Machine Company within which he continued to improve his designs and supply statistical systems for government and a number of large corporations.

In order to bow out of business management and devote time to his inventions, Dr. Hollerith sold his patents to a holding company in 1912. He became a consultant, while his old company was absorbed into the new conglomerate which was to become International Business Machines Corporation.

CHAPTER 1

INTRODUCTION TO DATA MANAGEMENT

HISTORY

In the early 1800's Charles Babbage, a man ahead of his time, designed the first mechanical calculating machine which had all of the components of a modern computer, including data storage areas, an output mechanism, a control unit for directing the machine's operations, and an arithmetic logic unit for performing additions at the "lightning" rate of one per second. Babbage did not call the components of his difference and analytical engines by these names, of course, but his design paved the way for later development of these concepts. Babbage's *Reflections on the Decline of Science in England and on Some of its Causes* (London, 1830) led to the foundation of the British Association for the Advancement of Science. His concern was that science not be pursued only by the aristocracy but that it really should be a profession of those who could apply it in business and manufacturing.

After 1842, Babbage's collaborator in computer design was Ada Byron, Countess of Lovelace, the daughter of the poet, Lord Byron. Ada developed the concept of a programming loop and earned the reputation of the first computer programmer. Unfortunately, Ada and Babbage were frustrated in their designs because the technology of the time simply was not capable of building a full-scale difference engine. Babbage's son, after the turn of the 20th century, did have the machine built, and proved that it really worked—unfortunately, long after cancer had claimed Ada's life at age 36.

Virtually all computers before 1950 were calculating machines. When the Electronic Numerical Integrator and Calculator (ENIAC) was built in the early 1940's by John Mauchley and J. Presper Eckert, it could perform 3000 multiplications per second. The ENIAC contained several thousand vacuum tubes. Since the mean lifetime before failure (MLBF) of a vacuum tube was about 3000 hours, one could expect to run the ENIAC for approximately 14 minutes before a breakdown. In those days, backup of data was already very important. The computer would be run for 10 (or, if you were brave, 20) minutes; then the contents of memory would be dumped onto a secondary storage medium, so that a relatively smooth startup could be achieved when the computer did go down. Often, hours were spent diagnosing the source of the failure before the defective tube was found and replaced.

In those early days programming a computer was a very different task from now. Rather than having the program stored in memory, the computer had to be rewired or instructions entered by switches for each program change. Though slow and ponderous, the machines still represented a tremendous breakthrough; even with hours of downtime and hours of programming, calculations were performed much more rapidly and accurately than could be done by hand.

John von Neumann is given credit for developing the concept of storing programs in the computer, along with the data, in the late 1940's. Thereafter, changing a program simply meant changing the contents of the memory locations where the program was stored. The development of codes for storing instructions and distinguishing them from data was a major accomplishment of this period.

By the mid 1950's most programmers began to tire of writing their own routines for driving auxiliary memory and input/output (I/O) devices each time a new program was written. From each other, they were borrowing stacks of cards which contained prewritten programs to handle I/O operations. Ultimately, a number of general purpose I/O subroutines were written which could be loaded with appropriate interpreters each time a program was run. By the late 1950's FORTRAN compile-and-go routines had been composed. The programmer needed only to load program and data into the computer; the routines for compilation and I/O were already within the computer memory or readily accessible to the computer from magnetic tape or another card reader. By the early 1960's Input/Output Management Programs and routines to control the flow of jobs through the machine were built into most large computers. These programs were stored as *Operating Systems* on tape, drum, or disk auxiliary storage known as the "system residence" devices.

OPERATING SYSTEMS

Why An Operating System?

Operating Systems are a set of programs stored more or less permanently within the computer memory for handling tasks that have to be done for most jobs. They made it easier for programmers and began to open entirely new possibilities for using computers. Until the 1960's most computers had been run in an "open shop"; when programmers wanted to run their jobs, they signed up on the schedule for a block of time when they could use the computer. (For some reason this seemed to occur most often in the wee hours of the morning.) It was their responsibility to learn how to operate the computer, much as personal microcomputer owners now do. The programmers would load whatever decks of cards they needed, including compilers and I/O handlers if necessary, into the card reader, punch the button, and wait to see what happened. Much of their time was spent looking at lights on the console and flipping switches to correct errors. The computer was idle much of the time while the programmer/operators were trying to figure out why their programs were not working. Often they performed a core dump, listing out the contents of primary memory, and took the listings home to study before their next turn at the machine.

It was apparent that the "open shop" was a tremendous waste of programmer talent, computer time, and money. Computers were so expensive that only the elite in science and engineering (government labs, huge corporations with large research budgets, etc.) could afford them, and time was scarce. It was too expensive to buy more machines. What was to be done? Why not put programs into the Operating System to allow several jobs to be run in sequence? If one job bombs, dump the core automatically, provide the output for the programmer, and proceed to load and process the next job. This was the concept of Batch Processing. It shortened turnaround time considerably and relieved the programmer of the burden of learning how to run the computer. A new job description, that of computer operator, was created.

The next obvious step was to overlap operations. Why couldn't the Operating System handle input/output operations on the peripheral devices while the central processing unit (CPU) was processing another program or another segment of the same program? This could further reduce equipment time, improve turnaround, and make more efficient use of the machines.

By the early 1970's operating systems had been developed which would even allow concurrent processing, two or more users on the same machine, sharing the facilities at small intervals of time. Jobs could be swapped on an *event-driven* basis; when one job ended a particular task, the status of the job could be saved, and another task could be performed. By allowing more than one job at a time on the computer, greater interchangeability of data between programs was possible, and the process of turning raw data into (hopefully) useful information was speeded up even more.

The next obvious step was time sharing. Without sophisticated operating systems, stored permanently within each computer, this process was impossible. Now many users can sit at remote terminals, all believing they have complete control of the machine. Their jobs are switched in and out of the CPU at such rates that, by the time they get control after each break, only a few milliseconds have elapsed, often in time periods shorter than the persistence of vision. Time-sharing is *time-driven;* that is, each user gets a fixed block of time, usually a millisecond or two, in order.

Another major benefit of Operating Systems is that errors are reduced when the machine is under program control rather than operator control. The user's program is separated from the computer system. Either can be modified without changing the other.

Tasks and Problems Which Must Be Handled by an Operating System

The tasks performed by an operating system must include:

JOB SCHEDULING. Of all the jobs entered into the computer, whether in an event-driven environment or in a time-sharing situation, whose job gets run when? Ideally, a good operating system would be able to distinguish between high and low priority jobs and also schedule tasks for the most efficient use of the CPU and peripherals. The scheduler part of a control program is responsible for these tasks.

SUPERVISION. How is the core memory allocated to the jobs which need it? Are entire programs loaded into core at one time, or are they divided into segments or pages and an algorithm applied (such as Least Recently Used) to determine which pages or segments get swapped out when new ones are needed? The operating system keeps track of what locations in memory are used for which tasks. The user need not be concerned about memory allocation. What if the program page swapped out happens to be the next one needed? Such a situation results in program segments being swapped in and out vigorously with no processing being done; the computer is said to be *"thrashing."* A good operating system will be capable of recognizing this situation and correcting it by choosing another swapping algorithm, at least temporarily.

RESOURCE ALLOCATION. If two users need the same tape drive at the same time, the operating system must be capable of allocating and deallocating, temporarily suspending operation of one program until the other releases the device. If program 1 is using Drive A and program 2 is using Drive B, what happens when program 1 requests drive B and program 2 requests drive A? Both programs would normally stop and wait for the other to release the requested drive. Such a situation is called *deadlock* or "deadly embrace." The operating system must be aware of such problems and be written to avoid situations when the computer is doing nothing.

COMMUNICATION WITH THE OPERATOR AND RECOVERY FROM FAILURES. An operating system must communicate with the operator, providing messages about I/O devices, machine status, which jobs are running, which tapes or disks need to be loaded or unloaded, etc. Also, should there be a failure—whether it be with the building power, a problem in memory, or of any other type—a good operating system should be able to store and then find and restart on the status at some time before failure. The operator must be given the status information and instructions by the operating system on how restart is to proceed. Ideally, data and status will be stored automatically by the operating system at short intervals so that it can be easily retrieved and updated, not just during failure but also on demand from the user.

ACCOUNTING. Most computer systems require detailed statistics on who uses the machine and its peripherals for what periods of time so that appropriate billing can be done. It is a fact of life that someone must pay for the computers and their operations. Unless a machine is entirely dedicated to one department or operation (which is usually not economically feasible), the costs must be divided. For the computer to stop each time a new user signs on or off, so that the operator can record the time from the clock on the wall, would not only be wasteful of computer and operator time, but also would not give a true picture of how much CPU time was used, how much peripheral time of what type was used, etc. Operator error would inevitably lead to arguments and problems regarding who gets charged how much. Therefore, these functions are now usually written into the operating system. If you have used a large computer you are aware that at log off you are usually told how much time you have used.

I/O HANDLING. Historically, the I/O handler part of operating systems is the justification for their development. Now I/O handlers are just one part of a comprehensive system on most machines. I/O handler programs tell the computer exactly how to write or read data to or from specific peripheral devices. Generally, each device is different; they use different data formats and have different data transfer rates, different buffer sizes and different methods of data transfer. Programs are stored within the operating system to handle these differences. Even if you are using a microcomputer, you will have some I/O handling operations built into the system, such as how to print onto your printer, how to write on the CRT, how to read information from the keyboard, and how to store information on and read from a disk or cassette.

The I/O handler allocates devices and auxiliary storage space to your programs and data. It controls how the devices operate, open, organize, and close data files; maintain catalogs, and store and retrieve data. It should be noted that I/O handlers are *machine dependent.* They must be written for a specific computer and a specific peripheral attached to a machine. Also, they are not entirely self-sufficient; the user must tell the computer the parameters to be used by the data handler when information is to be transferred.

EFFICIENCY. A perfect operating system should operate as efficiently as possible. It should be apparent that instructions for moving data from one point to another in the system are probably by far the most heavily used instructions in an operating system. These must be quickly accessed and executed. Providing status in an easily stored and retrievable form to recover from *interrupts,* whether anticipated in the form of time-driven swapping in a time sharing environment or unexpected error conditions, is critical.

Testing a newly written operating system is a difficult task at best. It is impossible to predict the uses to which the programmers will put it. Inevitably, someone wants to do something that the system was not designed to do or performs a procedure in an unexpected fashion that causes the system to fail. Normally, because of the myriad of situations encountered that could not be anticipated by the system designer, it takes months of operation on a large machine to get the bugs out of an operating system. Also, until a system is installed at its permanent location, the designer does not know what devices the operating system should be designed to support. Everybody wants something different, and operating systems must be writtern as generally as possible with the realization that changes and additions will be inevitable.

UNITS OF DATA

Before beginning a discussion of types of data storage and modes of computer operation, it is important to understand the basic concepts of how data is organized. This will be discussed in more detail in the next chapter, but for now you should be aware of the following fundamental concepts.

All information in a digital computer is written in binary form. That is, in terms of binary digits, 0 or 1, called *bits.* A binary sequence of 8 bits is called a *byte;* e. g., 10110011 would be a byte. Normally, one byte is required to represent an alphabetic or numeric character, using one of the common codes to be discussed in the next chapter. A computer *word* consists of a small number of bytes. For example, a small microcomputer may have an 8-bit (one byte) word, whereas a large scientific mainframe may have as many as 8 bytes per word. The computer word is a physical concept, having reference to the computer itself and how it stores information. The word is usually the smallest amount of information that can be stored or retrieved at one time.

Logically, the way we like to see our data, a character is generally the smallest unit of data. Remember, usually a character is physically one byte long. Characters are grouped logically into fields. A *field* would be a string of characters representing an employee identification number, a name, etc. Fields are collected in *records.* A record might contain, for example, all of the information for a given student, such as student number, year in school, age, address, courses enrolled in, etc. A collection of records, such as all of the records for the students in a given course, would be called a *data file,* or simply a *file.*

TYPES OF STORAGE

Data and programs are stored in two main locations in a computer. Ideally everything would be stored in high-speed main memory within the Central Processor. This memory is called *primary memory* or core storage. Before 1970 most primary memory was made of magnetic beads or "cores" approximately one millimeter in diameter, threaded on wires. Each core was capable of holding a binary bit, 0 or 1, depending upon the direction in which it was magnetized. Core memory was bulky as well as difficult and expensive to build. Now primary memory is almost always "semiconductor" memory, integrated circuits in which, roughly speaking, a current flowing past a point represents a binary 1 and no current is a binary 0. Semiconductor memory has advantages over core; it is much easier to build, thousands of binary bits can be packed into one small integrated circuit chip, and it is relatively cheap. Its major disadvantage is that it is "volatile"; that is, when the power goes off, no more current flows, and the memory has been lost. Core memory was permanent; a loss of current did not affect its contents. Primary memory is often still called "core" memory, even though it may not consist of magnetic cores at all.

The other location for storing data is in *auxiliary* (or secondary) *memory*. Secondary memory is always a peripheral medium such as cards, magnetic tape, disks, drums, etc. Two things make auxiliary memory more attractive than primary memory for large storage capacity. First, for keeping large amounts of data, auxiliary storage media are cheaper than main memory. More information can be stored per unit cost. Second, and perhaps more important, on machines with a small number of bits per computer word, if only one or two words are reserved for addressing, the amount of primary memory which can be directly addressed (whose addresses fit within one or two computer words) is quite small. For example, if an address is limited to 16 binary bits, then the maximum number of directly addressable memory cells is $2^{16} = 65{,}536$. This is the situation in many small microcomputers where the address registers are indeed two bytes long.

The properties of auxiliary storage media and devices will be discussed in considerable detail throughout this text.

OPERATING MODES

The methods of storing and processing data can be categorized in many different ways. It is especially informative to consider the operating modes of the computer which is handling the data.

Batch

In *batch* processing mode, jobs are entered into the computer and processed one at a time sequentially. Indeed, there may be at any one time a number of different tasks waiting at the gate, for the computer to process. However, each job is completed before the next job is started. In batch mode, data is collected and sorted before being entered into the computer memory. When the data is recorded in auxiliary memory a *master* file is created; that is, the permanent file of data is recorded in sequential order. The order of the information in the file is determined by one field, called a *key,* in each record.

Updating a master file, inserting new information or deleting some records, generally requires a complete rewrite of the file. New information is collected and sorted into order by keys in a *transaction* or *detail* file. Updating is performed by a merge sort. The first records are read from the master file and from the transaction file and compared. The one which comes first (as determined by the order of keys) is written to a new master file. Then the next records are compared, and so forth until the entire file has been rewritten. By this time a new master file has been created which contains all of the changes (updates). The old master and transaction files are kept as *backup* at least until the next update of the file, so that information can be retrieved in case something happens to the new master file.

Example 1–1

Assume that a master file contains records with information about types of small computers: their cost, memory size, peripherals, dealers, etc. The key by which each record is identified is the name of the company which makes the computer. The master file contains records for

1. Apre	5. Olson
2. Ather	6. Tarpen
3. Crab	7. Tinbox
4. JCN	8. Unvar

We wish to update from a transaction file which contains names of records to be added, changed, or deleted. A separate field indicates which action is to be taken. The transaction file contains

1. Brown (NEW)	3. JCN (CHANGE)
2. Homer (NEW)	4. Tinbox (DLTE) - Delete

A new file is created by the steps illustrated in Table 1–1 and Figure 1–1.

Batch processing mode allows considerable flexibility in scheduling jobs. They can be done in priority order or in an order which can be most efficiently handled by the central processor. Resource use—of peripheral devices and human resources—can be efficiently scheduled; accounting (who pays for what time) and rerunning of jobs are facilitated. This operating mode is especially useful when producing lengthy printed reports of items in key sequential order.

Multiprogramming

In 1960 IBM built a computer for the Los Alamos Scientific Laboratory which was called STRETCH. This was the first example of a multiprogramming machine. In a multiprogramming machine, two or more jobs can be run concurrently with a single central processing unit (CPU). It is important to

TABLE 1–1. Merging a Master File and a Transaction File to Create a New Master File.

Step	Read from Master File	Read from Transaction File	Compare in Central Processor	Write to New Master File
1	Apre	Brown(NEW)	Apre, Brown	Apre
2	Ather	—	Ather, Brown	Ather
3	Crab	—	Crab, Brown	Brown
4	—	Homer(NEW)	Crab, Homer	Crab
5	JCN	—	JCN, Homer	Homer
6	—	JCN(CHANGE)	JCN, JCN	JCN (changed)
7	Olson	Tinbox(DLTE)	Olson, Tinbox	Olson
8	Tarpen	—	Tarpen, Tinbox	Tarpen
9	Tinbox	—	Tinbox, Tinbox(DLTE)	—(Tinbox deleted)
10	Unvar	—(end file)	Unvar	Unvar

distinguish between the words *concurrent* and *simultaneous*. If two events happen simultaneously, they take up exactly the same place in time. Events which are happening concurrently occur at different times, but the time intervals between the events are so short that they may appear to be occurring simultaneously. On the STRETCH computer and most subsequent large machines, two or more jobs can run in the computer together, with the CPU performing the tasks alternately for each job in such short time intervals that it appears that the jobs are executing at the same time.

Multiprocessing

Computers periodically shut down, usually of their own volition and at the worst possible time (a corollary to Murphy's Law). This occurs with such regularity (or rather at such unpredictable, irregular intervals) that machines appear to have a diabolical nature of their own, running perfectly when routine work is being done, but inevitably shutting down when their use is most urgently needed. This problem was much more serious in the past than now, because microminiaturization has made circuits not only smaller but more reliable. However, an urgent need has been felt and is still felt in most critical situations to provide a standby backup system. Buying two identical computers is one solution to the problem, available unfortunately only to affluent corporations or laboratories, rarely to the indvidual.

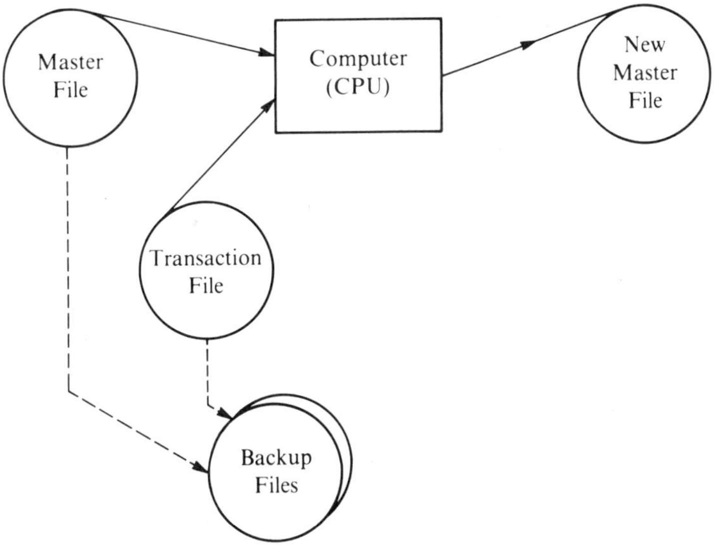

FIGURE 1–1. Three Tapes May Be Needed to Update a Master File; Old Master, Transaction, and New Master

An alternative to having two identical computers is to have a single computer with more than one CPU, a *multiprocessing system*. If the CPU's are *symmetric,* they can be used interchangeably for doing a number of jobs. Alternatively, the CPU's can be used for doing different jobs at the same time. For example, one CPU might be controlling an I/O operation while the other is sorting data, or one might be searching a file for the desired data while the second is performing arithmetic operations.

CPU's in a multiprocessing system may even be *asymmetric,* if the standby characteristic is not critical. For example, one CPU may be designed specifically to handle only I/O; all operations involving input and output are routed through that unit, allowing the other (which is designed for processing) to continue its tasks without ever having to be involved in I/O operations.

Time Sharing

In a time-sharing environment, whether with one or more CPU'S, each user is "on-line" with the computer from a remote terminal. The time-sharer interacts directly with the computer. Pressing a RETURN or ENTER key causes some action in the computer. The response is so rapid that the users feel like they are the only users of the machine. We have become spoiled, and if we have to wait more than a second for reponse to our requests, we complain about degradation of the response time.

Programs are swapped in and out of primary memory from an auxiliary storage system as needed. Programs can be interchanged either in their entirety or in pieces, called pages or segments. In the latter case, the computer appears to have essentially unlimited core memory for programming, because the user need not worry about what pieces of a program are in the memory. It used to be that programmers had to handle program *overlays* themselves when programs were larger than the computer memory could handle all at once. Programmers had to decide how best to divide their programs up into small segments and then load and run the pieces one at a time, performing the required processing before the next overlay was loaded. Now on a large computer an operating system does all of that. The computer is said to have *virtual memory,* as much memory as is needed to run any job (within reason, of course). The limit to the number of users who can use a large machine at any one time is usually determined not by the size of memory but by the number of lines attaching I/O devices to the computer and by the degradation in response time which the users are willing to tolerate.

Virtual memory tends to make large computers cheaper because a smaller core is required. Data is processed as it is received, the time between runs is reduced, and computer programmers can concentrate on making their programs do the job they wish rather than on the details of how the program will run in the computer. Another important consideration is that a large capacity direct access auxiliary storage device where tens or hundreds of megabytes* are available is quite different from a tape library where hundreds of tapes are stored. With a tape library, operator intervention is constantly required to find, mount, demount, and return tapes. Errors happen often. Data is easily lost or misplaced for long periods of time. With a large capacity direct access storage device, operator intervention is minimized and data is much more secure.

Remote Job Entry

Closely related to the concepts of time sharing and virtual memory is the *remote job entry* operating mode. In this case, many users are connected to the machine, just as in time-sharing. However, instead of providing a re-

*One megabyte = approximately 1 million bytes = exactly 1024^2 bytes = 1,048,576 bytes.

sponse as soon as a RETURN or ENTER key is pushed at the end of each line or record, the computer generally waits until the entire job has been transmitted before it begins any program execution or data processing operations.

Direct Processing

With the exception of batch sequential processing, all the modes of operation discussed above require some kind of direct processing. In direct processing mode, the data and programs can be used and stored as they are needed. It is not necessary to collect data and sort it before placing it into memory. Access to the required data or programs is "instantaneous," or at least much more rapid than having to look at all the contents of auxiliary memory in order to retrieve the particular records desired. Direct processing has been made possible by *Direct Access Storage Devices* (DASD's) represented by disk and drum type auxiliary memory. You can see that direct access to data would be very difficult to achieve if that data were stored on cards or magnetic tape.

In general, direct processing mode allows more effective management of data and better controls on its security than batch mode; however, this may be at the expense of wasted space in secondary memory (to be discussed later). As time progresses, and DASD's become larger and faster, batch mode processing is being replaced more and more by direct modes of operation. Time-sharing is the accepted way of handling users on mainframe (very large) computers and on many intermediate-sized minicomputers. Even some larger microcomputers, especially those used in educational institutions, are capable of handling time-sharing, direct access mode processing.

WHAT DIRECT ACCESS METHODS HAVE MADE POSSIBLE

Here are more specific examples of programming which are possible only with direct mode devices and operating systems.

1. Data files which require large amounts of storage and fast access are now feasible. For example, assume you have an inventory requirement for an automobile parts store. There are more than 8000 items in your inventory, and you need to be able not only to print out the

inventory periodically but also to keep a running total of parts on hand, so that when supplies are low you can order more immediately. Thus you can avoid having overstocks of items which tie up your capital. With direct access storage, when a part is sold or a shipment arrives, the inventory of that part can be updated immediately, without rewriting the entire inventory file. You can demand reports of items which are low in number, you can have the computer automatically warn you when an item is in short supply, and you can get your complete inventory reports when they are due.

2. We would all be very upset if we had to wait for hours (or even minutes in some cases) for a response to a request. How many of us would visit the office of a travel agent more than once if we were told to come back tomorrow or next week to find out if our airline reservations had been made? Virtually all airline reservations are now made on-line. A computer terminal shows flights available, a punch of a button confirms your reservation or puts you on a waiting list. Access to flight times and bookings is immediate. There is no waiting for long distance telephone calls or for a clerk to go through a file of thousands of cards or to read a magnetic tape.
3. In a bank it is impossible to predict which accounts will be active on any given day. Customer accounts must be retrievable rapidly and randomly. If there are 30,000 accounts at the bank, and the average rate of activity is 400 accounts per day, it would be absurd to have to read all accounts sequentially to find the balance for each customer who asks. In such a *low activity* situation direct access processing is ideal and could not be done efficiently at all without direct access devices.
4. Suppose the management of a company wishes to expand the plant and change the way billings and payroll are handled. If that happens rarely, the files can be searched sequentially and updated by rewriting the master files. The programs can be rewritten, and the entire processing procedure can be changed. Suppose, however, you are building computers or some other high technology product, and daily changes are necessary in your programs or accounting methods. Then you want to be able to get at the exact data and the exact program segments which you wish to change, without having to change the entire package.
5. Each evening all salespersons on your force report their daily sales, what items were sold, how many, and to whom. Your records must store this information for each salesperson, temporarily, in the order

in which it is reported. Then, at the end of the pay period, the computer takes the information stored temporarily on the DASD's, sorts it, updates the master payroll records, and calculates the commissions. This *intermediate storage* of information saves untold hours of processing time, which would be necessary if the information had to be sorted and processed piece by piece as it was collected.

6. Suppose you have 40 terminals in a student computer lab, and only one high-speed printer. If each student wrote directly to the printer from the computer, the system would become deadly slow, since most printers print information at a maximum rate of only a few hundred characters per second. Instead, your direct access storage device handles *spooling* (Simultaneous Peripheral Operations On Line). When printer output of a file is requested, the computer instead sends the data to a spool area on the DASD. The printer constantly polls the spool area to see what is there. When information is to be printed, it is read from the spool area of the DASD, not directly from the computer. Hence the computer does not have to slow down for the printer. If the spool area becomes full faster than the printer can empty it, the operating system may not allow you to write into the spool area until there is room.

THE COMPUTER SYSTEM

Let's look briefly at the computer system needed to perform the operations we have discussed above. Every computer must have at least one *central processor,* where control of operations and processing is actually done. Every central processor will have a *control unit,* whose job is to fetch and decode instructions and to keep track of where the next instruction is located. Also within the processor will be an *arithmetic logic unit* where calculations are performed and which directs the computer where to store results. Main or *primary memory* is also directly attached to or part of the central processing unit.

In addition, on large systems there will be *I/O channels* which run the programs necessary to drive the peripheral units. Also, one *controller* is required for each type of input or output device attached to the machine. *Auxiliary memory* storage devices, whether sequential or direct, are simply specialized input/output peripherals. A typical computer configuration is shown in Figure 1–2.

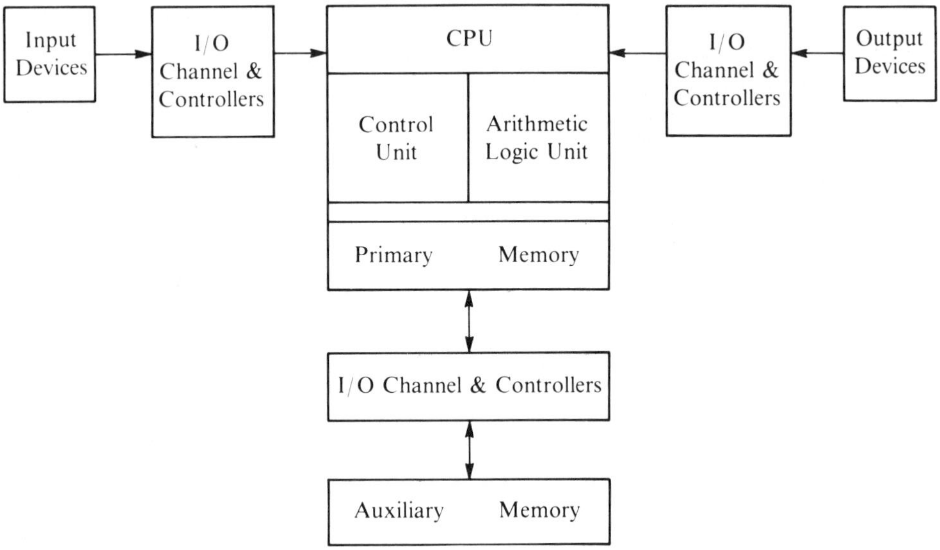

FIGURE 1–2. Block Diagram of a Computer System

QUESTIONS

1. Describe briefly the differences between batch processing, multiprogramming, multiprocessing, and time-sharing
2. Explain why updating a sequential file involves a complete rewrite. From where does one obtain a backup file in this situation?
3. If an operating system with 500,000 instructions were punched into a stack of cards with one instruction on each card
   a. how high would the stack be (assume 140 cards per inch)?
   b. how many tons would the cards weigh (assume 16 cards per ounce)?
   c. how long would it take to read the cards with a typical card reader at the rate of 600 cards per minute?
4. Magnetic tape is used extensively in batch processing. Suggest at least two reasons why magnetic tape is less used in time-sharing.
5. Assume 100 engineers would experience 15 percent improvement in efficiency by using a new, large computer. Would the purchase of

the computer be justified? Assume an engineer's time is worth $25 per hour, that she or he works 220 eight-hours days per year, that the computer costs $180,000 and has a five-year lifetime with no resale value. Ignore any other factors. How much money would be saved or lost by the purchase of the computer?

6. Distinguish between a bit, byte, computer word, character, field, record, and data file.
7. Give at least two examples of how DASD's can be used for intermediate storage.
8. Assume you have been asked to recommend to a large brokerage house whether they should install a batch processing or a direct processing computer system to handle customer records. Stocks are bought and sold almost continuously, billings and payments of customers are made weekly.
   a. What questions might you want to ask in your investigation?
   b. Based on the answers to those questions, what kind of processor would you recommend? Why?
9. What is the function of a "key" in a data record?
10. Why do we not build computers with very large primary memories so we can do everything internally? Wouldn't this save a lot of I/O handling and concern about compatibility of devices for storing data?
11. Assume that the new master file created in Example 1–1 is updated with the following records from a transaction file:

```
Brown, CHANGE     Gnu, NEW      Horner, DLTE - Delete
  Mort, NEW      Witch, NEW
```

List the final updated master file after this has been accomplished.

CHAPTER 2

DATA REPRESENTATIONS

UNITS OF DATA

Binary Numbers

The fundamental units in which data are stored in computer memory, whether primary or secondary, are binary digits (0's and 1's). Binary digits are used because it is easier to use two states than numerous states in a computer. For example, in the old core memory or on a magnetic tape or disk, a bead or spot is magnetized in either one direction or in the opposite direction. On a punched card, either there is a hole at a given position or there is no hole. A lamp is lit or it is off; a switch is on or it is off; etc. It would be considerably more difficult to create 10-state devices to represent decimal numbers directly. How would you measure, for example, whether a lamp is 3/10 lit, or a hole is 7/10 punched? One could conceive of a 10-position switch or a magnetization or current which is some fraction of its maximum possible value, but such devices would be difficult to use and expensive to construct. Dr. John V. Atanasoff, a physicist at Iowa State University, agonized in the late 1930's about whether people would really accept a machine which performed calculations in binary. His decision to build such a machine, with assistant Clifford Berry, led to the construction of the first electronic digital computer, called the Atanasoff-Berry Computer (ABC, for short).

Thus, in representing characters within a computer, or for use by a computer, we are restricted to two states, which we represent numerically by zero (0) or one (1), logically by False or True. It is relatively simple to count and write numbers in binary. The first few binary numbers are shown in Table 2–1. These can easily be reproduced by noting that the units column alternates between zero and one with each new number, the second column (representing $2^1=2$) alternates every two numbers, the third column (representing $2^2=4$) alternates every four numbers, the fourth column ($2^3=8$) alternates every eight units, etc. The leading zeros in the binary numbers of Table 2–1 are meaningless, just as leading zeros in decimal numbers are meaningless; they have been included for the sake of symmetry and for the discussion of hexadecimal numbers later.

Each digit in a binary number is called a *bit*, an abbreviation for *bi*nary digi*t*. Eight bits together form a *byte*. Most computers store information in

TABLE 2–1. The First Few Binary and Hexadecimal Numbers.

Decimal	*Binary*	*Hexadecimal*	*Decimal*	*Binary*	*Hexadecimal*
0	0000	0	16	0001 0000	10
1	0001	1	17	0001 0001	11
2	0010	2	18	0001 0010	12
3	0011	3	19	0001 0011	13
4	0100	4	20	0001 0100	14
5	0101	5	21	0001 0101	15
6	0110	6	22	0001 0110	16
7	0111	7	23	0001 0111	17
8	1000	8	24	0001 1000	18
9	1001	9	25	0001 1001	19
10	1010	A	26	0001 1010	1A
11	1011	B	27	0001 1011	1B
12	1100	C	28	0001 1100	1C
13	1101	D	29	0001 1101	1D
14	1110	E	30	0001 1110	1E
15	1111	F	31	0001 1111	1F
			32	0001 0000	20

memory in smallest quantities, called computer words, a small integer number of bytes. For example, small microcomputers have memory words which are one byte long; information is moved from place to place in the computer memory and CPU eight bits at a time. Newer versions of microcomputers have two-byte (16-bit) words, and larger machines may have 32-bit (four bytes) or even 64-bit (eight bytes) or longer computer words. Some advantages of longer words are that information is transferred between CPU, memory, and input/output devices more rapidly and that the central processor can address more memory locations directly.

Consider the transformation of binary numbers into their decimal equivalents. If you were asked the value of the binary number 1101 0011, for example, you would probably wish to state the answer in terms of numbers we use every day, namely, base 10 or decimal. To convert a binary number to decimal, use the definitions of the columns as in the following example.

Example 2–1

Convert the binary number 1101 0011 to decimal.

Solution:

Note first that any decimal number can be expanded in powers of 10. For example, the decimal number 5368 is really

8 units	$= 8 \times 10^0$	$= 8 \times$	$1 =$	8
plus 6 tens	$= 6 \times 10^1$	$= 6 \times$	$10 =$	60
plus 3 hundreds	$= 3 \times 10^2$	$= 3 \times$	$100 =$	300
plus 5 thousands	$= 5 \times 10^3$	$= 5 \times$	$1000 =$	5000

1000	100	10	1		
10^3	10^2	10^1	10^0		
5	3	6	8	=	5368

Since in binary we count by two's rather than 10's, each column is represented by a power of two, just as each column in the decimal number is represented by a power of 10. So that 1101 0011 is

128	64	32	16	8	4	2	1
2^7	2^6	2^5	2^4	2^3	2^2	2^1	2^0
1	1	0	1	0	0	1	1

equals $1 \times 128 + 1 \times 64 + 0 \times 32 + 1 \times 16$
$+ 0 \times 8 + 0 \times 4 + 1 \times 2 + 1 \times 1 = 211_{10}$

Note that any number raised to the power 0 has a value of 1, and the subscript $_{10}$ simply means decimal or base 10.

The binary number 1111 1111 is exactly one less than the number 1 0000 0000, which has a decimal value of $1 \times 2^8 = 1 \times 256 = 256$. Thus, the largest number which can be represented by eight binary digits is 1111 $1111 = 2^8 - 1 = 255_{10}$.

In general, the largest number which can be represented by n binary digits is $2^n - 1$. Obviously, the smallest number which can be represented by any number of binary digits is 0, so that the range of numbers which can be represented in n binary bits is 0 to $2^n - 1$, or 2^n different integers. Thus, if your computer uses only one eight-bit word to represent a memory address, there can be only $2^8 = 256$ different addresses in the memory which are directly addressable by the computer. Most eight-bit word machines use two words (= 16 bits) for the address register so that $2^{16} = 65,536$ different addresses are directly available.

You may have heard that the maximum memory size of an eight-bit microcomputer is 64K. This stands for 64 kilobytes of memory. Normally, in metric notation, the prefix *kilo* stands for a multiplier of 1000. However, in computer terminology, one kilo is defined to be the closest power of 2 to 1000, namely, $2^{10} = 1024$. Hence, 64K (= 64 kilobytes) $= 64 \times 1024 = 65,536$, the same number we saw above. Thus, an eight-bit microcomputer which accesses 64K of memory must use two words for its address registers.

Example 2–2

Suppose you wish your small computer to be able to address 16 *mega*bytes of memory. How large must the address register be?

Solution:

Normally, in metric terms, the prefix *mega* stands for 1,000,000 or $1,000 \times 1,000$. In computer terminology, one megabyte $= 1024 \times 1024 = 2^{20} = 1,048,576$ bytes. So 16 megabytes $= 16 \times 1024^2 = 16,777,216$ bytes. A bit of experimentation with your hand calculator will convince you that $2^{24} = 16,777,216$, so that the address register in your computer would have to be 24 bits long in order to be able to address 16 megabytes of memory directly.

Hexadecimal Numbers

You may have noticed already that there is another column in Table 2–1 which lists hexadecimal numbers. Hexadecimal is a base 16 number system, and is convenient to use when representing binary numbers in a more readable form for the user. Just as in base 2 only two symbols are needed to represent all the numbers, and in base 10 we need 10 symbols, in base 16 we will need 16 symbols to represent numbers. We generally use the numerals 0 through 9 and the letters A through F for these 16 symbols, but we could make up any set of symbols we desired. Note, from Table 2–1, that the first 16 decimal numbers, 0 through 15, are represented in binary by a maximum of four digits, namely 0000 through 1111. These same 16 numbers are represented in hexadecimal by the symbols 0 to 9, then A to F. Beginning with decimal 16, the hexadecimal numbers repeat with a carry, so that

$31_{10}=1F_{16}$, $47_{10}=2F_{16}$, $159_{10}=9F_{16}$, $175_{10}=AF_{16}$, $255_{10}=FF_{16}$, $256_{10}=100_{16}$, etc.

Note also that the patterns of four binary digits begin to repeat at decimal 16. Hence, translation of binary integers to hexadecimal is a matter of grouping the binary numbers into groups of four beginning from the right (the least significant bit), and writing each group of four bits in terms of its hexadecimal equivalent.

Example 2–3

Write the binary number 1101 0011 in hexadecimal.

Solution:

1101 0011 can be divided into two groups of four digits each, namely
1101 which, from Table 2–1, equals hexadecimal D
and 0011 which, from Table 2–1, equals hexadecimal 3.

Thus, binary 1101 0011 equals hexadecimal D3.

Hexadecimal is converted to decimal by considering the value of each column as we did for binary numbers.

Example 2–4

Convert hexadecimal D3 to decimal.

Solution:

Remember that the value of 1101 0011 in decimal was 211, which we obtained by considering the columns to be successively higher powers of two as we move left from the units column. We can obtain the same result by converting the hexadecimal number D3 directly into decimal, letting each column to the left of the units column represent higher powers of 16.

$$D3 = \begin{matrix} 16 & 1 \\ 16^1 & 16^0 \\ D & 3 \end{matrix} = D \times 16 + 3 \times 1.$$

But the decimal value of D_{16} is 13 (see Table 2–1). Therefore, $D3_{16} =$

$13 \times 16 + 3 \times 1 = 208 + 3 = 211_{10}$.

Example 2–5

A 16-bit address register contains the hexadecimal number FACE. What is the decimal value of the address to which this register refers?

Solution:

We could express $FACE_{16}$ in binary form, namely

$$FACE_{16} = 1111\ 1010\ 1100\ 1110,$$

and convert the binary number to decimal. Let's do this just for fun.

$$\begin{aligned} 1111\ 1010\ 1100\ 1110 &= 1 \times 2^{15} + 1 \times 2^{14} + 1 \times 2^{13} + 1 \times 2^{12} + 1 \times 2^{11} \\ &\quad + 0 \times 2^{10} + 1 \times 2^{9} + 0 \times 2^{8} + 1 \times 2^{7} + 1 \times 2^{6} + 0 \times 2^{5} \\ &\quad + 0 \times 2^{4} + 1 \times 2^{3} + 1 \times 2^{2} + 1 \times 2^{1} + 0 \times 2^{0} \\ &= 1 \times 32{,}768 + 1 \times 16{,}384 + 1 \times 8192 + 1 \times 4096 \\ &\quad + 1 \times 2048 + 0 \times 1024 + 1 \times 512 + 0 \times 256 + 1 \times 128 + 1 \times 64 \end{aligned}$$

$+0\times32+0\times16+1\times8+1\times4+1\times2+0\times1$
$=32{,}768+16{,}384+8192+4096+2048+512+128+64$
$+8+4+2=64{,}206_{10}$

It is simpler to convert $FACE_{16}$ directly to decimal by considering the powers of 16.

4096	256	16	1
16^3	16^2	16^1	16^0
F	A	C	E

$=F\times4096+A\times256+C\times16+E\times1$
$=15\times4096+10\times256+12\times16+14\times1$
$=61{,}440+2560+192+14=64{,}206_{10}$

If a binary number cannot be divided evenly into groups of four digits, you may supply leading zeros to complete the leftmost group before converting to hexadecimal.

Example 2–6

Convert binary 111010 to hexadecimal.

Solution:

$111010_2=0011\ 1010_2=3A_{16}$.

The justification for the use of hexadecimal numbers is that it is particulary easy to convert from binary numbers to hexadecimal. Long strings of binary numbers are hard to read and compare, while their hexadecimal equivalents are shorter and easier to read. Asked to compare 1110000100101101 with 101010111101111, you might find it easier instead to compare $E12D_{16}$ with $55EF_{16}$. For this reason, if you ask your computer to dump the contents of various locations of memory or of the registers, the dump will most likely be given to you in terms of hexadecimal numbers.

Converting Decimal to Binary and Hex

We have not yet discussed the conversion of decimal numbers to binary or to hexadecimal. We will very quickly show two examples which illustrate one method of doing that here. With a little practice you can begin to feel comfortable with such conversions. However, as you work with binary and hexadecimal numbers, you will probably find yourself simply using them and beginning to have a feeling for their magnitudes without having to convert at all.

In order to convert a decimal number to binary, one of the easiest ways is repeated division by 2, keeping track of the remainders at each step of the division.

Example 2–7

Find the binary equivalent of the decimal number 169.

Solution:

Perform the following operations:

169 divided by 2 = 84	Remainder 1
84 divided by 2 = 42	Remainder 0
42 divided by 2 = 21	Remainder 0
21 divided by 2 = 10	Remainder 1
10 divided by 2 = 5	Remainder 0
5 divided by 2 = 2	Remainder 1
2 divided by 2 = 1	Remainder 0
1 divided by 2 = 0	Remainder 1

Now read the remainders from the bottom up. That is,

$169_{10} = 1010\ 1001_2$.

You can check this result by converting $1010\ 1001_2$ back to its decimal equivalent using the methods discussed above.

To convert the number $656{,}171_{10}$ to hexadecimal, we could divide it repeatedly by 2 to convert it to binary, then group the binary number into groups of four digits and convert to hexadecimal. You might wish to try this and see that there are an awfully lot of division steps involved. Instead, we will convert $656{,}171_{10}$ directly to hexadecimal by repeated division by 16, keeping track of the remainders just as we did above. Example 2–8 shows the steps.

Example 2–8

Convert $656,171_{10}$ to hexadecimal.

Solution:

656,171 divided by 16 =	41010	Your calculator shows remainder 0.6875; which is 11/16, thus Remainder = 11
41,010 divided by 16 =	2563	Remainder = 2
2,563 divided by 16 =	160	Remainder = 3
160 divided by 16 =	10	Remainder = 0
10 divided by 16 =	0	Remainder = 10

Thus, reading the remainders from the bottom up,

$656,171_{10} = 10\ 0\ 3\ 2\ 11$
But 10 = A, and 11 = B, so that
$656,171_{10} = A032B_{16}$

which of course you could now convert to $1010\ 0000\ 0011\ 0010\ 1011_2$ if you wished.

We have discussed how these numbers are used as addresses in the computer memory. Of course the data stored in those addresses is also represented by binary numbers, so that whether we are talking about memory itself or the numbers stored in that memory, we must be able to read and interpret binary and hexadecimal numbers.

Octal Numbers

Even though most modern computers will display numbers in hexadecimal form, there are some which use octal (base 8) instead. Octal numbers use digits 0 through 7 only. Converting octal numbers to and from binary and decimal is accomplished as in the examples above, except that the base is 8 instead of 2 or 16. More detail is shown in question 7 at the end of this chapter.

ALPHANUMERIC CHARACTER STRINGS

In the discussion so far we have considered only how integers are represented by binary numbers. Other types of numbers such as floating point numbers with decimal points and fractional parts are handled in the computer by using several binary integer fields to represent the sign of the number, the significant digits in the number, and the power to which the number is to be raised. You may wish to refer to a text with more detail on binary arithmetic for information on handling fractions, negative numbers, and other representations.

More important in our consideration of data management and file design concepts is how alphabetic characters are stored. Simply stated, alphabetic characters (as well as numerals when they don't need to be used immediately for calculations) are represented in codes of binary digits.

Cards and Paper Tape

One of the first significant codes was invented by Hermann Hollerith for tabulating the 1890 U.S. census. In this system, holes were punched in cards, with each combination of holes representing a specific item of data. Figure 2–1 shows an example of Hollerith's original card codes and the

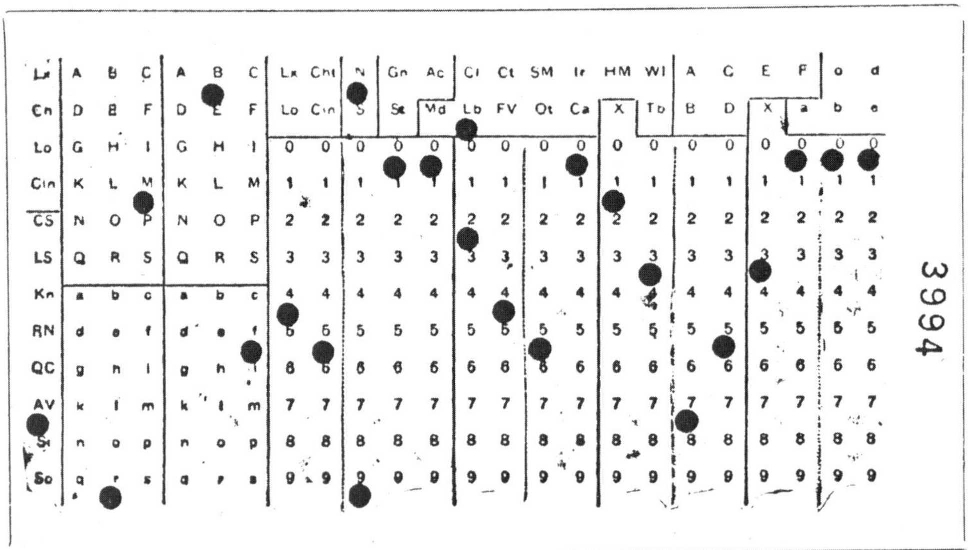

FIGURE 2–1(a). Hollerith's Original Card Code *(Courtesy of International Business Machines Corporation)*

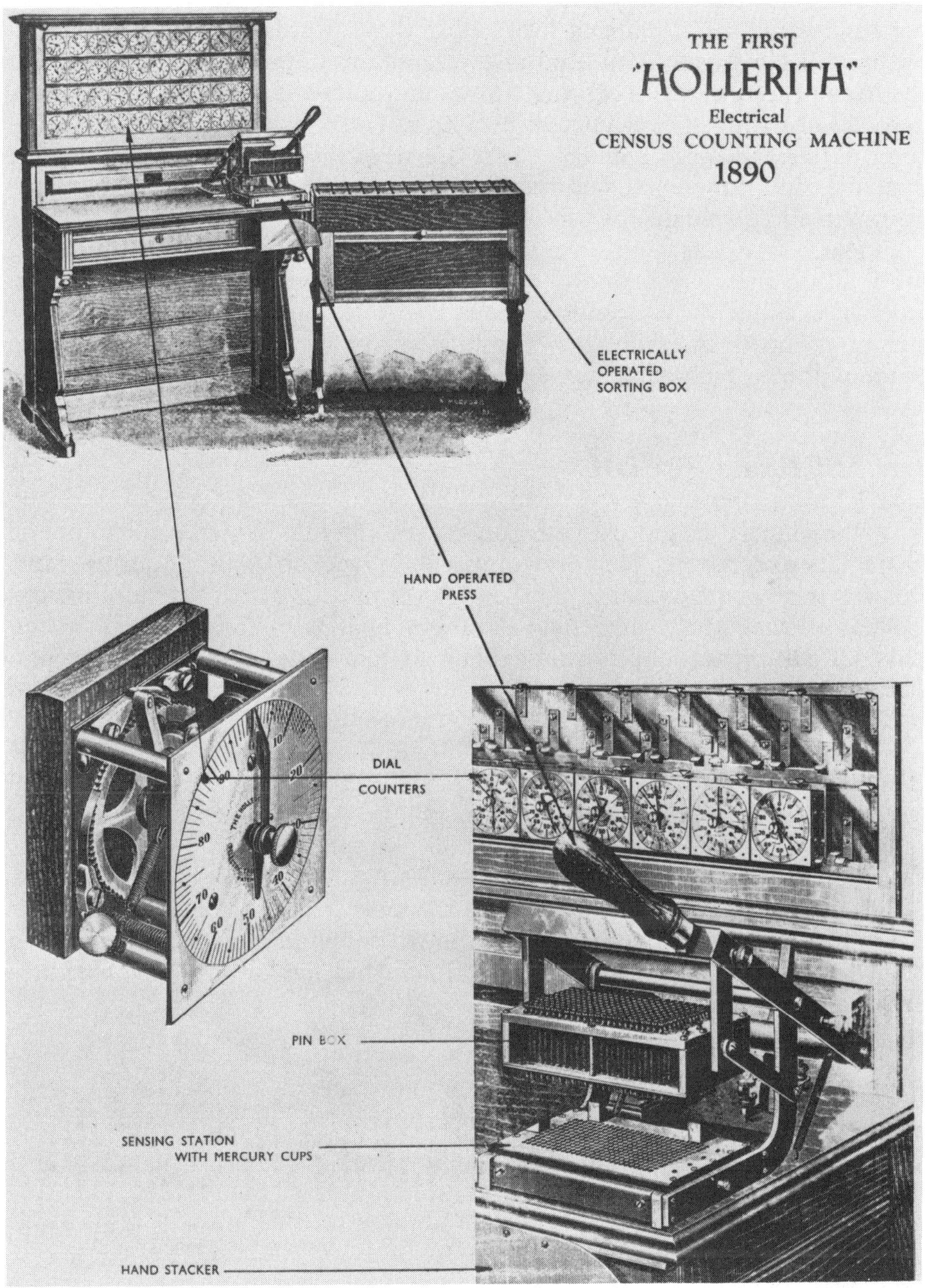

FIGURE 2–1(b). The First "Hollerith" Electric Census Counting Machine, 1980 *(Courtesy of International Business Machines Corporation)*

machine which he developed for reading them. Cards fashioned after Hollerith's concepts have been used in nearly every computer installation since the beginning of the 20th century. However, the use of punched cards is gradually disappearing as direct access devices and on-line keyboard terminals become faster and more popular. There are nevertheless still applications for punched cards, where magnetic tapes or disks are impractical, and batch processing is most valuable.

Paper tape was another popular medium for storing data in punched form. Again there were a number of formats, but one of the common ones, an eight-channel format standardized by the American National Standards Institute, is shown in Figure 2–2. The meaning of the "CHECK" track in this figure will be discussed later.

ASCII and EBCDIC

Two binary codes are commonly used for representing alphanumeric characters in computer memory, on magnetic tape, on disks, or during transmission from one medium to another. One of these is called Extended Binary-Coded Decimal Interchange Code, developed by IBM and referred to by its initials EBCDIC (pronounced Eb-see-dick). In this code, characters are represented by eight binary digits. The EBCDIC code for some characters is shown in Table 2–2.

Another code for alphabetic and numeric characters is one adopted by the American National Standards Institute (ANSI). This code is called ASCII (generally pronounced as-key) which stands for American Standard Code for Information Interchange. Each character is represented by seven bits, as shown in Table 2–3.

Often a leading 0 bit is added to the code for each ASCII character to make it exactly one byte long. However, in some circumstances (discussed below) it is more important to reserve the eighth bit for error checking purposes.

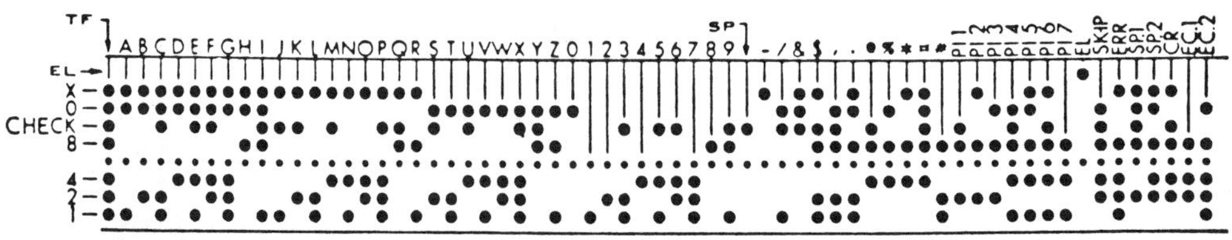

FIGURE 2–2. A Punched Paper Tape Code

TABLE 2–2. Extended Binary Coded Decimal Interchange Code—EBCDIC.

Symbol	*Binary*	*Decimal*	*Symbol*	*Binary*	*Decimal*
SPACE	0100 0000	64	s	1010 0010	162
¢	0100 1010	74	t	1010 0011	163
.	0100 1011	75	u	1010 0100	164
<	0100 1100	76	v	1010 0101	165
(	0100 1101	77	w	1010 0110	166
+	0100 1110	78	x	1010 0111	167
¦	0100 1111	79	y	1010 1000	168
&	0101 0000	80	z	1010 1001	169
!	0101 1010	90	A	1100 0001	193
$	0101 1011	91	B	1100 0010	194
*	0101 1100	92	C	1100 0011	195
)	0101 1101	93	D	1100 0100	196
;	0101 1110	94	E	1100 0101	197
¬	0101 1111	95	F	1100 0110	198
-	0110 0000	96	G	1100 0111	199
/	0110 0001	97	H	1100 1000	200
,	0110 1011	107	I	1100 1001	201
%	0110 1100	108	J	1101 0001	209
–	0110 1101	109	K	1101 0010	210
>	0110 1110	110	L	1101 0011	211
?	0110 1111	111	M	1101 0100	212
:	0111 1010	122	N	1101 0101	213
#	0111 1011	123	O	1101 0110	214
@	0111 1100	124	P	1101 0111	215
'	0111 1101	125	Q	1101 1000	216
=	0111 1110	126	R	1101 1001	217
"	0111 1111	127	S	1110 0010	226
a	1000 0001	129	T	1110 0011	227
b	1000 0010	130	U	1110 0100	228
c	1000 0011	131	V	1110 0101	229
d	1000 0100	132	W	1110 0110	230
e	1000 0101	133	X	1110 0111	231
f	1000 0110	134	Y	1110 1000	232

TABLE 2–2. Continued

Symbol	*Binary*	*Decimal*	*Symbol*	*Binary*	*Decimal*
g	1000 0111	135	Z	1110 1001	233
h	1000 1000	136	0	1111 0000	240
i	1000 1001	137	1	1111 0001	241
j	1001 0001	145	2	1111 0010	242
k	1001 0010	146	3	1111 0011	243
l	1001 0011	147	4	1111 0100	244
m	1001 0100	148	5	1111 0101	245
n	1001 0101	149	6	1111 0110	246
o	1001 0110	150	7	1111 0111	247
p	1001 0111	151	8	1111 1000	248
q	1001 1000	152	9	1111 1001	249
r	1001 1001	153			

TABLE 2–3. American Standard Code for Information Interchange (ASCII).

Symbol	*Binary*	*Decimal*	*Symbol*	*Binary*	*Decimal*	*Symbol*	*Binary*	*Decimal*
NUL	000 0000	000	+	010 1011	043	V	101 0110	086
SOH	000 0001	001	'	010 1100	044	W	101 0111	087
STX	000 0010	002	-	010 1101	045	X	101 1000	088
ETX	000 0011	003	.	010 1110	046	Y	101 1001	089
EOT	000 0100	004	/	010 1111	047	Z	101 1010	090
ENO	000 0101	005	0	011 0000	048	[	101 1011	091
ACK	000 0110	006	1	011 0001	049	˘	101 1100	092
BEL	000 0111	007	2	011 0010	050	]	101 1101	093
BS	000 1000	008	3	011 0011	051	^	101 1110	094
HT	000 1001	009	4	011 0100	052	←	101 1111	095
LF	000 1010	010	5	011 0101	053	°	110 0000	096

TABLE 2–3. Continued

Symbol	Binary	Decimal	Symbol	Binary	Decimal	Symbol	Binary	Decimal
VT	000 1011	011	6	011 0110	054	a	110 0001	097
FF	000 1100	012	7	011 0111	055	b	110 0010	098
CR	000 1101	013	8	011 1000	056	c	110 0011	099
SO	000 1110	014	9	011 1001	057	d	110 0100	100
SI	000 1111	015	:	011 1010	058	e	110 0101	101
DLE	001 0000	016	;	011 1011	059	f	110 0110	102
DC1	001 0001	017	<	011 1100	060	g	110 0111	103
DC2	001 0010	018	=	011 1101	061	h	110 1000	104
DC3	001 0011	019	>	011 1110	062	i	110 1001	105
DC4	001 0100	020	?	011 1111	063	j	110 1010	106
NAK	001 0101	021	@	100 0000	064	k	110 1011	107
SYN	001 0110	022	A	100 0001	065	l	110 1100	108
ETB	001 0111	023	B	100 0010	066	m	110 1101	109
CAN	001 1000	024	C	100 0011	067	n	110 1110	110
EM	001 1001	025	D	100 0100	068	o	110 1111	111
SUB	001 1010	026	E	100 0101	069	p	111 0000	112
ESC	001 1011	027	F	100 0110	070	q	111 0001	113
FS	001 1100	028	G	100 0111	071	r	111 0010	114
GS	001 1101	029	H	100 1000	072	s	111 0011	115
RS	001 1110	030	I	100 1001	073	t	111 0100	116
US	001 1111	031	J	100 1010	074	u	111 0101	117
SPACE	010 0000	032	K	100 1011	075	v	111 0110	118
!	010 0001	033	L	100 1100	076	w	111 0111	119
"	010 0010	034	M	100 1101	077	x	111 1000	120
#	010 0011	035	N	100 1110	078	y	111 1001	121
$	010 0100	036	O	100 1111	079	z	111 1010	122
%	010 0101	037	P	101 0000	080	{	111 1011	123
&	010 0110	038	Q	101 0001	081		111 1100	124
'	010 0111	039	R	101 0010	082	}	111 1101	125
(	010 1000	040	S	101 0011	083	~	111 1110	126
)	010 1001	041	T	101 0100	084	del	111 1111	127
*	010 1010	042	U	101 0101	085			

The symbols in column one of Table 2–3 represent special control characters such as BEL = ring the terminal bell, BS = backspace, LF = line feed, FF = form feed, CR = carriage return, del = delete the previous character, etc.

A legitimate question might be, "Why are there two popular codes?" If you wish, you may create your own code, but of course that may lead to considerable extra work when using a system which already uses one or the other of the standard codes. It should be observed that EBCDIC, the code used by IBM, was in widespread use long before ASCII was accepted. At the time ANSI settled on ASCII, most devices and most previously recorded data used eight-bit EBCDIC. It would have required the redesign of equipment and a complete rewrite of massive amounts of data in order to change to seven-bit ASCII. Thus, IBM as well as some other manufacturers and users prefer to continue the use of EBCDIC.

Just how many bits are required in a code depends on the number of different characters to be represented. For example, if the numerals 0 through 9 and upper case letters A through Z are all that are needed, the code needs to be capable of representing only 36 characters. Five binary digits can represent $2^5 = 32$ different symbols, and six bits can represent $2^6 = 64$ symbols. Thus, if you use six bits, as in the paper tape code in Figure 2–2 (ignoring the check and EL bits) you can represent all of the numerals, the upper case letters of the alphabet, 12 punctuation and special symbols, and still have 16 combinations left over for control characters or whatever you wish to use them for.

In order to represent 26 upper case and 26 lower case letters, 10 numerals, and 12 or more punctuation symbols (at least 74 symbols), you will need seven bits (since $2^6 = 64$ is too few, and $2^7 = 128$ gives us more than a sufficient number of combinations). Seven bits allows many extra codes for control and special characters, as the ASCII chart in Table 2–3 shows.

Obviously, the eight-bit EBCDIC code leaves room for many extra characters if desired, since $2^8 = 256$. You should observe that many possible binary combinations have been left out of Table 2–2.

Parity

The eighth bit needed to complete a byte in ASCII code is often used for error-checking purposes. Similarly, an error-checking ninth bit is often appended to character codes in EBCDIC. This extra bit is called the *parity* bit.

To determine what the parity bit should be for a given character, you must first decide whether you wish the parity to be *even* or *odd;* then the parity bit is chosen to be a 0 or a 1, so that the sum of the ones in the character (including parity) is an even number or an odd number respectively.

Example 2–9

For *odd* parity, what are the parity bits in ASCII and EBCDIC for characters A, a, and 5?

Solution:

Character	*Parity*	*ASCII*	*Character*	*Parity*	*EBCDIC*
A	1	100 0001	A	0	1100 0001
a	0	110 0001	a	1	1000 0001
5	1	011 0101	5	1	1111 0101

You should be able now to examine the paper tape in Figure 2–2 and convince yourself that the CHECK bit there is really an odd parity bit.

Sorting

It is important to emphasize that a medium for storing EBCDIC with parity would require spaces for nine bits per character, while ASCII with parity requires exactly one byte per character. Another important reason to be aware of whether your computer considers characters to be coded in EBCDIC or ASCII involves the process of sorting. Generally, the computer sorts character strings as we alphabetize names by hand; i. e., by comparing the first letters of the strings, then the second letters (if the first letters are identical), etc. As long as the character string which you wish to sort contains all upper case letters, all lower case, or all numeric, the order in which they are sorted will not differ from one computer to another. If upper and lower case letters or letters and numerals are mixed, however, the order will be different. For example the words "Chance" (capital C) and "dearly" (lower case d) would be sorted in the order

dearly   Chance

by EBCDIC, since EBCDIC for "d" is a smaller value than EBCDIC for "C"; while the same words would appear sorted in the order

Chance   dearly

by ASCII, since ASCII for "C" is a smaller value than ASCII for "d".

Sorting methods will be discussed in some detail in Chapter 9.

LARGER UNITS OF DATA

Characters are generally collected into *fields* of data. A field would contain such information as a name, an address, an identification number, etc.

A collection of logically related fields is called a *record.* An example of a record could be the information on a given employee containing the fields of name, address, age, pay rate, history with the company, etc. Records can all be of fixed length; i. e., the employee records could very well contain the same number of fields each of the same length for name, address, age, etc. On the other hand, if you were keeping track of customer orders, you might wish to make records of variable length, so that more orders could be added to a given customer's record without having to make all of the customer records equally long and waste valuable storage space.

A college professor may wish to have a collection of all the records for the students in his class. Such a collection of records would be called a *data file,* or simply a *file.* Other examples of data files might be payroll files, inventory files, or maintenance reports. Files may be organized sequentially, with each record located in the file by the relationship between its identifying *key* and all the other keys. Every record must have a key which distinguishes it from all other records. Typical keys are names or identification numbers. On the other hand, a file might be organized so that the position of any record can be determined directly by converting its key to the address where it is stored on a disk or similar device. Such a file is called a *random* or *direct access* file, since each record can be accessed, read, and updated immediately without regard to its location with respect to the other records. These file organizations and variations on them, such as linked lists and indexes, are discussed and illustrated in Parts II and III of this text.

An organization may find it useful to have a *data base,* a collection of files all of which may be accessed by a set of programs and all of which contain related data. In such a data base for a large university, for example, you might find the student files, payroll files, inventory of equipment, historical records, etc. Or the data base may be limited to one type of file, such as student academic records, student financial records, student history and personal information, etc. Ideally, these files would be organized so that appropriate administrators could access the information in any file as the need arose.

The character, field, record, file, and data base are *logical* concepts, referring to the way the computer user sees the data and organizes it. There are other ways in which the computer organizes the data. These are the *physical* units, which correlate more or less with the logical concepts discussed above.

We have already defined a computer *word.* It may not always be convenient for data to be transferred from point to point within the computer system one byte (character) at a time. In fact, by organizing the machine so that several bytes are transferred or stored together, a much greater efficiency and speed can be attained. Hence a computer word, the amount of information transferred from point to point simultaneously (in parallel), is generally a small integral number of bytes.

It may also be wasteful of space or time to transfer one logical record at a time between primary and secondary memory. A more efficient way may be to group the records into physical *blocks,* units of data storage appropriate to the physical system. A physical block is roughly equivalent to a logical record, except that the computer may group several records into one physical storage space or may even break a single long record into several smaller blocks for convenience of storage and transfer. Fixed length blocks may also be called *pages*.

Often the location in which a file is stored is called a physical *area* on the storage device. Again, an area may contain one file, a number of files, or only part of a very long file, depending upon which is the most economical in terms of space and time.

Table 2–4 summarizes the descriptions of the physical and logical concepts discussed above.

TABLE 2–4. Logical and Physical Units of Data.

Logical Organization	*Physical Organization*	*Description*
	Bit	One binary digit
Character	Byte	In most codes one character is represented by approximately one byte.
Field	Word	A field is a related set of characters. A computer word is a fixed, small number of bytes.
Record	Block (pages = fixed length blocks)	Records can be blocked into more convenient storage units.
File	Area	Several files may be stored in one storage area.
Data base		A collection of related data files may be organized into a data base.

INPUT/OUTPUT DEVICES AND MEDIA

Before discussing in detail how data looks on auxiliary storage devices, we should examine some kinds of I/O devices and how data is actually transferred from point to point.

There are four main types of I/O devices: data preparation devices, end-use machines, serial storage devices, and direct access storage devices.

The Data Preparation Device

The first type of device is that used by a *data entry operator,* a person who does not necessarily have any direct contact with the computer. This kind of equipment is called a *data preparation* device and is exemplified by a keypunch machine, a key-to-tape, or a key-to-disk entry device. The user—a programmer entering a program, a clerk, or a data entry secretary—sits in front of a machine and types in data. On a keypunch machine the data is transferred to punched cards. On a key-to-tape or key-to-disk device, the information goes to a magnetic tape or disk. The tape or disk is usually a cassette or a diskette with relatively small capacity so that the data entry operator need not type in huge amounts of data at one sitting. These devices are not directly attached to the computer. They have the advantage of requiring no computer time while the data is being typed. Their major disadvantage is that they introduce one or more extra steps in which the data must be handled by humans before the computer actually sees it. Of course such extra steps can introduce errors. Typical of this type of device is the keypunch machine, where data is typed directly onto cards. In a second step the punched cards are often inserted into a verifier machine where the data is typed again, and the machine either verifies that the typing was done the same the second time or indicates by a notch along an edge that something has changed. Usually, the cards are then sorted and tabulated (the contents printed out) before they are submitted to the computer for processing. Large machines which performed sorting and tabulating made up a major part of older computing centers. In fact, often this was the only processing done.

The End-Use Machine

A second category of I/O device is the *end-use machine.* These are the card readers, the keyboards, card punches, CRT's (Cathode Ray Tubes, television type displays on which information is displayed), printers, etc. These devices are attached more or less directly to the computer and provide the path for data to and from the computer. In the case of batch processing, the card reader may be the endstep of punching, verifying, sorting, tabulating, etc. In on-line processing, the operator or programmer will type the data or program directly into the computer from a keyboard and may see the results displayed on a CRT. Formerly, the end-use device was called a source or sink of data. In the 1960's and early 1970's a teletype machine was a convenient way of entering data directly into the computer from a keyboard or an attached paper tape reader.

The user should be aware that the above two types of I/O devices may turn out to be more expensive than many small computers on which they are used. Printers have been quite costly, for example, because they are primarily mechanical rather than electronic devices. Inexpensive printers such as thermal devices are available, but they often require expensive special paper, so that the user ends up spending more money in the long run. Character printers, which print at a rate of a few dozen to a few hundred characters per second, can be found in dot matrix, high speed form, where the characters are formed by an array (generally about 9×7) of dots or points on the paper. More expensive and slightly slower character printers are called letter quality printers, which use plastic or metal "daisy" wheels with characters on the ends of petal-like extensions. With these printers you can send out business letters, typed by the computer, which appear to have been typed by hand. Higher speed chain, drum, or band printers print an entire line at once and usually run at rates of a few lines to a few hundred lines per minute. Of course, if you have lots of cash you could consider very high speed printers which use lasers or other technologies and which print entire pages at once at the rate of dozens of pages per minute. With one of these printers, a programming error could send half a box of paper onto the floor before you could press the stop button.

The Serial Storage Device

The other two types of I/O devices are also used for secondary data storage. One of these is the serial storage device, typified by magnetic tape. Magnetic tapes are a major improvement over data cards or paper tape, because data can be stored much more densely and can be accessed more rapidly. A disadvantage of magnetic tape is its inherently sequential nature. A record can be found only by considering its location relative to all other records on the tape. Locating a record, without reading or at least scanning all of the records which come before, is so difficult that it is seldom tried. Thus, updating a file on a magnetic tape nearly always requires a complete rewrite of the tape, as illustrated in Table 1–1 and Figure 1–1 of Chapter 1.

Direct Access Storage Devices

Direct Access Storage Devices (DASD's), such as disks and drums, form the fourth type of I/O storage device. This equipment runs rapidly, and the physical addresses of data can be precisely located, so that any data record can be retrieved immediately, and updating and locating of records is very quick.

COMMUNICATIONS

When data is transferred to or from an I/O device it must be in appropriate form for the device and the computer to handle. Often this involves translating or reorganizing the data before and/or after the transfer. Every large computer will have a communications front end processor which performs this task. This may be a simple circuit which sets up conditions for the transfer; or it may be another, smaller computer called a channel or peripheral processor which actually directs other Input and Output control devices.

If data is transferred over telephone or other communications lines, its format and the method of transfer must be precisely specified. A modem (*mo*dulator-*dem*odulator) performs the task of transforming a digital signal supplied by the computer or device to an analog signal which the telephone lines can handle and then transforming back to digital at the other end. The *baud rate* at which a modem operates specifies roughly how many bits per second will be transferred. A modem which communicates at 110 or 300 baud will be quite inexpensive, whereas a modem which communicates at 1200, 4800, 9600, or 19,200 baud may cost considerably more. Computer communications can occur either in half duplex or full duplex mode, meaning that signals can be transferred in only one direction or in both directions at one time, respectively. A full duplex communications line is the most common. When setting up communications between machines you must also specify which machine is the originator and which is the receiver of the signal, what is the minimum wait time to be allowed between characters, how many start and stop indicators are to be expected between fields, etc.

A Typical Serial Port

As an example of the communications process, consider the transmission of data using the popular RS232C interface. The RS232C is an Electronics Industries Association (EIA) standard configuration for a serial input/output (I/O) port. Serial I/O means that one bit is transferred at a time. This is contrasted with high speed, parallel I/O ports through which all of the bits in an entire computer word can be transmitted simultaneously. In serial transmission, each bit is removed in turn and proceeds, one bit at a time, across a single wire or data path. In parallel I/O there are eight or more data paths, and all of the bits in a word could be transmitted simultaneously.

Data can be transmitted in full duplex mode through a serial port over as few as three wires—one to transmit bits, one to receive bits, and one to provide a zero signal reference (ground); although there are a total of 25 pins on a standard RS232C connector, which can be used if desired for other purposes. One such other use, for example, might be for device status (ready to send or receive) signals. When the RS232C interface is used in *asynchronous* transmission mode, the bits of one character are always preceded by a *start bit* (one interval representing binary zero) and always end with at least one *stop bit* (an interval representing binary one). Then the transmission line is kept "high" (representing continuous binary ones) until the next start bit is sent. Because start and stop bits are used, characters can be transmitted at irregular intervals. For example, the two eight-bit (with odd parity) ASCII characters, OH, sent over a line at 300 baud might appear as in Figure 2–3, where the time interval between characters is arbitrarily long, but the time interval between bits within a character is a fixed quantity, the reciprocal of the baud rate, in this case 1/300 sec. (=0.00333 sec.=3.33 millisec.).

In *synchronous* mode a signal, such as the ASCII synchronous idle character SYN, would be transmitted continuously so that clocks on the sender and receiver could be synchronized. Then, when a different character is transmitted, beginning at the precise synchronization interval, it is received and read without the need for start and stop bits.

Actual transmission takes place over normal telephone lines or radio waves at a high frequency, where, using the RS232C interface as an example, a binary 1 may be a signal such as 1270 Hertz (cycles per second) for a period equal to the reciprocal of the baud rate; then the binary 0 would be 1070 Hertz. Impressing a small frequency change on a high frequency signal like

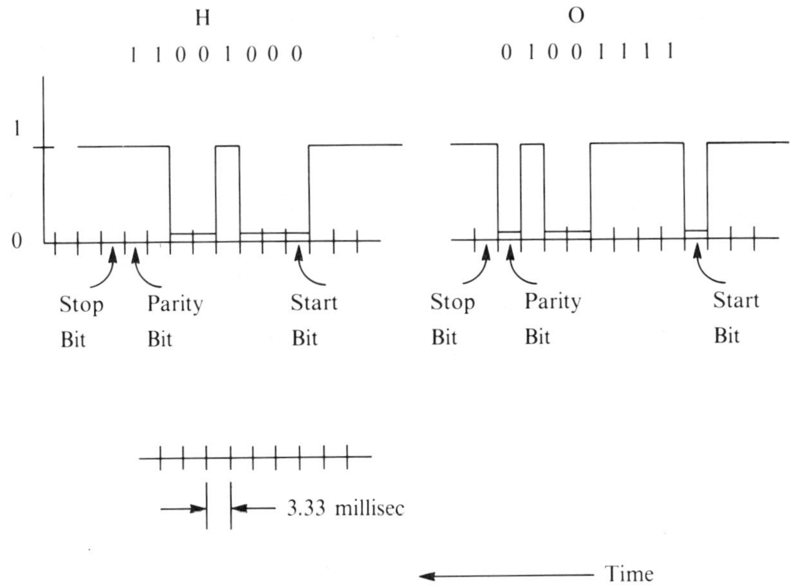

FIGURE 2–3. RS232C Asynchronous Transmission of "OH" in ASCII with Odd Parity

this is called frequency modulation (FM) and is the same process by which FM radio and television signals are transmitted.

QUESTIONS

1. Convert the following binary numbers to hexadecimal and to decimal:

   a. 11010 b. 1101110 c. 11010110 d. 11110010111

2. What would be the number of directly addressable words in the memory of a computer which uses an 18-bit address register? How many kilowords is this?
3. Suppose you wish your computer to be able to address directly 4,294,967,296 = 4 gigabytes directly, where 1 gigabyte = 1024^3 bytes. How many bytes long would your address register have to be?

4. What are the binary and decimal values of the following hexadecimal numbers?

   a. E3 b. C2A5

5. What is the largest number which can be written with 20 binary digits, expressed in

   a. binary b. hexadecimal c. decimal?

6. Convert the following decimal numbers to binary and hex:

   a. 23 b. 193 c. 485 d. 5962

7. Binary numbers are converted to octal by dividing into groups of three, beginning at the radix point. Thus

   $101111001110_2 = 101\ 111\ 001\ 110_2 = 5716_8$
   and
   $4326_8 = 100\ 011\ 010\ 110_2$.

   To convert an octal number to binary, simply write down the three-digit binary equivalent of each octal digit.

   $736_8 = 111\ 011\ 110_2$,
   and
   $3721_8 = 011\ 111\ 010\ 001_2$.

   To convert an octal number to decimal, consider each column as a power of 8.

   $$54613_8 = 3\times 8^0 + 1\times 8^1 + 6\times 8^2 + 4\times 8^3 + 5\times 8^4$$
   $$= 3\times 1 + 1\times 8 + 6\times 64 + 4\times 512 + 5\times 4096 = 22{,}923_{10}.$$

   One way to convert a decimal number to octal is to divide repeatedly by 8 and read the remainders from the bottom up.

   4327_{10} divided by 8 = 540 Remainder 7
   540 divided by 8 = 67 Remainder 4
   67 divided by 8 = 8 Remainder 3
   8 divided by 8 = 1 Remainder 0
   1 divided by 8 = 0 Remainder 1

   Thus, $4327_{10} = 10347_8$.

   a. Convert the following binary numbers to octal:

      (1) 101110 (2) 11110101 (3) 1111010100010110

b. Convert the following octal numbers to decimal and binary:

(1) 361 (2) 1411 (3) 23674

c. Convert the following decimal numbers to octal and binary:

(1) 23 (2) 496 (3) 73165

8. How many different characters could be represented by punching holes in the 12 rows of one column on a Hollerith card? Hint: Characters could be no punches, one punch, two punches, . . . , 12 punches; so you should calculate the sum of the combinations of 12 things taken 0 at a time, one at a time, two at a time, . . . , 12 at a time. The number of combinations of n things taken r at a time is given by ${}_nC_r = n!/((n-r)! \times r!)$, where $n! = n$ factorial $= 1 \times 2 \times 3 \times \ldots . \times n)$. Can you find an easier way to work this problem? (Hint $2^{12} = 4096$.)

9. Suppose, on the paper tape shown in Figure 2–2, that a punched hole is represented by a one and no hole is represented by a zero. If thc bits are written in the order b_1 b_2 b_4 b_8 b_0 b_x, what is the code and odd parity CHECK bit for each of the following characters?

	Character	*Parity*	*Code*
Example:	D	0	001011
	E		
	A		
	R		
	Space		
	J		
	O		
	H		
	N		

10. In what order would the list of character strings

C3PO Radar Luke bang 31flavors

be sorted (a) by a machine using EBCDIC? (b) by a machine using ASCII?

11. What are hexadecimal codes for the following ASCII characters:

a. if the leftmost bit is to be zero?

b. if the leftmost bit is to be an *odd* parity bit?

	Character	a. ASCII	a. Hex	b. Parity	b. ASCII	b. Hex
Example:	L	0100 1100	4C	0	100 1100	4C
Example:	e	0110 0101	65	1	110 0101	E5
	m					
	o					
	n					
	Space					
	A					
	i					
	d					
	Space					
	4					
	Space					
	S					
	a					
	1					
	e					

12. Suppose you wished to develop a binary code similar to ASCII or EBCDIC which could represent 450 different Chinese characters.

    a. How many bits would you need?

    b. What is the total number of characters which you could represent in your code with this number of bits?

13. Describe the difference between each of the elements in the following pairs, and give an example of each.

    a. block and record

    b. character and (computer) word

    c. file and data base

    d. field and area

    e. data preparation device and end-user device

14. Define briefly

    a. modem b. baud rate c. full and half duplex transmission

15. What is the minimum number of wires needed for a half duplex communications line?, for a full duplex line? What are the advantages of a full duplex line?

16. Draw a diagram similar to Figure 2–3 to illustrate continuous repeated transmission of ASCII character SYN with *odd* parity. Explain how sender and receiver clocks can synchronize by repeated transmission of a single character at regular intervals.
17. Draw a diagram like Figure 2–3 to show how the asynchronous transmission of the word My (capital M, lower case y) would appear if the transmission rate were 1200 baud. Assume the characters are ASCII code with *even* parity.
18. Research and describe briefly how using optical fiber technology could permit the transfer of binary data much more rapidly and efficiently than is possible with wires.

CHAPTER 3

DATA STORAGE EQUIPMENT

SERIAL DEVICES

Cards and Paper Tape

Two data storage media—the punched card and punched paper tape—and the way data is stored on them were discussed briefly in Chapter 2. Certainly these media were extremely useful in their day, but storing data on punched cards or paper tape is very bulky, and retrieving the data is quite slow. Loading the BASIC language into a small computer in the early 1970's required reading the language from a paper tape. A mechanical reader took nearly half an hour to read the language tape, and it was quite likely that the tape would have to be read two or three times before the mechanical reader read it completely correctly. Thus it was a major task to change from one language to another. Putting files on paper tape or cards made the search of those files a bulky, time-consuming task. Consequently, much work had to wait for better ways of storing data.

Magnetic Tape

A major improvement over cards and paper tape was the magnetic tape. Although magnetic tape has been used extensively since the 1950's, its popularity for small machines was limited before the late 1960's because of its expense. A good tape drive would cost a few thousand dollars, which made it appropriate for large installations but out of reach of the small user. However, most home microcomputers now allow the user to store programs and data on cassette tapes, using the same recorders and the same tapes which they use for audio recordings. In fact, this is now the least expensive method of auxiliary storge for small systems. Though still quite slow, four or five minutes to search and read a short cassette tape is a major improvement over half an hour to read from paper tape.

The industry standard for magnetic tapes, since the 1950's, is 1/2 inch (1.27 centimeters) wide and 2400 feet (732 meters) long when new. Magnetic tapes tend to get a few feet shorter with age and use. One side of the tape is coated with a magnetic oxide. A constant magnetization, aligning the magnetic spins of collections of atoms along the tape, creates a detectable signal which represents a binary 1. Changing the magnetization of the domains of atoms to the opposite direction represents a binary 0.

A magnetic tape drive is shown in Figure 3–1. The tape, loaded on a supply reel, passes in a loop through a "vacuum" (really a low pressure) column, between rollers and capstans, which pull the tape past the read/write heads, then in another loop through another "vacuum" column, and finally onto the take-up reel. The vacuum columns are absolutely essential to the smooth operation of this device and add to the complexity and expense, of course. Most standard computer tapes travel past the read/write heads at a speed of approximately 200 inches per second (about five meters per second or 11 miles per hour). There are interblock gaps (IBG's), generally 0.6 inches (1.5 centimeters) long, between blocks of data on the tape. The tape comes to a complete stop within about two milliseconds* in the interblock gap, after reading or writing a block, and then accelerates again to 200 inches per second by the time it begins to read the next block. Hence the tape has to accelerate from rest to top speed within two milliseconds and over a distance of less than 1/4 inch. It might be fun but somewhat less than wise to watch a cassette tape snap when you try to accelerate it to that speed within 1/4 inch (0.64 centimeter). The loops in the vacuum columns are necessary to take up the slack while the take-up and supply reels catch up.

The width of a standard magnetic tape is divided into either eight or nine tracks as shown in Figure 3–2. When data is stored in EBCDIC, nine

*1 millisecond = 1/1000 second

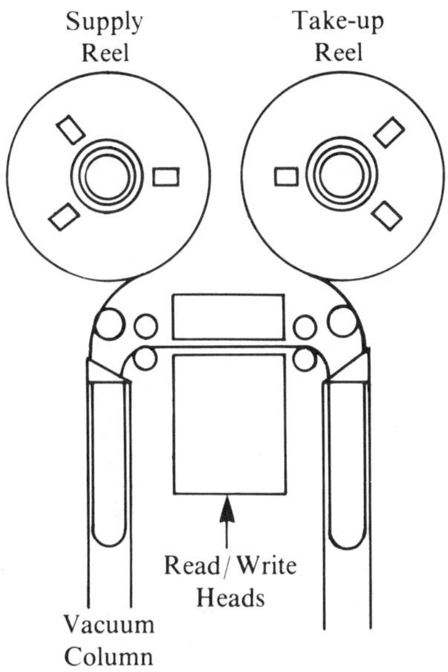

FIGURE 3–1. Magnetic Tape Drive

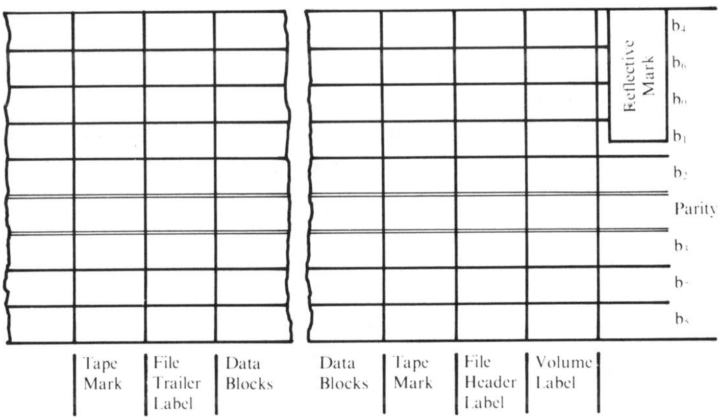

FIGURE 3–2. General Magnetic Tape Format

tracks are used, eight for the code plus one for parity. In ASCII only eight tracks are necessary, seven for the code plus one for parity. Standard data density in recent years has been 1600 bpi. The expression *bpi* means either bits per inch or bytes per inch; both are the same, since one byte is written across the width of the tape, and the number of bits per inch in any track is the same as the number of bytes per inch along the tape. Other densities, such as 800 bpi, are used by some tape drives; it is not unusual now to have data recorded at much higher densities, such as 6250 bpi.

A few feet from the beginning of each tape is a metallic reflective marker, which indicates the physical start of the tape. When the tape is mounted on the drive and the load button is pushed, the tape is automatically positioned at the reflective marker. Following the reflective marker may be a volume label, perhaps 80 bytes or so in length, containing information about the contents of the entire tape, which by definition is a "volume" of data. The volume label will contain such information as the serial number of the volume, whether the tape is write-protected (can information be written on or erased from the tape, or is access restricted to reading from the tape only?), who is the owner of the tape (whose data is it?), etc. At the beginning of each file on the tape, of which there may be many, there will be a file header label, also usually of the order of 80 bytes in length. In the file header label are specified such things as the name of the file, which version it is, when it was created, when it can be erased, who has access to it and whether access is restricted to read only, how many blocks of data are in the file, and other information.

Between blocks of data in the data area are the 0.6 inch long interblock gaps (IBG). These gaps are not empty. The definition of "empty" is a matter of philosophy anyway, since something (0's or 1's or randomized domains with no detectable net magnetization) must be on the tape. A section of tape can't simply be missing. The interblock gap may contain information about how many bytes are in the block preceding the gap and how many bytes are in the block following the gap. Often two consecutive interblock gaps, the first indicating that the next block has zero length and the second indicating that the previous block has zero length, are used to indicate the end of file (EOF) on a tape. Before the end of a file, a file trailer label may be written which contains information similar to that on the file header label. Labels are generally written automatically by the operating system when the user requests a new file to be written on a tape. Of course, if you were writing your own operating system or your own tape handling routines, you would have to be certain that you included label writing routines.

Between each element on the tape, between labels and data blocks, between files, etc. are "tape marks." These are indicators to the tape reader that one element has been read and that a new one is about to begin. A typical way of indicating a tape mark is to record at least one byte which is all binary 1's or some other special combination of bits which the computer will recognize as an indicator of the end of a section.

The bits of a character are not necessarily recorded in order across the width of the tape. If the bits of an EBCDIC character are represented by

parity b_0 b_1 b_2 b_3 b_4 b_5 b_6 b_7

then, from Table 2–2, the character "D," using *odd* parity, would be

0 1 1 0 0 0 1 0 0.

However, as seen in Figure 3–2, the bits might be recorded in the order

b_4 b_6 b_0 b_1 b_2 parity b_3 b_7 b_5

so that the character "D" would be recorded across the tape in the order

0 0 1 1 0 0 0 0 1.

The reason for this is an attempt to store the most significant bits, the ones most critical for identifying the character or for testing whether it has been recorded correctly, toward the center of the tape. Stray magnetic or electric fields or even physical mangling of the tape are more likely to affect the outer edges of the tape than the central tracks.

Because it is confusing to read a representation of a tape from paper if it is organized this way, in the examples and exercises we will assume that the bits are recorded in order across the tape even though we are aware that is not generally true. We will put the parity in the middle of the tape so that you begin to get some feeling for the true situation, however.

To illustrate some other features of recording data on magnetic tape, consider the situation shown in Figure 3–3. Here we assume that the message "DEAR Space JOHN Space" is recorded on a tape in EBCDIC code, with the bit pattern as indicated in the figure. You should verify from Table 2–2 that the codes are correct. The parity bit for each character has been calculated for *odd* parity.

A longitudinal check byte and lateral check bit are often recorded at the end of each block as shown. Various methods are used to create the longitudinal check byte. One of the simplest, illustrated in Figure 3–3, is to assign each bit in the check byte so that each track of the block has the same parity (even or odd) as is assigned to each byte. This is done for all tracks, including the parity track. The lateral check bit is the parity bit for the longitudinal

	Longitudinal Check Byte	SP	N	H	O	J	SP	R	A	E	D	
	1	0	1	1	1	1	0	1	1	1	1	b_0
	1	1	1	1	1	1	1	1	1	1	1	b_1
	1	0	0	0	0	0	0	0	0	0	0	b_2
	1	0	1	0	1	1	0	1	0	0	0	b_3
Lateral Check Bit	1	0	0	0	0	1	0	0	0	1	0	Parity
	1	0	0	1	0	0	0	1	0	0	0	b_4
	1	0	1	0	1	0	0	0	0	1	1	b_5
	0	0	0	0	1	0	0	0	0	0	0	b_6
	0	0	1	0	0	1	0	1	1	1	0	b_7

FIGURE 3–3. Longitudinal Check Byte and Lateral Check Bit

check byte. If you are using odd parity, the longitudinal check byte may have either even or odd parity. For ASCII (or any code with an odd number of bits per character) the longitudinal check byte will have odd parity when there are an odd number of characters in the block, and the check byte will have even parity when there are an even number of characters in the block. The opposite is true for EBCDIC (or any code with an even number of bits per character). If you are using even parity, the longitudinal check byte will always have even parity, regardless of the code or of the number of characters in the block. If you were writing an operating system, you would want to make certain that you take this effect into account.

The longitudinal check byte and lateral check bit serve to check to see if the entire block has been recorded or read correctly. If there is only one error in the block (a 1 was changed to a 0 or vice versa) then the parity of the longitudinal check byte will be incorrectly recorded in the lateral check bit. Then the user will either want to reread or rewrite the entire block or to check the parity of each character to determine which character has the incorrect parity and was read or written incorrectly.

Another popular way of writing the longitudinal check byte, which was used extensively with paper tape, is to record in that byte the total number of 1's written in the entire block. When the block is read, the number of 1's read is counted; the total read is checked against the total written, which would have been recorded in the longitudinal check byte. If the numbers do not agree, then the block would be read again.

Storing Files on Tape

It should be apparent, with bytes of data stored 1600 to the inch, and interblock gaps 0.6 inches long, that the most efficient utilization of tape space is with long blocks and few interblock gaps. However, a limit to the maximum length of blocks is imposed by the computer, which is reading from or writing to the tape. All information which is read from the tape, for example, must be moved one block at a time through the input *buffer* (an intermediate memory). With very long blocks, the amount of memory which must be set aside as the input buffer (or the output buffer when writing) is very large. Hence there is a definite tradeoff between efficient use of space on the tape (minimizing the number of interblock gaps), and having a reasonable amount of data transferred to the computer at one time. Typically, blocks do not exceed a few hundred bytes.

The way data is written to a magnetic tape defines a sequential file. Data can be read from the tape or written onto the tape only in sequential order. If you wish to read record 246, you must at least scan records 1 through 245. Unless tape is provided with special timing marks, it cannot support update in place. You cannot locate a specific spot on a tape within 1/1600th of an inch. It is asking for incredible accuracy to expect the tape drive to be accurate to within 1/1600 inch over a distance of hundreds or thousands of inches; you would be expecting about one part per million accuracy, which is difficult to achieve in any situation. Also, tape length changes slightly with temperature and with use; thus, even if you had the drive accuracy, it would not be feasible to try to use it. Recording densities, tape motion speed, and tape dimensions all vary slightly. When writing to a magnetic tape, the computer considers all data after the point last written as illegible; i.e. an end of file (EOF) is considered to be after the last record you just wrote. Trying to go to a spot on a tape and change or insert data simply tells the computer that the remainder of the tape is blank. A file can be extended but not updated in the middle. There are no physical boundaries on a tape other than the metallic starting point marker, so all processes performed on the tape are relative to the current position.

Most tape drives are capable of the following operations:

1. Read or Write forward one block
2. Skip forward to the next IBG
3. Skip backwards to the previous IBG (available on some drives only)
4. Skip forward to the end of file
5. Rewind to the beginning of the tape
6. Read backward one block (available on a limited selection of drives)

Each of these operations is relative to the current position. Thus, the data is considered sequential, and data on which only these or similar operations can be performed is said to be sequentially organized.

Writing to a magnetic tape involves write, read, and compare operations. If what is read does not match what was to have been written, a sophisticated tape drive will backspace and retry once. If this fails, then a few inches of the tape may be erased, and the write operation tried again. This is called "redundancy during a write failure."

"Redundancy during a read failure" may cause the tape to be backspaced and reread up to 10 times. If this is not successful, the "detergent" effect may be tried; that is, backspace about five blocks, then space forward and try to read again. This is the "detergent" effect, because the philosophy is to "get the dirt out" from between the tape and the read/write heads.

If a read failure occurs and cannot be recovered easily by the "detergent" effect, the block of data may simply be ignored as a "noise" block, especially if it is only a few bytes long. The computer assumes that this is an imperfection in the surface of the tape (which occurs often), ignores the space, and continues to try to read the rest of the tape. Thus, if you expect the computer to warn you of errors rather than just to ignore a region which cannot be read, all recorded data blocks should contain more than the minimum number of bytes which your device will assume to be noise.

Cassettes

The cassette tapes used with a home microcomputer and the microcassettes used on other systems contain the same magnetic oxide coated tape as the industry standard. However, the tape is less than 3/16 inch (1/2 centimeter) wide, and there is only one head, which performs both read and write functions. Thus bits are recorded serially along one track rather than on eight or nine tracks across the tape. The read and write speed of most commercially available cassette recorders is 1.875 inches (4.76 centimeters) per second. The density of data bits along the tape depends upon the speed at which data is transferred by the computer and varies from a few bits per inch for a very slow system to more than 800 bits per inch for faster machines. There are no automatically recorded gaps between data blocks, during which the cassette stops, although some spaces between data blocks are defined by the distance which the tape travels when no data is being transferred. Consequently, the time to read from or write to a cassette tape is several hundred times longer than that for a standard 1/2 inch tape.

Rarely is provision made on inexpensive cassettes for redundancy during read or write failures. A longitudinal check byte, if written, will be a simple expression, such as the total number of 1's in the entire file. Header and trailer labels similar to those recorded on larger tapes may be written as determined by the operating system. Skipping and rewinding must be performed manually by the person operating the recorder; of course, with only one read/write head, no write and read compare operations are possible while recording data.

Streaming Tapes

For the purpose of copying large amounts of data quickly, such as backup of several megabytes of data from a disk pack in a small system, other tape drives have been developed which store data on cartridges or reels of tape which stream past the read/write heads at high speed. These units are called *streaming tapes* and can store large quantities of data in a short time and in a relatively small space.

Typically, a streaming tape drive is designed to transfer the entire contents of the tape at once, with no interruptions, although most may be used in start/stop mode if desired. Tape formats vary widely between manufacturers. Some use eight tracks across the tape, others may provide as many as 24 tracks. Some will store a few megabytes at densities as low as 1600 bytes per inch while others can handle hundreds of megabytes at densities approaching 10,000 bytes per inch. Tape transport likewise varies from about 10 inches per second in the slowest models up to 200 inches per second in high speed versions.

Interblock gaps are recorded without stopping and starting the tape and are usually only about 10 to 20 bytes long rather than the 1000 bytes or so on start/stop standard tape drives. If tapes do have to be stopped, then of course the performance drops drastically. Software designed to transfer data to the streaming tape may, in its simplest form, transfer all data, non-data gaps, and noise blocks from a disk to the tape in what is called a mirror image approach. A more sophisticated method, which will be considerably slower, but which ultimately saves lots of tape, collects noncontiguous areas for an entire file and transfers them to one contiguous block on the streaming tape. A bit format method transfers data blocks, but not non-data or defective blocks, in sequence from the disk to the tape. Recovery of data from a bit-formatted streaming tape generally means copying the entire tape without performing any other file handling functions.

Video Tapes

Any device which uses magnetic tape can be adapted to data recording. Some effort has been made to use video tape recorders for this purpose. On video tapes large quantities of data must be stored in the form of several hundred thousand television screens full of information, where each screen represents several kilobytes. Thus a typical video tape may be able to store several gigabytes* of data. Of course, data will be retrieved sequentially from a video tape just as from any other serial storage medium. Since video recorders drive tapes at only a few inches per second, it may require several hours to read an entire tape. However, because the data density is so large, if the tape can be accurately positioned using a revolution counter or timing marks, retrieval of short blocks of data may occur within a few milliseconds.

A popular use of video tape recorders is for interactive computer-video applications, such as computer aided instruction (CAI). The computer is interfaced with the recorder so that the search and read operations necessary to call high quality graphics images from the video tape can be performed without tying up the huge quantities of primary memory which would otherwise be necessary for storing those images.

DIRECT ACCESS STORAGE DEVICES

Magnetic tape is considered a serial or sequential storage medium. Direct access storage devices (DASD's) include disks, drums, strips, cards, and a variety of other equipment.

Magnetic Strips and Cards

Magnetic strips and cards are becoming popular as banking tools, though there is some opposition for social reasons. Wallet-size cards are now avail-

*1 gigabyte = 1024^3 bytes = 1,073,741,824 bytes

able which have magnetic backings or which actually contain a microchip. Your entire financial status can be stored on such a card. With these cards you can charge items in establishments which have appropriate devices. Not only will the transaction be relayed directly to your bank, but your card will be updated immediately at the point of sale. Such devices are called "direct access" because the records or fields on the card can be accessed directly, without reading or processing the entire set of information on the card.

Magnetic Drums

Magnetic drums were among the first popular genuine high-speed direct access devices. A magnetic drum, such as that shown in Figure 3–4, is a cylinder of between one and three feet in diameter. The outside of the drum is coated with magnetic oxide, just like a magnetic tape or disk surface, and the drum spins at several hundred revolutions per minute. The surface of the drum is divided logically into strips, called tracks, on which data is stored. There is a separate, fixed, read/write head for each track. Switching from one track to another to find data is done by switching electronically from one read/write head to another. This can be done within microseconds at most, so that the data can be found extremely rapidly. Generally, any byte on an entire drum can be found within 10 milliseconds or less.

Drums, though they are still the fastest direct access devices, have two disadvantages. First, the amount of memory space on the drum is limited. Even with a very large diameter drum, it is rare to have more than 200 tracks, partly because the large numbers of read/write heads are expensive, and partly because there is a physical limit to how closely read/write heads can be packed next to each other. Five megabytes is considered a large memory for

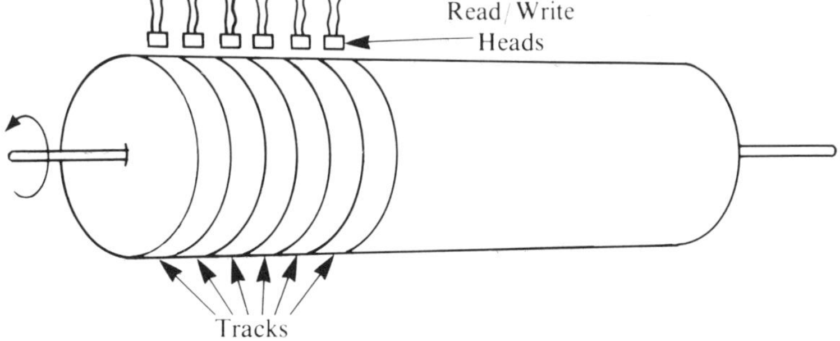

FIGURE 3–4. Magnetic Drum

a drum. A second disadvantage of a drum is the difficulty of balancing a high speed rotating cylinder. A small aberration can result in vibrations which, in the extreme, can cause the entire computer which contains the drum to "walk" across the floor. This can easily wipe out read/write heads and badly damage the drum surface, requiring costly replacement.

Floppy Disks

The most popular direct access storage devices at present are magnetic disk drives. There are a number of fundamental types of disks which you may encounter.

Many small computers use "floppy disks," flexible disks enclosed within a permanent envelope. Three standard floppy disk sizes are eight inches (20.3 cm), 5 1/4 inches (13.3 cm), and now approximately three inches (7.6 cm) in diameter. A floppy disk may have one usable side (single-sided) or two (double-sided). It may be recordable at single or double density. Typical capacities for 5 1/4 inch disks are, for example,

single-side; single-density; 80 kilobytes
single-side; double density; 160 kilobytes
double-side; double-density; 320 kilobytes

However, these may vary depending upon the computer and disk drive manufacturer. Capacities for three-inch and eight-inch disks may be scaled down and up accordingly. Newer three-inch diskettes are packaged in rigid envelopes which allows higher speed of rotation and denser packing of data so that they may be able to contain more data than some of the larger disks.

Typical diskettes are shown in Figure 3–5. The disks are read through the slot in the envelope, and most are driven at about 300 revolutions per minute by a hub on the disk drive which fits through the center of the disk. There is also a small hole in the disk envelope just outside the center hub. This hole is used by the disk drive to find the beginning of each track, a concentric ring on which data is stored.

If the disk is soft-sectored, there will be one hole through the disk itself. When the hole in the envelope and the hole in the disk are aligned, a photoelectric cell detects light through the hole and informs the drive controller that this is the beginning of every track. Typically, on a 5 1/4 inch disk there will be about 40 tracks, the outermost track being designated track 1 or 0, depending upon the operating system being used, and the innermost track

FIGURE 3–5. Flexible Diskettes *(Courtesy of International Business Machines Corporation)*

having the highest number (e. g., 40). Each track is divided into sectors. The collection of sectors in a fixed position for every track gives the appearance of a wedge shape, like a piece of pie. Typically, on a 5 1/4 inch disk there will be about 18 sectors per track, though this may differ considerably depending on the computer manufacturer. If a disk is hard-sectored, there will be as many holes through the disk as there are sectors. In this case the photoelectric cell picks up the beginning of each sector through the window in the envelope.

Note that the sector itself is not wedge shaped. One sector is simply a piece of a track (e. g., 1/18th of the circumference of a given track). Usually the same number of bytes is stored in each sector, even though the sectors of the tracks along the outer edge of the disk are physically much longer than the sectors along the inner tracks. Thus data is stored more densely toward the center and less densely along the outer circumference. This is because reading and writing on the disk is done as a function of time; one bit is sent and recorded in a fixed amount of time, no matter at which track the read/write head is located. It takes the same amount of time for one "short" sector at the center of the disk to pass under the read/write head as for a "long" sector at the outer edge. Hence the same number of data bytes will be recorded (typically 128, 256, or 512 bytes per sector) Given the incentive, you could design a disk drive such that the recording rate could be changed or the speed of the disk could be changed as the read/write head moved from edge to center. With this type of device you can pack much more information on a floppy disk; some manufacturers are designing disk drives with this feature. A variety of other, different concepts are also being used to achieve closer packing of the data on a disk, such as aligning domains across the width of a track or in the depth of a track rather than along the track, or enclosing the disks in rigid envelopes so that higher access speeds can be reached.

You may observe that the 5 1/4-inch diskette in Figure 3–5 has a notch punched along the edge of the envelope. This is the write enable notch. When this is covered, by a piece of tape or a label, the disk is write-protected. That is, you may read only; you may not change, delete, or write new data to the disk. On the other hand, the standard eight-inch disk comes without a notch and may be write-protected by punching a notch in the appropriate location in the envelope.

When a floppy disk is being accessed, the disk itself is pinched gently between a soft pad on one side of the disk and the read/write head on the other. Thus the read/write head actually rides on the surface of the disk. The highest quality disks should have highly polished surfaces to minimize scratching of the disk surface and the build-up of oxide deposits on the read/write head.

5 1/4-inch and eight-inch disk sizes are standard. Thus, for example, you should expect that any soft-sectored, single-sided, double density, 5 1/4-inch diskette should work in any drive which uses that format. Before you store data on the disk it is usually necessary to run a program which records non-data addresses and flags on the tracks in the format required by your operating system.

Winchester Disks

Another type of disk drive which you might find on small business systems is called a *Winchester* drive. A Winchester disk differs from a floppy disk in that the disks are rigid rather than flexible and are either sealed permanently within the drive or are sealed within a removable cartridge. In either case, the disks never see the light of day. Great care is taken to see that they are kept away from dust and dirt. This is important because the data on a Winchester disk is typically recorded much more densely than on a floppy disk, and the drive spins the disk at several thousand revolutions per minute rather than several hundred rpm as for a floppy. Rather than riding on the disk surface, the read/write heads of a Winchester drive "fly" on a cushion of air about 10 millionths of an inch (0.25 micrometers) thick. This air cushion is created by the aerodynamic design of the head and the air dragged by friction on the surface of the rapidly spinning disk. At these densities and speed, the disk could easily be damaged severely by smoke, dust, or human hair coming between the read/write head and the disk. Typical capacities for Winchester disks range from a few megabytes to a few hundred megabytes, and because of the much higher rotation speed, access to the data on the disk is much faster than for a floppy disk. Winchester disks range in size from about five-inches (approximately 13 cm) to more than 17 inches (43 cm) in diameter, the larger disks holding more data, of course, for a fixed density.

Hard Disks

Very large capacity disk drives use stacks of several rigid disks, mounted on a central spindle so that they all spin together. Typically, these hard disks spin at about 3600 rpm and are eight to 14 inches (20 to 36 cm) in diameter. You may find a few models which use even larger disks. The capacity of the largest stacks of disks is about 1000 megabytes, and smaller drives range downward from that figure to as low as five megabytes. Access time to find any particular byte of data on a typical hard disk ranges from about 25 to 150 milliseconds.

As with the Winchester disks, the read/write heads float on very thin cushions of air, considerably smaller than the thickness of a human hair. Figure 3–6 illustrates how the read/write heads are mounted on an access arm which resembles a comb in appearance. All of the heads move in and out together.

Hard disks are generally recorded on both top and bottom surfaces. Thus, if there are 11 platters on a spindle, there should be 22 recordable surfaces. However, there are two reasons why the number of surfaces on which you can record data is less than twice the number of platters. First, most hard disk drives reserve one surface to be used as a control surface for monitoring where the access arm is positioned. Thus, for virtually all disk drives the number of data surfaces is at least one fewer than twice the number of platters.

In some disk systems, the *disk pack* is *removable* from the drive so that disks can be interchanged and data can be stored *off-line* as well as *on-line.* In these cases the top surface of the top disk and the bottom surface of the

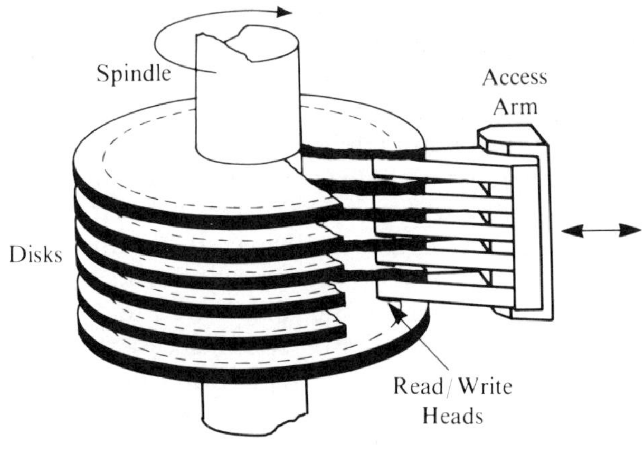

FIGURE 3–6. A Hard Disk Pack with Access Arm

bottom disk are most likely to get dirty and scratched, so their use is generally avoided. Hence, for a removable disk pack, two more surfaces are unavailable for data storage. If we look at a removable pack of 11 platters, there may be only 19 surfaces for data storage (11 platters × 2 surfaces per platter − 1 surface for control − 1 top surface − 1 bottom surface = 19 surfaces). See Figure 3–7.

DISK CHARACTERISTICS

General Organization

Virtually all hard disks are organized physically in the same manner with only minor differences. The surface of a hard disk is divided into concentric tracks, just as is the surface of a floppy disk or a Winchester. The obvious difference is that there are more tracks, since the data can be recorded more densely.

Typically, on a floppy disk, consecutive data is recorded on consecutive tracks on the same surface. For example, after track 5 is filled the data is continued on track 6 if space is available there, then on track 7, etc. On a hard disk with several platters, consecutive data is recorded vertically through the stack of disks on cylinders. A *cylinder* is the set of all corresponding tracks on all surfaces. If you could cut one cylinder out of a disk pack, it would ap-

FIGURE 3–7. A Removable Disk Pack *(Courtesy of International Business Machines Corporation)*

pear as a stack of rings all the same diameter, one on top of another. The reason for filling up a cylinder before going to a new track is simple. To transfer recording from track 5 on one surface to track 5 on the next surface requires only that the appropriate write head be activated. Switching read/write heads is done electronically within a few microseconds. On the other hand, moving from track 5 to track 6 on one surface requires that the access arm be moved physically. Moving the access arm is time consuming, from a minimum of about 10 milliseconds to move to the next adjacent track, to much longer to move to tracks further away. Thus, switching from surface to surface on one cylinder may be thousands of times faster than moving from track to track on one surface. Reading and writing of data is speeded up considerably by recording by cylinders rather than by tracks.

Some disk tracks are divided physically into a fixed number of sectors, each with the same number of bytes. Such disk drives are called *Fixed Block Architecture* machines, in contrast with *"conventional"* machines where the user may determine how long each physical block of data is to be on a track.

All of the data recorded on one disk pack constitutes a *volume.* Sometimes, if there are a large number of tracks per surface, these tracks will be grouped logically into two *bands,* an outer band and an inner band; the cylinders defined by the bands will define a volume. In this terminology, if there are two bands per surface, the disk pack would be said to contain two volumes.

The concepts of sector, track, cylinder, and band on a hard disk pack are illustrated in Figure 3–8.

Many companies build Direct Access Storge Devices (DASD's). Specific characteristics of disk drives will be found in the manuals which accompany the drives. The DASD's described here are representative of the different options available.

Specific DASD Types

The computer to which DASD's are attached is commonly called the *host* machine. Most drives made by a given company can be connected to any host computer made by that company, although there are limitations, which one must inquire about when purchasing a system. Just as floppy disk operating systems and drives for various microcomputers are rarely compatible with other brands, so one must also be careful about which hard disk drive is purchased for a given large host. The concept of *compatibility* among machines and drives is relatively new, and although attempts are being made to improve the situation, it is still not as simple as buying a lightbulb from the hardware store and fitting it into a standard socket.

It is important when considering disk drives to recognize that the servo motors, read/write heads, access arms which hold the read/write heads, electronics, and other hardware are much more expensive than the disks themselves. Therefore, manufacturers attempt to pack more and more data onto a disk in order to decrease the cost per megabyte of the storage.

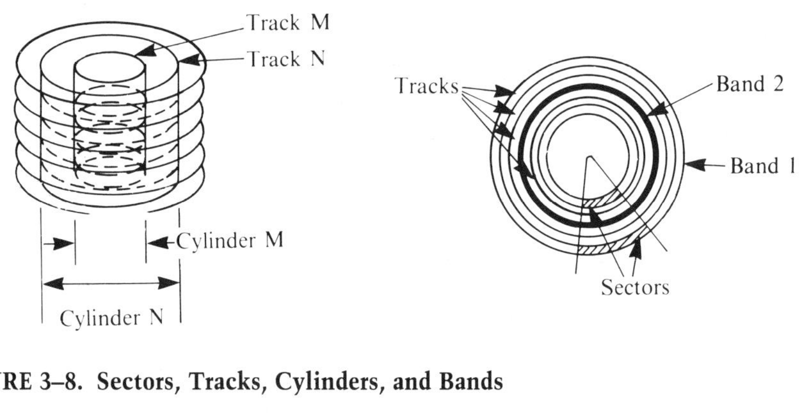

FIGURE 3–8. Sectors, Tracks, Cylinders, and Bands

Fixed Block Architecture

A number of disk drives use fixed block architecture (FBA), in which the lengths of physical blocks are determined by the hardware. On these machines the tracks on a disk are divided into fixed length sectors, typically with 256 or 512 bytes per sector. When data is written to the disk or read from the disk it must be done in integer multiples of the sector length. The user has no choice in the matter. The advantage of fixed block architecture is that the operating system is simpler, and the data is easily read or written. There is no doubt about the block length as there may be on "conventional" drives where the user has more choice in determining the recording format. The major disadvantage of an FBA machine is that some space may be wasted in the process of storing the data. For example, if you wish to store 448 byte records on an FBA disk with 512 byte sectors, it is likely that you would store one record per sector. In this case, the last 64 (512–448) bytes of each sector would be unused, and you would be wasting at least one-eighth of the available space on the disk.

Fixed block architecture is generally used on floppy disks. Some larger disk drives also use FBA. Let's consider some important parameters for a typical small FBA drive with three platters.

A typical small fixed block architecture disk pack:

153 tracks per surface (plus one alternate)

25 sectors per track (plus one alternate)

256 bytes per sector

five tracks per cylinder (2×3 platters less one control surface)

Example 3–1

What is the maximum byte capacity of the small FBA drive described above?

Solution:

$$\frac{153 \text{ tracks}}{\text{surface}} \times \frac{25 \text{ sectors}}{\text{track}} \times \frac{256 \text{ bytes}}{\text{sector}} \times \frac{5 \text{ surfaces}}{\text{volume}}$$

$= 4{,}896{,}000$ bytes per volume.

Removable Disk Units

In a computer facility where much of the processing is done in batch mode, it is convenient to have disk packs which can be removed from the drive and stored off-line. The disk volumes can be loaded manually as needed, and one or two disk drives can service large numbers of programs and very large quantities of data. Of course, if the computer is used in time-sharing mode, users may be quite unhappy to find that their programs and data are often not on-line. In this situation a removable disk pack may not be suitable.

When removable hard disk packs are used, the top and bottom surfaces are most susceptible to damage and are generally not used for data storage. One surface is often reserved to be read by a synchronizing servo head to maintain alignment of the access arm. Hence the number of tracks per cylinder would normally be twice the number of platters less top, bottom, and control surfaces. Most removable disk packs are conventional architecture in that the user may format the data blocks on a track as desired, without concern for fixed length sectors.

Removable disk packs come in a wide variety of configurations, depending upon the vintage and the manufacturer, but a typical removable, conventional architecture disk pack may have characteristics similar to the following.

A typical removable, conventional disk pack:

11 14-inch diameter disks

19 data tracks per cylinder

13,000 bytes per track

800 tracks per surface (plus seven alternates)

Nonremovable (Fixed) Disk Packs

In circumstances where many machine users must have data and the programs on-line at all times it is desirable to use nonremovable, or fixed, media. On this type of disk it is even more critical than on removable media to provide as much storage capacity as possible. Running out of disk space on a fixed medium implies either a large expense for another drive or a large expenditure of time to reorganize and delete or retire unused data. Thus fixed media disk drives with capacities approaching a gigabyte are not unusual.

Often a fixed disk pack is divided logically into two volumes; each surface then has two bands. One band contains half of the tracks on the surface, and the other band contains the remaining tracks. A volume then consists of the set of cylinders containing the tracks in a given band.

These units vary in configuration also, but typical large capacity characteristics may be similar to those of the fixed drive described below.

A typical nonremovable (fixed), conventional architecture disk pack:

four 14-inch diameter disks

two bands per surface

600 cylinders per volume

26,000 bytes per track

14 tracks per cylinder

You may note that on a fixed medium all disk surfaces are generally used, including top and bottom. One surface may be reserved for control. Thus, one would expect the fixed drive described above, which has four platters, to have seven (2×4 platters $-$ 1 control surface) tracks per cylinder. In fact, it is not unusual for large capacity devices such as this to be configured with two read/write heads per surface, so that each cylinder (the area which can be accessed without moving an access arm) contains two tracks rather than one from each surface. Thus, the device described above has 14 tracks per cylinder, rather than seven.

Example 3–2

a. What is the capacity (in megabytes) of each volume on the nonremovable, conventional architecture drive described above?

b. What is the total capacity of the drive?

c. How many tracks are on each surface?

Solution:

a. $$\frac{600 \text{ cylinders}}{\text{volume}} \times \frac{26000 \text{ bytes}}{\text{track}} \times \frac{14 \text{ tracks}}{\text{cylinder}} = 218{,}400{,}000 \text{ bytes/vol.}$$

$$= 281{,}400{,}000/(1024)^2 = 208.3 \text{ Megabytes per volume}$$

b. $\frac{2 \text{ volumes}}{\text{drive}} \times \frac{208.3 \text{ Megabytes}}{\text{volume}} = 416.6$ Megabytes per drive

c. Each cylinder contains two tracks from each surface. Thus there would be 1200 (2×600) tracks per band and *2400 (2×1200) tracks per surface*. Another way to see this result is

$$\frac{\text{tracks}}{\text{surface}} = \frac{218{,}400{,}000 \text{ bytes}}{\text{volume}} \times \frac{2 \text{ volumes}}{\text{disk pack}} \times \frac{\text{track}}{26000 \text{ bytes}} \times \frac{\text{disk pack}}{7 \text{ surfaces}}$$

$$= 2400 \text{ tracks/surface}$$

Because the removable disk pack requires more complex mechanics than the fixed disk machine, nonremovable disks are often the least expensive and most reliable.

Data Modules

In order to improve reliability while preserving the capability of removable disks, some manufacturers have designed equipment in which the disks, access arms, and read/write heads are all enclosed in a sealed module, which can be removed from the drive. Obviously, this helps prevent dirt from getting inside the module, but makes the cost of replacement modules somewhat more expensive. Total data capacity may be changed in some of these devices by using different modules, and the integrity (resistance of accidental change to the data) is enhanced because the head which wrote the data to the disk is always the head which reads it. For very quick access to part of the data, some modules have separate read/write heads, fixed in place, for each of the tracks in the first few cylinders. Data recorded on these cylinders can be accessed very rapidly because no motion of an access arm is required. A typical data module may have capacities similar to the following.

A typical removable data module:

1400 tracks per surface

8000 bytes per track

12 tracks per cylinder

It may not be necessary in such a module to reserve an entire surface for control. Also, the top and bottom surfaces may be used without undue concern. So with one read/write head per surface, the module just described would have to have six platters. If there were two read/write heads per surface, the module would need only three platters.

Fixed Head Drives

A quite different type of disk drive is the fixed head device. In this drive, the disks are fixed permanently within the machine, and each track on each disk has its own read/write head, just as each track on a drum has its own read/write head. For this reason, this type of drive is often loosely called a "drum."

One typical fixed head drive contains approximately

64 tracks per surface (plus eight alternates)

15,000 bytes per track

24 tracks per cylinder

Thus, counting the eight alternate tracks per surface, there have to be 72 read/write heads per surface, which of course adds to the expense of the device. However, the reliability is increased enormously. On this particular device, there are four fixed access mechanisms containing 18 heads each, with every other track being read by a given mechanism, as shown in Figure 3–9.

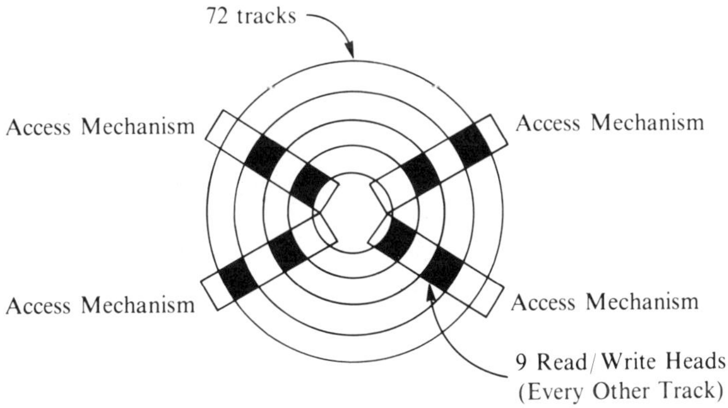

FIGURE 3–9. Head Configuration on a Typical Fixed Head DASD

Other Configurations

In order to achieve very high capacities, some devices use a combination of conventional and fixed block architecture concepts. For example, faster access speeds may be achieved by allowing the user to format a track as desired but with the restriction that each Count, Key, or Data area must be recorded in short, fixed length blocks, perhaps 16, 32, or 64 bytes long.

Some very large drives have multiple access arms which may access different cylinders independently and simultaneously, provided the necessary control electronics are available. The attempt is constantly being made to achieve higher capacity and faster access through an increase in density in terms of more tracks per inch across a disk surface and more bytes per inch along the tracks. Also, new developments in VLSI (very large scale integration) technology allow high capacity disk drives to occupy much less floor space, require considerably less power, and perform some of their own failure diagnostics.

Some storage equipment is being designed to allow data to be moved from older devices without having to be completely reformatted to match the new device. Generally, when used in "compatibility mode" like this, the storage capacity is somewhat less than when the device is used in the "native mode" for which it was designed; but manufacturers seem to be showing more and more concern about providing urgently needed compatibility.

Video Disks

On magnetic disks data can be packed along a track at typical densities of several thousand bytes per inch; however, to accommodate the positioning of a mechanical access arm, the track density across the disk can be only a few hundred tracks per inch. On optical disks, the tracks can be placed as closely together as the bits along a track. Hence track densities as high as several thousand tracks per inch can be achieved, and overall data densities approach 200 million bits per square inch (bpsi), compared with fewer than 10 million bpsi on even the most precise magnetic disks. Thus, video capacities can be in the gigabyte range.

Most video disks used for data recording are preformatted with servo tracking signals to allow precise radial positioning of the head. Data is recorded by producing a bubble about one micrometer (39 microinches) in diameter on the surface of the disk. Reading the data is a matter of measuring changes in the intensity of a low power laser beam as it is reflected from the spots on the disk suface.

Video disks are direct access storage devices, since any spot on the surface can be found and examined within milliseconds. This technology lends itself better to permanent recording than to erasable data; thus video disks are particularly suited to the distribution of large data bases such as legal, scientific, and medical files. One exciting use of video disks is in education, where the disk, used to store video information, interfaces with a computer. The computer can provide graphics and text and allow the student direct interaction with the video frames on the disk.

Memory

It is not unusual to see tapes and disks used only for backup purposes. Very Large Scale Integrated (VLSI) circuits, with tens of thousands of circuit elements on one semiconductor chip, have led to computers, both large and small, with very large primary Random Access Memory (RAM). RAM capacities have grown from one kilobit in 1970 to 256 kilobits or more per chip now.

For fastest access, memory is often designed so that each bit of a word resides on a different chip. Thus a computer with 16-bit words would have at least 16 RAM chips and sufficient data lines so that bits could be transferred from all chips simultaneously. Many computers now use extra banks of semiconductor memory for high speed secondary storage, avoiding the delays associated with motion of a tape, an access arm, or rotation of a disk. Such auxiliary memory is random access, by definition, since any byte or word can be stored and retrieved directly.

One problem with most semiconductor memory as a secondary storage medium is its volatility. When the power dies, so does the memory. However, most semiconductors require very small currents and can be protected easily by battery backup power. In addition, there are some nonvolatile technologies such as read only memory (ROM) and bubble memory chips. ROM is used for storage of information that does not change frequently, such as operating systems; thus it has limited application to the secondary storage of data. On the other hand, there are bubble memories which store the data in the form of magnetic domains with opposite magnetic field from the rest of the medium. These are quite fast, can be reprogrammed quickly, and are used commonly in portable devices where disk drives are too cumbersome.

Even when semiconductor memories are used for secondary storage, backup on disk or tape is generally critical to maintaining adequate data security and integrity.

Alternate Tracks and Sectors

In the discussion above we have referred briefly to *alternate* tracks and sectors. Disk surfaces are rarely flawless. Although disks are carefully analyzed, even at the factory there may be defects in some of the surfaces of the disks. For this reason alternate tracks are provided on high capacity DASD's, which can be used in place of defective *primary* tracks on which data cannot be stored.

Before hard disks are shipped from the factory, any defective primary track will be *flagged,* and an indicator may be recorded concerning which alternate track is to be used instead. Utility routines in the access methods at user installations will be provided for detecting and flagging bad tracks or sectors which occur subsequently.

On most drives, when a track has a defective area, the entire track is flagged defective, and an entire alternate track is designated as its replacement. However, some devices have a "skip displacement" feature, which allows the remainder of a track to be used even if part of it is found to be defective. On fixed block architecture machines, alternate sectors may be provided on each track for use in place of defective sectors.

The use of alternate tracks slows down data access. When a track is determined to be defective, a motion of the access arm is usually required to find and read the alternate. Most floppy disk drives do not provide the option of alternate tracks.

Head Crashes

One way of creating defective tracks, or of causing complete disaster, is the *head crash.* A head crash occurs when foreign material comes between the read/write head and the disk surface or when loss of the thin cushion of air causes the read/write head to ride on the surface of the disk. Figure 3–10 shows how serious foreign matter can be in a disk drive. The air cushion between the head and the disk is a few 10-millionths of an inch wide. In contrast, smoke, lint, or human hair are enormous. Supervisory personnel should get quite upset with smoking and dirt in the computer room. A head crash is usually accompanied by considerable noise, a pungent odor, and some smoke of its own. With luck, only a few tracks of a disk surface will be scratched and a small amount of data lost. By Murphy's Law, the lost data will always be the most critical on the disk pack. The read/write head may even be damaged to the point that through a microscope it looks something like shredded wheat. A few specialists throughout the country perform a valuable service

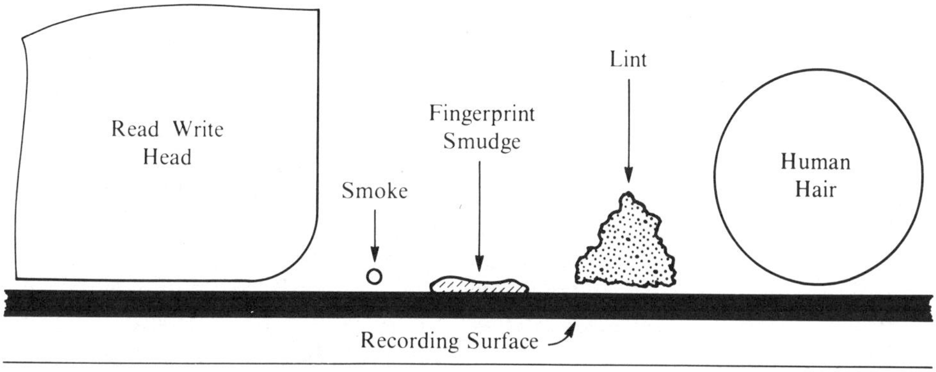

FIGURE 3–10. Contrasting Sizes of Head-Disk Air Cushion, Smoke, Lint, and Hair

by recovering as much information as possible from crashed disks. Obviously, replacing disk packs, recovering data, and replacing read/write heads is costly in both money and time. Great effort should be made to keep head crashes to a minimum.

INTRODUCTION TO DATA STORAGE ON DISKS

Data is recorded serially along a disk track, one bit at a time, along its circumference. A track has practically no width, so the most inexpensive units make no attempt to store bits across the width of a normal track. However, some drives can pack bits more densely along a track by magnetizing domains in the depth of the disk or perpendicular to the track.

On most disk drives the disk spins at a constant speed, and read/write signals are transmitted at a constant rate. This results in the data being recorded more densely toward the center of the disk than along the outer tracks. A sector containing 512 bytes, for example, will be much shorter on an inner track than on an outer track. Again, some drives have been made with variable speeds, with the disk spinning more slowly as the access arm moves toward the outer tracks, so that more data can be recorded on a track. This results in considerably higher capacities for such devices and is popular for some floppy disk drives.

There is a considerable amount of non-data information stored on each track of a disk. This includes such information as error checking and error correction bytes, physical addresses, flags (defective or good), which head number is used to read this track, etc. Maximum data storage capacity is achieved only with *full track blocking,* when there is only one physical block of information per track. In all other situations, the number of gaps between blocks and the amount of non-data information required to describe the blocks is larger, and the track capacity for storing data will be diminished. The key for a block or record can be stored within the data block, or it can be recorded as a separate field immediately preceding the remaining data. In the case where the key is stored separately, an extra gap and more non-data information are required, and track capacity is reduced. On fixed block architecture machines, of course, we have no choice—the block (sector) lengths are fixed by the machine; and the capacities quoted are always the capacities available.

Timing

Four factors affect the speed with which data can be retrieved from a disk. Roughly in order of decreasing importance, these are

1. the motion of the access arm, *seek time*
2. the *rotational delay* or *latency*
3. the *data transfer rate*
4. the *head selection* time

Other factors to consider are the response of the computer, how long it takes the user's program to request and analyze the transferred data, the transmission delays in lines and controllers, etc. However, these are variable quantities which must be estimated for each specific system and program. These variables cannot be discussed in general, even though in some cases they may be as significant as some of the factors we will discuss.

Most units of disk access time are expressed in terms of fractions of a second, defined as follows:

1 millisecond = 1/1000 sec.
1 microsecond = 1/1,000,000 sec.
1 nanosecond = 1/1,000,000,000 sec.

Light travels at a rate of approximately one foot (about 30 centimeters) per nanosecond. Electronic signals travel at about the same speed, so that any operation which is expected to occur in less than one nanosecond must involve signals which travel less than one foot (30 centimeters) in distance.

Although there is a wide range of speed for devices, Figure 3–11 gives typical value of seek times, rotational delay (sometimes called "latency") and transfer rates. The *minimum seek time* is the time required for the access arm to come up to speed and move from one cylinder to an adjacent cylinder. The *average seek time* is the time for the access arm to move across half of the cylinders on the disk pack, and the *maximum seek time* time is the time required to move all the way from the outermost track to the innermost track or vice versa.

Latency or *average rotational delay* is the time required for the disk to rotate through half of one revolution, and *maximum rotational delay* is the time required for one complete revolution of the disk. Rotational delay occurs because the desired data is rarely passing under the read/write head at the instant the access arm places the head over the appropriate track. On the average, the disk will have to spin through one half-revolution before the data is positioned correctly.

The *data transfer time* depends on the density at which data is packed on the disk and the speed of rotation of the disk. It is the time required to transfer data to the host computer from the DASD.

Head selection, which determines from which track on a given cylinder data will be read, is accomplished electronically. Typically, this occurs in microseconds rather than the milliseconds required for the other operations; its effect on the timing is generally ignored.

	TYPICAL SEEK TIME (milliseconds)			TYPICAL LATENCY (milliseconds)		TYPICAL DATA TRANSFER RATE (kilobytes per second)
Device ↓	Min.	Avg.	Max.	Avg.	Max.	
Hard Disks	10	25	50	8.4	16.8	1000
Floppies	20	100	200	83	167	500
Winchester	10	40	80	8.4	16.8	800

FIGURE 3–11. Typical Seek Times, Rotational Delays, and Data Transfer Rates

Consider the following two examples:

Example 3–2

Assume a hard disk contains 410 cylinders and that the access arm is resting at cylinder 1. One block of data five kilobytes long is to be read from cylinder 402. How long does it take to find and transfer the data to the host computer?

Solution:

The access time will be in four parts,

1. seek time = maximum = 50 millisec (ms), because the access arm has to move all of the way across the disk.
2. rotational delay, since not predictable, will be assumed to be the average rotational delay = 8.4 millisec.
3. data transfer time =

$$5 \text{ kbytes} \times \frac{1 \text{ second}}{1000 \text{ kbytes}} = 0.005 \text{ sec} = 5.0 \text{ msec.}$$

4. head selection time = a few microseconds, which will be neglected

Thus the *total time* to find and transfer the data is approximately 50 + 8.4 + 5.0 = 63.4 milliseconds.

Example 3–3

Assume, on a typical hard disk with 1000 tracks per surface, that the access arm is at rest on cylinder 1. Fifty blocks of data are to be read from cylinders 346 and 347. Each block contains two kilobytes of data. How long does it take to find and transfer the data to the host?

Solution:

In this problem, the situation is slightly different because many blocks of data are to be transferred. While the computer is processing one block, the disk continues to spin, so that an average delay of approximately one half-rotation occurs while finding successive blocks. Thus the total access time will be approximately

1. seek time = 25 millisec. (ms) to move from cylinder 1 to cylinder 346, plus
2. seek time = 10 millisec. to move from cylinder 346 to 347.
3. data transfer time =

$$\frac{2 \text{ kbytes}}{\text{record}} \times \frac{1 \text{ second}}{1000 \text{ kbytes}} \times 50 \text{ records}$$
$$= 0.1 \text{ seconds} = 100 \text{ millisec.}$$

4. After one block of data is transferred, the disk will spin about one half-revolution before it is positioned for the next read operation. Thus the total rotational delay is approximately 50 times the average rotational delay $= 50 \times 8.4$ millisec. $= 420$ millisec.

Therefore, the approximate total time to find and transfer the data = $25 + 10 + 100 + 420$ millisec. $= 555$ millisec. $= 0.56$ seconds.

Usually, when reading one block of data the seek time is most significant; when reading many blocks, the rotational delay or data transfer time may be much more important.

DIMENSIONAL ANALYSIS

When performing calculations such as for the transfer times, there are two significantly different ways of knowing whether to multiply or divide by an expression. First, we could memorize the formula. However, if we spend our lives memorizing formulae, we will inevitably forget some of them and get others confused. On the other hand, we could write down the dimensions with the numbers, as we have done in the examples. If the dimensions cancel appropriately in order to obtain the dimensions which the answer should have, we can be pretty certain that we have done the problem correctly. In most cases this procedure, called *dimensional anlaysis,* will help us find the correct formula. In Example 3–3, we wanted to find the number of seconds.

Quantities given to us were

$$\frac{\text{kilobytes}}{\text{record}} \qquad \frac{\text{kilobytes}}{\text{second}} \qquad \text{and records}$$

We wrote the expression that contained the answer, seconds, so that "seconds" appeared on the top (in the *numerator*) of the fraction, namely

$$\frac{\text{seconds}}{\text{kilobyte}}$$

To eliminate the kilobyte dimension, we had to multiply by kilobytes; so we looked for another expression which contained kilobytes and wrote it with kilobytes in the numerator, namely

$$\frac{\text{seconds}}{\text{kilobyte}} \times \frac{\text{kilobytes}}{\text{record}}$$

Now to get rid of "record" we multiply by records. Thus

$$\text{seconds} = \frac{\text{seconds}}{\cancel{\text{kilobyte}}} \times \frac{\cancel{\text{kilobytes}}}{\cancel{\text{record}}} \times \cancel{\text{records}}$$

If we had tried in Example 3–3 to multiply by 1000 kilobytes per second instead of dividing, we would have ended up with

$$\frac{2 \text{ kbytes}}{\cancel{\text{record}}} \times \frac{1000 \text{ kbytes}}{\text{second}} \times 50 \ \cancel{\text{records}} = \frac{100{,}000 \text{ kbytes} \times \text{kbytes}}{\text{second}},$$

which is a nice number, but certainly not the number of seconds we wanted.

Virtually all of the problems in this text can be solved in this way. For example, in Example 3–1, calculating the number of bytes per volume, we chose the multiplication factors carefully to put bytes in the numerator of the fraction, volume on the bottom (in the *denominator*), and to cancel sectors, tracks, and surfaces.

MASS STORAGE SYSTEMS

Suppose that in a large installation you have more data than you can store on the DASD's attached to your computer. This situation inevitably occurs sooner or later on every system. What do you do with the excess data?

In the past, it has been common to dump the contents of the DASD's onto magnetic tapes and store them in a tape library. Such a procedure soon leads to rooms with racks full of magnetic tapes. Computer operators and tape librarians have to be hired and trained to retrieve tapes from the library and load *(mount)* them onto the computer's tape drives when requested, or *demount* and return them to the appropriate library rack; also, the tapes have to be read by the computer before processing can begin. At best, reading tapes is slow, much slower than DASD access. At worst, tapes can get lost, dropped, or erased accidentally; hours are wasted in delay, or data is lost completely. Tapes can be read only sequentially and generally there is only one set of data per tape reel. Scheduling the tape drives and allowing multiple user access to the data on a tape is a complex, often nearly impossible, task. There has to be a better way.

A mass storage facility, to replace the tape library, would be ideal if it had the following characteristics:

1. Capacity must be at least equal to that of the tape library.
2. The system mounts and demounts volumes without operator intervention.
3. Data can be organized in storage in ways other than just sequentially.
4. The cost per megabyte is significantly less than the cost of more DASD's.
5. Users should have rapid access to multiple files quickly.
6. Data security (preventing unauthorized tampering with data) must be better than in a tape library.
7. Mounting and demounting time and reading the data into the computer should be significantly faster.
8. Floor space should be significantly reduced.

This is a big order, which has been solved in part by a variety of mass storage systems developed by IBM and other manufacturers.

In one type of mass storage system, data is recorded on magnetic tapes, two to three inches wide and several hundred inches long. The tape is wound on a spool and forms a cartridge about two inches in diameter and four inches long. Data is recorded on stripes across the tape with several kilobytes per stripe, and the entire spool of tape in a cartridge may contain 50 to 100 million bytes of data. The cartridges are stored in a honeycomb array and are accessed from one side of the array by a robot arm, which picks the requested cartridge and moves it to a high speed reader where the tape is unwound and read rapidly. Then the tape is rewound on the cartridge and replaced in the appropriate bin by the robot arm. No operator intervention is required to load the data from a cartridge; since cartridges can be read within a few seconds, access is rapid. Figure 3–12 illustrates the cartridges, honeycomb storage, robot access arm, and the data stripes on the tape. The Mass Storage System (MSS) is an auxiliary device to the DASD's. Data can be moved from the MSS into the DASD within a few seconds. Just as the DASD itself gave rise to the virtual memory concept, where the computer appears to have unlimited primary memory, so the MSS gives the system the appearance of *virtual drives,* where the computer appears to have access to almost unlimited DASD storage space. More jobs can be run concurrently.

Staging

The system consisting of the computer, DASD, and Mass Storage System with appropriate intermediate controllers is said to form a *hierarchy.* Data migrates up (toward the computer) and down (toward the MSS) in the hierarchy as it is needed. This process of moving data from one point in the hierarchy to another is called *staging,* and is managed by the utility software provided with the system. Staging with a mass storage system requires time, often of the order of tens of seconds, and slows down the system; however, the time involved is orders of magnitude less than that involved in staging data from a tape library. Also, the probability that data integrity (protection from exposure to accidental damage) or data security (protection from expo-

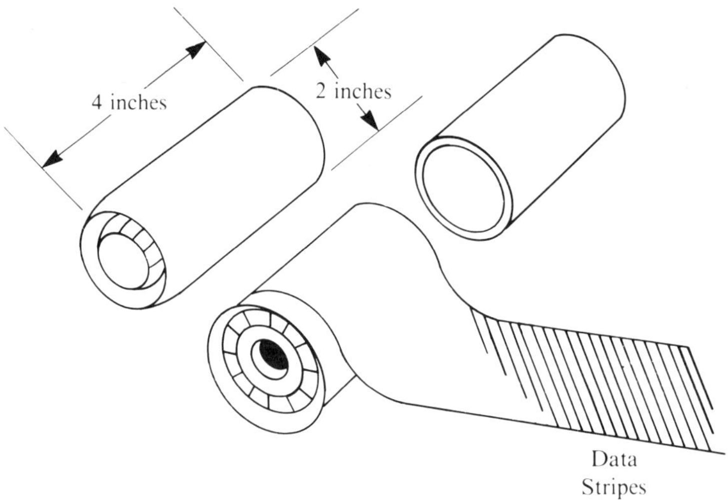

FIGURE 3–12(a). Mass Storage System, Data Cartridge and Stripes

FIGURE 3–12(b). Mass Storage System, Honeycomb Storage and Access Mechanism *(Courtesy of International Business Machines Corporation)*

sure to unauthorized access) will be compromised is reduced by a mass storage system.

Staging from a mass storage system provides flexibility in scheduling and makes the system more responsive to user demands. For example, without great difficulty, data and programs can experience *roll-out* (motion in the direction from the processor toward the storage system) when jobs of higher priority need the system and *roll-in* (motion toward the processor) when external demands are reduced. The MSS also provides economy of storage, since if properly managed, data need only be stored on one cartridge, not on a separate medium for each user. Nonconsecutive processing of data is easier; large quantities of data can be referenced repeatedly without having to keep it all within the computer or on the DASD; and data can be used by several programs simultaneously, thus reducing the size of the system by not requiring separate I/O devices for each user to mount his or her own data.

Another feature facilitated by staging and greatly enhanced by the mass storage system is *remote job entry*. Data and programs can be requested from a remote terminal, located quickly from the mass storage facility, and moved to the computer for execution.

DATA SECURITY AND INTEGRITY

Data security is the protection of data from intentional change or access by unauthorized persons. *Data integrity* is the protection of data from accidental change or deletion. Hardware is built very carefully to try to prevent accidental changes to the data. Circuits are designed to check the transmission of data from one point to another. Redundant checks on the data itself, such as parity bits or check characters, are calculated and recalculated as data is written and read. Special coding methods are devised to allow a limited burst of errors to be corrected by the computer. Labels on tapes and mass storage cartridges are both external and internal. An *external* label is generally a sticker attached to the package on which is written a description of the information recorded on the medium. An *internal* label is the same information, and usually more, recorded on the medium itself, such as header and trailer labels on a magnetic tape, or similar information on an MSS cartridge. Addresses of data, whether on disk, tape, or MSS, are usually recorded at least twice in different locations to prevent loss. However, no matter how careful you are, data will inevitably be changed accidentally. It is critical, therefore, that backup copies be kept for data which cannot be reproduced easily, so that accidental changes may be inconvenient but not disastrous.

Data security is becoming more complex as more people gain access to computers and data. Not only do more users imply a larger number of persons who might try to violate security, but more sensitive data is being recorded in computers, and the social problems associated with security are more critical than ever before. Most of your financial history is probably stored within at least one computer file. It is not necessarily to your advantage for everyone in the world to have access to that information, and certainly you would not want unauthorized persons to be able to change it. Thus extensive measures must be taken to protect data within computer systems and as it is moved between systems.

On most computer systems, where more than one user has access, each user is assigned a unique name which the system recognizes. Authorization to use the computer is assigned with the name, and priorities are assigned so that not every user has access to the entire system. Passwords can be assigned and must be reassigned periodically to ensure that the system is under control and data is available only to those who should see it. Audits are made periodically to determine who has had access to the computer and what use they have made of it. Nevertheless, no matter how tight security becomes, no matter how many different codes are used, no matter how clever systems managers are at devising "fail-safe" methods, someone invents a way to crack the security. A disgruntled employee, a bored student looking for a challenge, even a saboteur, can eventually violate the security of any system given sufficient incentive. What to do? Keep trying to provide better security on sensitive data, change the system regularly, and try to keep from becoming paranoid.

QUESTIONS

1. If the read rate from a magnetic tape is 200 inches per second and the density of data is 1600 bpi, what is the read rate in bytes per second?
2. Assume that you have a magnetic tape with a read/write speed of 200 inches per second, length of tape = 2400 feet, tape width = 1/2 inch, recording density = 1600 bytes per inch, interblock gaps = 0.6 inches. The file you wish to write on the tape contains records each with a length of 200 bytes:
   a. If the records were all recorded in one long block with no gaps and no labels, how many bytes and records could be recorded on the tape?
   b. How long would it take to read the entire tape?
   c. Suppose the records are blocked with a blocking factor = 5 (5 records per block)
      (1) How many bytes are in each block?
      (2) Counting the interblock gap at the end of each block, how many inches of tape are required for each block?
      (3) How many blocks can be recorded on the tape?
      (4) How many records could be stored on the tape in this format?
      (5) How many data bytes could be stored on the tape in this format?
      (6) What percent of the tape is used in this format for actual storage of data?
   d. In the real world we usually don't even get close to the number of bytes stored on a tape which are indicated above, nor can we read the tape as quickly as item b indicates. Why not?
3. On a magnetic tape you have stored the message "I LOVE YOU" in seven-bit ASCII code with an eighth *odd* parity bit. Complete the diagram in Figure 3–13.

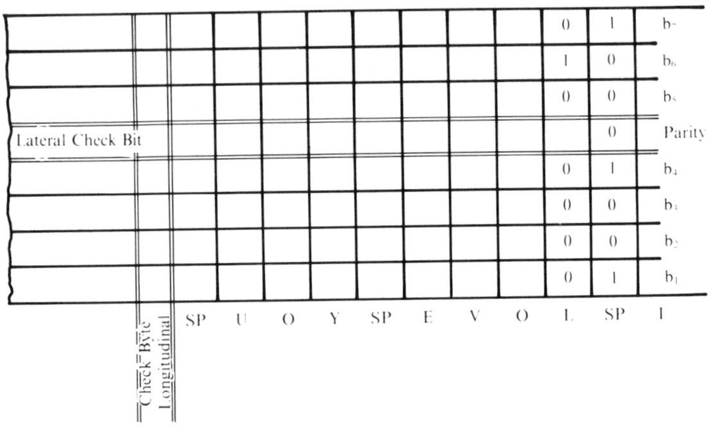

FIGURE 3–13. Parity and the Longitudinal Check Byte, Question 3–3

4. How would you discover if there were an error of one bit in a message such as the one recorded on magnetic tape in problem 3? How could the computer find out which byte was incorrect?
5. Compare the time required to read a file from a standard tape and from a cassette tape. Assume that the cassette has a read/write speed of 1.875 inches per second, a data density of 800 bits per inch, and that data is recorded in seven-bit ASCII plus parity. Asume that the standard tape reads the entire file, with no stops for gaps, at 200 inches per second, that it has a data density of 800 bpi, and that data is recorded in seven-bit ASCII plus parity.
6. A high capacity streaming tape drive operates at 25 inches per second. Data is stored on 24 tracks at a density of 9600 bytes per inch. a.) How many feet of tape are required to store 300 megabytes? b.) How long should it take to read 300 megabytes from this tape?
7. a. How many bytes long is a 0.6 inch gap on a 1600 bpi standard magnetic tape? b. How many inches long is a 13-byte-long gap on a streaming tape which moves at 60 inches per second and is recorded at a density of 1000 bytes per inch?

8. Assume that a video tape recorder is to be used to record data. On this particular recorder you can record three hours of television programming.

   a. How many screens full of information is this if the recorded screen on the tape is updated 30 times per second?

   b. If one video screen contains 240 lines with 320 pixels (picture elements) per line, and it require three bits to specify each pixel, how many bytes are required to record one video screen?

   c. How many bytes of data could be recorded on the entire tape?

   d. How long would it take to read a 10-kilobyte block of data from the tape?

9. Given a removable disk pack with 10 platters and one surface dedicated to control,

   a. on how many surfaces would you expect to be able to record data?

   b. how many data tracks per cylinder would you have?

10. Suppose that an old eight-inch-diameter floppy disk stores 256 kilobytes of information on one side. The disk format is fixed block architecture (FBA) with eight 512-byte sectors per track. How many tracks have to be on the disk?

11. An old, 5 1/4-inch-diameter, single-sided, floppy disk has 40 tracks and 18 sectors per track. It stores 90 kilobytes. How many data bytes are there on each sector?

12. A given video disk player uses 12-inch diameter disks which have 40,000 tracks, spaced 70 microinches apart. The disks store one gigabyte of data and spin at about 1100 rotations per minute.

    a. What is the average number of data bits per track?

    b. If the outermost track has a diameter of 10.80 inches, what is the diameter of the innermost track? How many data bits per inch must be on the innermost track if it is to contain the number of bits calculated in part a?

    c. How many textbook pages (at 500 words per page, eight characters per word, eight bits per character) could be stored on the disk?

13. A 16-bit-word computer has a memory constructed of 16 256-kilobit RAM chips and stores one bit of each word on a separate chip.

a. What is the minimum number of data lines which would be required to transfer data to and from this memory?

b. How many kilobytes are available in this storage configuration?

c. How many bits long would the address register of this machine have to be if every byte were to be directly addressable?

14. Given that the access arm is positioned at cylinder 1 on a DASD with the following characteristics:

    1110 tracks per surface

    Seek time (millisec.): Min. = 10, Avg. = 25, Max. = 50

    Latency (millisec.): Avg. = 8.4, Max = 16.8

    Data Transfer Rate = 1198 kilobytes per second

    You wish to read 20 blocks (each 2.5 kilobytes long) from cylinder 1100.

    a. Approximately how long is the seek time?

    b. How long would it take to transfer the 50 kilobytes to the computer once they have been located?

    c. What would be the average total rotational delay?

    d. What is the total approximate elapsed time in finding and transferring this information?

15. If a 14-inch-diameter hard disk spins at 3600 revolutions per minute, how fast (in feet per second or miles per hour) is a point on the edge moving? Note: Circumference = PI × Diameter where PI is approximately 3.14.

16. Of those discussed in this chapter,

    a. which type of DASD is often loosely called a "drum"? Why?

    b. on which type of DASD are the read/write heads removed with the disk pack?

17. What is the purpose of an "alternate" track?

18. A given nonremovable disk pack on a conventional drive has 30 data tracks per cylinder, 19,000 bytes per track, and 1110 tracks per surface. How many bytes are there

    a. per cylinder? b. per surface? c. per disk pack?

    d. How many pages of a textbook (at 500 words per page, eight characters per word) could be stored on this disk pack?

19. a. How many 2400 foot magnetic tapes recorded at 6250 bpi would it take to backup (record all of the data from) a very high capacity fixed drive which has 15 tracks per cylinder, 1770 cylinders per volume, and 47,500 data bytes per track? Assume 40% efficiency (40% of the space on the tape actually contains data) and that the DASD is recorded in a format using maximum capacity.

    b. How many tapes would it take at 20% efficiency and 6250 bpi?

    c. How many tapes would it take at 40% efficiency and 1600 bpi?

    d. How many tapes would it take at 40% efficiency and 800 bpi?

20. Given that 1 millisecond = 1 sec./1000 and that 1 microsecond = 1 sec./1,000,000, use dimensional analysis to find how many microseconds are in one millisecond; that is, find microseconds/milliseconds.

21. You are given a Mass Storage Facility cartridge about four inches long and two inches in diameter, which contains 50 million bytes. The three-inch wide tape in the cartridge is 770 inches long, and there are 4096 bytes per stripe:

    a. How many stripes must be on the tape?

    b. How many stripes per inch are on the tape?

    c. Approximately how many layers deep is the tape on the cartridge?

22. Describe briefly the "virtual drive" concept.

23. If one mass storage system could manage 9000 mass storage cartridges at 50 million bytes each, approximately how many library books could be stored on the system? (Assume one character per byte, 8 characters per English word, 500 words per page, and 500 pages per book.)

24. Briefly define

    a. staging

    b. roll-out and roll-in

    c. remote job entry compared with time-sharing

    d. data security compared with data integrity

CHAPTER 4

INTERFACES, CHANNELS, AND CONTROLLERS

INTERFACE EQUIPMENT

Controllers and Channels

The transfer of information from a computer to secondary storage and vice versa doesn't just happen. A number of functions must be performed, including physical movement of the tape or disk, motion of the access arm, rotational positioning of the disk, error detection, and execution of the commands to find, transfer, and read or write the data.

It is the function of a *Controller* to tell an I/O device exactly how the data is to be recorded or read. Every device will have a controller, whether it is a CRT display, a keyboard, a printer, a magnetic tape drive, or a DASD. The controller interprets instructions from the computer and instructs the device to perform such functions as positioning the access arm at the appropriate cylinder or drawing the correct symbol on the screen. The controller may also detect and correct errors or at least make the user aware of their existence, so that there is some control over data integrity. Often an electronic controller is located physically within the I/O device itself, although this does not have to be the case; it can be a completely separate unit.

Most computers larger than single user microcomputers, and even some of those, use an I/O *channel* or *peripheral processor* to direct input and output operations. A channel or peripheral processing unit (PPU) is a small, auxiliary computer. If the channel is large enough it may contain the input and output program instructions itself. Otherwise it executes an I/O program which it reads, one instruction at a time, from the host's primary memory. The channel forwards commands to the controller which actually directs the operations of the I/O device.

A peripheral processor is important for a machine which is not dedicated to just one user; it may be desirable even on a small computer. Input and output devices *all* run much more slowly than central processing units in the host computer. When the host CPU must itself direct the I/O operations, it runs very slowly, because it literally spends most of its time waiting for the attached devices to perform their functions. When there is a PPU or channel, the host is free to perform those operations while the PPU runs the I/O programs.

Computer System Configuration

Thus input and output are not simple one-step operations. There is always a set of one or more units between the device and the computer. In fact, if all units were in separate boxes, most computer systems would have the minimum configuration shown in Figure 4–1.

If you own a microcomputer with floppy disk drives, a cassette tape, or a printer you may wonder where all these boxes are. Your printer, for example, may be in one case with a cable which connects it directly to the cabinet containing the computer. Similarly, the disk drives may appear to be attached by a single cable to your machine. If you examine the ends of those cables, however, you probably will find electronics at one or both ends, inside the respective units. This will be the control electronics for the device. You may not find a peripheral processor on a microcomputer, but be assured it will be there for a machine which is large enough to support time sharing.

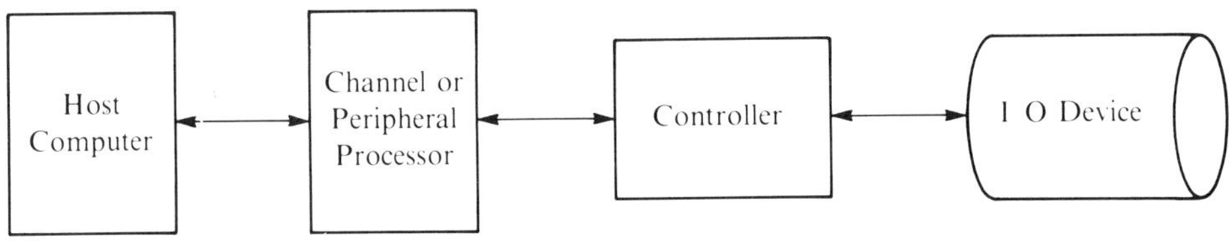

FIGURE 4–1. Minimum Computer System Configuration

The channel or peripheral processing unit and controller may be called different things in the literature, depending upon how the system is configured, how it looks. If the channel and controller are in the same physical box, that box may be called, obviously, a channel and control unit. If the channel and control electronics for a DASD are both physically within the host computer the system is said to have *integrated* storage controls or an integrated file adapter. If the control unit is physically located within the first in a string of DASD's (more than one DASD attached to a single host through a single control), then that DASD and the controller are called the *head of string*. If a large control unit is able to control a number of DASD strings independently, the box which contains the separate controllers may be called a *storage director*. Thus many different names are given to the same devices. Obviously this leads to confusion. In this text we will use the words *channel* and *controller* for these units unless it is desired to make an explicit distinction about where the units are located; but you should be aware that different names may be used elsewhere.

Channel Commands

A channel directs the flow of data by executing a program similar to a user's program. When data is to be transferred, the CPU instructs the channel to begin execution of a channel program or a PPU detects data in an I/O buffer and begins execution automatically. Once the channel takes over, the CPU is free to pursue other operations while I/O proceeds under the channel's direction. The channel commands are quite simple, but each different I/O device may require its own channel program. For a DASD, for example, the channel program may include commands such as

Search, compare the request for data with that stored on the DASD, and find the appropriate information.

Read, read the records, transfer them to the designated place in main memory, and check for errors.

Write, transfer data from main memory to a specified area on the DASD.

Wait, delay execution of the next read or write command until the previous operation has been completed.

A typical output operation, for example, might proceed as follows:

First, the user's program in the central processor chooses a device, a channel, and a control unit, which are to be used for transfer of the information.

Second, the CPU initiates the channel program.

Third, the channel requests the data from the main memory and controls the flow of the data to the device controller.

Fourth, the controller codes the data in the form needed by the output device.

Finally, the device responds to the signals from the controller and records the information.

Although the CPU initiates the execution of a channel program, it is often necessary for the CPU to resume control during the channel operations; it is certainly necessary for control to be returned to the CPU after the channel program has been executed. Remember that the channel is usually a very small computer. It reads and writes. If anything unusual happens, it must request help from the central processor. Most channels simply do not have sufficient memory to handle all possible situations. For example, all of the data may have been transferred, the data may fail to record properly, the device may not be ready to send or receive, a requested block of data may not be found, or there may be no more space on a storage device to record the data. All of these conditions, and many more, would be considered unusual and would require special handling by the central processor. When such a situation occurs, the channel sends a message called an *interrupt* to the CPU, which tells the central processor that the channel needs help. At the first opportunity, what the CPU is doing is interrupted and a routine is initiated to handle the situation. After the problem has been solved, the central processor may then resume the process that was "interrupted." On the other hand, some machines are designed with PPU's large enough to contain programs which operate quite independently of the central processor. Indeed, in order to speed processing, some CPU's are given no control at all over a PPU once execution of a PPU program has begun.

Most programmers do not concern themselves with channel programming. Packaged I/O systems generally take care of all of those details, and only systems programmers normally worry about such things. However, you may find yourself in a situation one day where you will be interested in channel programming. Such a situation could occur when you desire to attach a device to your computer for which the I/O programming has not already been written. Then you may wish to write or modify channel programs to accommodate that device.

A number of situations occur in writing channel programs, which must be carefully considered by the programmer. Especially important is program timing. In most cases, the channel is capable of executing instructions much faster than the I/O device can handle. Wait loops must be included in the channel program, so that program execution proceeds at a rate which is acceptable to the I/O device. Failure to match the channel program to the timing of the device results in a situation called *overrun* where the channel provides data too fast or fails to execute commands fast enough. Timing is especially critical when transferring data to or from a DASD since the disk continues to rotate at a constant rate, stopping for nothing. Much time could be wasted if data were transferred at too slow a rate, since at least one complete rotation would have to occur before the disk were again at the appropriate position.

Controller Functions

The control unit has four major functions in most data transfer operations. These are

1. Interpret and execute channel commands. What do the commands such as search, write, and read actually mean in terms of operation of the device?
2. Provide *status information* to the channel or computer as commands are executed. Status may include such information as whether the device is ready or whether all of the data has been transferred.
3. Convert data between the form which is acceptable to the host and that which is acceptable to the device. For example, most host computers will transfer at least some of the data in parallel form, several bits at a time, while most I/O devices want the data in serial form, one bit at a time. If many bits are transferred to the controller at one time by the channel, the controller must hold them, separate them, and transfer them one at a time to an output device. In the other direction, the controller must read the individual bits from the input device, collect them into bytes or blocks, and transfer them in parallel through the channel to the computer.
4. Check and correct errors in transmission. When data is transferred to a DASD, if the data contains parity bits, those bits are removed by the controller, and two or more bytes (called cyclic check characters, CC) are calculated for each block of information. These bytes are a function of the bits of code transmitted, and the algorithm for their calculation depends upon the device. The cyclic check characters are recorded with each block of information. When the blocks are read at a later time, the check characters are recalculated and compared with what was recorded in the block, to make certain that the information

read is the same as was stored. Upon reading data from the DASD, the cyclic check characters are removed from the data, and the parity bits may be restored to each byte. On some systems (those using fixed block architecture) the cyclic check characters are called cyclic redundancy check characters, CRC. In addition, some systems calculate four or more bytes per block called error correction code (ECC). These codes are added to the data block on the DASD for the purpose of giving the computer the capability to correct short bursts of errors.

Rotational Position Sensing

One option available on some controllers is rotational position sensing (RPS). With RPS, every track on a disk, whether it is a "conventional" drive or a fixed block architecture machine, is divided into sectors, and each sector on a track is assigned an address, just as each track has its own address. When data is to be written to or read from the disk, the channel remains available for other operations until immediately before the desired sector passes under the read/write head. From eight to 80 milliseconds (a long time for processors), while the disk spins, may be available to the channel for performing other tasks between read or write operations. Obviously such a capability saves time and increases the utility of the channel.

Typical DASD Configurations

Providing for compatibility of DASD's and computers is not a strength of the computer industry, although much work is being done to improve the situation. Theoretically, at least, given the appropriate controller, any I/O device could be made to work with any host. However, most users do not want to build electronics, so it is important to make certain when a device is purchased that there is a controller and a channel program that will allow the device to be used with the machine you have.

Most computers are not limited to the use of just one I/O device. You may have, for example, even on your personal computer, the capability of driving a keyboard, a CRT display, a printer, a cassette tape recorder, and/or floppy or hard disks all at the same time. Similarly very large systems can drive multiple tape drives, printers, DASD's, terminals (keyboards and CRT's), and other devices concurrently or even simultaneously. Each device must have a path to the host computer through its own controller and a channel.

To very large computers, for example, you may attach very powerful DASD control devices in which there may be more than one independent controller. Each controller provides a separate data path for communicating through a channel to the computer. These controllers may be attached to the same channel, or to different channels. If attached to different channels, the channels may be on the same computer or on different computers. Each storage director may then control a number of strings of DASD's. Figure 4–2 illustrates a very large configuration in which several strings of DASD's are connected to each controller within a storage director. Each DASD string may contain several disk drives, provided the first drive in the string also contains some control hardware for the string. The first DASD in the string would then be called the "head of string." The set of DASD's and the controllers in this situation are together called a *DASD Subsystem.*

The distance between controller and channel is usually limited. Normally 100 feet (30 meters) is considered a maximum distance over which information can be transferred at rates up to one megabyte per second without becoming garbled. Even with special options, most DASD controllers may not be placed more than 400 feet (120 meters) from the channel, and data transfer rates are limited to a maximum of two or three megabytes per second.

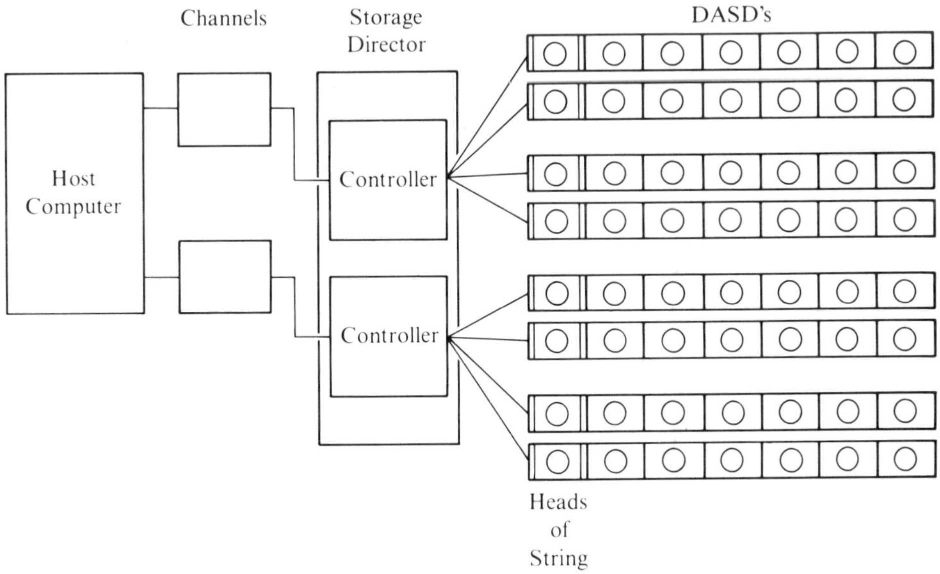

FIGURE 4–2. A Typical Large DASD Subsystem

SWITCHING

Path Selection

With several DASD strings attached to a host computer through two or more independent controllers, some switching capability must be present to choose the appropriate DASD and controller. Also, if data is to be transferred by different controllers to the computer simultaneously, there must be more than one channel between controllers and host. Figure 4–3 shows a possible system configuration with several channels and controllers on the same system.

DASD switching allows sharing of devices and can speed the flow of information from one part of the system to another. Switches may be physically wired and require the operator to actually set the switches manually. Such switches are called *static.* At other times the user may wish to have the program determine which DASD is to be accessed or which path the data is to take between host and DASD. Switching done under program control is called *dynamic* switching. Most computer systems allow switching of both kinds.

In *channel switching,* the path which the data is to take between computer and controller must be chosen either by the computer or by the controller, depending upon whether the data is to be read or written. Channel switching may be static (under operator control) or dynamic. The channels may be attached to the same processor or to different processors. *String*

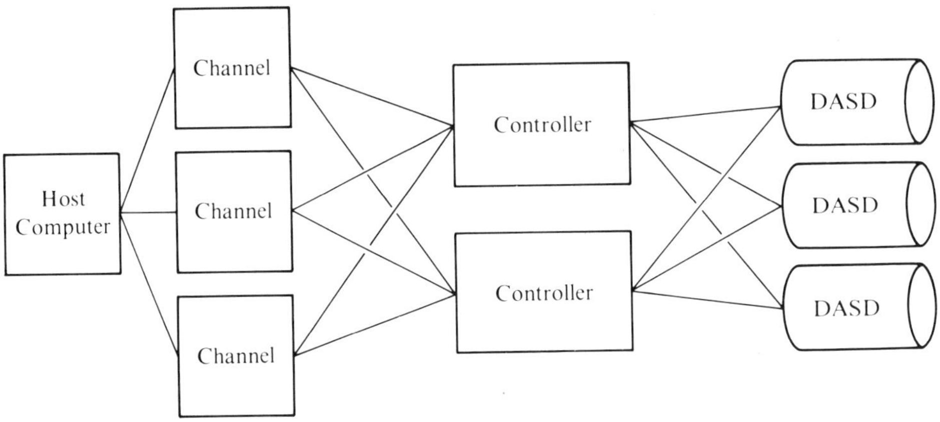

FIGURE 4–3. Switching

switching is done at the controller or at the head of string. Again, this may be done dynamically or under static control. A controller may select a particular string to which data is forwarded, or a head of string may choose which controller is to be used for transfer of information from that string. Most large systems have both channel and string switching capabilities.

Figure 4–4 shows how a set of external static switches might appear for switching between four different channels. Operation of the ENABLE-DISABLE switches for each channel is straightforward. If a switch is set to the ENABLE position, then that channel is available for use. In the DISABLE position, as far as the computer and the controllers are concerned, that channel is inoperative and is not to be used.

The Multitag switch requires a bit of explanation. Perhaps the easiest way to view the multitag switch is to consider children playing a game of "tag." In normal tag, the first child discovered is tagged and becomes "it." If the children were playing "multitag," then all of the children found would be tagged and could be "it" if they were willing to continue the game. Similarly, when the multitag channel switch is set to the OFF position, only the first available channel will receive the signal from the controller that the DASD is ready, i.e., that a disk pack has been loaded and the DASD can be used. When the Multitag switch is set to MULTITAG, all channels which are ENABLEd will receive the message when a DASD is ready; all enabled channels will know that a particular DASD is ready to send or receive data through its controller.

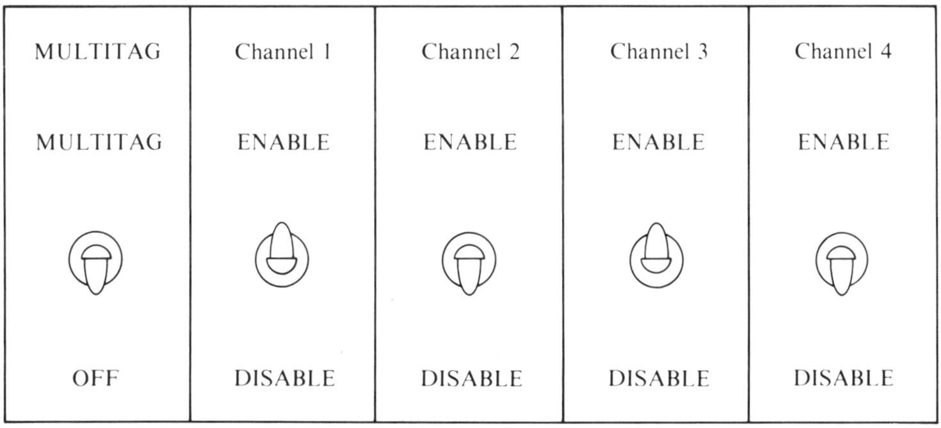

FIGURE 4–4. External, Static Channel Switches

Optional Channel Path and Shared DASD

Figures 4–5 and 4–6 illustrate the difference between *optional channel path* and *shared DASD* switching.

Optional channel path means that there are a number of different paths through the channels and controllers by which data on a given DASD can be accessed from a computer. The major advantage of this type of switching is that the data from a given DASD is available to the host even if some of the intermediate devices are busy or inoperative.

Shared DASD switching allows a particular DASD to be accessed from two or more computers. Even though the switching capability may be available either statically or dynamically, one DASD cannot be used simultaneously by more than one computer. Access to the DASD by the computers must be sequential, with each getting its turn as determined by the hardware and the programs. Sharing a DASD is not the same as sharing the same data set between two jobs in the same computer. The first processor to request the DASD establishes a path, and then the other processors get their paths to the device as it is released. Maintaining the integrity of the data is the sole responsibility of the user, since normally none of the computers will be aware that the others are accessing the same data on the same DASD. Generally a command is issued by the user that the device is reserved while it is being accessed by that user's processor. This locks out all other processors until the user is finished. A device-release instruction is then issued, and control of the DASD is transferred to another user. In many installations, data integrity is further preserved in such situations by allowing only one processor to write to the disk, while the others are always restricted to reading the data only.

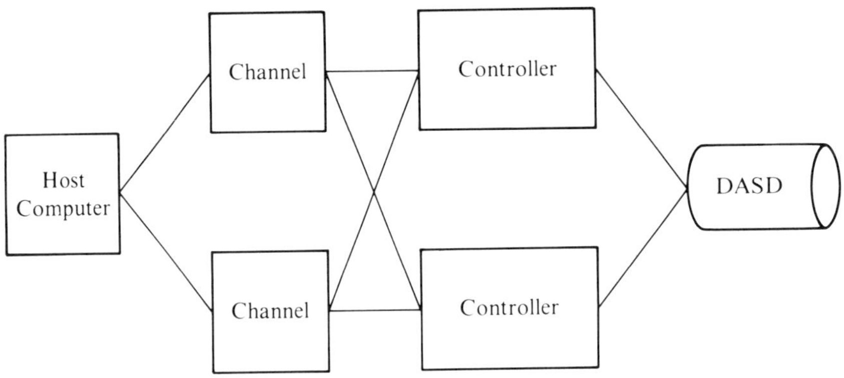

FIGURE 4–5. Optional Channel Path

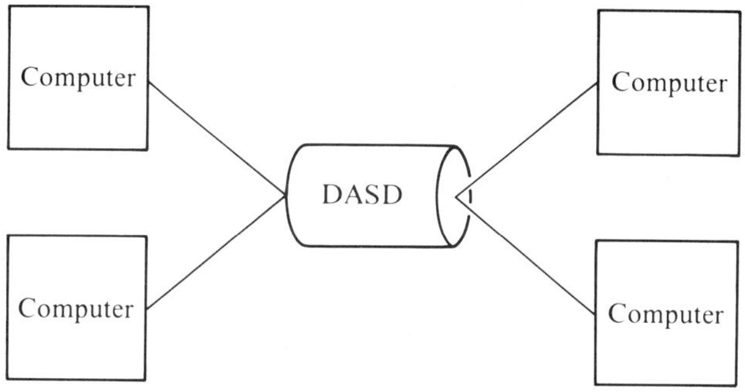

FIGURE 4–6. Shared DASD

This prevents users from changing the data on a disk without the knowledge of the primary user who controls its content.

Sharing of DASD's between computers simplifies scheduling of jobs; disks need not be moved from one facility to another. Operator intervention is minimized for the same reason, and the time and resources (other I/O devices and media) to maintain the file are minimized. Of greatest economic importance is that storage space is saved, since just one copy (plus a backup, always) of the data is all that is needed. However, use of one DASD by several computers should not be undertaken without careful planning; otherwise disastrous things could happen to your files.

QUESTIONS

1. Given the configuration in Figure 4–2,
   a. what is the maximum number of DASD's which could be attached to the host computer through the storage control unit shown?
   b. if each DASD were to have 1400 tracks per surface, 12 tracks per cylinder, and 8400 bytes per track, what is the maximum number of bytes available to the system in this configuration?
2. How must the first DASD in a string differ generally from the others in the string?
3. Name at least two operations performed by each of the following units:
   a. channel b. controller

4. Describe and distinguish
    a. parity
    b. cyclic check characters (CC)
    c. cyclic redundancy check (CRC)
    d. error correction code (ECC)
5. Distinguish between channel switching and string switching.
6. Describe each term and tell its benefits
    a. dynamic switching
    b. static switching
    c. optional channel path
    d. shared DASD
7. Suppose a control unit has four-channel switching capacity. Assume that the manual switches are set as follows:

    Channels 1, 3, 4 = ENABLE   Channel 2 = DISABLE

    Channels 3 and 4 happen to be busy at the moment, but channel 1 is not busy. A new disk is mounted on one of the DASD's controlled by the control unit. Which channels ultimately receive the message that the DASD is ready?
    a. when the multitag switch is OFF?
    b. when the multitag switch is ON?
8. How does rotational position sensing save time, improve device utilization, and improve throughput?
9. Describe two specific situations in which the CPU might be required to assist a channel during execution of a channel program.

CHAPTER 5

DATA FORMATS

INTRODUCTION TO FORMATS

Cards and Tapes

In Chapter 2 we illustrated one way, using Hollerith code, that data is stored on punched cards. Although punched cards were bulky and messy, they had some advantages over magnetic media such as magnetic tapes, drums, and disks; namcly, you could pick out any record, the data on any card, and examine it visually to determine exactly what was on the card. If you wished to make a change, you simply punched a new card and inserted it in place of the old one. If you wished to reorganize the data, you sorted the cards in a different order, although this was not always a simple job for large files with large numbers of records. On cards the record format was always fixed length (80 characters for Hollerith cards) and unblocked (read one record at a time).

Punched paper tape was a step toward flexibility in data formats. On a punched tape records could be as long as you wished to make them. Records were separated by tape marks, usually at least one row of 1's (holes) punched in every column across the tape. Now records could be fixed or variable length, but in a sense they were still unblocked; i. e., one record was read at a time. Again paper tape had the advantage that you could examine it, if you wished, and determine by sight exactly what was stored on it; but you could no longer change just one record or one character. If you wished to make changes, you had to repunch the entire tape. So data and instructions on paper tape were very much sequential.

On magnetic tapes, as we saw in Chapter 3, data can be stored much more densely. We lost the ability to look at the tape and see visually what was on it, so it became urgent that external labels (in the form of stickers applied to the reel or to the container) be faithfully recorded with a description of the data stored on the tape. In exchange for the ability to store a few million characters in a small space on one reel, we had to learn to use some of that space to carefully record internal labels describing the files and data. Also, space had to be reserved for parity bits and longitudinal check bytes to make certain we knew that the data was recorded correctly. Typical magnetic tape formats were illustrated in Figures 3–1 through 3–3 in Chapter 3. Again, the records could be variable or fixed length, separated by interrecord gaps, but it was usually more efficient to read them and write them in groups (blocks), so that we now had the option of blocking the records. For example, if records are grouped and read five at a time between interblock gaps and between stops of the tape drive, they are said to be blocked with a *blocking factor* of five.

Buffers

When data is transferred from a storage device to the computer or vice versa, it is always moved through a *storage buffer.* The buffer is a special part of main memory in which data waits to be transferred to the rest of memory or to a storage device. Buffers typically range from a few bytes, e. g., 128 bytes, to a few kilobytes in capacity. The buffer is important, because it is an extremely rare situation in which the rate at which secondary storage can accept or transmit data is the same as the rate at which the computer can send or receive it. Hence there must be an area where the data can be stored temporarily while waiting for a device. In addition, the computer must often examine the data being read before assigning it to a memory location; often it is desirable to collect small pieces of information into a larger block before transferring to an external device. The buffer is used for all of these purposes.

When data was always read from cards, punched on cards, or printed on a slow printer, the maximum record length was rarely more than 80 characters on a card or 132 characters on a printer line, so a buffer with 128 bytes for a card reader or punch or 256 bytes for a printer was more than sufficient.

Now, however, records may be blocked with several kilobytes per block or transferred at high rates. Many lines may be waiting for the printer at once. Consequently, buffer sizes must be large enough to accommodate more data being transferred at one time.

Drums, Disks, and Physical versus Logical Records

Magnetic drums, described in Chapter 3, can be used to store data in essentially the same format as on magnetic disks. Therefore, most of what will be said about disks is also applicable to the drum. However, compared with tracks on a disk, the tracks on a drum are often quite short. It is not unusual, instead of having several records recorded on a single track as on a disk, to find that a single long record takes up several tracks on a drum.

At this point it is important to draw the distinction between *logical* and *physical* concepts. A logical record or a logical file refers to data organized the way the user sees it. When you sit down to organize your data files, you will put together in logical records those things that logically go together, such as all of the data about one student in a class or all of the information about one particular customer order for your firm. However, the storage devices may not find this the most convenient way to store or to transfer the data. The tracks, cylinders, sectors, and surfaces on a disk drive are *physical* concepts, indicating the way things really look to the hardware. When you block records to be transferred and stored one or more at a time you are creating a *physical record,* a record the way the hardware sees it. Generally, physical records (or blocks) are closely analogous to collections of your logical records, but it is not absolutely necessary that that be true. If you are very limited in disk storage space, for example, you might wish to consider splitting logical records between physical blocks, tracks, cylinders, etc., in order to achieve the greatest density of data storage on the medium. At the same time you must realize that the *access method,* the programs which you use to read and write the data in this format, will be quite messy.

TRACK FORMATS

What's on a Track?

It may be a surprise that a considerable amount of non-data information gets recorded on the tracks of your DASD. This overhead, or excess baggage, is necessary to ensure that everything works properly and that data is kept as safe as possible; however, it reduces considerably the amount of space which is available for actual storage of your data. Of course, if you wish to program the computer at the operating system level, you could eliminate much of the non-data information, which is stored by normal operating system programs. But you might find that such information is valuable and wish you had used it. Also, few of us wish to write our own access methods, so we are stuck with what the programmers before us have decided is important.

To illustrate what gets stored on a track and how that affects the capacity of the disks, we will show here how a typical access method may handle the situation. On a fixed block architecture machine, block sizes (sectors) are fixed, preformatted if you will, and the data must fit into that format. On conventional devices the format can be prescribed by the central processor, and there will be system utility routines to allow you or the computer operator to format the disk to your specifications before it is used. If you have a microcomputer with floppy disks, you are probably aware that after you purchase a disk, unless you purchase it especially from the manufacturer for your machine, you will need to put the disk into your computer's drive and run a FORMATting program. The program divides the disk into the appropriate number of tracks and sectors per track for your operating system to handle in a fixed architecture form. Similar programs are used on large machines, except that often the format you may use is more flexible.

Figure 5–1 shows a typical conventional disk track format.

The Index Point

The index point marks the beginning of the track. On a floppy disk this is done physically by the hole in the envelope and the hole in the disk. When the disk drive detects that these holes are aligned, the beginning of the track is indicated. The index point on a hard disk may be a logical signal, such as a few bytes of all ones or another code indicating the beginning of the track.

The Gaps

Between every area on a track and between data blocks there are recorded gaps, much the same as the gaps between blocks of information on a magnetic tape. However, the gaps on a track of a disk are at most a few bytes long, a few hundredths of an inch. You will remember that the gaps on a magnetic tape were all 0.6 inches long, because the tape had to stop and start within the length of the gap. A disk continues to spin, so there is no need to

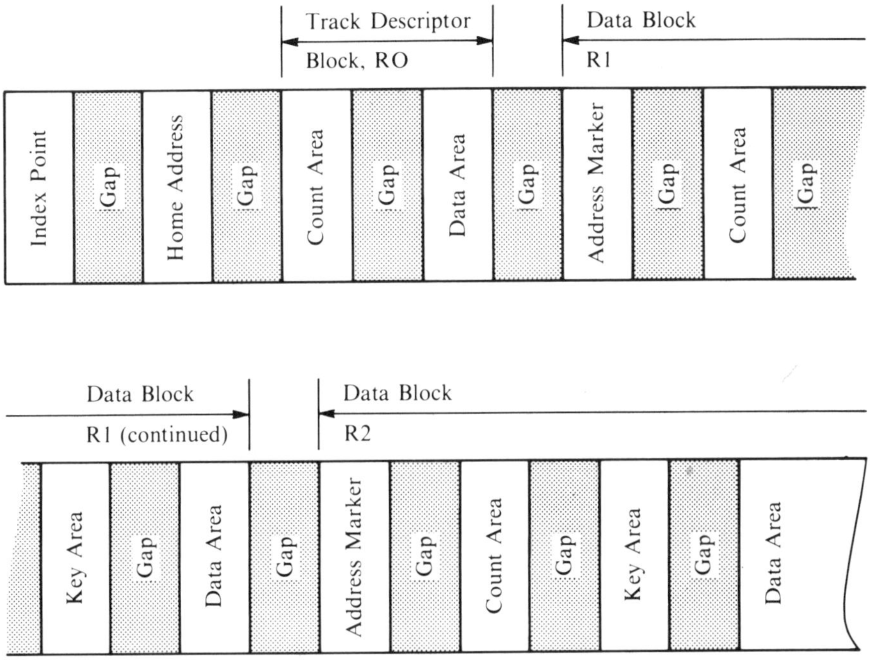

FIGURE 5–1. Typical Conventional Track Format

have gaps longer than necessary to indicate the division between areas on a track. The length of a gap may actually vary depending upon the length of the previous area. The more bytes recorded in an area, the longer could be the gap at the end of the area. The hardware performs some operations such as data transfer when a gap is under the read/write head. Gaps written by FBA machines are of fixed length and generally shorter than those on conventional drives.

Home Address

Most tracks begin, after the index point, with a number of bytes called the *home address.* Special channel programs use the information in the home address when utility programs for formatting the disk are executed.

In the home address, there will typically be several bytes of information. The physical address part of the home address, the first few bytes, relays information back to the CPU to verify that the access arm is positioned in the right place.

Another byte of the home address may be a *flag.* In programming, a flag is any piece of information which usually has one of two values, indicating one of two conditions. For example, suppose you have written a program which is to execute one set of routines if the result of a calculation is an even integer and a different set of routines if the result is odd. One way of doing this is to test the result and set a variable (the flag) to positive in one case and negative in the other case. Then, at each subsequent point in the program you need only to test the flag to determine which subroutine to execute. In the home address, the flag is a byte indicating whether the track is operative or defective and whether it is to be used as a primary track or an alternate track.

Other bytes in the home address indicate the cylinder number within which the track is found and the read/write head which reads the track (i. e., which disk surface the track is on).

Finally, the last few bytes of the home address may be cyclic check characters for the entire track, calculated and appended by the controller when the track is written, for error checking purposes.

Block R0, The Track Descriptor

The first physical record after the home address on each track is designated block 0 and contains information about the track which is used when channel commands read the information from the track. In standard format, this block generally contains a count area and a data area, as shown in Figure 5–1.

The count area of the track descriptor should contain three constants: the physical record number, which is always zero; the key length, which is generally also zero; and the length of the following data area, which is a few bytes. It may also contain information about the number of unused bytes following the last data block on the track. If the track has been flagged defective in the home address, the count area of block R0 may also contain the cylinder and head (surface) number of the alternate track which is to be used instead.

The data area of the track descriptor block is a few bytes long, including bytes for the cyclic characters calculated for block R0. The data area may contain information about the contents of the track, how many data blocks there are on the track, the lengths of the data blocks, etc. If you wish to write your own access programs, the data area of block zero could even contain data which you wish to store on the track.

Data Blocks

What is left of the track is available to store the data which you wished to put on the track in the first place. It seems that we have already used a lot of space on the track for non-data information. However, if you count it up, we have really used only a few bytes out of the thousands available, so most of the track is still left for data storage. The remainder of the track may be one or more data blocks. Remember that the maximum track capacity for each conventional device is achieved only if the remainder of the track is used for one long physical record. This situation is called full track blocking; i. e., the entire track is one block of information. Note that we are discussing physical records. You may indeed have several logical records within a block, which are all read by the computer as one physical record or one block of information.

Most physical data records begin with an address marker, a few bytes written by the controller to allow it to locate the beginning of the block when it is to be read. This would be a relative address, specifying which block this is on the track (1 or 2 or 3 . . .).

The count area of each data block generally contains much of the same information as the home address plus some additional information about this particular block. For every physical record, this area on a conventional machine is a few bytes long. Some of these bytes are the physical address again, used by the controller and the channel to determine that the access arm is indeed correctly positioned. (Note that these bytes may not be needed for a fixed head drive. Why?) Another byte is the flag, indicating the same information as the flag in the home address field, namely whether the track is defective or operative and whether the track is to be used as a primary track or an alternate track. A short identifier contains the cylinder and head number of the track (just as in the home address) as well as a relative block number (1 through 255), defining which physical record this is from the beginning of the file as defined by the user.

One byte of the count area in a data block may be used to specify how many bytes are in the key area which follows. The key area itself is optional; of course, if there is no key area, this byte will contain the number 0. Then there are N bits which define the length of the following data area in bytes. Theoretically, the data can be as many as 2^N bytes long. If these bytes defining the length of the data area indicate 0, then this record is generally considered to be the end of file. Finally, the cyclic check characters which provide error checking for this data block may be recorded in the count area. Count areas are not usually necessary on fixed block architecture machines, since keys are generally included in the data area, and every data sector is of the same, fixed length.

The Key Area

The *key area is optional.* Data may be formatted with or without keys. That statement requires a bit of explanation. Every data record will have a key, some field of information by which it is identified. The user may choose to store the key separately in an area of its own on the track so that it can be easily found and the record readily identified. Otherwise, the key may be included in the data area itself and not stored independently. In the latter case, the entire data will have to be read from the disk and the key separated logically by the CPU to identify the record. Storing the key as part of the data area, and not separately, saves some space on the track since there is one less area and one less gap. In order to make the judgment whether the data will be formatted with or without keys, the user will have to weigh the advantages of saving some disk space against the slightly longer time required to read the entire record and separate the key logically to identify the record. It is important that formatting the data "without keys" does not mean that the record has no key; it only means that no separate area aside from the data area is reserved for storing the key. Of course, if you so choose, the key may be recorded in a separate key area *and* also within the data area.

The Data Area

Finally, after all that, you now have some space to store your data on the track. There are many ways in which your data can be formatted, but the important concept is that the entire data area is yours to use. You specify what goes in it. The computer and controller need to know two things. One is how many physical records your data will have; this number can be changed dynamically as your file grows. The other is how long each data area will be.

DATA FORMATS

Data may be formatted on a disk with or without keys as explained above. Generally, when the data is formatted with keys the access method is simplest if all the keys in the file have the same length. Logical records may be blocked or unblocked, and their lengths can be fixed or variable. In fact, there are eight useful ways in which data can be arranged physically on a disk. These are summarized in Figure 5–2.

Record Length → / Blocking ↓	Fixed	Variable	Undefined
Unblocked	1. Long, Similar Random Records	4. Long, Differing Random Records	7. Read data between consecutive gaps
Blocked	2. Short, Similar Sequential Recs.	5. Short, Differing Sequential Recs.	8. Read a fixed number of bytes
Spanned	3. Compacting or Very Long, Similar Records	6. Compacting or Very Long, Differing Records	

FIGURE 5–2. Data Formats and Typical Uses

1. Fixed, Unblocked Format

When all the records in a file are the same number of bytes in length and when each data area contains exactly one logical record, the records are said to be fixed length and unblocked. Usually, if the keys are recorded in a separate key area, then the keys are not repeated in the data area. You will find that most major computer systems support recording data in this format, where one physical record is by definition the same as one logical record. Unblocked format is especially useful for storing long records which you wish to be able to process in random order. Fixed length is particularly valuable when all records are to contain approximately the same amount and type of information, such as a mailing list file.

2. Fixed Blocked Format

If all the records are to be the same length but are relatively short, access to the data may be more efficient if a number of logical records are collected into one physical record, or block. Remember, only one set of non-data information in the form of address marker and count area need be recorded for each physical record, and it may be faster for a long physical block of data to be transferred and sorted into logical records by the computer. This format is also supported by most computer systems.

When data in this format is also formatted with keys, the key for each logical record will be contained within the data for that logical record, and the *key for the block* will almost always be a repeat of the *last record key* of the logical records in the block as shown in Figure 5–3. This data format is particularly useful when short, constant length records are to be processed in sequential order.

A variation of the fixed, blocked format is called fixed, blocked, *standard* format where the blocking factor (number of logical records per block) may be allowed to vary, so that, even though all logical records are the same length, the physical records may have different lengths.

3. Fixed, Spanned

In fixed, spanned format both the logical record length and the physical block length are fixed but different. Logical records may span block boundaries either because the logical record length is longer than the block length or because the block will not contain a whole number of short records. This organization is particularly useful for very long records when the computer buffer through which the records are to be moved is too short to contain the entire record. However, it may also be used to compact short records in order to avoid undue wasting of space on a disk. Spanned format is shown in Figure 5–4. Note that in every case where records are blocked, if a separate key area is provided for the block, the block key is a copy of the key of the last logical record in the block.

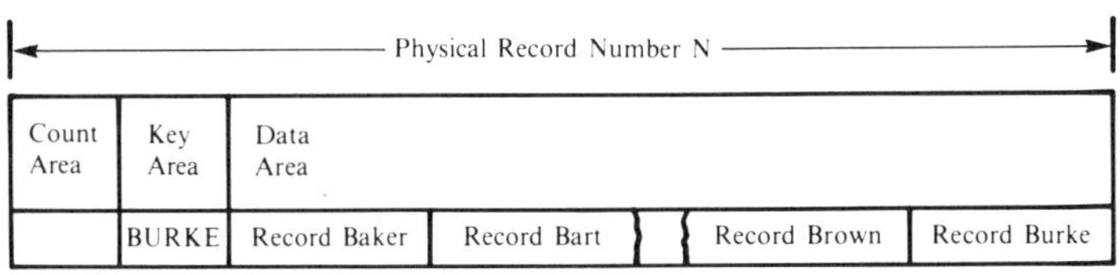

FIGURE 5–3. A Fixed, Blocked Record, with Key

4. Variable, Unblocked

Record lengths need not all be the same size in a file. Suppose, for example, that you have a company which makes 315 different kinds of fasteners, each of which sells for a different price, and that you maintain a large file of customers. During the month, some customers will order a few fasteners of one type. Other customers will order many different types of fasteners. You would probably not wish to make every customer record large enough to hold order information for 315 different fasteners; that would waste space. Hence you make your records of variable length so that the customer who orders only one fastener will have a very short record, and the customer who orders 300 different varieties will have a long record. When these records are stored, one per block on your disk, you have variable, unblocked format, which is supported by most large computer systems. The data area of the record in this format must contain two extra fields which specify the length of the block in bytes and the length of the record in bytes.

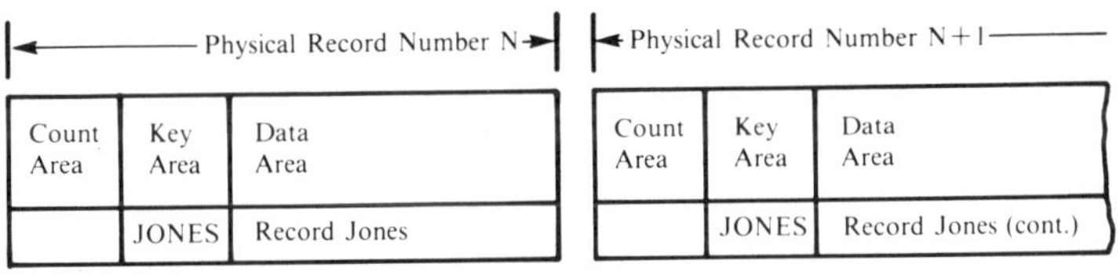

FIGURE 5–4(a). Spanned Records, Long Records

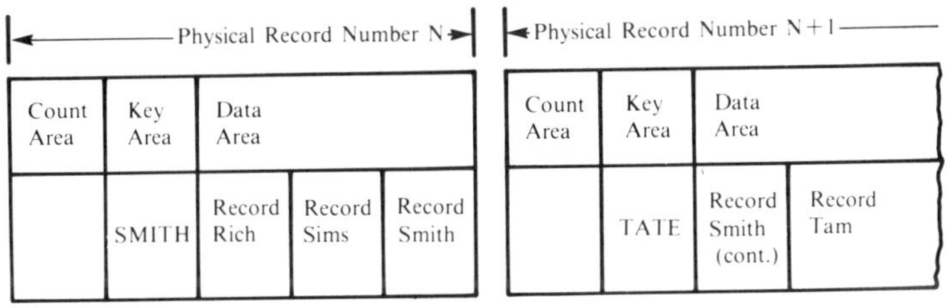

FIGURE 5–4(b). Spanned Records, Short Records

5. Variable, Blocked

If your variable records are mostly short, and mostly accessed in sequential order, it will be more efficient in terms of disk space and access time to write several of them into one physical record. Such variable, blocked format is supported by virtually all of the manufacturers who support the variable, unblocked format; this format is perhaps the more popular of the two, since it provides a fixed block size while allowing the records themselves to vary in length. Note again that the data area of variable records, whether blocked or unblocked, must contain two fields, one which indicates the length of the block in bytes and one per logical record which indicates the number of bytes in that record. The length of a record may not exceed the length of the block in this format.

6. Variable, Spanned

If your variable-length, logical records are longer than the physical blocks which you can reasonably handle, then you would want the option of letting the records span the block boundaries as shown in Figure 5–4 (a). In this case you will need to indicate in a special field, or as part of the field which specifies the block length, whether this particular block is the beginning, a mid-part, or the end of a logical record. This format is also quite useful, and you will find it supported on many computer systems.

7. Undefined, Unblocked

Suppose that you have data on a disk pack which was written years ago on an unknown machine in a forgotten format by a person who has long since left your company. If it is important to retrieve the data, you will need to do so in a format which does not require you to know the format in which the data was written. One such format is the undefined record length, unblocked format. Most computer systems support your access to the data in this form. You simply read all of the data between gaps, transfer it to your new disks, and/or examine it visually to determine what it contains. Without this option you could not copy a file unless you knew the format in which it was written. It is important to realize, however, that there must be some similarity between the way the data was written and the characteristics of the machine that will read it. If the devices have different numbers of tracks per disk, for example, the controller simply cannot position the access arm properly to read the disk.

8. Undefined, Blocked

Another way of reading data of unknown format is to read a fixed number of bytes at one time as if the data were in fixed-length blocks. This allows you to ignore gaps of odd lengths and other situations which might interfere with determining where one record ends and another begins. Many systems will allow you to do this.

Undefined, Spanned

Essentially, no computer system supports an undefined, spanned data format. If the record lengths are undefined, and the block lengths are undefined, it is meaningless to speak of records which span block boundaries. Hence, this possible format is difficult to define and is not used.

Blocking of Records

Maximum storage capacities for DASD's are achieved only when long physical records are recorded one per track.

Such a situation is called *full track blocking*. When there is only one block per track there will be only one count area, one address marker, one key area (at most), and one set of corresponding gaps. When there are many physical records per track, these areas will be repeated for each data area, and considerably less data can be recorded on a track. Thus, when it is stated that the capacity of a DASD is 13,000 bytes per track, that is an optimistic figure, achieved only when each track contains only one block which fills the track. Of course, in the case of full track blocking, the buffer through which the data is moved to the host memory must be able to hold the quoted maximum number of data bytes per track.

Blocking makes efficient use of storage space on a DASD. Less non-data information is required, leaving room for more data. Also, time is saved during read and write operations because there is always some rotational delay before a read or write of each block; the fewer the number of blocks required to read or write a given set of data, the shorter will be the access time.

If records are to be stored in sequential order by keys, and if buffers are sufficiently large, blocking makes a lot of sense. However, if records are stored in a random or direct access file, they rarely end up in key sequential order, and blocking can lead to serious difficulties in recovering data. Suppose, for example, you have a file which contains the records with keys MIDVALE, OGDEN, BOUNTIFUL, LOGAN, FARMINGTON, and MORGAN. The records are to be blocked with a blocking factor of three and stored in the order given. The key and data areas of the two blocks of the file would appear as in Figure 5–5.

If you were searching this file for the record with key MIDVALE, where would you look first? Of course, you would look at the second record, since you expect the key for the block to be the last and highest key in the block. The key for the first block is BOUNTIFUL. That is smaller than the key, MIDVALE, of the record you are searching for. The key of the second block is MORGAN, greater than MIDVALE, so you would expect to find the record for MIDVALE in the second block, and you would be wrong. Thus blocking of records is very useful for files in sequential order but poses some difficulties otherwise.

COMPACTION AND COMPRESSION OF DATA

On a new disk or in a clean area of memory, most access methods will record data in contiguous extents, filling the space most efficiently, and leaving no extra, unused areas. However, as records or files are moved, erased, or rewritten, the storage space becomes fragmented. Each time a new block or file is written it must fit into the space left by previously deleted blocks. Thus the computer must search for an area which is at least as large as, and usually larger than, the data to be written. Otherwise, the data must be written in several noncontiguous extents. The first process leaves holes throughout the storage area, and creates wasted space. Writing data into noncontiguous extents significantly increases access time and requires the allocation of excess space for recording tables of the addresses of the multiple extents.

Data should be *compacted* periodically in order to close in the small empty holes and leave larger, usable spaces. This is usually a time-consuming task, which involves moving most of the records on the medium, and is generally performed when more space is needed rather than every time data is stored. Often the same routines which perform compaction of data also han-

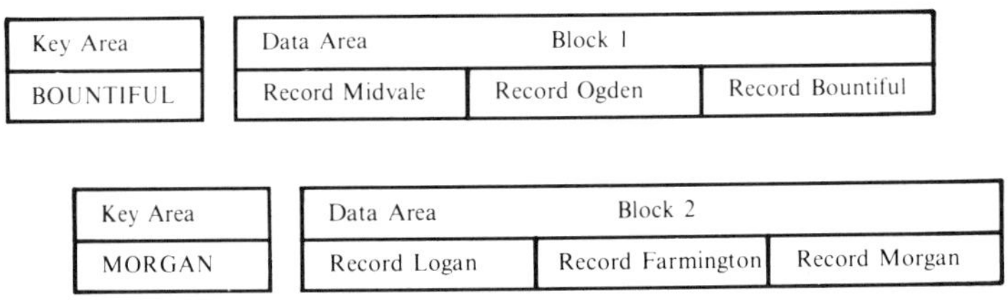

FIGURE 5–5. Blocked Records, Random Order

dle "garbage collection," physically eliminating from storage areas those records which have been flagged as logically deleted, or removing from memory those records which are not being used. You may even discover that in the middle of very long data access routines, such as sorting or writing large files, your computer automatically performs some garbage collection and compaction operations.

Other ways of conserving storage space involve using data *compression* techniques. There are many of these. A frequency-dependent code, such as Morse code or that described by Huffman*, assigns very short codes to the most frequently used characters. In this scheme, if we were coding the letters of the alphabet, frequently used characters such as E or T would require only a few bits, while the codes for Q or Z would be several bits longer. The total text then might occupy only 70 to 80 percent of the space required by ASCII or EBCDIC codes.

Another common data compression method is to remove most of the blanks from record fields. For example, if a name such as JONES, BOB requires space for only nine characters, an efficient program may not use the same storage space as for another record containing the name KLEINRINGER, WILHELM. In cases where blank spaces are critical, it may be much more efficient to record the number of spaces, such as binary 1101 for 13 spaces, rather than ASCII or EBCDIC characters for each space. Of course, common abbreviations, such as AZ for Arizona, or short codes for often repeated patterns of data, also reduce storage requirements. Many other data compression techniques are commonly used and are described in literature.**

DASD TRACK CAPACITIES

It is a rare file that can be efficiently stored with full track blocking. Thus finding how many bytes can be stored on a track or calculating how many tracks or cylinders a file may take on a given DASD generally takes a bit more effort than looking up maximum track capacities such as those given in Chapter 3. We will show how to calcuate track capacities in the case of several typical DASD's which illustrate a fairly complete set of problems that you might encounter in finding track capacities for different devices.

For every DASD, there will be a chart or a table, such as that shown in Table 5–1, which you can use to approximate track capacities, if you know

*David Huffman, "A Method for the Construction of Minimum Redundancy Codes," *Proc. IRE,* (International Convention Record issued by the Institute of Radio Engineers, now IEEE), Vol. 40, pp 1098–1101, Sept. 1952.

**See, for example, *Design of Database Structures,* by Toby J. Teorey and James P. Fry, 1982, Prentice-Hall, Englewood Cliffs, NJ, pp 196–201.

TABLE 5–1. Excerpt from a Track Capacity Table for a Typical DASD with 19 tracks per Cylinder, 13150 Bytes per Track, and 800 Cylinders per Disk Pack.

Bytes per Physical Record				*Physical Records (Blocks) per*		
Without Keys		*With Keys*				
Min	*Max*	*Min*	*Max*	*Track*	*Cylinder*	*Disk Pack*
...	...	...	...	...	...	...
...	...	...	...	...	...	...
946	1045	886	985	11	209	167200
862	945	802	885	12	228	182400
790	861	730	801	13	247	197600
727	789	667	729	14	266	212800
672	726	612	666	15	285	228000
...	...	...	...	...	...	...

the lengths of the physical records (blocks) and whether the records are formatted with or without keys. Reading those charts is a matter of looking down the appropriate column to find the capacity.

Example 5–1. Reading the Chart

Suppose you have a file which contains 5000 data records and which is to be stored on the device described in Table 5–1. Each logical record in the file is 190 bytes long. The records are blocked with a blocking factor of 4, and the blocks are formatted without keys. Find a) the number of blocks per track, b) the number of logical records per track, and c) the number of tracks and the number of cylinders required on the DASD to store this file.

Solution:

a. The length of each block is 4 records = 4 × 190 bytes = 760 bytes. From the chart, looking in the column for blocks without keys, we find that 760 bytes lies between 727 and 789 bytes. Thus, there are *14 blocks* per track. A total of 266 blocks can be written on a cylinder, and 212,800 of these blocks could be written on the disk pack.

b. Since there are four logical records per block, we have

$$\frac{\text{14 blocks}}{\text{track}} \times \frac{\text{4 logical records}}{\text{block}} = \frac{\text{56 logical records}}{\text{track}}$$

c. To find the total number of tracks needed to store the 5000 record file, we can use either the number of blocks in the file and the blocks per track or the number of logical records in the file and records per track. Let's use the blocks.

First, we need to know how many blocks are in the file.

$$\frac{5000 \text{ logical records}}{\text{file}} \times \frac{1 \text{ block}}{4 \text{ log. records}} = \frac{1250 \text{ blocks}}{\text{file}}$$

Then, we find the number of tracks needed.

$$\frac{1250 \text{ blocks}}{\text{file}} \times \frac{1 \text{ track}}{14 \text{ blocks}} = \frac{89.29 \text{ tracks}}{\text{file}}$$

Usually, we do not wish to start a new file on the 90th track, so we always take the next higher integer number of tracks, and we would then require *90 tracks* to store this file. Since there are 19 tracks per cylinder, it will require $90/19 = 4.74$ cylinders for the file, which we again adjust to the next higher integer. Thus it requires *5 cylinders* for the file.

Example 5–2. Reading the Chart

You again have a file of 5000 records to be stored on the same DASD used in the previous example. This time, however, the records are to be formatted *with keys,* where the record data length is 180 bytes and the key length for each record is an additional 10 bytes. The blocking factor is again 4. Find a) the number of records per track and b) the number of cylinders required to store the file.

Solution:

a. First, we must find the physical record or block length. The key and data areas for the block appear as shown in Figure 5–6. Thus, the block length is $4 \times (180 + 10)$ bytes plus 10 bytes for the block key length $= 760 + 10 = 770$ bytes.

Examining the Track Capacity Table, Table 5–1, we determine that for a physical record of 770 bytes, formatted with keys, there are *13 physical records per track,* and $13 \times 19 = 247$ physical records per cylinder. Since there are 4 logical records per physical record, we then have $4 \times 13 = 52$ *logical records per track*.

Key Area	Data Area			
10 bytes block key	Logical Record 180 + 10 bytes	Logical Record 180 + 10 bytes	Logical Record 180 + 10 bytes	Logical Record 180 + 10 bytes

FIGURE 5–6. One Block, Logical Records, 180 Bytes plus 10-Byte Key—Formatted with Keys, Blocking Factor = 4

b. In order to find the number of cylinders required to store the file, let's perform the calculations using logical records this time instead of blocks, just to be different. Fifty-two logical records per track × 19 tracks per cylinder = 988 logical records per cylinder (or we could have said 247 blocks per cylinder × 4 logical records per block = 988 logical records per cylinder). Now 5000 logical records divided by 988 logical records per cylinder gives us the result of 5.06 cylinders required for the file. Thus, it takes all of 5 cylinders and 6% of a 6th, so it requires *6 cylinders* on the DASD to store this file.

Using a Track Capacity Formula

Another method of calculating track capacities and the amount of DASD space required for a given file is to use a formula rather than a table. The formulae appear as indicated in Figure 5–7.

The track capacities given in this figure are larger than the maximum data capacities by the amount of the Constant, which is the number of non-data bytes required for a single block of data on the track. Thus, for example, the maximum capacity of Device II in Figure 5–7 with full track blocking would be 26,460 − 235 = 26,225 data bytes per track.

Now let's work the preceding examples again, this time using the Track Capacity Formula for Device I instead of the chart.

Example 5–3

Your file contains 5000 data records and is to be stored on Device I. The logical record length is 190 bytes. The blocking factor = 4. Records are formatted without keys. Find a) the number of blocks per track and b) the number of cylinders required for the file.

$$\text{Physical Data Records (blocks) per track} = \frac{\text{Track Capacity}}{\text{Constant} + C + D}$$

Where

Track Capacity = the number of bytes of data that could be stored on a track if no non-data information were required.

Constant includes overhead for address marker, count area, cyclic check characters, and gaps.

C = extra overhead (including an extra gap, among other things) for a block formatted with keys.

D = length of key area plus data area for the block.

Device	Track Capacity	Constant	C
I*	13,150	150	0 format without keys
(19 tracks/cylinder, 800 cylinders/disk pack)			60 format with keys
II	26,460	235	0 format without keys
(14 tracks/cylinder, 600 cylinders/disk pack)			96 format with keys
III	1500**	0	0 format without keys
(15 tracks/cylinder, 1800 cylinders/disk pack)			24** format with keys

* Device I is the one for which the track capacities are also given in Table 5-1.

** On Device III, all information is stored in 32 byte segments. Thus, for this device the track capacity, C, and D are all expressed as a number of 32 byte segments. D = number of 32 byte segments for the key plus the number of 32 byte segments for the data.

FIGURE 5–7. Track Capacity Formulae

Solution:

a. The length of each block is again 4×190 bytes $= 760$ bytes. Thus, in the formula $D = 760$, the value of $C = 0$ because the records are formatted without keys. Therefore,

$$\text{Physical records per track} = \frac{13{,}150}{150 + 0 + 760} = 14.45$$

So we can get 14 physical records plus 45% of another one on a track. The 45% would be placed on a different track, so we always take the next lower integer, and we can get *14 physical records per track* for this file. Note that this is the same result achieved in Example 5–1 by using the table. With four logical records per block, there are then $4 \times 14 = 56$ *logical records per track*.

b. Using logical records this time (compare with the calculation using blocks in Example 5–1), the number of tracks required for the file = 5000 logical records divided by 56 logical records per track = 89.29 tracks, which says that we need *90 tracks* for the file. Ninety tracks divided by 19 tracks per cylinder = 4.74 cylinders. Thus, we require *five cylinders* for this file.

Example 5–4

Our file of 5000 records is now to be formatted with keys and stored on Device I. Each record has a length of 180 bytes plus a 10-byte key. The blocking factor is 4. Find a) the number of records per track and b) the number of cylinders required for the file.

Solution:

a. The length of the block is $4 \times (180 + 10)$ bytes $+ 10$ bytes for the block's key $= 770$ bytes. This will be the number D in the formula of Figure 5–7. The number C is 60, since the data is formatted with keys. Thus,

$$\text{physical records per track} = \frac{13{,}150}{150 + 60 + 770} = 13.42$$

Therefore, there are *13 physical records (blocks) per track* or $13 \times 4 = 52$ *logical records per track*.

b. Thirteen physical records per track × 19 tracks per cylinder = 247 blocks per cylinder. There are 5000 logical records with 4 logical records per block. Hence, there are 5000/4 = 1250 blocks in the file.

$$\frac{1250 \text{ blocks}}{\text{file}} \times \frac{\text{cylinder}}{247 \text{ blocks}} = \frac{5.06 \text{ cylinders}}{\text{file}}$$

So it requires 6 *cylinders* to store the file.

To further illustrate this type of analysis, let's consider a file stored on Device II described in Figure 5–7. The data will then be transferred to a mass storage facility with a capacity of 50 million bytes per cartridge.

Example 5–5

A customer file for a large mail-order catalog store contains 150,000 records. The records are formatted with keys, each record being 512 bytes long plus an additional 128 bytes for the key. The file is unblocked and stored on Device II. a) How many records can be stored on a single track? b) How many records can be stored on a cylinder? c) What percentage of the total disk pack of the device is required to store the file? d) If the storage space for the file on the DASD is in contiguous (adjacent) cylinders beginning at cylinder 200, approximately how much time would be required to read the entire file and transfer it to the host computer? e) Approximately how many mass storage cartridges would be required for this file?

Solution:

a. Since the records are unblocked, the physical record (block) length equals the logical record length = 512 bytes plus 128 byte key = 640 bytes. Using this record length for the number D, we have from the formula for Device II in Figure 5–7,

$$\text{Records per track} = \frac{26{,}460}{235+96+640} = \frac{27.25 \text{ records}}{\text{track}}$$

Hence, there are *27 customer records per track.*

b. There are 14 tracks per cylinder on this disk pack. Thus there are 27 × 14 = *378 records per cylinder.*

c. 150,000 records divided by 378 records per cylinder = 396.83 cylinders. Therefore it will take 397 cylinders to store the file. The disk pack has 600 cylinders.

$$\frac{397 \text{ cylinders}}{600 \text{ cylinders}} \times 100 = 66.2\% \textit{ of the disk pack is required}$$

d. To calculate the approximate time needed to transfer the file to the host computer use the data for a typical hard disk from Figure 3–11 in Chapter 3. Assume that the seek time to find cylinder 200 is approximately the average seek time = 25.0 millisec
The seek time for each of the following 396 cylinders

= 396 × minimum seek time =
396 × 10 millisec = 3960.0 millisec

Data transfer time equals approximately

$$150{,}000 \text{ records} \times \frac{640 \text{ bytes}}{\text{record}} \times \frac{1 \text{ second}}{1000 \times 1024 \text{ bytes}} = 93.8 \text{ sec.}$$

Rotational delay will be approximately one half rotation after each data transfer to find the next record

= 150,000 × 8.4 millisec = 1,260.0 sec.

Thus the total transfer time to read the entire file to the host computer is approximately

seek time rotational delay transfer time
0.025 + 3.960 sec + 1260.0 sec. + 93.8 sec
= approx. 1358 sec. = approx. *23 minutes*

e. The data plus non-data information to be transferred to the mass storage cartridge is approximately 397 Device II cylinders which is 397 × 14 tracks per cylinder × 26,460 bytes per track = approx. 147,000,000 bytes. One mass storage cartridge holds 50 million bytes. 147/50 = 2.94. Thus it will take *3 mass storage cartridges* to contain this file.

Storing data on a DASD such as Device III in Figure 5–7 requires a bit of a change in the way the calculation proceeds, since data is stored in 32-

byte segments. The following example illustrates how to handle such a situation.

Example 5–6

Suppose you have an inventory which consists of 10,000 records, each 250 bytes in length plus a 20-byte key. The records are blocked with a blocking factor of 7 and formatted with keys on Device III. a) How many records are there per track on the DASD and b) how many tracks will it take to store the file?

Solution:

a. The physical record length must be calculated in two parts. First, not including the key for the entire block, there are $7 \times (250+20) = 1890$ bytes per block. Remember, however, that we must calculate how many 32-byte segments this takes. So, 1890 bytes divided by 32 bytes per segment equals 59.0625. Thus, it takes 60 of the 32-byte segments to store the data area of the physical record. The key area of the physical record is 20 bytes long, but again this area must be an integer multiple of 32 bytes. Hence it takes 1 segment of 32 bytes for the key area. Thus the physical record length, D, to be used in the formula from Figure 5–7, is $60+1=61$ segments.

   Therefore, the number of physical records per track, using the formula in Figure 5–7, is

$$\frac{1500}{0+24+61} = 17.65$$

   or *17 physical records per track* which equals $7 \times 17 =$ *119 logical records per track.*

b. 10,000 records divided by 119 records per track = 84.03 tracks.

   Thus it will take *85 tracks* on Device III to store the inventory file.

Fixed Block Architecture

On a fixed block architecture (FBA) disk drive, as some hard disks and most floppy disks are, the tracks are divided into sectors with a fixed number of data bytes per sector. A typical floppy disk will have 128 or 256 bytes per sector. Machines using rigid disks may have 512 bytes or more per sector.

A typical larger FBA disk may have 32 sectors per track with 512 data bytes in each sector. The total capacity of each sector may actually be more like 600 bytes, but 88 of those bytes would contain zeros, gaps, and non-data information. The non-data bytes generally include a flag indicating whether the sector is operative or defective, primary or alternate. On large devices, alternate sectors are provided for every track as well as alternate tracks for each surface. Generally, no alternate sectors or tracks at all are provided on floppy disks. Also included in the non-data bytes within a sector are address bytes giving the relative sector number with respect to the beginning of the track, the surface or head number for the track, and the cylinder number. Cyclic redundancy check bytes (CRC, essentially equivalent to the cyclic check characters on a conventional architecture DASD), error correction code (ECC) bytes for the sector, a few synchronizing bytes so that the controller can determine when the data area is positioned under the read/write head, and a number of bytes containing zeros complete the non-data byte area.

The amount of data transferred to or from an FBA machine during I/O operations must be an integer number of sectors. This quantity, roughly equivalent to a block or physical record on conventional devices, is called a *control interval* (CI) on a fixed block architecture machine. Hence the number of bytes in a control interval must equal an integer times the number of data bytes per sector. Note that the non-data information contained on a disk is generally not transferred to the host computer. Non-data is used solely by the controller or the channel (peripheral processor) for checking operations. An integer number of records must fit within a control interval. Generally, unless records are carefully organized to be 128, 256, 512, etc. bytes in length, there will be extra unfilled bytes at the end of the last sector in a control interval. These extra unused bytes are often filled with zeros.

The data storage capacity stated for an FBA machine is constant. The total number of bytes available for data on a disk equals the number of sectors times the fixed number of data bytes per sector, no matter how the data is formatted. For data stored on an FBA disk, there is no need for count areas, since the length of the data area in each sector is constant and need not be specified for each record. Also, keys are nearly always stored within the data area rather than in a separate key area.

On small computers, especially microcomputers using floppy disks, the minimum control interval size is usually fixed by the computer. Often this will be two or three sectors, and this minimum CI is called a *granule*. The user may then specify the control interval to be a small number of granules. The computer will usually pick one granule for the CI size if the user does not specify otherwise. On larger computers, the computer user is generally free to specify a CI size of from one to 64 or more sectors. The number of bytes in the control interval cannot be larger than can be contained at one time in the I/O buffer of the host computer, of course. A careful choice of the control interval size for a given record length can, in some cases, greatly reduce the number of unused bytes in the last sector and improve the efficiency of use of storage space on the DASD.

Example 5–7

Suppose that you have a computer which uses floppy disks. The disks have 18 sectors per track, with each sector capable of containing 256 bytes of data. The I/O buffer on your computer can hold 4 kilobytes. The minimum control interval size set by your computer is 3 sectors, which is defined to be one granule on your machine. Your file will contain 3000 records, each with 115 bytes. a) Choose a control interval size which will minimize unused data space on the disk. Then, b) calculate how many records you can put on one track and c) how many sectors and how many tracks will be required to store your file.

Solution:

a. To find an ideal control interval size, first consider that the minimum CI size is one granule = 3 sectors = 3 × 256 bytes = 768 bytes. So our control interval must be one of the following sizes:

3 sectors = 1 granule = 1 × 768 bytes = 768 bytes
6 sectors = 2 granules = 2 × 768 bytes = 1536 bytes
9 sectors = 3 granules = 3 × 768 bytes = 2304 bytes
12 sectors = 4 granules = 4 × 768 bytes = 3072 bytes
15 sectors = 5 granules = 5 × 768 bytes = 3840 bytes

Note that you cannot have 6 granules, since this gives a control interval size = 4608 bytes, which is greater than your I/O buffer can handle.

Now, which control interval size is best for your file? First, you will probably wish to choose 3, 6, or 9 sectors rather than the other two options, because you can get a whole number of these intervals on an 18-sector track. By choosing 12 or 15 sectors, either you would have to waste a large part of each track or you would greatly complicate the situation by having control intervals which spanned across more than one track. In a 3-sector, 768-byte CI you could get 768/115 = 6.68 records in the control interval; so you would store 6 records and waste 0.68 × 115 = 78 bytes. In a 6-sector, 1536-byte CI you could get 1536/115 = 13.36 records; so you would store 13 records and waste 0.36 × 115 = 41 bytes. Thus, the 6-sector CI would probably be a better choice than the 3-sector CI. However, in a 9-sector, 2304-byte CI you can get 2304/115 = 20.035 records; so you could store 20 records in the control interval and waste only 0.035 × 115 = 4 bytes.

Thus, your best choice by far in terms of maximum efficiency in use of storage space on the disk would be

1 control interval = 9 sectors = 3 granules = 2304 bytes with 20 records per control interval

b. With 9 sectors (3 granules) per control interval and 18 sectors (6 granules) per track, you can put two control intervals on a track. Since each control interval contains 20 records, you will be writing *40 records per track*.

c. 3000 records divided by 20 records per 9 sectors = *1350 sectors* for the file. 3000 records divided by 40 records per track = *75 tracks* for the file.

Example 5–8

On an FBA DASD with 400 tracks per surface, 32 sectors per track, 512 bytes per sector, and 11 tracks per cylinder, you wish to store a file containing 8000 records, each with a data length of 300 bytes and a key length of 80 bytes. You have already decided that you wish to block the records with a blocking factor of 5. Your host computer can handle up to 32 kilobytes in the input/output buffer. a) Find the length of a *logical block,* i. e., a block made up of the five logical records. b) Choose an appropriate control interval. c) How many sectors and how many tracks on the DASD will be required to store this file?

Solution:

a. The logical block length = 5 × (300 + 80) bytes = *1900 bytes*. Note that the 80-byte key is *not* added again as in earlier examples for blocked records on conventional DASDs, because no key is stored separately for the block on FBA machines.

b. To choose a control interval, note that the smallest control interval should be at least four 512-byte sectors = 2048 bytes, since that is the smallest integer multiple of 512 into which one 1900-byte physical record can fit. Using four sectors, note that there will be 2048 − 1900 = 148 bytes wasted. This is pretty good, and would make a reasonably good control interval. However, consider the following table of multiples of 512 bytes, i. e., possible sizes for control intervals:

TABLE 5–2. Multiples of 512, Possible Control Interval Sizes

N	*N*×*512*	*N*	*N*×*512*	*N*	*N*×*512*
1	512	22	11264	43	22016
2	1024	23	11776	44	22528
3	1536	24	12228	45	23040
4	2048	25	12800	46	23552
5	2560	26	13312	47	24064
6	3072	27	13824	48	24576
7	3584	28	14336	49	25088
8	4096	29	14848	50	25600
9	4608	30	15360	51	26112
10	5120	31	15872	52	26624
11	5632	32	16384	53	27136
12	6144	33	16896	54	27648
13	6656	34	17408	55	28160
14	7168	35	17920	56	28672
15	7680	36	18432	57	29184
16	8192	37	18944	58	29696
17	8704	38	19456	59	30208
18	9216	39	19968	60	30720
19	9728	40	20480	61	31232
20	10240	41	20992	62	31744
21	10752	42	21504	63	32256
				64	32768

Multiplying the logical block size for this file (1900 bytes) by 1, 2, 3, etc., and comparing with the possible control interval sizes in the table (Table 5–2), you will soon discover that $7 \times 1900 = 13300$ bytes, which is only 12 bytes different from 26×512 bytes $= 13312$ bytes. Hence, a very good control interval size for this file would be exactly *26 sectors = 13312 bytes*. This would make good use of storage space, wasting only 12 bytes out of every 13312; $(12 \times 100) / 13312 = 0.09\%$ waste.

c. There are $8000/5 = 1600$ logical blocks in this file. Seven (7) logical blocks require 1 control interval.

$$\frac{\text{1600 logical blocks}}{\text{file}} \times \frac{\text{control interval}}{\text{7 logical blocks}} = \frac{\text{228.57 CIs}}{\text{file}}$$

Thus, you will need 229 control intervals in which to store your file. However, a large capacity fixed block architecture DASD may require you to *add one more control interval* at the end of the file to indicate End of File. Therefore, the file would require *230 control intervals*. There are 26 sectors per control interval, so you will need $26 \times 230 =$ *5980 sectors* for the file. There are 32 sectors per track. 5980 sectors divided by 32 sectors per track $= 186.88$ tracks, so you will need *187 tracks* on the DASD on which to store your file. This is $187 \times 100 / 400 = 47\%$ of one of the 11 surfaces on the disk pack.

QUESTIONS

1. Data on Cards:
   a. What is the record length for data stored on IBM (Hollerith) punched cards? Why?
   b. How are punched cards similar to a fixed block architecture disk drive?
   c. Of the eight record formats in Figure 5–2, which combination best describes data stored on punched cards?
2. What is the purpose of two consecutive interblock gaps on a magnetic tape or a record which contains zero length key and data areas (hence at least two consecutive gaps) on a DASD?
3. List the differences, if any, in the information stored in the Home Address, Track Descriptor Record, Address Marker, Count, Key, Data, and Gap areas when records are formatted with keys, in contrast to when the records are formatted without keys.

4. Of the eight record formats in Figure 5–2
   a. Which would be the most useful for records processed in random order?
   b. Which would be the most useful for long logical records, which are larger than the buffer can accommodate?
   c. What is usually contained in the key area for a block in a fixed, blocked format with keys?
   d. Which format would you use to copy a file without concern for its contents?
5. Why is the two-byte physical address field in the count area of a data record not needed on a fixed-head DASD?
6. Assume that the inter-area gaps on a hypothetical 14-inch diameter disk are five bytes long and that there are 15,000 bytes per track.
   a. What would be the length of a gap (in inches) on a track which lies along the outer circumference of the disk?
   b. What would be the length of a gap on a track which has a six-inch diameter (that is, which lies three inches from the disk center)?
7. Assume that a hypothetical 5 1/4-inch diameter floppy disk is formatted with 18 sectors per track and has gaps between each sector. If the gaps between sectors along a track which is five inches (12.7 cm) in diameter are approximately 0.0264444 inches (0.672 cm) long, and if each track contains 4652 bytes (including gaps)
   a. How many bytes long would a gap be?
   b. How many bytes would be in each sector between the gaps?
8. Assume that a disk drive has tracks configured similar to Device II in Figure 5–7, with 26,460 bytes per track. The track is to be formatted for full-track blocking without keys. How many bytes would be left for the data area of the one block on the track if the index point required a 22-byte area, the home address were 19 bytes long, the count areas for record 0 and record 1 were each 21 bytes long, the data area for record 0 were 20 bytes long, the address marker in record 1 were 12 bytes long, and the gaps were each 20 bytes long?
9. In Table 5–1,
   a. Why are the numbers in the records per cylinder column equal to 19 times the corresponding numbers in the records per track column?

b. What is the ratio of the numbers in the records per disk pack column to the corresponding numbers in the records per track column? Why?

10. Suppose a frequency-dependent code had been developed such that all characters, including punctuation, require seven bits except for the following:

Character	*Bits in Code*	*Character*	*Bits in Code*
Space	3	r	6
e	4	y	9
t	4	k	10
s	5	x	10
n	6	j	11
o	6	z	11

How many bits would be required to store the first sentence in Chapter 5 of this text

a. in 7-bit ASCII with no parity?

b. in the frequency-dependent code described above?

c. What is the compression ratio (compressed text / ASCII text) for that sentence?

11. A department store keeps a record for each customer in a master file. Each record is 190 bytes long plus an 18-byte key (which is the customer's account number). The 15,000 records in the file are to be formatted with keys, blocked with a blocking factor of 4, and stored on Device I, described in Table 5–1 and Figure 5–7.

a. Use Table 5–1 to determine how many physical records (blocks) can be recorded on a track.

b. How many logical records are recorded on a track?

c. How many physical records can be recorded on a cylinder?

d. How many logical records would be on a cylinder?

e. How many tracks are needed for the file?

f. How many cylinders are needed for the file?

g. What percentage of the disk pack will be needed for the file?

12. A politician keeps track of his 10,000 "friends" in a file stored on Device II, described in Figure 5–7. His records are formatted without keys and are each 60 bytes long. The records are to be blocked in groups of 10.

    a. How many physical records (blocks) will fit on one track?

    b. How many tracks should be reserved for the file?

13. The records in a file stored on Device III, described in Figure 5–7, are each 300 bytes long plus a key for each record which is eight bytes long. The records are blocked with a blocking factor of five and formatted with keys.

    a. How many physical records per track are there in the storage area for this file?

    b. How many logical records are stored per track?

14. A 16,000-record inventory file is to be stored on the FBA device described in Example 5–8. The records are 240 bytes in length and will be blocked with a blocking factor of four. You have already decided that the control interval will be 10 kilobytes long.

    a. What is the logical block length for records in the file?

    b. How many logical blocks will fit in one control interval?

    c. How many data bytes will be left unused in each control interval?

    d. How many sectors on the device should be allocated for the file?

15. You have a master patient file for a small community hospital which is to be stored on the FBA device described in Example 5–8. The file will contain 500 records, each 3180 bytes long. The records are to be unblocked.

    a. Find an acceptable control interval which will give you fewer than 100 bytes wasted data storage space in each control interval.

    b. How many sectors on the device will be needed to store this file?

    c. What percentage of the total storage space on the device should be reserved for the file?

16. Your microcomputer has a maximum buffer size of four kilobytes and uses 5 1/4-inch diameter floppy disks. The disks are single side, formatted with 18 sectors per track, 256 bytes per sector, and 40 tracks per disk. The computer requires that control intervals be an integer number of granules, where for your computer one granule is

three sectors long. You wish to store 3,000 billing records in a file for your small business. The records are each 400 bytes long.

a. Find the control interval size such that you can get an integer number of CI's on a track and such that the minimum number of bytes is wasted.

b. In this situation what percentage of each control interval is wasted?

c. How many sectors are needed for your file?

d. What percentage of a floppy disk would be used for this file?

17. Retlaw Distributors keeps its master catalog on Device I, described in Table 5–1 and Figure 5–7. The catalog lists 50,000 items, each in a separate record which is 120 bytes long and has a 10-byte key. The records are formatted with keys and blocked with a blocking factor of eight.

a. How long is each logical record in the file?

b. How long is each physical record (block)?

c. How many physical records can fit on one track of the DASD?

d. How many physical records are there on one cylinder?

e. How many physical records are there in the file?

f. How many tracks on the DASD will be required for the file?

g. How many cylinders on the DASD will be required for the file?

h. What percentage of the disk pack is filled by the file?

i. What fraction of a 50-million-byte mass storage system cartridge would be needed for this file?

PART II

FILE DESIGN

PROLOGUE

GEORGE BOOLE

The formal development of the rules of logic which allow modern computers to manipulate symbols and files must be credited mainly to George Boole (1815–1864). He was born in Lincoln, England, the son of a cobbler, who in spite of his interests in mathematics and optical instruments was not particularly talented in business. Because of unsettled economic conditions in the family, George attended some elementary and trade school but gained his foundation and keen insight into mathematics through determined, independent study.

In 1849, Boole was appointed, without a college degree, professor of mathematics at Queen's College in Cork, Ireland. Here he was a conscientious, well loved teacher, regarded by the people in the town as an "innocent" to be protected and admired. In 1855, George Boole married Mary Everest, the daughter of a professor of Greek at Queen's College (after whom Mount Everest is named). Mary was resigned to the stream of visitors who came to her home to talk science with George because she knew of the good will generated in the community by her husband.

Boole's numerous papers and books covered wide areas of mathematics research, but he is best remembered today for his *Mathematical Analysis of Logic*. In this work he succeeded in reducing Aristotle's logic to an algebraic calculus, an effort which had been attempted by numerous mathematicians before him.

In kindness and adherence to principle George Boole endured to the end. In 1864, concerned about his students, he walked through the rain in frail health and conducted a lecture in wet clothes. To treat the resulting fatal illness he requested a physician who had been dismissed from Queen's College for misconduct. Boole's concern was to show friendship to someone who needed it.

CHAPTER 6

INTRODUCTION TO LINEAR AND NONLINEAR DATA STRUCTURES

LINEAR VERSUS NONLINEAR

"Linear and Nonlinear Data Structures"—it sounds ominous and impressive. Actually, all it means is that data is organized so that all of the records are read in sequence by keys (linear) or that it is accessed in some other order. The remainder of this text will discuss the organization of data in files, so that records can be retrieved either in key sequential order or randomly. The methods of file organization which will be discussed are those which have been commonly used and seem to work reasonably well in various circumstances. As files grow and as new data is added to old files, virtually all organization methods seem to deteriorate in efficiency, in how well data space is used, and in how fast records can be found. There is nothing sacred about the file organization methods which we will discuss. New organization methods are needed; perhaps you will be the one to discover powerful new techniques. However, for now, most data is organized according to one of the patterns discussed below.

If a data file is small, say fewer than a hundred records, the manner of organization is relatively unimportant. Any record or set of records in a small file can be read or updated quickly no matter which one comes first or whether they are read in some particular order. However, when a file gets large, hundreds or thousands of records, the organization is critical; the most efficient organization is very dependent upon what your data looks like and how you wish to use it. A rule of thumb is that the larger the file the more carefully it must be organized.

File Volatility

Suppose that you still have a file which contains the financial records for your small business for the year 1967. You would expect that the way you use that file would be different from the way you use your financial records for the current year. Your 1967 business records would be quite *static;* you would rarely want to add to or delete from records in the file. On the other hand, your current year records are *dynamic;* you will be adding and changing regularly. How often you add records to your file or delete them from your file is called the *volatility* of the file. A highly volatile, dynamic file should probably be organized so that any record can be accessed and updated quickly. A low volatility, static file would rarely require any updating of individual records.

File Activity

Another important characteristic of data in determining how it should be organized is its activity. When we speak of activity we should also refer to a time frame. In other words, the daily activity of a file may be quite different from the monthly activity, especially if it happens to be a payroll file for a company which pays its employees once a month. The *activity* of a file in a given time period is the ratio of the number of records accessed to the total number of records in the file. For example, if you call an automobile rental agency to reserve a car, the agent will be accessing an active file. The daily activity of a file containing records for all of the cars in a rental agency is high. Virtually all of the records will be accessed every day. In fact, the agent may have to search through a large fraction of the records in the file of cars at a particular location each time a request is made in order to determine which car is available and which one is suitable for your use. Suppose that out of 1000 cars at the Portland airport, records for 300 of them are examined on the average each time a request is made; the *immediate activity* of that file would be (300/1000) = 0.30 = 30%.

On the other hand, a record of prescriptions dispensed by a pharmacy during the year 1950 would be a low activity, static file. At the request of a physician, you may indeed on a given day wish to recover the data for 86-year-old Mrs. Jones, and find out exactly what was prescribed for her during the year 1950; however, that is probably the only record for all of the 5000 customers of that year which you need that day. Thus the activity of that file for the day would be about 1/5000 = .0002 = 0.02%.

You may wish to have the automobile rental file and the 1950 pharmacy records file organized quite differently because of the difference in their activity. In the case of the active file, you will very likely read and examine every record in order until you find the appropriate conditions. In the pharmacy records, you probably do not wish to read the records for every 1950 customer until you find Mrs. Jones. Instead, you would want to be able to pick the information for Mrs. Jones immediately. These two situations require different organization methods. For high activity files, linear data structures are usually quite valuable. For low activity files, linear organization of data may be quite cumbersome.

File Growth

When a data file is created, the wise programmer leaves space for future growth. A file can grow in *two dimensions*. First, *new records* are added to virtually every file as it matures. Rarely would the user know all the data which will be entered into a file when it is first created. The second dimension of growth of a file is the amount of data to be put into *each record*. If you set up a file containing all relevant data about students at a college, for example, inevitably somebody will need more data about the students than was planned for. If bytes were allowed in each record for expansion, it may be possible to add new information to the records fairly easily. Otherwise the file may have to be completely reorganized and rewritten. It is a corollary to Murphy's Law that no matter how much room is left in each record for future expansion and no matter how much room is provided for adding records to the file, somebody always needs more. No matter how much room is allowed in an address field for a street address, somebody will have a longer address for which there is no sensible abbreviation. You should plan ahead for some growth, at least, to avoid having to reorganize any more often than absolutely necessary. File organization programs should always be written so that they can be changed easily to handle unforseen circumstances.

FILE ORGANIZATION VERSUS FILE PROCESSING

In the discussion in this chapter so far we have been discussing *file organization*. This is the way data is stored, the way it is arranged physically on a storage device. In contrast, *file processing* is the way data is read from or written to a device, the way the user wishes to see the data.

Organization depends upon the physical characteristics of the device, but it also depends very much on the volatility, activity, and provision for growth of the file. Processing depends upon the user's desires for accessing the data. The two basic types of processing are batch and direct. They correspond closely with the concepts of linear and nonlinear organization, although not immutably so. Usually, in batch processing, all the data is to be accessed at once. Something is to be done to every record, even if it is only to be examined to see that it is not the one desired. A linear method of organization, where all records are read in order by key, is usually advisable. On the other hand, direct processing implies that the user wishes to access only a select few records in the file and generally not in a predictable order. In this case a so-called "nonlinear" organization method, which allows records to be picked at random from a file without reading the entire file, is probably most efficient. You may well be able to think of situations in which a linear data structure would be valuable for a direct access file and where a nonlinear structure would work best on a batch file, but these situations will be exceptions.

Another way of categorizing the processing of files is by how many records need to be accessed at one time. Files lend themselves very well to linear organization when one wishes to access many or all of the records in the file. Sequential data structures such as strictly sequential organization, linked lists, stacks, or queues are valuable in such situations. If accessing one unique record or a few records is desired, then nonlinear structures, such as direct organization or an indexed organization, would be more useful.

Linear file organization is possible on virtually every type of storage medium, including tapes, cards, a printer, etc. Yes, even a printer is a device for storing data in linear order; it is a bit difficult for a computer to retrieve data from a printed page, but it certainly is a good way to store information permanently. Other types of file organizations are possible only with high-speed direct access devices such as disks. "Life in the fast lane" would be much slower if all our data still had to be stored on and accessed from cards or tape. You may make your own judgments about whether that would be good or bad for society.

Managing the Data

Choosing a method of data organization is one small part of the total process of data management. Although the data may indeed just seem to grow from nothing, a good data file does not just grow. It needs to be carefully managed from creation to deletion if it is to be useful. Every useful data file must be consciously *created* at some time. You must decide on what *medium* the data is to be stored, how it is to be *organized,* and how it is to be *processed.* Once the data has been organized you will find that it is seldom a file that you just use and forget. The file will inevitably grow, and *growth* must be managed. Some means must be provided for handling the growth both in the number of records and in the record contents. You may even wish to *reorganize* periodically to keep access speed as fast as possible and utilization of storage space as efficient as possible. You definitely will wish to provide *backup* for your file on the same or a different medium, so that in case of problems, the file can be reproduced. Some method will probably be needed for *accounting,* for determining who uses the data for what purposes. You may even wish to *relocate* the file at some time on another device or medium, either because it outgrows the device on which it was originally located or because you are upgrading machines. Eventually, every file reaches the limit of its usefulness. At that time, if it is needed for future reference it can be *retired* to a library on magnetic tape, removable disks, or some other medium which is relatively inexpensive and easy to store. Finally, it should be *deleted* completely.

Data Handling Software

It might be interesting and informative to write your own programs to handle each data management problem as it occurs, and you may indeed find yourself writing software for unusual situations. However, the same problems are encountered repeatedly in virtually every computing facility. Good software has been written to handle common data management situations, so you need not write all of the programs to manage your data unless you really want to or unless something unusual happens.

The programs which handle how you access your data files are called *access methods.* This software is part of the operating system for the computer, auxiliary storage, and I/O devices of your system. It usually comes packaged with the system, or can be purchased "off the shelf" for your equipment. Many operating systems for handling data on disks will have the letters *DOS* (for Disk Operating System) or *OS* (for Operating System) somewhere in the name. However, you may find systems which deviate from this policy and use completely different symbols in reference to their control programs.

Access methods handle the details of reading from and writing to I/O devices, including secondary storage devices. Moving data through the I/O *buffer* to match transfer rates, to wait for status signals that the devices are ready for data transfer, etc., is a function of an access method program. GET, PUT, and FIELD are typical of the instructions which you may see performing these operations at some level. The FIELD instruction defines the buffer, what variables are to fill which bits in the buffer. The PUT instruction moves the contents of the buffer to an output device, and the GET instruction moves values into the buffer from an input device.

Blocking and unblocking data, collecting records for transfer as a block to the storage device, or separating blocks into individual records as the data comes from storage, are also performed by some access methods without the user's intervention. Formatting the data for a particular device is something that the typical computer user should not have to worry about.

You should not have to write an I/O *driver* program, a program to transmit the data properly and make certain it is transmitted and received in the correct format, each time you wish to send the data to a device. The access methods do that for you, so that in most situations you need not even know the details of how an I/O device works. This makes modern applications programming independent of the device. A WRITE or PRINT command or a READ or INPUT command simply calls an access method routine which handles all the unpleasant details for you.

While processing the block of data which has just been accessed, some access methods even anticipate what will be the next block to transfer, and will search for and move that data to the buffer. Such anticipatory buffering is called *queuing* and can be done only with linear data structures where it can be predicted which record is to be accessed next.

Using an Access Method

In many cases using an access method is as simple as giving an I/O command, such as READ or WRITE, in a high level language, and allowing the operating system to call the access routine for you when your program is compiled or interpreted (translated to machine language for execution by the computer).

At other times, you may wish to access the data directly from the terminal without writing a high level program to do so. You may then use JCL (job control language) commands on most machines to LIST, COPY, or examine your files. Other commands such as those for creating, renaming, protecting, or deleting file areas, or for giving a directory of files, will also be available to you.

Other access methods may have to be called from your job control language as special utility programs. Within your system there will undoubtedly be one or more EDitor routines available for writing data into a file in sequential order and for examining and changing individual records in the file. More sophisticated utilities may be available to help you create indexed or other nonlinearly organized files.

Types of Access Methods

Access methods can generally be divided into types by how they perform their tasks. *Basic* access methods read and write one physical record at a time. They do not perform extra functions such as anticipating the next record or blocking and unblocking records. They are indeed basic in the sense that all they do is transfer information; the programmers have the responsibility for blocking and organizing the data in the form they wish to use it. Because it is so fundamental, this type of access method can be used as part of the data handling programs for virtually any type of storage organization.

Queued access methods, on the other hand, do perform anticipatory buffering, anticipating what the next record will be. They can be used only for linearly organized data, since they must predict next records. These methods also generally perform blocking and unblocking functions for the programmer, and they handle more of the details of the data transfer than Basic access methods do.

Some common acronyms for access methods are

BSAM (Basic Sequential Access Method), a basic access method used for sequential files

BDAM (Basic Direct Access Method), a basic access method used for accessing data records randomly, rather than in sequential order

QSAM (Queued Sequential Access Method), used for anticipatory buffering, and blocking and unblocking, on sequential files only

There is no such thing as QDAM, which would be queued access method for direct (randomly organized) files. That is because a queued access method must be able to predict what the next record will be, which cannot be done if records are to be written or retrieved in random order. You may see other acronyms, such as VSAM, which stands for Virtual Storage Access Method. This is a powerful collection of programs which was developed by IBM and is typical of sophisticated packages which allow great flexibility in data organization and data management.

Linear and Nonlinear Data Structures

In the next three chapters we will examine linear data structures carefully. In Chapter 7 the sequential organization of data and two search methods which accompany that method of data organization will be discussed. Other linear data structures, such as linked lists, stacks, queues, and trees will be covered in Chapter 8. These are variations on sequential data storage. In linked lists the data may be stored in any order, but pointers in the data are used to link the records in sequential order. Binary trees require data to be stored in a hierarchical order. Stacks and queues allow a small number of records to be accessed quickly and easily in the order in which they are stored. Methods of sorting data in linear order will be examined in Chapter 9.

Some popular nonlinear methods of organizing data will be discussed in Chapters 10, 11, and 12. These include partitioned files, direct or random access files, indexed file organizations, and other special types of data structures. Direct access files are particularly useful when retrieval of one record from a file without reading all the records in order is desired. In direct organization, algorithms are used to convert record keys into the physical addresses where the records are stored. Given the algorithm, any record can be found by converting its key. In partitioned and indexed files, a directory or index is created to help locate parts of the file quickly. A partitioned file is a collection of members (or subfiles) in which each member is a set of records written and accessed sequentially. The partitioned file directory contains the names of the members so that a given member can be located quickly. In an indexed sequential file, all the records in the file are organized sequentially by key, so that they can be read sequentially quickly and easily. However, the index associated with the file allows you to find and access individual records as well.

In Part III, Chapters 13 through 15, you will find some algorithms and programs to help demonstrate these methods on your computer. You may wish to refer to them during the following discussions.

QUESTIONS

1. Explain why the method of organization is relatively unimportant for a very small data file.
2. What is the difference between file organization and file processing?
3. What is the difference between linear data structure and nonlinear data structure?
4. Classify each of the following files as to whether it is most likely to be dynamic or relatively static.
   a. a list of soldiers in the Union Army during the Civil War
   b. the master patient file for a large hospital
   c. an inventory for the stock of parts of Edsel automobiles (Edsel automobiles were a model of Ford built for two years in the 1950's and then discontinued. A few are still around as collectors' items.)
5. A large mail order department store maintains an inventory file of 10,000 items from its most recent catalog. If orders are placed daily for approximately 7000 of these items, what is the daily percentage of activity for the file?
6. Explain why the decision of the U. S. Postal Service to change from a five-digit zipcode to a nine-digit zipcode had many large mail-order firms quite upset.
7. How would you organize each of the following files in order to be able to access the data most efficiently? Your choices are sequential, indexed sequential, partitioned, direct.
   a. an alphabetical mailing list where your mailings always include everybody on the list
   b. a file of accounts for a large bank in which each account needs to be updated whenever a deposit or withdrawal is made
   c. Volume 4 of the *Encyclopedia Americana*
   d. an inventory file which needs to be updated quickly as items are shipped or received, and for which you need a complete printout every night
8. What functions would be filled by commands such as GET, PUT, and FIELD in data access programs?

9. What is an "access method"? Describe briefly the differene between a single access method command in job control language and an access method utility.
10. What are the differences between
    a. BSAM and QSAM?
    b. BSAM and BDAM?
    c. Why isn't there any QDAM?
11. If, on your home computer system, you have completed your personal income tax return for the past year, and you wish to make room for your financial records for the current year, would you *retire* your past year's records, or would you *delete* them? Why?

CHAPTER 7

SEQUENTIAL FILES AND SEARCHING

SEQUENTIAL FILES

A file in which records are located on the basis of their physical locations with respect to the preceding and the following records is called a *sequential file.* To be most useful, the records in such a file are generally stored in sequence according to their keys; however, that does not have to be the case. Any set of records which must be read one after another is sequential, whether they are in key order or not. We will assume that most of the sequential files we study in this text have been ordered by key, which means that the data must be *sorted* before it is stored in the file. In a sequential file, individual records cannot be located quickly, nor can records be changed without rewriting the entire file as illustrated for the update of a magnetic tape in Chapter 1. You may indeed see a sequentially organized file stored on a disk in which individual records can be found and updated without reading or writing the entire file; however, strictly speaking those files are not sequential, they are some modification of sequential organization. Sequential organization is the easiest of all the organization methods to use. Therefore, when files are small or when activity is high, files are nearly always organized sequentially.

Sequential Storage Media

A sequential file can be written on almost any storage medium. Cards, paper tape, magnetic tape, disk, even a printer, provide a good output device for a sequential file. You may not have considered a printer in this light before; but after all, what is written to a printer is just the records of a file in sequential order. Our concepts in this regard are somewhat narrow, because we are in the habit of thinking that a file must be written on a medium from which it can be read into the computer again; normally, unless we have a good optical reader or a secretary who does not mind retyping all the data, it is difficult to recover the records which have been stored on paper by a printer.

On all devices except DASD's, the *processing* of a sequentially organized file must be done sequentially. Sequential data on a DASD may be processed in other modes; however, if significant nonsequential processing is to be done, the user may wish to consider writing the data in one of the nonsequential organizations. Otherwise, access to the file may not be as efficient as was anticipated. Note, from Figure 7–1, that the additional capability of updating a single block of data makes DASD's considerably more versatile than other devices.

When records are written sequentially on any device, they may be fixed or variable length, blocked or unblocked. They may even be considered undefined length if the specific characteristics of the file are unknown. However, some formats are more convenient than others on some media. For example, on Hollerith, 80-column, punched cards, it is most convenient to consider the records to be fixed length (80 characters) and unblocked, one logical record to a physical block (one card). Records on punched paper tape are most conveniently considered to be either fixed or variable length and unblocked with one record between record delimiter marks (generally a punch in the otherwise unused eighth column, or eight punches across the tape as shown in Figure 2–2 of Chapter 2). On a magnetic tape or a DASD, formats are more flexible.

If the file is to be processed sequentially it is usually formatted without keys. Remember "formatted without keys" does not mean that the records have no keys. What it does mean is that keys are stored within the data area and not in a separate field. There is no need to take up extra storage space for keys and gaps if the records are to be read sequentially anyway and will not be sought by key. Of course, if the data is stored on a DASD, then key areas may be provided if it is anticipated that some nonsequential access may be needed.

There may be more than one key field identified within a record. For example, if you were maintaining a mailing list of newspaper subscribers, you

	Read Next Block	Read Previous Block	Write Next Block	Skip Next Block	Skip Back One Block	Skip to End of File	Skip Back to Last End of File	Update a Single Block
Printer			X					
Paper Tape Reader Punch	X		X					
Card Reader Punch	X		X	X				
Magnetic Tape Drive	X	X	X	X	X	X	X	
DASD	X	X	X	X	X	X	X	X

FIGURE 7–1. Maximum Capabilities of Data Storage Devices

might wish to use the subscriber names as the primary key or *major control field*. This is how you would identify the records normally. On the other hand, you might also wish to make a mailing each month to those whose subscriptions are about to expire. In this case you would also wish to be able to identify those records by subscription expiration date. Then you would use the expiration date field in the record as a secondary (alternate) key or *minor control field*. Generally, primary keys are chosen to be unique; every record has its own major control field, unlike any other record. Alternate keys need not be unique.

Storage Space

When data is stored in sequential manner the storage space required is simply enough space to hold all of the records, roughly the average record length (including necessary non-data information, gaps, and keys if present) times the number of records. This may seem obvious, but it is pointed out here because in other file organizations more storage space will be required to handle indexes, directories, etc., which are not present in sequential files. The user does not have to worry about providing extra space for future growth of the file, because, by definition of a sequential file, whenever records are added they must be appended to the end of the file or the entire file must be rewritten.

On a hard disk pack the records are written successively one track per surface until a cylinder is filled. Then the access arm moves to the next cylinder, and the records are again written track by track until another cylinder is filled, etc. This minimizes access time. If successive tracks were written across one surface before the next surface were used, then the access arm would have to move each time a track was full, rather than after an entire cylinder was filled. The areas on a disk which are occupied by a file are called *extents*. If all of the data is physically *contiguous* (with no breaks), then the file is said to require only one extent. If part of the data is written on one area of the disk, then extended to a different area because of space limitations or because previously written material on the disk prohibits the continuation of the present area, then the data is said to be physically *noncontiguous* and to require *multiple extents*. Generally multiple extents are *transparent* to the user. The device controller handles the situation without user intervention.

File Maintenance

It has been stated several times already that additions to a sequential file or updates of records generally require a complete rewrite of the file. Physical deletions also require a complete rewrite. Example 1–1, Table 1–1, and Figure 1–1 in Chapter 1 illustrate how this might be done for a sequential file stored on magnetic tape. On a DASD, if a complete rewrite is done, it does not require three disk packs as three tapes are required; however, it does require three disk areas to be accessed—one for the old master, one for the transaction file, and one for the new master file.

On a DASD, if we are willing to accept modifications of a strictly sequential organization, we *can* add records to the end of a file, find individual records and update them, and *delete records logically* without a complete rewrite of a file. Logical deletion of a record is accomplished by changing the first few bits of the record to a code which indicates that this record is to be ignored. Very often this is one or two bytes of all 1's, although other codes may be used, of course. In fact, most information which is to be deleted from computer memory or from a DASD is deleted logically rather than physically, unless data security requires that the data be completely eliminated. Logical deletion flags an area so that it is ignored when the old material is read and can be written over when new material is stored.

However, even on a DASD, as new records are added to the end of the file—not in key order of course—and as records are deleted logically, the search time to find a given record gets longer and longer until it degenerates to an unacceptable level. At that time the file must be reorganized and rewritten to physically eliminate the logically deleted records and to insert the additions into their proper order in the file. A number of different strategies may be used to accomplish file reorganization. Reorganization is often performed during a *file maintenance run* with a utility program written specifically for that purpose. It may take place while full or restricted access to the file is allowed, with a utility program written to handle that kind of task. Some reorganization strategies on a DASD are:

1. Reorganize *in place*. Do not remove the data from its disk area. Reorganize by moving the data within its assigned area. Of course, user access to the data should be prohibited during the reorganization. This method uses a minimum of space and does not interfere with other user areas on the disk, but it is slower than other methods.

2. *Unload* the data into another area or onto another medium. Then *reload* the data into the original area in the desired order and format. This is a faster and easier way to reorganize. However, it does require at least one more disk area equal to or larger than the size of the original file. Also, user access may be blocked to both disk areas while reorganization is taking place.

3. Reorganize *incrementally*, one piece of the file at a time. While users are allowed access to most of the file, part of it can be blocked and reorganized in place. For example, records which need to be deleted from the first 20% of the file can be removed, and records which should be placed there from the end of the file can be inserted, while only that part of the file is blocked from user access. Of course, there must be sufficient room in this area, after deletions, for storage of the added records.

4. Reorganize the file *while in use*. Take the risk of allowing user access to the file while deleting, moving, and adding records. This method, while appearing to minimize the time during which the file is blocked from use, may turn out to be the most frustrating to the user and the person who is maintaining the file, unless it is carefully planned and the utility program to do the job is designed very well. It could be quite disconcerting to access the same records at two different times during a user program and find that the locations of the data and/or the contents of the data have changed.

No matter how or when a file is reorganized it will be inconvenient at best. Usually file reorganization is postponed as long as possible simply to avoid interrupting more "productive" activities to do the job. Users will always be distressed when they cannot obtain access to a file for a time; since reorganization of a large file is quite time consuming, they may also be upset with the computer time that is being used for this purpose. At the very least, such a large job may degrade response time on the system while it is being performed. At worst, of course, the system will be unavailable while the reorganization is taking place.

Timing

The length of time required to find a record in a sequential file depends very much on the medium on which it is stored and the method used to search for the desired record. Strictly speaking, all searches on a sequential file would be done linearly; that is, from beginning to end. Certainly this is the way a record must be found on a magnetic tape. Reading a file linearly from a magnetic tape or paper tape or card reader is more easily accomplished than reading linearly from a DASD, although the latter may well be faster. On a tape or with a card reader, the device stops after reading each block, and proceeds when the next physical record is to be read. On a DASD, the disk does not stop spinning between block reads. Thus, after each data transfer, the disk will spin, on the average, one half-revolution to find the new block before the next operation can take place. On a DASD the current position of the file must be recorded each time a read is performed, so that the controller can relocate the position when the next block is to be read. Of course the same arguments apply when writing a sequential file. The tape drive or card punch will stop between physical records so that it is obvious where the next block is to be written. A disk does not stop spinning; the current position must be recorded, so that when the next write command is issued, the controller knows where to write.

Consider the following timing problems:

Example 7–1

Assume a magnetic tape drive which writes data on the tape at 1600 bpi. The gaps between blocks are 0.6 inches, and data is read at a rate of about 200 inches of tape per second. The time to stop the tape at a gap is about 2 milliseconds, and the time to restart is also approximately 2 milliseconds. During the stop + start time the computer can easily process the previously read record and issue the command to read the next record.

Your company's mailing list consists of 50,000 records, each 180 bytes long, written sequentially in alphabetic order by customer names on the tape. To save time and space, the records are blocked with a blocking factor of 10.

a. How many feet of tape will be required for the file?
b. How long will it take to read the entire file from the tape into the computer?

Solution:

a. In blocks of 10, the block length between gaps is $10 \times (180) = 1800$ bytes, and there are 50,000 divided by $10 = 5000$ blocks.
   Each block requires

$$\frac{1800 \text{ bytes}}{\text{block}} \times \frac{1 \text{ inch}}{1600 \text{ bytes}} = \frac{1.125 \text{ inches}}{\text{block}}$$

   plus 0.6 inches for the gap at the end of the block. Thus, the length of each block $= 1.125 + 0.6 = 1.725$ inches.

$$\frac{1.725 \text{ inches}}{\text{block}} \times \frac{5000 \text{ blocks}}{\text{file}} = \frac{8625 \text{ inches}}{\text{file}}$$

   So the file requires 8625 inches divided by 12 inches per foot = *718.75 feet of tape*.

b. The time to read the file from the tape can be divided into two parts, the time to read the data, plus the time spent stopping and starting at the gaps.
   Data is read from the tape at the rate of

$$\frac{200 \text{ inches}}{\text{second}} \times \frac{1600 \text{ bytes}}{\text{inch}} = \frac{320{,}000 \text{ bytes}}{\text{second}}$$

   The total number of bytes of data is 5000 blocks times 1800 bytes per block = 9,000,000 bytes.

Thus, the time to read the data bytes is

$$\frac{9{,}000{,}000 \text{ bytes}}{\text{file}} \times \frac{\text{second}}{320{,}000 \text{ bytes}} = \frac{28.125 \text{ seconds}}{\text{file}}$$

The time spent stopping and starting in one gap is 2 milliseconds to stop plus 2 milliseconds to start = 4 milliseconds. So the total time spent stopping and starting in gaps is approximately

$$\frac{4 \text{ milliseconds}}{\text{gap}} \times \frac{5000 \text{ gaps}}{\text{file}} = \frac{20{,}000 \text{ millisec}}{\text{file}} = 20 \text{ sec.}$$

So the total time to read the file is approximately 28.125 + 20 = *48.125 seconds*.

Example 7–2

Assume that you have the file from Example 7–1 stored on DASD Device I, described in Figure 5–7, Chapter 5. Seek times, latency, and data transfer rate are those given for typical hard disks in Figure 3–11, Chapter 3. The record length and blocking factor are the same as in Example 7–1 above. The records are formatted without keys, because it is anticipated that the file will always be read sequentially.

a. How many tracks on the disk pack will be required for the file? How many cylinders will be required? What percentage of the disk pack is this?
b. Assume that the file is stored in one contiguous extent beginning on cylinder 750 of the disk pack and that the access arm is resting at cylinder zero. Approximately how long will it take to find the data and transfer the entire file to the computer?

Solution:

a. Again there are 50,000 logical records divided by 10 logical records per block = 5,000 blocks in the file. Each block has a length = 10 × (180) = 1800 bytes.

Referring to the formula for DASD Device I in Figure 5–7 of Chapter 5, the number of blocks per track =

$$\frac{13{,}150}{150+0+1800}=6.74.$$

Thus there are 6 *blocks per track*.

Since each cylinder on the DASD contains 19 tracks, there are $6\times19=$ *114 blocks per cylinder*.
5000 blocks divided by 6 blocks per track = 833.33 tracks. Thus the file requires *834 tracks*.
5000 blocks divided by 114 blocks per cylinder = 43.86 cylinders. Thus the file requires *44 cylinders*.
There are 800 cylinders on this disk pack (from Chapter 5), thus this is $(44 / 800)\times100=$ *5.5% of the disk pack*.

b. The time to find and transfer the data to the computer can be divided into several parts. We will use the data in Figure 3–11 in Chapter 3 for this analysis.
Seek time to find cylinder 750. This equals approximately the maximum seek time, since the access arm moves from cylinder zero to cylinder 750, which is most of the way across the disk. So we can estimate this time (from Figure 3–11) to be approximately 50 millisec. = 0.05 seconds.
The seek time to find each of the remaining 43 cylinders as each previous cylinder is read is the minimum seek time (the time to move the access arm across one cylinder) = (from Figure 3–11) 10 milliseconds. Thus the total seek time to find the remaining 43 cylinders is approximately 43×10 milliseconds = 430 millisec. = 0.43 seconds.
The time to transfer the data depends only on the number of bytes of real data. Remember that *only the data gets transferred to the computer*. The non-data information is used by the channel and controller to find the data; it does not get transferred. Thus the time to transfer the data (using Figure 3–11) is

$$5000 \text{ blocks}\times\frac{1800 \text{ bytes}}{\text{block}}\times\frac{1 \text{ second}}{1000\times1024 \text{ bytes}} \qquad =8.8 \text{ seconds}$$

As each block is read, the disk continues to spin. Thus on the average there is about one half-rotation after each data transfer before the next record is found. Thus the total rotational delay is approximately $5000\times$ the average rotational delay. From Figure 3–11, that is 5000×8.4 milliseconds = 42,000 millisec. = 42.0 seconds.
The head selection time to move from track to track on each cylinder is at most a few tenths of one microsecond, since no physical motion of the

device is involved, and the process is carried out electronically. 843 head selections times approximately 1 microsecond is 0.000843 seconds, which is negligible when compared with the numbers above.
The total time to find, read, and transfer the data to the computer is then approximately

$0.05 + 0.43 + 8.8 + 42.0 = 51.3 =$ approximately *51 seconds*

Notice from Example 7–2 that the transfer time and the rotational delays seem to be most significant in transferring large amounts of data. This is because there are a large number of bytes to be transferred and a large number of rotational delays. Taken one for one, if you were going to search for one single record and transfer it to the computer, the seek time (10's of milliseconds) would be much more significant than the single rotational delay (a few milliseconds) or the time to transfer a few bytes to the computer. Certainly, if data were recorded on consecutive tracks to fill up a surface before using the succeeding surface, the times would be increased tremendously. In Example 7–2, we used 834 tracks to store the file. The seek time to find 833 consecutive tracks on DASD Device I, after having found the first track, would be 833×10 milliseconds $= 8330$ milliseconds $= 8.33$ seconds. When that is compared with the 0.43 seconds required to find successive cylinders, we see that our access time would have increased from approximately 51 seconds to 59 seconds.

Perhaps it is a surprise that the time to read a large file from a disk is about the same as the time required to read the file from a tape. Don't confuse this result with the fact that access to a single record is much faster and simpler on a disk.

Access Methods

Sequentially organized files are most easily and efficiently accessed by *sequential access methods.* That seems obvious, but when a sequential file is written on a direct access storage device, it becomes tempting to access it by other methods than sequentially. It certainly is possible to access a sequential file directly on a DASD; however, if that is to occur often, the user should consider whether a different method of organization might give faster access and better overall performance.

Off-the-shelf sequential access methods (SAM's) are of two fundamental types. BSAM, a basic sequential access method, simply allows you to write or read a sequential file in sequential order. Typically, no blocking or unblocking is done by the program and no error checking is performed. The users themselves are responsible for writing the programs to perform those operations if they are needed.

QSAM, a queued sequential access method, generally does have blocking and unblocking functions built into it, and it also checks parity or cyclic check characters for errors. These burdens are thus removed from the user. In addition, QSAM queues the next record. That is, it anticipates what record to read next, so that it can be found and moved to the buffer while the previous record is being processed. Thus some I/O operations can be happening concurrently with processing by the CPU.

If a BSAM performs so many fewer functions than a QSAM, why would you wish to use the former? The answer depends upon what your needs are as the user of the file. You may wish simply to find the data quickly and have more flexibility than a QSAM allows in determining the format of that data. In addition, you may wish occasionally to access your data, if it is on a DASD, in other than strictly sequential order. You may wish to have the option of telling the computer which next record is to be read, rather than having the computer decide that in advance. It should be emphasized again that if this is to occur often, you may wish to organize your data other than sequentially. In this case you would use a BSAM, or perhaps even a BDAM (basic direct access method), rather than using the anticipatory buffering feature of a QSAM.

Figures 14–1 through 14–4, Chapter 14, illustrate a simple basic sequential access method for writing to and reading from sequential files.

SEARCHING

Examples 7–1 and 7–2 illustrated the situation in which a sequential file is read linearly, i.e., one record at a time in the order in which the records are written. If you wish to find a particular record in a sequential file, especially if the file is stored on tapes or cards, you would use a *linear search,* start from the beginning and look at each record until you find the one you are looking for. Indeed, on these devices you have no choice but to execute your search linearly. On the average, if there are *N* records in your file, you will need to examine about *N*/2 records before you find the one you need. Figures 15–5 through 15–11, Chapter 15, illustrate linear search methods on both sequential and random access files.

If your telephone directory were stored on a magnetic tape, and you wished to find the number of Gustav Holtz, you would have to start with Aaron Aardvark and proceed to read every listing until you found Gustav Holtz. If Mr. Holtz did not happen to be in the directory at all, or if he were added late in a supplement at the end, you could read thousands of entries until you arrived at Zelda Zwumbly before you discover that Mr. Holtz is not there. On the other hand, you could test every record as you read it, and as soon as you reached Heinrich Holtz, the computer could inform you that Gustav Holtz was not in his proper place, and ask if you would like to continue to read to the end of the file to see if he is in the supplement or just give up and call directory assistance. If there were 20,000 entries on your phone directory tape, in all your searches for names you would average about 10,000 reads per search before you locate what you are looking for. Now obviously we don't read a telephone directory in a linear search mode, but we would have to if it were stored on a magnetic tape.

If we stored the telephone directory on a disk, we might be able to search it in another manner than linearly. First of all, if we insisted that the file of names and telephone numbers were to be organized sequentially, but that we did not wish always to do a linear search, we should consider organizing the file with keys. We would probably find it most convenient if the records were unblocked, so that when we find a record it would contain just the information we need. Since every physical record on a DASD is accompanied by a count area, every record has an address, either absolute in terms of the cylinder and surface on which it is found, or relative in terms of which record it is from the beginning of the file. These addresses make it possible, then, for us to find a record more swiftly. One method is to use a *hash code* to transform the key directly into an address. This method will be discussed in detail in later chapters dealing with nonlinear data organizations.

Another way to use the features of the DASD is to perform a *binary search* on the data such as that illustrated in Figures 15–13 through 15–15, Chapter 15. The binary search approximates the way we actually use a telephone book, by estimating where the name is likely to be, opening to a page in that area, and looking to see if the names on that page are greater than or less than the one we are looking for. Greater than and less than are used in the sense that a name which occurs toward the end of the alphabet is greater than one which occurs toward the beginning. Each name in the directory is "greater than" all of the names which precede it in the directory. This defines alphabetical order for us, and a computer language which handles strings of characters always defines "greater than" and "less than" in this manner.

Now, the computer cannot "guess," as we do, just where a name might be expected to appear. So when the computer executes a *binary search* it looks as close to the middle of the file as it can. The key which it reads at midfile is compared with the key for which we are looking. If the midfile key is greater than the key we are seeking, then the computer looks at the middle of the first half of the file, and compares that key with the one we want. If the midfile key is less than the search key, the computer looks at the middle of the last half of the file and compares keys again. As the search proceeds, the search area becomes progressively narrower until precisely the record we need is found. The examples and figures below illustrate the method.

The average number of searches required to find a record with a binary search is approximately LOG_2N-1, where N equals the total number of records in the file. The worst case will be LOG_2N+1. Don't panic about the LOG_2. LOG_2N equals $LOG_{10}N$ divided by $LOG_{10}2$ or $LOG_{10}N$ / 0.3010. The latter is a calculation which you can perform on your scientific calculator. For example, if we take the 20,000-name telephone directory, which we have now stored on a DASD, the average number of reads which we would need to perform to find a name and number by a binary search would be $LOG_2 20000-1=(LOG_{10}20000\ /\ LOG_{10}2)-1=(4.301\ /\ 0.3010)-1=14.3-1=$ 13.3. Thus it should take 13 or 14 searches.

Example 7–3

Consecutive records with keys 501 through 1300 are formatted with keys and stored sequentially on 16 consecutive tracks of a DASD. We know that the records are stored as shown in Figure 7–2, but of course the computer doesn't "know" that. The computer performs a binary search by examining the largest key on each track.

a. Show the steps taken by the computer to find record number 726 using a binary search.
b. What is the average number of reads to find a record in this file by a linear search?
c. What is the average number of reads required to find the track on which a record is located in this file if a binary search is used?

Solution:

a.

Step	*Look at Track No.*	*Largest Key on Track*	*Is Key Larger Than 726?*
1	8	900	Yes
2	4	700	No
3	6	800	Yes
4	5	750	Yes
5	Track 4 has records with keys not greater than 700. Track 5 has records with keys not greater than 750.		

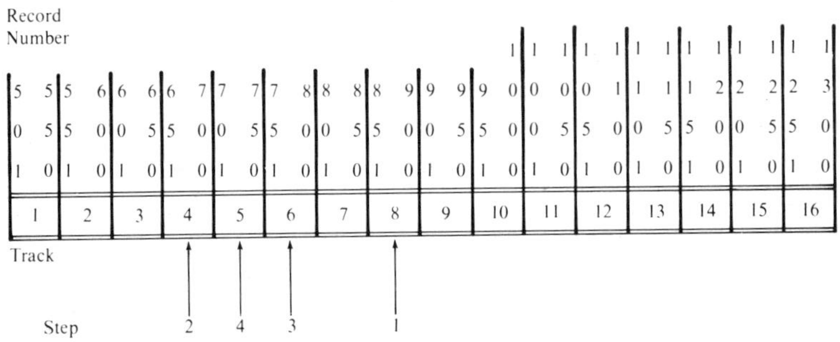

FIGURE 7–2. A Binary Search

Therefore, record 726 lies on track 5. Read track 5 to find record 726.
You will note that this procedure requires four reads to find track 5 plus 26 reads to find record 726 on track 5. Thus the total number of records read was $4+26=30$. A linear search would have required reading all of the records from 501 through 726—that is, 226 reads.

b. The average number of reads in a linear search would be the number of records, N, divided by 2. $N=1300-500=800$ records. Therefore, the average number of linear reads would be $800 / 2 = 400$ *reads.*

c. The number of reads to find the track on which a record is located, using a binary search, equals LOG_2N-1, where $N=$number of tracks used by the file ($=16$ in this problem). $LOG_2 16-1=(LOG_{10} 16 / LOG_{10}2)-1=(1.20412 / 0.30103)-1=3.0$ *searches*. (Those who are familiar with logarithms may have recognized that $LOG_2 16=LOG_2 2^4=4.0$)

Things don't always turn out as nicely as in the previous example. However, if we approximate the middle of section, we will always converge on the correct result, even though the sections may not be able to be divided exactly in half.

Example 7–4

Assume that a file contains the names, addresses, and party affiliations of the five top political leaders in each of the following U.S. cities.

1. Albuquerque
2. Baltimore
3. Boise
4. Chicago
5. Cincinnati
6. Dallas
7. Denver
8. Detroit
9. Fresno
10. Galveston
11. Honolulu
12. Houston
13. Indianapolis
14. Jacksonville
15. Kansas City
16. Los Angeles
17. Louisville
18. Miami
19. Milwaukee
20. Nashville
21. New York
22. Omaha
23. Philadelphia
24. Phoenix
25. Pittsburgh
26. Reno
27. Salt Lake City
28. Santa Fe
29. Seattle
30. Tampa
31. Toledo
32. Tulsa
33. Wichita

The file is stored in sequential order alphabetically by city name on a floppy disk with six 256-byte sectors per control interval (CI). The first sector in each CI contains the name of the city; each of the other five sectors in the CI contains the name and information about a leader in that city. Assume that the sectors are contiguous and numbered relatively 1 through 198 (6×33).

a. Show the steps in finding the leaders of Santa Fe by a binary search.
b. What is the average number of control intervals which would need to be read in finding a city in this file by a linear search?
c. What is the average number of control intervals which would need to be read in finding a city in the file using a binary search?

Solution:

a.

Step	*Read the CI Numbered*	*City Named in Interval*	*Is City Greater than Santa Fe?*
1	33/2 = approx 17	Louisville	No
2	(17 + 33)/2 = 25	Pittsburgh	No
3	(25 + 33)/2 = 29	Seattle	Yes
4	(25 + 29)/2 = 27	Salt Lake City	No
5	(27 + 29)/2 = 28	Santa Fe	

It took five searches to find the control interval containing Santa Fe. It would have required the reading of 28 control intervals to find Santa Fe using a linear search.

b. The average number of control intervals to be read in a linear search for a record in this file would be $N/2 = 33/2 \sim$ *17 reads*.

c. The average number of control intervals to be read in a binary search $= LOG_2 N - 1 = (LOG_{10} N \;/\; LOG_{10} 2) - 1 = (LOG_{10} 33 \;/\; LOG_{10} 2) - 1 = (1.5185 \;/\; 0.3010) - 1 = 4.04 \sim$ *4 or 5 reads*.

QUESTIONS

1. a. How can a printer be considered a device for storing sequential files?

   b. Name at least two other devices which can be used for storing sequential files.

2. Why are records usually formatted without keys for sequential files?

3. What is the most time-consuming operation in

   a. finding a single record from a sequentially organized file on a DASD?

   b. finding and transferring a very large sequential file, with many physical records, from a DASD to a host computer?

4. On a magnetic tape, each read or write operation automatically positions the medium for the next operation on a sequential file.

   a. How does this happen?

   b. Why can't this happen on a DASD?

   c. How does a DASD handle this situation?

5. List three functions which may be performed by a QSAM that, as a result, need not be performed by user application programs.

6. Your new magnetic tape drive writes data at a density of 6250 bpi. Gaps between blocks are 0.6 inches long, and data is read from the tape at a rate of 200 inches per second. The stop time in a gap is two milliseconds and the start time is also two milliseconds. During the stop plus start time, the computer can easily process the previously read records and issue the command to read the next record.

The historical records for your national organization for the year 1982 are written on the tape. There are 100,000 records, each 300 bytes long. The records are blocked into blocks of 12.

a. How many feet of tape will be filled by the file?

b. How long will it take to read the entire file from the tape into the computer?

7. Suppose the historical file from problem 6, with 100,000 records, is stored on DASD Device II, described in Figure 5–7, Chapter 5. The seek times, latency, and data transfer rates are those shown for a typical hard disk in Figure 3–11, Chapter 3. Each record is 300 bytes long plus an 18-byte key. Approximately half of the file is stored in one extent beginning on track 2. The other half of the file is stored in another extent beginning at track 300. Assume that the access arm is resting at track zero before reading the file. The records are blocked with a blocking factor of 12 and formatted with keys.

   a. How many cylinders will be required for the file on the disk pack? What percentage of the entire disk pack is this?

   b. Approximately how long will it take to find and read the data from the file in sequential order and transfer it to the computer?

8. A sequential file is stored on a DASD. It has 16,000 records. What is the approximate average number of reads to find a record

   a. by a linear search? b. by a binary search?

9. Consecutive records 1 through 509 are formatted with keys and stored sequentially on a DASD as follows:

Record Numbers	*Track*
1–9	1
10–19	2
20–29	3
.....	...
.....	...
500–509	51

   You wish to locate record 186.

   a. How many reads would you have to perform to find record 186 by reading linearly from the beginning of the file?

b. Illustrate the steps which you would have to perform to find record 186 by a binary search, where you look at the largest key on each track until you find the correct track and then read the track linearly to find record 186 on that track?

c. What is the total number of reads which you had to perform in part b?

10. A directory of members for a local club contains 624 records of members' names, addresses and occupations. Each record is 256 bytes long. The file is organized sequentially, alphabetically by name, and is stored on a floppy disk. The disk is fixed block format with 18 sectors per track, 40 tracks total, and 256 bytes per sector. The control interval (CI) size is one sector. Assume that the club membership is very unusual, with an equal number of members' names beginning with each letter of the alphabet. (How did they find so many people whose last names begin with Q and X?) Approximately how many reads would have to be performed to find the record for UZZRAH, ZELDA (the last one beginning with U) by

    a. reading linearly from the beginning of the file?

    b. using a binary search? Illustrate the steps of this binary search. Make up appropriate names which would be found at each step in your search.

    How many reads would have to be performed on the average to find records in this file by

    c. reading linearly?

    d. binary search?

11. Prove that the average number of reads in a binary search is $\mathrm{LOG}_2 N-1$. Hint: in m reads, you have narrowed the search to $1 / 2^m$ of the file. $1 / N$ th of the file would be one record, $2 / N$ th of the file is two records.

Chapter 8

LINKED LISTS, QUEUES, STACKS, AND TREES

Other linear data structures, besides sequentially organized files, are used commonly. Four of these, linked lists, stacks, queues, and trees, are the subject of this chapter. A linked list is a way of logically organizing data in sequential order without having to sort the data physically. Stacks and queues are convenient methods for storing data temporarily and retrieving it in a manner related to the order in which it was written. Trees are methods of relating and searching data in a hierarchical order.

LINKED LISTS

In a linked list, records are not stored physically in sequential order, but they are easily read in that order. Each record in such a list contains at least one *pointer,* a field which specifies the address of the next record in sequence. In fact, records may contain several pointers, specifying several different orders for reading the file; however, nearly always, one of the pointers will be specified as the primary or major pointer and the others will be secondary or minor pointers. The major pointers define the way the records would be read if organized sequentially by primary key. Some pointers may even point backward allowing the file to be read in reverse order.

To illustrate the linked list concepts, consider the following example, where just one forward pointer is used.

Example 8–1

A file is to contain the names, addresses, and telephone numbers of your friends. At first the file is small, but you wish to add names to the file and still be able to read it alphabetically without having to completely reorganize it. In Figure 8–1 (a) you have the file with five names, as you originally set it up. Figures 8–1 (b) through 8–1 (f) illustrate adding one name at a time to the end of the list and changing the pointers so that the list can still be read in order.

As each record is added, its place is found in the list. The pointer in the record, which comes logically before the added record, is changed to point to the location of the added record. The pointer in the added record then reads what the pointer in the record logically before it read previously.

In Figure 8–1 (b) we have added a record, Gregory, physically to the end of the file. However, Gregory was added logically to its position following Friar. In Figure 8–1 (c) the record, Carver, is also added logically into the file by changing the pointer in Burns to point to Carver, and by giving the pointer in Carver the value which Burns had before. Figure 8–1 (d) shows what happens when a record larger than any of those already in the list is added. In this case the pointers are changed as before, except that the new largest record now becomes the End. Figure 8–1 (e), adding Smith, is the same as before, but Figure 8–1 (f) illustrates what happens when the new record, Adams in this case, is to be the first one in the list.

Record Number	Name	Pointer	
1	Burns	2	← Start
2	Cramer	3	
3	Friar	4	
4	Richards	5	
5	Thomas	End	

(a)

Record Number	Name	Pointer	
1	Burns	2	← Start
2	Cramer	3	
3	Friar	~~4~~ 6	
4	Richards	5	
5	Thomas	End	
6	Gregory	4	

(b)

FIGURE 8–1. Adding to a Linked List

Record Number	Name	Pointer
1	Burns	~~2~~ 7 ← Start
2	Cramer	3
3	Friar	6
4	Richards	5
5	Thomas	End
6	Gregory	4
7	Carver	2

(c)

Record Number	Name	Pointer
1	Burns	7 ← Start
2	Cramer	3
3	Friar	6
4	Richards	5
5	Thomas	~~End~~ 8
6	Gregory	4
7	Carver	2
8	Williams	End

(d)

Record Number	Name	Pointer
1	Burns	7 ← Start
2	Cramer	3
3	Friar	6
4	Richards	~~5~~ 9
5	Thomas	8
6	Gregory	4
7	Carver	2
8	Williams	End
9	Smith	5

(e)

Record Number	Name	Pointer
1	Burns	7
2	Cramer	3
3	Friar	6
4	Richards	9
5	Thomas	8
6	Gregory	4
7	Carver	2
8	Williams	End
9	Smith	5
10	Adams	1 ← Start

(f)

FIGURE 8–1. Continued

Note that the position of the starting record must be recorded somewhere, so that when we wish to read the file in order, we know where to begin. It is common to store starting addresses for all pointers in the first record of the file, which we may call record 0 (zero) and reserve for that purpose.

Example 8–2 illustrates a file which uses multiple pointers.

Example 8–2

Consider a file which contains the records of students living in a dormitory. The primary key for a record, of course, is the student's name; most of the time we will wish to list the records in alphabetical order by name. However, we may also wish to have a list of which students live in which rooms, in order by room number; and at times we may even wish to list them by home state. The room number and the home state will be secondary keys; in a linked list, pointers are provided for each key.

Figures 8–2 (a), (b), (c), and (d) below show how such a file is created, and then show four additions to the file. Observe carefully how, when a record is added to the file, its place is found with respect to each list of keys. The pointer of the record which comes logically before the new record, is changed to point to the new record. The new record pointer is the old value of the pointer of its logically preceding record. The first record of the file is often used to hold pointers which indicate the starting point of reading the file and other housekeeping information about the file.

Record Number	Name	Name Pointer	Room	Room Pointer	State	State Pointer
79	Name Pointer Start = 80		Room Pointer Start = 81			
	State Pointer Start = 83					
80	Baker, Charlie	81	169	End	Ut.	End
81	Cramer, Robert	82	113	83	Mont.	82
82	Garrett, Samuel	83	126	84	Or.	80
83	Smith, John	84	114	82	Ala.	84
84	Wilson, Fred	End	150	80	Cal.	81

FIGURE 8–2(a). The New List

Record Number	Name	Name Pointer	Room	Room Pointer	State	State Pointer
79	Name Pointer Start = 80		Room Pointer Start = 81			
	State Pointer Start = 83					
80	Baker, Charlie	81	169	End	Ut.	~~End~~ 85
81	Cramer, Robert	~~82~~ 85	113	83	Mont.	82
82	Garrett, Samuel	83	126	~~84~~ 85	Or.	80
83	Smith, John	84	114	82	Ala.	84
84	Wilson, Fred	End	150	80	Cal.	81
85	Davis, Michael	82	140	84	Wyo.	End

FIGURE 8–2(b). The First Addition

Record Number	Name	Name Pointer	Room	Room Pointer	State	State Pointer
79	Name Pointer Start = 80		Room Pointer Start = ~~81~~ 86			
	State Pointer Start = 83					
80	Baker, Charlie	81	169	End	Ut.	85
81	Cramer, Robert	85	113	83	Mont.	82
82	Garrett, Samuel	83	126	85	Or.	80
83	Smith, John	~~84~~ 86	114	82	Ala.	84
84	Wilson, Fred	End	150	80	Cal.	~~81~~ 86
85	Davis, Michael	82	140	84	Wyo.	End
86	Thomas, Gary	84	101	81	Maine	81

FIGURE 8–2(c). The Second Addition

You may have noted in Figure 8–2 (d) that Burns was added before Wilson (both records have a California key) so that when the list is read in order by state, Burns and Wilson will be listed in alphabetical order.

Record Number	Name	Name Pointer	Room	Room Pointer	State	State Pointer
79	Name Pointer Start = 80		Room Pointer Start = 86			
	State Pointer Start = 83					
80	Baker, Charlie	~~81~~ 87	169	End	Ut.	85
81	Cramer, Robert	85	113	83	Mont.	82
82	Garrett, Samuel	83	126	~~85~~ 87	Or.	80
83	Smith, John	86	114	82	Ala.	~~84~~ 87
84	Wilson, Fred	End	150	80	Cal.	86
85	Davis, Michael	82	140	84	Wyo.	End
86	Thomas, Gary	84	101	81	Maine	81
87	Burns, Kenneth	81	132	85	Cal.	84

FIGURE 8–2(d). The Third Addition

Linked lists are not as messy as they appear. To practice their use you may wish to do some of the exercises at the end of the chapter and examine the List Linker program in Figures 14–15 and 14–16, Chapter 14. The secret to handling them efficiently is to add only one record at a time and calculate new pointers progressively, rather than trying to find the entire list of pointers at one time.

The linked list is very useful when additions are made regularly to a sequential file. This method eliminates (or at least postpones) the necessity of reorganizing the file. Of course, deletions can be made from a linked list file simply by changing the pointer of the record preceding the one to be deleted, to the pointer contained in the deleted record. Then the record has been deleted logically, and will never be read. Try it! It may be wise to write an indicator into the record that it has been deleted, so that when the file is eventually reorganized that record will be recognized as deleted.

QUEUES

Sequential files and linked lists are relatively permanent structures for storing large quantities of data. Often, however, we wish to store a relatively small amount of information in an organization that allows access to it quickly. Queues and stacks are two types of organization that allow us to do this.

In the United States we get in line for tickets to the theater. In Britain we would "queue up." A queue is simply a line or a linear structure in which the first one in the line is the first one out. *First in, first out* is abbreviated

FIFO. (This should not be confused in any way with the concept that you must put meaningful data into your computer if you expect to get meaningful information out. Failure to do this results in what is called a "garbage in, garbage out," or GIGO condition.)

Assume you wish to set up a waiting list of customers for items which you can stock only at rare intervals in your store. Normally, such a waiting list would be set up with a queue organization; the first customer to sign up would be the first to be notified and have the opportunity to purchase the item when it arrives. On the other hand, you might have some favorite customers or other reasons for giving one preference over another. We will not discuss whether this is morally "fair" or not, just what happens. Then, you might assign *priorities* to the customers in the queue. Although customers would in general be called in the order in which they appear in the queue, those with first priority would be called first in the order in which they appear, before the others are called.

Such a system of priorities in a queue is common in computing. An example is I/O requests. When I/O devices request use of a bus or attention of the Central Processor, the requests are placed in a queue in the order in which they occur. Normally, such requests are handled on a first in, first out basis. However, some devices may require more immediate attention than others. For example, a high-speed disk drive cannot stop and wait when it needs to transfer information to the buffer. It needs an immediate channel to the system. A printer, however, can wait for use of a channel or a bus; it does not require immediate access. Thus priorities may be assigned to the devices; although the request to send information to the printer may have been placed in the queue before the request to send data to the host from the DASD, the DASD operation occurs first because it has higher priority.

In the computer, a queue is usually handled by setting aside a small set of memory locations or a few registers in which the data for the queue is stored. As data is received by the computer, it goes into the memory or registers in sequential order and is generally retrieved in the same order in which it was received. Since information is being inserted and removed from the queue at periodic intervals, the queue would "walk" through memory or registers as shown in Figure 8–3 and eventually exhaust the memory, or at least run off the top, unless some provision were made to prevent this.

To avoid this situation, where the queue progresses through the memory, a *circular queue*—a circular memory or register area—is set up for the queue, where a limited number of locations are set aside and used. The limits of the queue area are stored as data in records which we will call FIRST and LIMIT. When the queue progresses past the end of the area (LIMIT) it starts again from the beginning of the area (FIRST). Pointers are kept to indicate the bottom of the queue (last in) and the top of the queue (first in). Let's call these pointers IN (indicating at which location the next new record should be en-

Location	Contents				
800	Smith				
801	Jones	Jones			
802	Howard	Howard	Howard		
803	Rich	Rich	Rich	Rich	
804		Adams	Adams	Adams	Adams
805		Courts	Courts	Courts	Courts
806			Bale	Bale	Bale
					Green
Operation	Create with Smith Jones Howard Rich	Remove Smith Add Adams Courts	Remove Jones Add Bale	Remove Howard	Remove Rich Add Green

FIGURE 8–3. A Queue Progresses through Memory

tered) and OUT (indicating from where the next record should be removed). If IN equals OUT, the circular queue is full, and nothing more can be placed in the queue until something is removed. A circular queue is illustrated in Figure 8–4, and a circular queue program can be found in Figures 14–18 and 14–19, Chapter 14.

Deques

A *deque,* pronounced "deck," is a double-ended queue in which insertions and deletions may be made either at the beginning or the end of the queue. There are, then, four distinct types of deque:

1. Insert at the end, remove from the beginning. This is the FIFO algorithm described for queues above, where the queue begins at a low address and proceeds to progressively higher addresses with IN and

OUT getting progressively larger as records are added and deleted. Of course, an upper LIMIT may be placed on the values of IN and OUT, so that the FIRST address in the queue logically follows LIMIT, forcing the queue to be circular.

2. Insert at the beginning, remove from the end. This is another first in, first out algorithm, i. e., a queue. However, in this case the queue begins at a highest address, FIRST, and records are added at successively lower addresses. IN and OUT get progressively smaller as records are added to and removed from this type of queue.
3. Insert at the end, remove from the end. This is the last in, first out (LIFO) algorithm. A deque in this form called a *stack* which begins at a low address with additions being made at successively higher addresses.
4. Insert at the beginning, remove from the beginning. Again this is a last in, first out algorithm, another stack. The difference between this stack and that described immediately above is that this stack begins at a high address and additions are made at successively lower locations. Both types of stack will now be discussed in detail.

STACKS

Two forms of deque data structures are called *stacks.* A stack works similarly to a pile of books on a table, a stack of cafeteria trays, etc. The first item on the stack ends up on the bottom, the last item on the stack ends up on the top, and it is the last item which is picked up first. Thus the organization of a stack is *last in, first out* (LIFO).

In a computer which supports the use of stacks, or with software for using stacks, a set of memory locations or registers will be reserved for the stack. One register will be called the stack pointer, which always tells where the top of the stack is. For example, consider the following situation.

Example 8–3

You may wish to create, in a stack, a short temporary catalogue of the minerals you have found during recent expeditions, so that you can recall the most recent discovery first. You could set aside register R1 as your stack pointer, and memory locations 32,740 through 32,767 to accommodate a list of 28 items or fewer. You then begin to fill the stack by PUSHing the name of the mineral, a sample number, and the discovery date onto the stack as shown in Figure 8–5.

In Figure 8–6 we perform combinations of PUSH (add to the stack) and POP (remove the top item from the stack).

Register	Contents				
R0	Pear		Apple	Apple	Apple
R1	Fig	Fig		Apricot	Apricot
R2	Kiwi	Kiwi	Kiwi	Banana	Banana
R3	Peach	Peach	Peach	Peach	
R4		Grape	Grape	Grape	
R5		Cherry	Cherry	Cherry	Cherry
R6		Guava	Guava	Guava	Guava
R7			Mango	Mango	Mango
Operation	Create with Pear Fig Kiwi Peach	Remove Pear Add Grape Cherry Guava	Remove Fig Add Mango Apple	Remove Kiwi Add Apricot Banana	Remove Peach Grape
Pointers FIRST = R0 LIMIT = R7	IN = R4 OUT = R0	IN = R7 OUT = R1	IN = R1 OUT = R2	IN = R3 OUT = R3	IN = R3 OUT = R5
				Queue is Full	

FIGURE 8–4. A Circular Queue Using Eight Registers

Operation:	PUSH Quartz	PUSH Barite	PUSH Galena	PUSH Halite
Location:				
32740	Quartz 12115 Dec. 22	Quartz 12115 Dec. 22	Quartz 12115 Dec. 22	Quartz 12115 Dec. 22
32741		Barite 12116 Jan. 5	Barite 12116 Jan. 5	Barite 12116 Jan. 5
32742			Galena 12117 Mar. 17	Galena 12117 Mar. 17
32743				Halite 12118 Apr. 12
R1 Stack Pointer Top of Stack	32740	32741	32742	32743

FIGURE 8–5. Operations on a Stack

Operation:	PUSH Argenite	POP (Remove Argenite)	POP (Remove Halite)	PUSH Gneiss
Location:				
32740	Quartz 12115 Dec. 22	Quartz 12115 Dec.22	Quartz 12115 Dec. 22	Quartz 12115 Dec. 22
32741	Barite 12116 Jan. 5	Barite 12116 Jan. 5	Barite 12116 Jan. 5	Barite 12116 Jan. 5
32742	Galena 12117 Mar. 17	Galena 12117 Mar. 17	Galena 12117 Mar. 17	Galena 12117 Mar. 17
32743	Halite 12118 Apr. 12	Halite 12118 Apr. 12		Gneiss 12120 Jul. 7
32744	Argenite 12119 Jun. 18			
R1 Stack Pointer Top of Stack	32744	32743	32742	32743

FIGURE 8–6. More Stack Operations

Observe in Example 8–3 that there are two stack operations. *PUSH* adds an item to the top of the stack and increments the value of the stack pointer by one. The other operation is *POP*, which removes the top item from the stack and decrements the stack pointer by one.

Some computers have commands built into their machine language which PUSH data onto the stack and POP data from the stack into the accumulator, the register which is used for arithmetic operations. These instructions can be very short, generally not more than eight bits long, because they do not have to refer to any address from which data is to be retrieved or to which data is to be stored. The address is automatically the top of the stack as indicated by the stack pointer register, and the incrementing and decrementing of the stack pointer register is taken care of automatically by the PUSH and POP commands. Other zero address instructions can be provided to handle all arithmetic operations as illustrated in Example 8–4.

Example 8–4

Suppose you have a computer which supports stack arithmetic. The commands available to you are

PUSH m	Pushes number m onto the top of the stack
LOAD	Pops the number from the top of the stack, and replaces the contents of the accumulator with the number
STORE	Pushes the contents of the accumulator onto the top of the stack
ADD	Pops the number from the top of the stack and adds it to the accumulator
SUB	Pops the number from the top of the stack and subtracts it from the accumulator
MUL	Pops the number from the top of the stack and multiplies the value of the accumulator by the number
DIV	Pops the number from the top of the stack and divides the accumulator by the number
XCH	Interchanges the top two elements of the stack
PRN	Pops the number from the top of the stack and transfers it to a buffer for printing
HALT	Stops the execution of the program

Now you wish to use this computer to perform the operation

$$[A - (B \times C)] / D$$

where A = 76, B = 4, C = 9, and D = 5. Table 8–1 shows a program to perform the calculation in your machine, using register RO for a stack pointer and memory locations 101 through 104 for the stack contents.

TABLE 8–1. Using a Stack and the Accumulator.

Operation	Comments	Stack	Pointer
1. PUSH 76	A(=76) onto the stack	101 76(A)	←101
2. PUSH 4	B(=4) onto the stack	101 76(A) 102 4(B)	←102
3. PUSH 9	C(=9) onto the stack	101 76(A) 102 4(B) 103 9(C)	←103
4. LOAD	C(=9) into accumulator	101 76(A) 102 4(B)	←102
5. MUL	B×C(=4×9 = 36) in accumulator	101 76(A)	←101
6. STORE	B×C(=36) on the stack	101 76(A) 102 36(B×C)	←102
7. XCH	Interchange the top two stack entries	101 36(B×C) 102 76(A)	←102
8. LOAD	A(=76) into accumulator	101 36(B×C)	←101
9. SUB	A−(B×C) = 76−36 = 40 in accumulator	Empty	
10. PUSH 5	D(=5) onto the stack	101 5(D)	←101
11. DIV	Answer:[A−(B×C)]/D = 40/5 = 8 in accumulator	Empty	
12. STORE	Answer(=8) on stack	101 8(Ans)	←101
13. PRN	Move answer to the print buffer	Empty	
14. HALT			

The algebra we just used in Example 8–4 is called *postfix* or Reverse Polish Notation, *RPN*. In this algebra the two operands are specified before the operation which is to be performed, rather than operand-operation-operand as in the direct algebraic, or *infix* notation with which most of us are familiar. Stack arithmetic is, almost by definition, postfix in nature. All *dyadic* operations (those which require two operands) are performed upon the top two elements of the stack. If you consider the subtraction operation in Table 8–1 above, for example, note that an interchange had to be made so that the minuend was on top of the stack and the subtrahend second on the stack, because the subtract operation which we needed was [(top of stack) (second on stack) subtract]. The subtract operation performed in Table 8–1 above would be written in postfix or Reverse Polish notation, 76 36 −, in contrast with the direct algebraic, infix, notation 76 − 36. You may be familiar with calculators which use Reverse Polish notation and stack arithmetic.

Example 8–5

Perform, on a calculator using stack arithmetic, the calculation

$[76 - (4 \times 9] / 5$

To solve this problem we will illustrate the keystrokes normally performed on a postfix calculator and how the stack appears at each step. You need to remember that, unless an operation key is pressed, you should press the ENTER key to tell the calculator that you are finished entering a number. An arrow (→) will be used to indicate the top of stack. Note that the top of the stack always contains the number which is shown on the calculator display.

Operation	76 ENTER	4 ENTER	9	MUL	SUB	5	DIV
Stack	→76	76	76	76	→40	40	→8
		→4	4	→36		→5	
			→9				

The answer = 8.

Stack arithmetic or postfix notation is called Reverse Polish Notation (RPN) because it was created by Jan Lukasiewicz, a Polish mathematician and logician, in 1951. Dr. Lukasiewicz (1878–1956) studied and taught mathematics at the University of Lvov, then at the University of Warsaw. He was minister of education in Poland in 1919 and, with his friend Stanislaw Lesniewski, founded the Warsaw School of Logic. Following World War II, during which he and his wife Regina were exiles in Belgium, he accepted a professorship at the Royal Irish Academy in Dublin, where he remained until his death. In 1951 he developed the parenthesis-free Polish notation, which we have used above.

In the examples, we have shown the stack beginning at a low numbered address and filling successively higher locations as additions are made. In this situation, the top of stack pointer is incremented by one each time an addition is made. On some systems, the stack may well begin at a high numbered address and fill successively lower locations as additions are made. The differences are that location numbers will get progressively smaller, and the top of stack pointer will be decremented by one when an addition is made. Some algorithms for handling stacks and stack arithmetic are shown in Figures 14–9 through 14–12, Chapter 14.

One other major use of stacks is for storing return addresses when subroutines or procedures are called within a program. As routines are called, the addresses from which they were called must be remembered. Then these addresses are recalled in the reverse order as RETURN commands are executed.

Procedures A and E in the example below are *recursive procedures,* routines which call themselves. A string of procedures in which the procedure, which initiates a string of calls, is itself called again—e. g., P calls Q, Q calls R, R calls P—is called a *daisy chain.* In procedures A and E below, we have placed conditions on when the procedure calls itself. Without conditions, both a recursive procedure call and a daisy chain inevitably result in an infinite loop.

Example 8–6

Suppose a program contains routines which are called in the order shown:

Main Program

Location

0 Begin Program

. . . .

```
32          Call A
. . . .
38          Call D
. . . .
46          Call F
. . . .
55        End Program

          Procedure A
          Location
          100          Begin A
          . . . .
          105            Call B
          . . . .
          112            Call C
          . . . .
          118          If 1st time Call A,
          . . . .        otherwise
          132          Return
                       End A

          Procedure B
          Location
          140          Begin B
          . . . .
          148            Call D
          . . . .
          157          Return
                       End B

          Procedure C
          Location
          160          Begin C
          . . . .
```

```
167           Return
              End C

Procedure D
Location
180           Begin D
. . . .
188           Return
              End D

Procedure E
Location
210           Begin E
. . . .
212           If 1st time Call E,
. . . .         otherwise
230           Return
              End E

Procedure F
Location
250           Begin F
. . . .
280           Return
              End F
```

Now let's look at the stack of return locations at each Call and each Return command. The top of stack in each case is indicated by an arrow(←).

	Run	*Call-Return Command*	*Return Address Stack*
1.	Program	32 Call A	32←
2.	A	105 Call B	32 105←
3.	B	148 Call D	32 105 148←

4.	D	188 Return	32 105 ←
5.	B	157 Return	32←
6.	A	112 Call C	32 112←
7.	C	167 Return	32←
8.	A	118 Call A	32 118←
9.	A	105 Call B	32 118 105←
10.	B	148 Call D	32 118 105 148←
11.	D	188 Return	32 118 105←
12.	B	157 Return	32 118←
13.	C	112 Call C	32 118 112←
14.	C	167 Return	32 118←
15.	A	132 Return	32←
16.	Program	38 Call D	38←
17.	D	188 Return	Empty
18.	Program	46 Call F	46←
19.	F	280 Return	Empty
20.	Program	55 End	Empty

TREE STRUCTURES

Still another linear organization method is the Tree Structure. Access to a tree is linear in the sense that the normal order for reading the file is determined by the hierarchical relationships between the records. A tree will always begin with a single element, which is called the *root*. The root of a tree is said to "own" *descendants,* called *nodes* or branches, which in turn may be roots of subtrees. Nodes which own no subtrees are called *external nodes* or leaves; all others, except for the root of the tree, are called *internal nodes.*

A *binary tree* is a tree for which each node owns at most two branches. A good example of a binary tree is an ancestral chart such as that shown in Figure 8–7. The root of this tree is Theodore Wilson. He "owns" descendants represented by the nodes Samuel Wilson and Linda Baker (which in this case of course are Theodore Wilson's parents). Linda Baker owns descendants Richard Baker and Susan French (Theodore Wilson's grandparents), etc. Theoretically, all people listed on an ancestral tree represent internal nodes; i. e., every person has parents, so every node owns descendants. In practice, of course, the tree does have external nodes at the points where the genealogical research has ended.

A tree need not be binary. Nodes may own any number of descendants, as illustrated in Figure 8–8, the organizational chart for a small business. Here the root of the tree is the company president, whose descendants are the

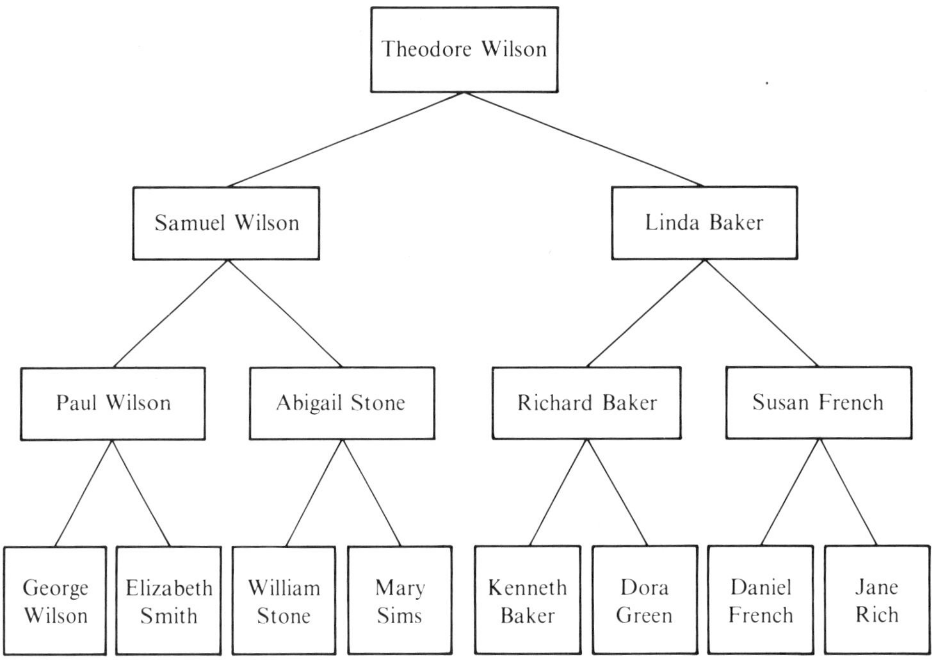

FIGURE 8–7. A Binary (Ancestral) Tree

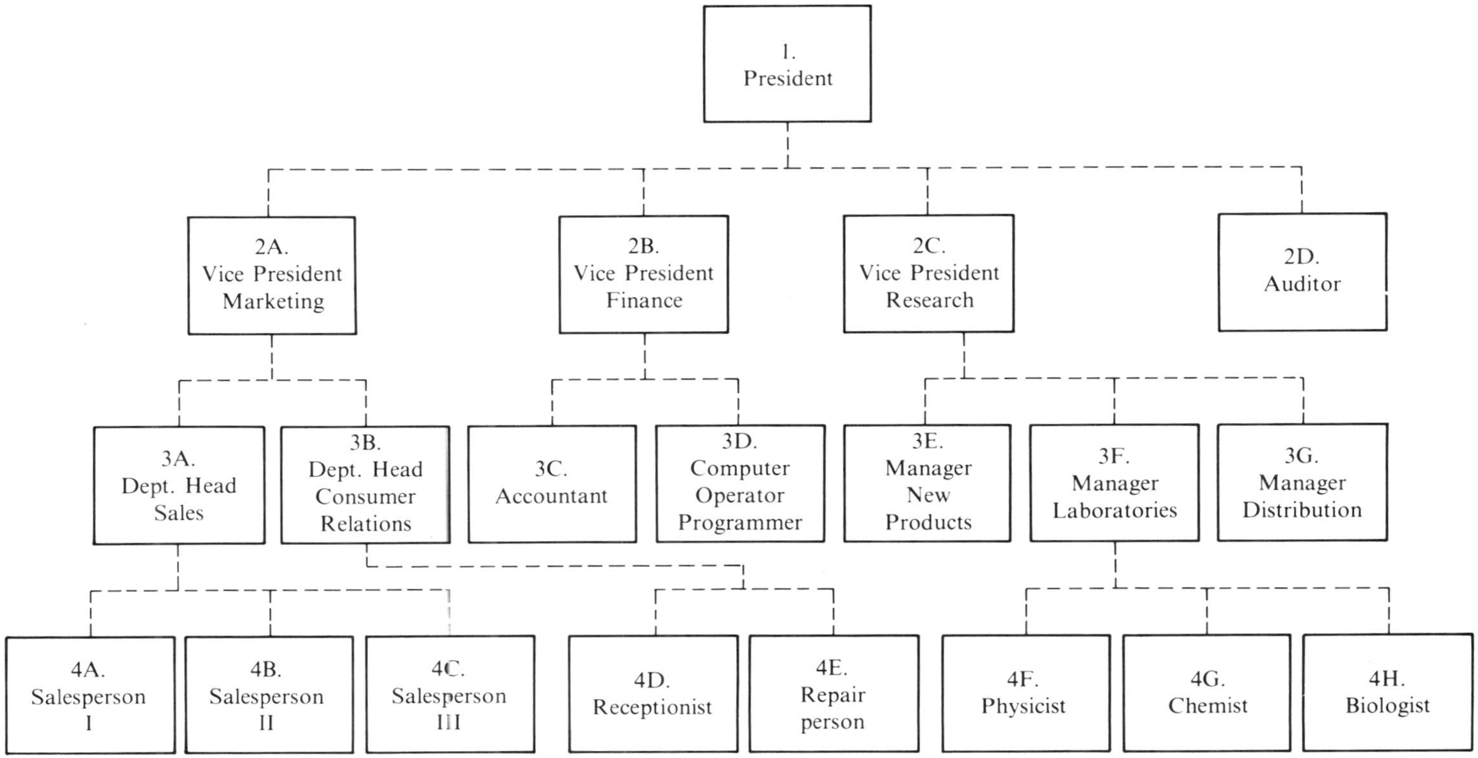

FIGURE 8–8. An Organization Chart, a General Tree

vice presidents of marketing, finance, and research, and the auditor. Except for the auditor, each vice president in turn owns descendants. The auditor is an external node, or leaf. Similarly, the salespersons, accountant, chemist, etc. are other leaves on this tree.

Searching a Tree

In searching a tree, we may desire to process the entire file sequentially or to access a single record as quickly as possible. There are many ways in which all of the records of a tree may be retrieved sequentially. One method requires the use of a stack according to the following algorithm:

1. Read the record for the root of the tree.
2. Read the records of the nodes owned by the root until a node is reached which is the owner of a subtree.
3. PUSH a pointer onto the stack indicating the next record in the owner level, and begin reading the nodes in the subtree.
4. Whenever an external node is encountered, POP a pointer and resume following the owner chain.

Example 8–7

a. Use the algorithm specified above to search the organization chart in Figure 8–8 sequentially.
b. How many reads are required to find
   (1) Salesperson III? (2) the Vice President of Finance?

Solution:

a. To illustrate the search we reproduce, in Figure 8–9, the organization chart showing only the labels and arrows indicating the order of search. The following operations are performed:
   1. Read the root, 1, the President.
   2. Read internal node 2A, VP Marketing, PUSH 2A onto the stack.
   3. Read internal node 3A, Dept. Head Sales, PUSH 3A onto the stack.

4–6. Read external nodes 4A, 4B, 4C. 4C is Salesperson III.

7. POP 3A from the stack and read internal node 3B, Dept. Head Consumer Relations. PUSH 3B onto the stack.

8–9. Read external nodes 4D and 4E.

10. POP 3B from the stack. POP 2A from the stack and read internal node 2B, VP Finance. PUSH 2B onto the stack.

11–12. Read external nodes 3C, 3D.

13. POP 2B from the stack, read internal node 2C. PUSH 2C onto the stack.

14–15. Read external node 3E and internal node 3F. PUSH 3F onto the stack.

. . . .

b. Salesperson III, leaf 4C, was found on the 6th read. The Vice President Finance, internal node 2B, was found on the 10th read.

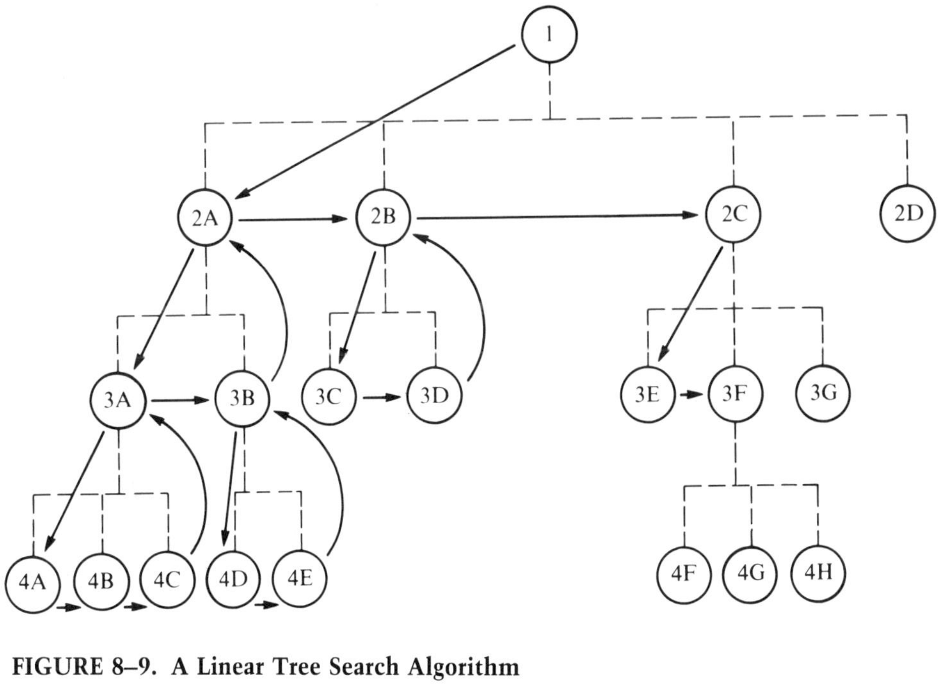

FIGURE 8–9. A Linear Tree Search Algorithm

Just as with any linear search of N records, it requires an average N/2 reads to find a particular record by this method.

Another type of search of a tree is a direct search similar to the binary search of an ordered file, discussed in Chapter 7. The number of branches which have to be followed from the root of the tree to any node is called the *path length* of that node. Thus the path length of the root is one, the path length of the direct descendants of the root is two, etc. If pointers to every direct descendant are provided at the root and at each internal node of a tree, then the file may be searched by following the pointers.

If the search must rely on examining records to determine whether to choose another path, the average path length for a binary tree with N nodes is approximately 1.386 LOG_2N. In other words, the average number of comparisons which have to be made or the average number of records which must be read, is about 1.4 LOG_2N. For a tree with N nodes, where each internal node had M direct descendants, the average path length is of order of magnitude LOG_MN. Of course, the better the rule which predicts the order of records in the hierarchy, the shorter the actual path length will be.

Example 8–8

a. In the ancestral tree of Figure 8–7 find the name of Theodore Wilson's great-grandmother on his mother's father's side of the family. What was the path length of this search?

b. In a general binary tree of the size shown in Figure 8–7, what would be the average number of comparisons needed to find any record?

Solution:

a. In this case, the rules (or pointers) are:

Follow the left branch if referring to a father.

Follow the right branch if referring to a mother.

Theodore Wilson's great-grandmother on his mother's father's side can be restated as Theodore Wilson's mother's father's mother. Hence from Theodore Wilson we proceed right branch, left branch, right branch, reading in order, 1. Theodore Wilson, 2. Linda Baker, 3. Richard Baker, and 4. Dora Green. The great-grandmother is Dora Green. The path length is 4; four records were read.

b. The average number of reads to find any record is 1.4 LOG_2N where N is the number of nodes in the tree. In the tree of Figure 8–7 there are 15 nodes (including the root). Thus the average path length would be approximately $1.4\ LOG_2 15 = 1.4\ (Log_{10} 15\ /\ LOG_{10} 2) = 1.4 \times 1.1761\ /\ 0.3010 = 1.4 \times 3.907 = 5.5$ *reads.*

QUESTIONS

1. Suppose you have records stored in a linked list file as indicated. Show what the linked list file would look like after you added the names SMITH, THOMAS, GRAHAM, and YOUNG in that order and you still wish to access the file in alphabetical order.

Location	*Key*	*Pointer*
1	ADAMS	2
2	BAKER	3
3	DOLBY	4
4	MCHENRY	5
5	WILSON	End

2. Given the following linked list

Location	*Key*	*Pointer*
100	Start Pointer =	101
101	AKRON	102
102	BUTTE	103
103	CHINO	104
104	DALLAS	105
105	FRESNO	106
106	JACKSON	End
107		
. . .		

Show how the file and pointers will appear after you add FURTH and CAMERON and then logically delete DALLAS and AKRON, in that order.

3. Members of an organization are to be recorded in a linked list beginning at location 101 (location 100 will contain starting pointers and

other pertinent information). You wish to be able to read the records alphabetically by the name of the member and also in order of increasing age.

a. Show how the linked list and pointers will appear for the following records:

Name	*Age*
Jones	52
Patterson	18
Richards	26
Sims	34
Tripp	40

b. Now add the following records, in the order shown, to the end of the list and show how the pointers will appear:

Lowry	29
Barnes	63
Young	34

4. If you were standing in line for a bus, which do you feel would be more fair, if the bus loaded passengers by stack organization or by queued organization? Why?
5. A typical *distributed computer network* is shown in Figure 8–10. In a distributed network, the terminals, such as A, B, C, D, and E, are

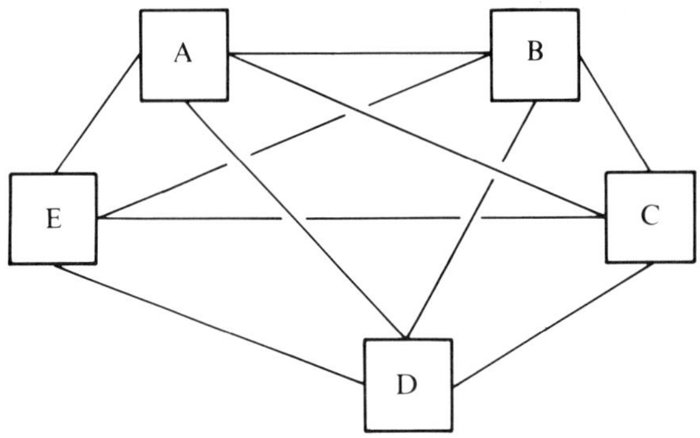

FIGURE 8–10. A Distributed Network

connected to each other by many different paths, so that if any one breaks down the others can still communicate. The terminal points are called *nodes.* At each node there may be a computer which is capable of storing a limited number of incoming messages until the lines are available to forward the messages. Should the messages waiting at a node be stored in a linked list, on a stack, or in a queue? Why?

6. A queue in a 64-kiloword computer begins at location 65,520.

   a. Initially five records are placed in the queue. Thereafter, whenever a record is removed from the queue another record is added. If the queue is *not* circular, how many removal-addition steps can occur before the queue overflows memory?

   b. If the queue is circular and runs to the end of memory, what are the values of the variables FIRST and LIMIT?

   c. Assume the queue is circular. Five records with keys ANTON, BERTHA, CAESAR, DORA, and EMIL are written initially in the queue.

      (1) What are the values of IN and OUT?

      Thereafter, whenever two records are added to the circular queue, one record is removed *after* the two records are added.

      (2) What will be the values of IN and OUT after the records FRIEDRICH, GUSTAV, HEINRICH, and IDA have been added to the queue and ANTON and BERTHA have been removed?

      (3) At which record in the following list will the queue be full if you continued adding two then removing one? JACOB, KAUFMANN, LUDWIG, MARTHA, NORDPOL, OTTO, PAULA, QUELLA, RICHARD, SIEGFRIED, THEODORE, ULRICH, VICTOR, WILHELM, XRAY, YPSILON, ZED, AAL, ABLE, ACRE, ADZE, AETNA, AFTON, . . .

7. Repeat problem 6c where the beginning of the queue is at the top of memory, records are added to locations with successively smaller addresses, and the LIMIT of the queue is at address 65,520.

8. Use the commands of Example 8–4, a top of stack pointer in register R1, and a stack beginning at memory location 32,760 to perform the arithmetic

A / [B − (C × D)]

where A = 63, B = 45, C = 4, and D = 9.

9. Use the commands of Example 8–4, a top of stack pointer in register R9, and a stack using memory locations 200 through 207 to perform the arithmetic

   [A + (B × C)] / [D − (E × F)]

   where A = 10, B = 5, C = 7, D = 45, E = 4, and F = 9.

   a. Assume that the stack begins at location 200 and that records are added at successively higher addresses.
   b. Assume that the stack begins at location 207 and that records are added at successively lower addresses.

10. Use the calculator described in Example 8–5 to perform the operation

    63 / [45 − (4 × 9)]

    where the numbers are to be entered in order from left to right. Assume that the calculator has an unlimited stack size, an ENTER key, keys for ADD, SUB, MUL, DIV, and XCH (interchange the top two entries on the stack).

11. Use the calculator described in Example 8–5 to perform the operation

    [10 + (5 × 7)] / [45 − (4 × 9)]

    where the numbers are to be entered in order from left to right. Assume that the calculator has an unlimited stack size, an ENTER key, keys for ADD, SUB, MUL, DIV, and XCH (interchange the top two entries on the stack).

12. You wish to perform the calculation [5(4 + 2) − 3] / 9 using a stack and entering numbers in order from left to right. The operations available to you are

PUSH m	pushes a number m onto the stack
POP	pops the number from the top of the stack into a temporary arithmetic register
ADD	adds the two numbers most recently POPped from the stack
SUB	subtracts the number previously POPped from the stack from the number most recently POPped
MUL	multiplies the two numbers most recently POPped from the stack
DIV	divides the number previously POPped from the stack into the number most recently POPped from the stack
XCH	interchanges the top two elements on the stack

Complete the table of operations and stack contents shown in Figure 8–11. (Note that the stack is shown with Top of Stack first and previously PUSHed values in order below. This is different from our earlier example but is another way stacks are often represented.)

Operation	PUSH 5	PUSH 4	PUSH 2	POP 2 POP 4 ADD PUSH SUM	POP 6 POP 5 MULT PUSH PRODCT
Top of Stack	5	4 5	2 4 5	6 5	

FIGURE 8–11. Stack Calculations

13. A rather useless BASIC program appears in Figure 8–12. As subroutines are called, the return addresses are stored on a stack. Show how the stack appears after each GOSUB command and after each RETURN command is executed. What does this program do?

```
10 REM PROCILUS
20 INPUT "WHAT'S YOUR NAME";NM$
30 GOSUB 1000
40 REM NEW ROUTINE
50 INPUT"HOW MANY TIMES";NUM
60 GOSUB 2000
70 REM DO IT AGAIN
80 GOSUB 1000
90 GOSUB 2000
100 REM WRAP IT UP
110 GOSUB 3000
120 PRINT "THAT'S ALL"
130 STOP


1000 REM WELCOME
1005 PRINT
1010 PRINT "WELCOME ";NM$
1020 PRINT "I'M HAPPY TO SEE YOU"
1030 PRINT
1040 GOSUB 4000
1050 RETURN


2000 REM COUNT
2010 PRINT "LET'S COUNT"
2020 FOR I=1 TO NUM
2030   PRINT "THE COUNT IS ";I
2040 NEXT I
2050 PRINT
2060 RETURN


3000 REM WRAP IT UP
3010 PRINT "GOODBYE ";NM$
3015 PRINT
3020 Y$=Y1$
3030 GOSUB 6000
3040 Y$ = Y2$
3050 GOSUB 6000
3060 PRINT
3070 RETURN


4000 REM FRIENDS
4010 PRINT "WHO'S YOUR FRIEND";
4011 INPUT Y1$
4015 Y$=Y1$
4020 GOSUB 5000
```

FIGURE 8–12. A BASIC Program for Problem 8–13

```
4030 PRINT "ANOTHER FRIEND";
4031 INPUT Y2$
4035 Y$=Y2$
4040 GOSUB 5000
4050 RETURN


5000 REM FRIEND WELCOME
5005 PRINT
5010 PRINT "I'LD LIKE TO KNOW ";
5012 PRINT Y$;" TOO."
5020 PRINT
5030 RETURN


6000 REM GOODBYE
6010 PRINT "SAY GOODBYE TO ";
6012 PRINT Y$;" FOR ME."
6020 RETURN


7000 END
```

FIGURE 8–12. Continued

14. a. Complete the linear sequential search illustration of Example 8–7.
    b. How many reads are required to find the biologist? the Manager of Distribution?

15. What would be the average number of reads to find a record in
    a. a binary tree with 255 nodes?
    b. a tree with 16,383 nodes in which the root and each internal node have four descendants?

16. In the ancestral tree of Figure 8–7
    a. (1) Find the name of Theodore Wilson's great-grandfather on his mother's mother's side of the family. (2) What is the path length of this search? (3) Using the method of a sequential search with a stack, illustrated in Example 8–7, how many reads would it have taken to find this person?
    b. Find Linda Baker's grandfather on her mother's side. What is the path length of this search (1) if we know the rules for finding an-

cestors? (2) if the tree were more general and the rules were not so well defined?

c. If one more complete generation (great-great-grandparents) were added to Figure 8–7, what would be the *average* path length to find any record in the tree?

17. A tree has the following characteristics:

The root and all internal nodes have four direct descendants.

The path length of a direct search from the root to any external node is five.

a. How many nodes (root, internal, and external) are on the tree?

b. What is the approximate average path length for a general direct search from the root to a node in this tree?

18. a. Show that a direct path length from the root to an external node of a tree with N nodes and M branches per node is exactly

$$L = \text{path length} = \text{LOG}_M\,[1 + ((M-1)/M) \times N]$$

b. Show that for large M that result in part a is approximately

$$L = \text{LOG}_M\,(N + 1)$$

or for large N

$$L = \text{LOG}_M\,N$$

c. How could you reason that this might be approximately the average path length in a direct search for any node? (HINT: Show that the number of nodes N, excluding the root, for a tree with M branches per node and a path length from root to external node L is given by the geometric series $N = M + M^2 + M^3 + \ldots + M^L$ and solve the equation for L in terms of M and N.)

19. Given that (1) the average path length for a binary tree is defined to be

$$P = \sum_{i=1}^{L} (n_i \times i)/N$$

where n_i = number of nodes at level i; e. g.
level 1 = root, $n_1 = 1$

level 2, $n_2 = 2$ level 3, $n_3 = 4$
level 4, $n_4 = 8\ldots$ level i, $n_1 = 2^{i-1}$

(2) $N = \text{total number of nodes} = \sum_{i=1}^{L} 2^{i-1}$

(3) $\sum_{i=1}^{L} (i \times 2^{i-1})/N = \text{approx.}2(\ln N)$
where $\ln = \log_e = $ natural logarithm

Show that the average path length is approximately $P = 2 \ln 2$ ($\text{LOG}_2 N$) = approximately 1.386 $\text{LOG}_2 N$

20. Suppose that you have a very small computer which uses stack arithmetic. The machine language Operations Code (OPCODE) for each instruction is four bits long. Some OPCODEs must be followed by an address to specify the location of an Operand. The instructions listed here without operands are the same as in Example 8–4 with a few additions:

CODE	*Instruction*		*CODE*	*Instruction*	
0000	NOP	No Operation	1000	DIV	Divide
0001	PUSH		1001	XCH	
0010	POP		1010	PRN	
0011	LOAD		1011	JMP	Jump to address specified by Operand
0100	STORE				
0101	ADD		1100	JIF	Jump if Accumulator contains 0
0110	SUB				
0111	MUL		1101	RTL	Rotate Accumulator left one bit
1111	HALT		1110	CLR	Clear the stack and the Accumulator

a. Illustrate how a binary tree can be used to decode instruction OPCODES. HINT: Let the instruction interpretations be records stored at external nodes of the tree. Each level of the tree represents a different binary digit position in the OPCODE.

b. Show on your diagram the path to find the interpretation of the instruction with OPCODE 0110.

CHAPTER 9

SORTING

SORTING PHYSICALLY

In Chapter 7 the process for searching sequential files to find a record was discussed. It was stated there that to find a record in a file containing N records, the average number of reads, using a linear search, is $N/2$. Also, finding a record using a binary search requires, on the average, only about LOG_2N-1 reads. What was not emphasized is that if a linear search is to be performed, where the file is read from beginning to end, it is unimportant whether the file is sorted into any particular order. Even in the most random order, it will still take $N/2$ reads on the average to find a record. On the other hand, a binary search requires that the file be ordered by search key.

If you had 1000 records which were not in key sequential order, and you wished to find record number 762, a linear search would eventually find 762 for you. In fact, if you were lucky, 762 might be closer to the beginning of the file than the end, and this particular record might be found faster than otherwise. Of course, for those of us who might not be so fortunate, Murphy's Law ensures that 762 would be the next to last record in the file. A binary search for record 762 would be impossible, however, unless 762 were in its appropriate order. Suppose, for example, that 762 were the 25th record from the beginning of the file. Then the first record we read in a binary search would be close to the middle of the file. Who knows whether this would be 500 or not? If it were, then we would look at the third quarter point, and even find, perhaps, a record number close to 750. At this point we eagerly believe we are getting close to the target of 762, when in fact we are in the wrong part of the file completely.

Card Sorters

Thus, there need to be methods of sorting records if we wish to be able to find the data quickly. Sorting of data used to be done with large machines designed specifically for the purpose of sorting cards. Some of the machines were quite sophisticated and could sort up to 2000 cards per minute. Card

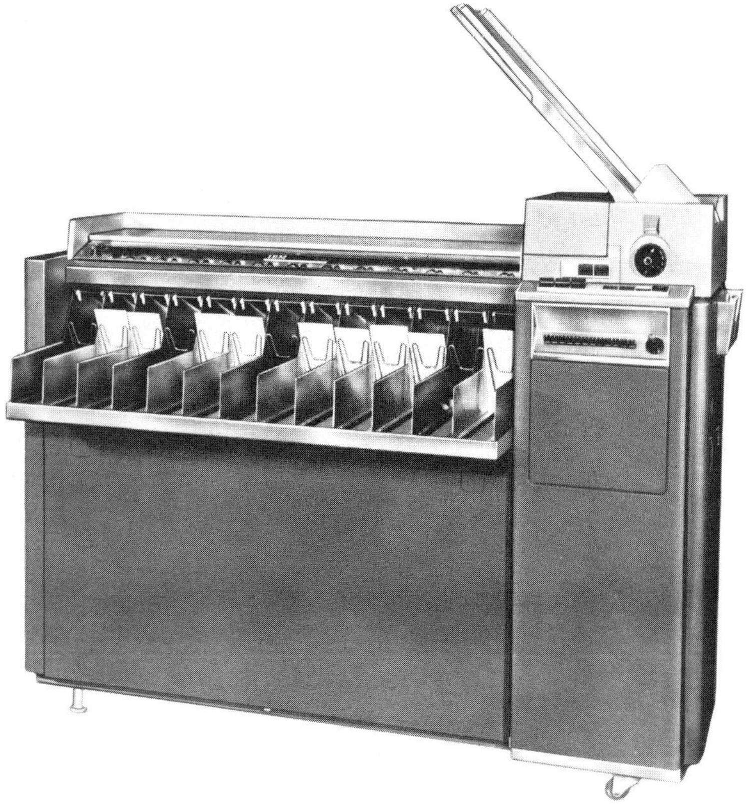

FIGURE 9–1. A Card Sorter *(Courtesy of International Business Machines Corporation)*

sort operators became adept at sorting on one column, stacking the cards, sorting on another column, and stacking again until the entire stack was in order. A lot of computing was done in this manner without even touching the computer. Nevertheless, sorting cards, though inexpensive, was at best slow and prone to errors. With large computer memories it soon became feasible to read the data into the computer and sort the data in the machine.

Just as there are dozens of different high-level computer languages, each one developed for a special purpose and each one considered by someone to be the best possible, there are also literally dozens of different sort algorithms, developed for special purposes and each one considered by someone to produce the best possible sort. In this chapter we will discuss three sort methods in detail and touch on a number of others, being fully aware that the ones we discuss are perhaps only the most popular and not necessarily the "best." You may find other sorting methods more to your liking or even create some of your own.

Bubble Sort

Perhaps the most popular of all sorting methods is the *bubble sort,* so called because the smallest or "lightest" element is allowed to "float" to the top of the list. In practice, it may be slightly more efficient to allow the heaviest element to "sink" to the bottom instead. The method is to compare successive elements and interchange when the first is larger than the second. The algorithm is

1. Let $I=1$.
2. Compare the Ith element in the list with the $I+1$st. If the Ith element is larger, interchange element I and element $I+1$.
3. Increment I and repeat step 2 until the bottom of the list has been reached, i. e., until $I=N-1$. At this point the largest element will be at the bottom of the list.
4. Reduce the length of the list by 1, set $I=1$, repeat steps 2 and 3.
5. Continue to repeat steps 2 through 4 until the list has a length of two elements. At this time the list will be sorted.

The bubble sort requires $(N-1)+(N-2)+\ldots+3+2$ comparisons $=$ $[(N-1)\times N\ /\ 2]-1=(N^2-N-2)\ /\ 2$ comparisons. At worst, every comparison would require an interchange. Bubble sort interchanges (worst case) $=$ $(N^2-N-2)\ /\ 2$.

For a file with 100 records, the bubble sort requires fewer than 5000 comparisons, which can be done rapidly. However, a file of 1000 records would require almost half a million comparisons, and a bubble sort of a file of 10,000 records would take about 50 million comparisons, a long process indeed. A short program for performing a bubble sort is given in Figures 14–5 and 14–6, Chapter 14.

Example 9–1

Perform a bubble sort on the list

N(1) = Sue, N(2) = Bob, N(3) = Tom, N(4) = Sally, N(5) = Adam

The solution is shown in Figure 9–2 where the arrows (←) indicate which elements are compared.

Sorted List: N(1) = Adam, N(2) = Bob, N(3) = Sally, N(4) = Sue, N(5) = Tom

Selection Sort

Another sort, which will require about the same number of comparisons as the bubble sort, is the *selection sort*. In this method, the list is examined and the largest element is found, then the largest element is interchanged with the bottom of the list. The algorithm is

1. Let $I=1$, let Maximum $= N(I)$ and Number of largest element $= I$.
2. Compare element $I+1$ with Maximum. If $I+1$ is larger, let Maximum $= N(I+1)$ and let the number of largest element, $N = I+1$.
3. Increment I and repeat step 2 until the bottom of the list has been reached. Then interchange the element at the bottom of the list with Maximum at the position N of largest element.
4. Reduce the length of the list by 1, set $I=1$, Maximum $= N(I)$, Number of largest element, $N=I$, repeat steps 2 and 3.
5. Continue to repeat steps 2 through 4 until the list has a length of two elements. At this time the list will be sorted.

The number of comparisons in the selection sort is the same as in the bubble sort, namely

$$\text{Selection Sort Comparisons} = (N^2 - N - 2)/2.$$

However, a maximum of one interchange is required on each pass through the data, so

$$\text{Selection Sort Interchanges (worst case)} = N - 1.$$

Length of List = 5

	I = 1	I = 2	I = 3	I = 4	
N(1)	Sue ←	Bob	Bob	Bob	Bob
N(2)	Bob ←	Sue ←	Sue	Sue	Sue
N(3)	Tom	Tom ←	Tom ←	Sally	Sally
N(4)	Sally	Sally	Sally ←	Tom ←	Adam
N(5)	Adam	Adam	Adam	Adam ←	Tom

Length of List = 4

	I = 1	I = 2	I = 3	
N(1)	Bob ←	Bob	Bob	Bob
N(2)	Sue ←	Sue ←	Sally	Sally
N(3)	Sally	Sally ←	Sue ←	Adam
N(4)	Adam	Adam	Adam ←	Sue

Length of List = 3

	I = 1	I = 2	
N(1)	Bob ←	Bob	Bob
N(2)	Sally ←	Sally ←	Adam
N(3)	Adam	Adam ←	Sally

Length of List = 2

I = 1	
Bob ←	Adam
Adam ←	Bob

FIGURE 9–2. A Bubble Sort

See Figures 14–7 and 14–8, Chapter 14, for an illustrative Selection Sort program.

Example 9–2

Perform a selection sort on the list

N(1) = Sue, N(2) = Bob, N(3) = Tom, N(4) = Sally, N(5) = Adam

The solution is shown in Figure 9–3 where the arrows (←) indicate the largest element and the bottom element with which it will be interchanged.

Sorted List: N(1) = Adam, N(2) = Bob, N(3) = Sally, N(4) = Sue, N(5) = Tom

Length of List = 5

	Before Interchange	After Interchange
N(1)	Sue	Sue
N(2)	Bob	Bob
N(3)	Tom ←	Adam
N(4)	Sally	Sally
N(5)	Adam ←	Tom

Length of List = 4

Before Interchange	After Interchange
Sue ←	Sally
Bob	Bob
Adam	Adam
Sally ←	Sue

Length of List = 3

	Before Interchange	After Interchange
N(1)	Sally ←	Adam
N(2)	Bob	Bob
N(3)	Adam ←	Sally

Length of List = 2

Before Interchange	After Interchange
Adam ←	Adam
Bob ←	Bob

(Note: No interchange necessary)

FIGURE 9–3. A Selection Sort

Quick Sort (Partition-Exchange Sort)

Another type of sort, which we will illustrate, is the partition-exchange or *quick* sort. This sort will appear to be much more difficult on paper than the bubble or the selection sort; however, it is usually much faster on the computer than the other two, as can be shown by running the programs in Figures 14–13, 14–14, 15–12, and 15–13, Chapters 14 and 15. In this sort, we compare opposite ends of a list and interchange if the element at the beginning is greater than the element at the end. Pointers are moved in alternately from each end and the elements designated by the pointers are compared and interchanged if necessary. When the pointers are at adjacent elements, then the list has been divided into two sublists, neither of which is necessarily sorted yet; but all of the elements in the first sublist have smaller values than any element in the second sublist. The limits of one of the unsorted sublists are stored on a stack, and the other sublist is sorted. The procedure continues until all sublists have been sorted, and the entire file is in sequential order.

The algorithm is

1. Assign two indexes, $I=1$ and $J=N$, where $N=$ the number of elements in the list.
2. Compare element I with element J. If element I is greater than element J, then interchange elements I and J.
3. If no interchange was made in step 2, then decrement J by 1, and repeat step 2. If an interchange was made in step 2, then hold J fixed and increment I by 1 before repeating step 2.
4. Repeat steps 2 and 3 until $J=I+1$.
5. At this point, the original list has been partitioned into two sublists. Every element in the first sublist is less than any element in the second sublist.
6. Sort each sublist. Store the boundary values of the other sublist on a stack, so that it can be sorted later.

Example 9–3

Sort the list

N(1) = Fred, N(2) = Dan, N(3) = Bill, N(4) = Tom, N(5) = Sue, N(6) = Bet, N(7) = Greg, N(8) = Adam, N(9) = Sam, N(10) = Mary

using a quick sort.

The solution is shown in Figure 9–4 where the arrows (←*I*) and (←*J*) indicate the pointer positions.
The quick sort of the list is illustrated also in Figure 14–14, Chapter 14.

SORTED LIST:

N(1)	Adam	N(6)	Greg
N(2)	Bet	N(7)	Mary
N(3)	Bill	N(8)	Sam
N(4)	Dan	N(9)	Sue
N(5)	Fred	N(10)	Tom

In a quick sort, the number of comparisons is approximately

$$(N-1)+2(N/2-1)+4(N/4-1)+8(N/8-1)+\ \ldots,$$

since there are $N-1$ comparisons for the entire list, then two lists each with approximately $(N/2)-1$ comparisons, four lists with $(N/4)-1$ comparisons, etc. After multiplying factors, this is

$$(N-1)+(N-2)+(N-4)+(N-8)+\ \ldots\ +\ 2.$$

Reverse this series and add to itself to obtain

$$[(N-2)+2],\ [(N-4)+4],\ [(N-8)+8],\ \ldots$$

Therefore, twice the number of comparisons is

$$N+N+N+N+\ \ldots\ +N-2.$$

How many N's are there? Just as in the binary search, with each term we reduce the size of the list to half of its previous length. Thus (see problem 11, Chapter 7) the number of terms is LOG_2N-1. The average number of comparisons in a quick sort therefore is given approximately by

$$\text{Quick Sort Comparisons}=(N/2)\times(LOG_2N-1)$$

In the worst case, every comparison would require an interchange, so the number of interchanges in this type of sort could also be as great as

$$\text{Quick Sort Interchanges (worst case)}=N/2\times(LOG_2N-1)$$

N(1)	Fred ← I	Fred ← I	Fred ← I	Adam	Adam
N(2)	Dan	Dan	Dan	Dan ← I	Dan
N(3)	Bill	Bill	Bill	Bill	Bill ← I
N(4)	Tom	Tom	Tom	Tom	Tom
N(5)	Sue	Sue	Sue	Sue	Sue
N(6)	Bet	Bet	Bet	Bet	Bet
N(7)	Greg	Greg	Greg	Greg	Greg
N(8)	Adam	Adam	Adam ← J	Fred ← J	Fred ← J
N(9)	Sam	Sam ← J	Sam	Sam	Sam
N(10)	Mary ← J	Mary	Mary	Mary	Mary
			Exchange Fred ↔ Adam		

N(1)	Adam	Adam	Adam	Adam	Adam
N(2)	Dan	Dan	Dan	Dan	Dan
N(3)	Bill	Bill	Bill	Bill	Bill
N(4)	Tom ← I	Fred ← I	Fred ← I	Bet	Bet
N(5)	Sue	Sue	Sue	Sue ← I	Fred ← I
N(6)	Bet	Bet	Bet ← J	Fred ← J	Sue ← J
N(7)	Greg	Greg ← J	Greg	Greg	Greg
N(8)	Fred ← J	Tom	Tom	Tom	Tom
N(9)	Sam	Sam	Sam	Sam	Sam
N(10)	Mary	Mary	Mary	Mary	Mary
	Exchange Tom ↔ Fred		Exchange Fred ↔ Bet		
				Exchange Sue ↔ Fred	

FIGURE 9–4. A Quick (Partition-Exchange) Sort

Now I = 5 and J = 6. Thus J = I + 1 and the sublist

N(1) = Adam, N(2) = Dan, N(3) = Bill, N(4) = Bet, N(5) = Fred

contains elements all of which are less than any element in the other sublist

N(6) = Sue, N(7) = Greg, N(8) = Tom, N(9) = Sam, N(10) = Mary.

We now set up a stack that contains the limits of the first sublist and begin to sort the second sublist.

Stack (← = Top)

N(1) Adam, N(5) Fred ←

N(6)	Sue ← I	Mary	Mary	Mary	Mary
N(7)	Greg	Greg ← I	Greg	Greg	Greg
N(8)	Tom	Tom	Tom ← I	Sue ← I	Sam ← I
N(9)	Sam	Sam	Sam	Sam ← J	Sue ← J
N(10)	Mary ← J	Sue ← J	Sue ← J	Tom	Tom

Exchange Sue ← Mary   Exchange Tom ← Sue

Exchange Sue ↔ Sam

I = 8, J = 9; thus J = I + 1

Store the limits of the unsorted sublist on the stack and sort the sublist N(9) Sue to N(10) Tom.

Stack (← = Top)

N(1) Adam, N(5) Fred

N(6) Mary, N(8) Sam ←

N(9)	Sue ← I	
N(10)	Tom ← J	SORTED

FIGURE 9–4. Continued

Go back and sort the sublist whose limits are on the top of the stack.

Stack (← = Top)
N(1) Adam, N(5) Fred ←

N(6)	Mary←I	Mary←I	Greg←I	
N(7)	Greg	Greg←J	Mary←J	
N(8)	Sam←J	Sam	Sam	SORTED
		Exchange Mary↔Greg		

I = 6, J = 7; thus J = I + 1

Sort the sublist whose limits are on the top of the stack.

Stack
Empty

N(1)	Adam←I	Adam←I	Adam←I	Adam←I
N(2)	Dan	Dan	Dan	Dan←J
N(3)	Bill	Bill	Bill←J	Bill
N(4)	Bet	Bet←J	Bet	Bet
N(5)	Fred←J	Fred	Fred	Fred

I = 1, J = 2; thus J = I + 1

Store unsorted sublist limits

N(1) Adam to N(1) Adam on the stack

and sort N(2) Dan to N(5) Fred.

Stack (← = Top)
N(1) Adam, N(1) Adam ←

FIGURE 9–4. Continued

N(2)	Dan←—I	Dan←—I	Bet
N(3)	Bill	Bill	Bill←—I
N(4)	Bet	Bet←—J	Dan←—J
N(5)	Fred←—I	Fred	Fred
		Exchange Dan←→Bet	

I = 3, J = 4; thus J = I + 1

Store limits N(2) Bet to N(3) Bill on the stack and sort N(4) Dan to N(5) Fred.

<u>Stack</u> (←——= Top)
N(1) Adam, N(1) Adam
N(2) Bet, N(3) Bill ←——

N(4)	Dan←—I	
N(5)	Fred←—J	SORTED

Sort N(2) Bet to N(3) Bill.

<u>Stack</u> (←——= Top)
N(1) Adam, N(1) Adam ←——

N(2)	Bet←—I	
N(3)	Bill←—J	SORTED

Sort N(1) Adam to N(1) Adam.

N(1)	Adam	SORTED

FIGURE 9–4. Continued

For a quick sort of 100 records there would be approximately 280 comparisons. For 1000 records you obtain approximately 4500 comparisons, and for 10,000 records the average number of comparisons would be about 61,500, which is much fewer than the 50 million comparisons needed for a selection or bubble sort of 10,000 records.

Radix or Tree Sort

A number of other sorting methods are more or less popular. One of these is the tree or *radix sort*. In this method, the elements of the list are categorized depending upon what is contained in the element. The categories are then divided into smaller categories, etc. until the list is sorted. For example, as illustrated in Figure 9–5, if you wished to sort 500 cards, each with a unique key between 000 to 999 (but not all keys in this range are represented on the cards), you could place those cards whose key ends with 0 in one pile, those with keys ending in 1 in a second pile, those ending with 2 in a third pile, etc., until you had ten piles. The "3 pile" for example might contain cards with keys such as 003, 363, 143, 873, 513, etc., not in order. Now take the "3 pile" and sort them into 10 piles according to the 10's digit. You now

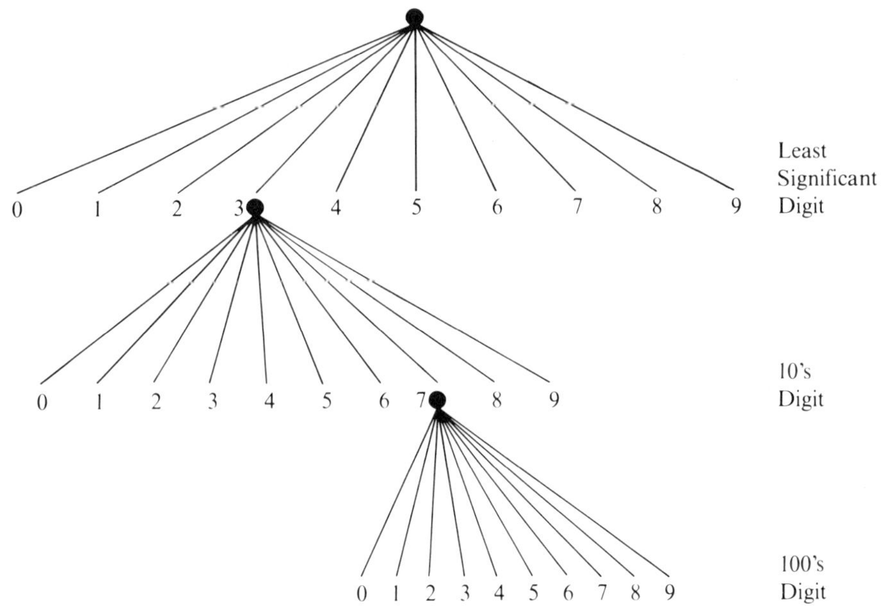

FIGURE 9–5. Part of a Sort Tree

have 10 piles for each of your previous piles. Sort each of these into 10 piles on the 100's digit, and you end up with $10 \times 10 \times 10 = 10^3$ piles, half of which, in this example, are empty, since there are only 500 records. If you carefully pick up the cards in order, they will be sorted.

In practice, you may place the units piles in order, one on top of the other, then sort the entire pile of cards by the 10's column, place the piles in order on top of each other again, sort on the 100's column, and place the piles on each other in order. Now you have the entire deck of cards sorted in numerical order. This version of the tree sort is called a radix sort and is the way the mechanical card sorters were used. Sorter operators became adept at sorting on a row, stacking the cards, and sorting again so that all came out right. Now, of course, you could write an algorithm to do a tree or radix sort within the computer. The number of characters compared in these sorts equals approximately the number of elements N in the list to be sorted times the number of characters M in each key (such as three characters in the keys from 000 to 999) times the number of possible different characters D (such as 10 different digits). In this example there are 500 cards, three characters in each key, and 10 possible digits for each character. Thus $N = 500$, $M = 3$, and $D = 10$, so that

$$\text{Radix Sort Comparisons} = N \times M \times D.$$

In this case $N \times M \times D = 500 \times 3 \times 10 = 15{,}000$ character comparisons.

Merge Sort

One last type of sort to be discussed here is the *merge sort*. In this case we assume that we have two lists already sorted and wish to merge them into one sorted list. It takes one pass through the lists to merge them. If the lists have a total of N elements with approximately the same number, $N/2$, in each list, then the number of comparisons in one pass will be approximately $N - 1$. A good example of a merge sort is inserting the items from a transaction file into a master file such as that illustrated in Example 1–1 and Table 1–1 (Chapter 1).

A number of lists can be merged in pairs, then merged in pairs again, etc. until the entire file is merged. This requires K passes to merge 2^K lists. In the extreme, any list with N elements can be considered to be N different lists with one element each. Doing a merge sort on one completely unsorted list becomes a process requiring LOG_2N passes. The average number of comparisons on these passes will be approximately $(N - 1)$. Thus

$$\text{Merge Sort of a Completely Unsorted List} = (N - 1) \times LOG_2 N \text{ comparisons.}$$

SORTING LOGICALLY

When we think of sorting the items in a list we usually think of putting all of the items in physical order. After all, that is the way we usually see sorted lists. In a computer, however, it may be more efficient to create or change link pointers associated with the list and *logically sort* the linked list without physically moving anything. The following example, as well as Figures 14–15 and 14–16, Chapter 14, illustrate this process.

Example 9–4

Sort the following list logically by creating linked list pointers.

Record Number	*Contents of Record*
1	Sue
2	Bob
3	Tom
4	Sally
5	Adam

Solution:

1. Read the list to find the smallest element (requires $N-1$ comparisons), namely 5 Adam. Assign the Start Pointer to 5 Adam and store Start Pointer = 5 in a separate location. Add the number 5 to a list of records considered.
2. Read the list (skip record 5) to find the smallest element ($N-2$ comparisons), namely 2 Bob. Assign a pointer to record 5 Adam to point to 2. Add the number 2 to the list of records considered.
3. Read the list (skip 2 and 5) to find the smallest element ($N-3$ comparisons), namely 4 Sally. Assign a pointer to record 2 Bob to point to 4. Add number 4 to the list of records considered.
4. Read the list (skip 4, 2, and 5) to find the smallest element ($N-4$) comparisons), namely 1 Sue. Assign a pointer to record 4 Sally to point to 1. Add number 1 to the list of records considered.
5. Note that there is now only one element (3 Tom) which has not been considered ($N-4=1$). Assign a pointer to record 1 Sue to point to 3.
6. Assign the End pointer to 3 Tom.

The sorted list is now

Record Number	*Contents of Record*	*Linked-List Pointer*
XXX	Start Pointer	5
1	Sue	3
2	Bob	4
3	Tom	End
4	Sally	1
5	Adam	2

The number of comparisons made in this sort, where $N-4=1$, is

$$(N-1)+(N-2)+(N-3)+(N-4)=(N-1)\times N/2$$

However, there are a few hidden comparisons, namely comparing each record examined with the list of those considered already. This is also $(N-1)\times N/2$. Thus

$$\text{Logical Sort Comparisons}=(N-1)\times N.$$

Virtually no interchanges were made. Essentially, in Example 9–4 we have performed a selection sort. Given sufficient incentive, we could sort the list using any of the methods discussed in this chapter.

QUESTIONS

1. Illustrate the following list after each pass through the entire list, sorting alphabetically

   a. by a bubble sort (moving the largest to the bottom)

   b. by a selection sort (interchanging the largest with the bottom)

      JUNEAU
      CARSON
      SEATTLE
      WAUSAU
      BOISE
      TRENTON

2. Illustrate a complete quick sort on the records with the following numerical keys. Show the contents of the stack after each pass.

A(1)	553	A(5)	921	A(8)	186
A(2)	486	A(6)	205	A(9)	874
A(3)	321	A(7)	613	A(10)	722
A(4)	988				

3. Keys for records in a given file are four characters long (such as C3PO, R2D2, RX37, or 2H13) and may be capital letters A through Z or digits 0 through 9 in any order.

   a. How many "branches" would you ultimately have on a complete binary tree for the file? How many of those branches would be empty, if the file contained 5000 records with unique keys?

   b. How many character comparisons would you have to make in order to perform a radix sort of 5000 such records?

   c. How many comparisons would be made in a bubble or a selection sort of a file with 5000 of these records?

4. Records for 250 students in a small school are stored in a file. Assume in a sorting process that one comparison or one interchange requires reading two records and that your equipment can read 1000 records per second. Assume also that the number of interchanges in a sort is approximately one half of the worst case.

   a. What is the average number of records which would be read with a linear search for a student in the unordered file?

   b. What is the average number of records which would be read with a binary search of the file if it were sorted in order?

   c. What is the average *time* to find a record with a linear search?

   d. What is the average *time* to find a record with a binary search?

   e. What is the average time required to perform the comparisons needed to sort the file using a bubble sort or a selection sort?

   f. What is the approximate time required to perform the interchanges in a bubble sort of the file?

   g. What is the approximate time required to perform the interchanges in a selection sort of the file?

   h. What is the approximate *total* time required to sort the file using a bubble sort?

i. What is the approximate *total* time required to sort the file using a selection sort?

j. How many times would the file have to be searched linearly in order to justify taking the time to perform a selection sort and do binary searches instead?

5. Work problem 4 again with a file containing the information for a college with 10,000 students.

6. How much time would be required to perform a quick sort on a file containing records for 10,000 students? Assume that one comparison or one interchange requires two reads and that your equipment can perform 1000 reads per second. Assume also that the number of interchanges required is one half of the worst case.

7. Sort the file with the following record keys *logically* by assigning pointers.

Rec. No	*Key*
1	FRED
2	DAN
3	BILL
4	TOM
5	SUE
6	BET
7	GREG
8	ADAM

8. Two sorted lists consist of records with the indicated keys.

a. Illustrate a merge sort of the lists.

List 1	*List 2*
Apple	Cherry
Banana	Grape
Date	Kiwi
Lemon	Mango
Pear	Orange
Raspberry	Quince
Tomato	Strawberry
Watermelon	

b. How many comparisons did you have to make?

c. What is the average number of comparisons which you would have needed if you had assumed that both lists were one long unsorted list and performed a (1) merge sort? (2) quick sort?

9. Develop a *general* algorithm for a *logical* selection type sort of N records, such as that shown for five records in Example 9–4.

CHAPTER 10

RANDOM ACCESS FILES

NONLINEAR ORGANIZATION

Until now our discussion has centered primarily on linear or sequential organization of files. Sequential organization is usually the simplest method of organizing files and is likely to be used when the number of records is small and the method of organization is not critical. Also, when the "instantaneous" activity of a file is high—that is, when a large fraction of the records must be accessed each time the file is read—sequential organization is convenient.

Suppose, however, that you have a file of accounts for customers in a large bank. When a customer comes in to find out the status of an account, you probably would not wish to have to search the entire file of accounts in order to find this particular one. Even a binary search might be time consuming, and updating such a file, keeping it in order so that a binary search could be used, would be a lengthy job which might need to be performed at least daily. In this situation you must have some way of finding the customer's record immediately, no matter where it is in the file. You wish to have the file *directly organized.*

In a direct, nonlinear organization there will be a predictable relationship between the key of a record and its physical storage address. This relationship is called the *hash function* or the *hash code,* and applying a hash code to a key in order to create or find a storage address is called *hashing.* There are many popular hash codes which are used, but you may find it necessary to invent your own functions when the popular ones are not satisfactory for your application. Hashing allows you to convert any record key, the *external identifier* of the record, into its physical storage address, *the internal identifier,* and to locate any random record immediately. Hence direct organization of files is said to give *random access* to the records in the file.

Activity and Response

It may seem that a direct organization is the best of all possible worlds, that all files should be organized this way so that any record can be found immediately. It turns out however, that storage of directly organized files is feasible only on direct access storage devices (DASD's) such as disks or drums, and that, unless activity is low or "instantaneous" response is critical, other methods of organization may be more efficient.

Certainly, if you always wish to access one record at a time, such as the accounts in the bank, you would wish a direct organization. However, hashing functions rarely convert keys to addresses which are in the same order as the keys. That is, hashing usually results in nonsequential storage of the records.

Suppose, for example, that you have an inventory file. The identifying key for each record is the part number of the item for which information is stored in the record. You wish to be able to update a record immediately as a part is removed from or added to the inventory. Obviously, then, the file should be directly organized, so that each record can be found and updated quickly. However, you also need a complete printout of your inventory, in order, by part numbers, available to your stock manager every morning at the beginning of the workday. For this you need to be able to read the file sequentially, and this may be quite difficult for a large, random file.

In order to read a random file in sequential order you have two options, both of which are considerably slower than reading a sequentially organized file.

1. You may sort the file before printing it. Obviously, if you sort it physically, you have lost the predictable relationship between keys and physical addresses. If you sort the file logically, by assigning link pointers to each record, you have consumed a lot of time, and will need to be absolutely certain that pointers are updated whenever records are added to or deleted from the file. If the file is volatile, this

may be an unbearable burden to lay upon your access method. On the other hand, if you do not keep pointers up to date, you will have to sort the file again every time you wish sequential access.

2. You may keep a cross-reference list in your file cabinet or in a separate finder or "tickler" file within your computer system, in which all the keys of the files are listed in sequential order. Then sequential access will mean reading the cross-reference list or tickler file, finding each record, converting its key, looking up the storage address, retrieving the record, looking at the next key in the finder file, converting its key, etc.

Thus, you see that if a low activity file is always to be accesseed randomly, direct organization may indeed be best. However, if you need to access the file sequentially very often, random access may not be the best of all possible worlds. In fact, if file activity is high, direct organization may result in very slow, cumbersome access. In such situations, if "instantaneous" response is absolutely necessary, an indexed method, such as one of those described in the next chapter, may be required.

Record Formats and Storage Requirements

Records in a directly organized file may be recorded in practically any format. Records may be of fixed or variable length. The count area of each record descriptor should contain the length of the record, especially if the lengths are variable. Records are usually formatted *with keys* to facilitate identification.

In the rare case where record keys can be converted *directly* to addresses such that the addresses are in the same order as the keys, records can be blocked. In this case, it will make sense to assign the highest key of any record in the block to the block itself, and a record's location will be determined by a search for the first block key which is not less than the desired record key.

In most cases, however, record keys do not convert directly to addresses in the same order. In fact, hashing may put the records quite randomly into an address area. This is the most common situation and is called *indirect addressing*. Then it is almost essential that records be stored in *unblocked* format, so that each logical record is also a physical record. For example, if record keys were converted to random addresses, with the records blocked as shown in Figure 10–1, it would be virtually impossible to find the location of the record with key WREN by examining block keys with a "not less than" algorithm.

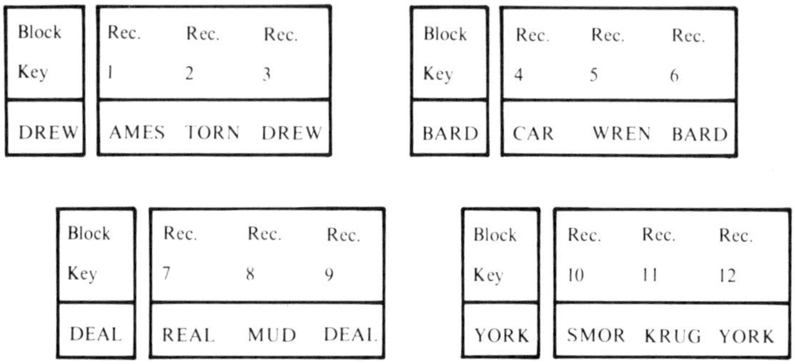

FIGURE 10–1. A Difficult Blocked Random File

In addition to the storage area required for the records in the file, a direct organization must provide for extra storage space. The file itself may be more or less sparsely loaded. That is, the *loading factor* or *packing factor* is less than 100%. The loading, or packing, factor equals the number of records actually stored in an area, divided by the number of locations reserved in that area for those records. This is demonstrated in Example 10–1.

Example 10–1

a. A file with 7500 records is to be loaded into an area containing space for 12,500 such records. What is the packing factor?

   Solution: Packing factor = 7500/12,500 = 0.60 = 60%

b. A file contains 9000 records. It is to be loaded with a packing factor of 80%. How many locations must be reserved for the file?

   Solution: Locations reserved = 9000/0.80 = 11,250.

The packing factor is usually chosen to be less than 100% to help alleviate problems encountered while trying to place some records in the file, whose keys convert to the same address as other records. Such records are called *synonyms*, and their addresses are called *collisions*. Synonyms and collisions will be discussed in detail later in the chapter. Another reason for a packing factor of less than 100% is to provide for the addition of records to the file.

In addition to leaving empty spaces in the file, other storage space is needed for directly organized files. If a finder or tickler file is needed for rare sequential access, space must be provided for that. One record area, usually record 0, on each track is usually reserved for specific information about the number of records on the track. Some provision must be made for storing the hash function which was used to convert the keys to storage addresses, so that same function can be used to find the records. The function itself may be stored in an easily accessible record, or a table may be created in which all of the keys are recorded along with their storage addresses. In either case extra storage space must be provided.

DIRECT ADDRESSING

In an ideal situation, all of the record keys could be converted to a closely packed set of relative addresses with few or no holes and no synonyms or collisions. In such a case the internal keys, the storage addresses, could be in the same order as the external keys. Records could be stored in key sequential order, and both direct access and sequential access to the file would be easy. In the rare case when this situation occurs, it is called *direct addressing*.

Example 10–2

Suppose you have started a small car rental agency. When you go to buy license plates for your fleet of 100 cars, you are given plates with numbers *ATC 456* through *ATC 555* in sequential order. Set up a file with records for each of your automobiles, so that you can find the record for a particular car quickly if you know its plate number. The records will be fixed length, unblocked, formatted with keys, and 512 bytes in length each, including the key.

Solution:

The simplest hash function in this case is to take the three digits of the plate numbers, 456 through 555, and subtract 455 from each. This gives a set of relative addresses running from 1 through 100, namely

Plate No.	*Address*	*Plate No.*	*Address*
ATC 456	1	. . .	
ATC 457	2	ATC 553	98
ATC 458	3	ATC 554	99
. . .		ATC 555	100

Note that the records can be found quickly by applying the hash function and looking up the record. Also, since the records are in key sequential order, a sequential read of the file will be straightforward. This is a case of direct addressing.

You might consider what will happen to this file when, six months later, you add 50 more cars to the fleet and acquire plates *BLT 007* through *BLT 056*. Now the code you used to create the file runs into some problems with synonyms, and other measures will have to be taken.

Example 10–3

The addresses, 1 through 100, in Example 10–2 are relative addresses. Suppose that you wish the file to start at the beginning of track 6 on cylinder 281 of DASD Device I of Figure 5–7, Chapter 5. How can you assign absolute addresses? Where would you find the record with key ATC 502?

Solution:

First we need to determine how many of these records will fit on a track of the DASD.

From Chapter 5, Figure 5–7, the number of records on one track of the DASD is given by

Physical Records per track = 13,150 / (150 + C + D).

Since the records are unblocked, the number of physical records per track is the same as the number of logical records per track. C = 60, since the records are formatted *with* keys, and D (the data length, including key) = 512 bytes. Thus 13,150 / (150 + 60 + 512) = 18.21; so there are *18 records* per track.

Also note that 100 records / 18 records per track = 5.56; so it will require six tracks for the file.

Now *take the relative record number,* 1 through 100 in this problem, *subtract one,* then *divide by the number of records which will fit on one track.* The *quotient plus one* will be the *relative track number,* and the *remainder plus one* will be the *relative record number* on that track.

Thus relative record numbers will convert to relative track and record numbers as shown below:

Relative Record No.	*Record No. Minus 1*	*Quotient*	*Remainder*	*Track (add 1)*	*Record (add 1)*
		(divide by 18 rec/track)			
001	000	0	0	1	1
002	001	0	1	1	2
. . .					
018	017	0	17	1	18
019	018	1	0	2	1
020	019	1	1	2	2
. . .					
035	034	1	16	2	17
036	035	1	17	2	18
. . .					
047	046	2	10	3	11
. . .					
098	097	5	7	6	8
099	098	5	8	6	9
100	099	5	9	6	10

Because record ATC 502 has relative record number $502-455=47$ (from Example 10–2) the chart above shows that it is the eleventh record on the third track for this file.

Since the file begins on track 6 of cylinder 281, the third track occupied by the file is $6+3-1=$ track 8.

Thus record ATC 502 is *record number 11 on track 8 of cylinder 281.*

Example 10–4

A file is to consist of the weather data for Salt Lake City for every day of the year 1984. The record keys are to be the dates, namely month and day. Find a set of relative record numbers for the file.

Solution:

We would like to convert the keys directly, with the records stored in order by keys, no synonyms, and in 365 consecutive spaces, if possible. One hash function which approximates this is to subtract one from the month, multiply by 31, and add the day. This produces the following results:

Key (Date)	*Month mm*	*Day dd*	*(Month − 1)×31*	*Address 31×(mm−1)+dd*	
Jan. 1	1	1	$(1-1)\times 31=0$	$0+1=$	1
Jan. 2	1	2	$(1-1)\times 31=0$	$0+2=$	2
. . .					
Jan. 31	1	31	$(1-1)\times 31=0$	$0+31=$	31
Feb. 1	2	1	$(2-1)\times 31=31$	$31+1=$	32
Feb. 2	2	2	$(2-1)\times 31=31$	$31+2=$	33
. . .					
Feb. 28	2	28	$(2-1)\times 31=31$	$31+28=$	59
Feb. 29	2	29	$(2-1)\times 31=31$	$31+29=$	60
Mar. 1	3	1	$(3-1)\times 31=62$	$62+1=$	63
Mar. 2	3	2	$(3-1)\times 31=62$	$62+2=$	64
. . .					
Mar. 31	3	31	$(3-1)\times 31=62$	$62+31=$	93
Apr. 1	4	1	$(4-1)\times 31=93$	$93+1=$	94
. . .					
Dec. 31	12	31	$(12-1)\times 31=341$	$341+31=$	372

In this solution we have required 372 spaces for 365 records, but there have been no collisions. Because there is no record at address 61 for Feb. 30, for example, the packing factor equals 366/372 = 98.4%. This is a very good packing factor for such a simple hashing algorithm; less than two percent of the space is wasted. Had we been more determined, we could have used a formula for calculating Julian date, number of consecutive days since sometime way back when, and had 100% loading, but the hash function might not have been quite so simple as we found it here.

INDIRECT ADDRESSING

Unfortunately, life is rarely as simple as in Examples 10–2 through 10–4 above. The record keys usually do not convert easily to a nice compact set of addresses in the same order as the keys, and we generally do have to deal with synonyms and collisions. These conditions are lumped under the title of *indirect addressing* to distinguish them from the direct addressing cases illustrated above.

Hash Functions

It may be quite difficult to find a hashing algorithm which works well for a particular set of records. First of all, we would like for our hash function to be as *simple* and as *compact* as possible. Certainly, if a simple addressing method (such as picking three digits from a key) will work, we would not want to make life more difficult by choosing something more complex.

As a second consideration, there should be as *little wasted space* as possible in the area in which our file is stored. It would normally be unacceptable to take the last four digits of the social security numbers for 200 employees and use those as the storage addresses. You would end up with 200 records spread out over addresses 0000 to 9999, 10,000 record spaces long. The loading factor here would be about 200/10,000=2%, with 98 percent wasted space. In this case you must find a different hash function, which packs the records considerably closer together in the address space. An 80 percent or greater packing factor is generally considered acceptable.

Third, you would wish to have as few record keys as possible converting to the same addresses; i. e., as *few synonyms* as possible. Usually, more than 20 percent collisions between addresses is difficult to handle, and our hash functions should be chosen, if at all possible, to produce fewer than 20 percent collisions.

Finally, the *average number* of searches or *reads* necessary to locate a record should be close to 1.0. If you have to look at a dozen records before you find the one you want, the access time may be unacceptably long, and a better organization, using a different hash code, may be in order. An average of 1.2 reads per record or less is considered good in most situations.

Synonyms, Collisions, Buckets

As indicated, when two different record keys convert to the same address, the keys are said to be *synonyms*, and the records are said to be in *collision* within the address storage area. There are a number of ways to handle collisions. The most common way is to store the colliding record at the next available higher address. Then, when the record in question is not found at the address to which its key has converted, a search to find it begins consecutively through the file from the current position. A variation on this is to provide pointers in the storage area, so that the records forming each set of synonyms form a linked list in the storage area.

Another way to handle synonyms is to provide sufficient space for them when the file is first organized. In this situation, it is anticipated that every address will have to accommodate a number of synonyms. Thus, instead of providing space for one record at each address, space is provided for two or three or more. This space is called a *bucket,* and all synonyms with a given address go into the same bucket. When a record key is converted to an address, all of the records in the bucket at that address are searched until the desired record is found. Although the bucket approach is very simple and requires no linked lists or extended searches, it has two inherent problems. First, the packing factor is small. A lot of space is wasted unless the hash function is specifically designed to put more than one record into each bucket (such as converting record keys to track numbers, and considering each track to be a bucket). Second, buckets never fill up uniformly. As a file grows, there will always be empty space in some buckets while other buckets are overflowing. For the overflowing buckets, some algorithm must be chosen to handle the overflow, with overflowing records being put in the next available bucket, or requiring a separate overflow area for the file and providing pointers to indicate where to search for the bucket overflow records.

A third way of handling synonyms of numerical keys is to use the result of the hash conversion as a new key and apply the hash function again. If the result is another collision, apply the hash function to this result again. If this process is repeated a sufficient number of times, eventually you hope to generate a new address which does not collide with the internal identifier of a previous key.

Still another way is to write all synonyms in a separate overflow area on the disk. In this case, room will have to be provided in each record so that, whenever a collision is generated, a pointer can be placed in the record which already occupies the addressed space. That pointer would specify the absolute address of the synonym. Similarly, if a second collision occurs, a pointer is placed within the record of the first synonym to indicate the address of the second, and so forth, with all of the pointers forming a linked list of a set of synonyms. If the tracks for overflow can be reserved on the same cylinder on which the primary records are located, then access to the synonyms will be quite fast, not requiring any motion of the access arm. However, it may be difficult to predict just how many tracks will be needed for this purpose on a given cylinder; and, rather than risk wasted space or overflow from the overflow tracks, a completely separate cylinder or cylinders may be provided. The user of this method of handling synonyms must decide whether it is better to have some wasted space or to have slower access. Some systems use a combination of synonym overflow areas, providing a limited number of tracks for that purpose on each cylinder and separate cylinders for overflow from the overflow tracks.

HOW TO MAKE HASH

There is no set hash recipe, for converting keys to addresses, which works well every time. In fact, often in your search for an effective hash code you will have to try a function on all or most of your keys to determine whether the loading factor is acceptable (80% or better), that you have few synonyms (20% or fewer), and that the average number of reads per record is reasonable (1.2 or less). If these conditions are not satisfied you will probably wish to choose another hash function and try again. Obviously, if you have lots of records, this procedure will be tedious at best, maddening at worst. Generally you will find it necessary to write a short computer program which reads your keys from a file (sequential will do), tries a hash function, tests the results, and tries again with a new hash function until you see what you like. At some point you may decide to use the best hash function found so far, because the time you spend trying to find a better one may never be recovered in faster access, or because you have exhausted all of the simple functions you can think of, and the ones you are trying now are so complex that it would take too long to apply them to find a record.

There are a few hashing algorithms which are popular because they have been found to work well for many sets of keys. We will discuss some of those here; however, remember that none of these may work acceptably for your file and occasionally you may have to invent your own.

Quotient/Remainder Method

The most popular method of converting keys to relative record numbers is the *quotient/remainder method.* This algorithm is based upon the fact that when you divide by any number N, the remainder from the division is a number between 0 and $N-1$. Thus, if you divide a (numerical) key by the number of spaces to be reserved for the records of the file, the remainder plus one forms a convenient relative address.

Example 10–5

In your small company the 200 employees are identified by Social Security numbers. Devise a hash function to store your employee records with a packing factor of 80 percent.

Solution:

For a packing factor of 80% you will set aside 200/0.80 = 250 spaces for your records.

Social Security numbers have nine digits, such as 468-39-7482. The last four digits should be reasonably random.

Thus, for the hash function, you might take the last four digits of the Social Security numbers and divide by the number of spaces allocated for the file, 250. The remainders plus one will be a set of numbers between 1 and 250, which can be used as a set of relative addresses for the records.

For example, for an employee with Society Security number 468-39-7482, a relative address can be obtained by

$$7482 / 250 = 29.928 = 29 \text{ Remainder } 232,$$

where the remainder is simply the fraction .928 times the divisor 250 ($.928 \times 250 = 232$). Why?

Thus the relative address for a record with key 468-39-7482 would be 233 ($232 + 1$).

Notice that the quotient (29 in this case) is irrelevant. Only the remainder is significant. Indeed the quotient may not be in the appropriate range to use as an address even if we wished to do so.

Now that we have relative addresses between 1 and 250 in Example 10–5, we could apply the direct addressing method of Example 10–3 to find absolute track and record addresses if we desire. You may note that the hash function of Example 10–3 is also a type of quotient/remainder method.

We hope that the quotient/remainder method of Example 10–5 will result in fewer than 20 percent synonyms. The only way we can be sure is to test it on the keys for all 200 employees.

A *variation* on the quotient/remainder method which may produce fewer synonyms is to *divide* the key *by the closest prime number* not greater than the number of record spaces. In this case the packing factor will be slightly larger than we chose because the address space will be only as large as the prime number divisor.

Example 10–6

Use the closest prime number not greater than the number of record spaces in Example 10–5 to determine the relative address of the record for the employee whose Social Security number is 468-39-7482.

Solution:

We will use the last four digits of the Social Security number, 7482, in this case again. The closest prime number not greater than 250 is 241. Then

7482 / 241 = 31.0456. . . = 31 Remainder 11,

so the relative record address is 12 (11 + 1).

Note that the packing factor is no longer 80 percent. We now have 200 records in 241 spaces, so the packing factor is 200 / 241 = 83%.

The address (12) calculated in Example 10–6 is not even close to the address (233) calculated in Example 10–5. This is not a problem; we simply get a different set of addresses. The records are stored in a different order, which points out that an indirect addressing method rarely puts the records in key sequential order. In fact, each different hashing function is likely to put the keys in a different order.

Folding

A very simple hash method is called *folding*. Split a large key into segments and add the segments to obtain an address or a number which can be converted to an address.

Example 10–7

Use folding to reduce a set of Social Security numbers to relative addresses between 1 and 1000.

Solution:

For the Social Security number 468-39-7482, write the number 468397482, split it into three parts, and add

468 + 397 + 482 = 1347.

This is still not an address between 1 and 1000. You may now use the quotient/remainder method (divide by 1000 and take the remainder plus 1), or you can achieve the same answer in this case by taking the last three digits of the result and adding one. Why? The address in this case would be 348.

In folding you are free to choose whether to split the number in two or three or however many parts you wish. Be aware, however, that the parts should be large enough that their sum is not less than the relative addresses which you need.

If you wish your addresses to be in a range other than from 1 to some power of 10 (such as 10, 100, 1000, etc.), it is probably simplest to apply the quotient/remainder function after folding in order to convert to the proper range. So why bother to use folding at all, if you are going to apply the quotient/remainder method anyway? The answer is that it may reduce the number of synonyms, and the method is so simple that it is worth a try.

Radix Transformation

Another way of trying to minimize synonyms is to assume that the key is written in a base other than base 10, then convert to base 10. Besides possibly reducing collisons, this method has the added advantage of making the keys larger if the base chosen is greater than 10 and creating smaller keys if the chosen base is less than 10.

Example 10–8

A total of 720 records are to be loaded with a 96 percent loading factor. Convert the following typical keys for these records:

2345 and 6973

to relative addresses in the appropriate range by radix transformation assuming that the keys are written in

a. base 16
b. base 8.

Solution:

With 96 percent loading factor we need 720 / 0.96 = 750 spaces in which to load the records.

a. If we assume the keys are written in base 16 then

$$\begin{aligned}2345_{16} &= 5\times16^0+4\times16^1+3\times16^2+2\times16^3\\ &= 5\times1+4\times16+3\times256+2\times4096\\ &= 5+64+768+8192\\ &= 9029_{10}\end{aligned}$$

and

$$\begin{aligned}6973_{16} &= 3\times16^0+7\times16^1+9\times16^2+6\times16^3\\ &= 26995_{10}\end{aligned}$$

To convert these to relative addresses between 1 and 750, since we are trying to minimize collisions, let's divide by the closest prime number not greater than 750, namely 743.

9029 / 743 = 12 Remainder 113
26995 / 743 = 36 Remainder 247.

Thus the record with key 2345 will be stored at relative address 114 (113 + 1), and record with key 6973 will be stored at relative address 248 (247 + 1).

b. If we assume that the keys 2345 and 6973 are written in base 8, there is a minor problem; namely, 6973 is not a valid octal (base 8) number. (Remember, base N numbers use only digits between 0 and $N-1$. Thus 9 is an illegal octal digit.) However, since we are only assuming that the keys are written in base 8, and the numbers themselves are only considered to be sets of symbols, we can ignore this problem and convert the numbers anyway. Thus

$$\begin{aligned}2345_8 &= 5\times8^0+4\times8^1+3\times8^2+2\times8^3\\ &= 5\times1+4\times8+3\times64+2\times512\\ &= 1253_{10}\\ 6973_8 &= 3\times8^0+7\times8^1+9\times8^2+6\times8^3\\ &= 3707_{10}\end{aligned}$$

Then 1253 / 743 = 1 Remainder 510, and 3707 / 743 = 4 Remainder 735.

Thus, record 2345 will be stored at relative address 511 (510 + 1), and record 6973 will be at relative address 736 (735 + 1).

Digit Analysis

Sometimes by analyzing the digits of a set of keys we can pick out the ones which are more or less evenly distributed. Then we can use those for relative addresses or to calculate relative addresses, and minimize the number of synonyms in that manner. For a large set of keys the analysis of digits may well require a computer program in order to be able to accomplish the analysis in a reasonable amount of time.

Example 10–9

Given the following set of 12 keys

12345	12865	13185
13014	13454	13997
12229	12579	12474
13607	13734	12964

a. Perform a digit analysis to convert them to relative addresses between 1 and 20.
b. Perform a digit analysis to convert them to relative addresses between 1 and 200.
c. Would digit anlaysis be a reasonable way to convert these keys to relative addresses between 1 and 2000?

Solution:

Counting the digits in the keys (which we can do by hand for this short set, but which would require a computer program if we had lots of keys to analyze) results in the table shown in Figure 10–2.
Note that the 10 thousands digit is not distributed at all, all 12 keys have a 1 in that position. So we would create lots of synonyms if we used this digit in our address. The thousands digit is almost as bad, all 2's and 3's, though it may be useful for us to recognize that about half are 2's and half 3's. The hundreds and tens digits are quite well distributed, so we could use them as part of our addresses. The units digits are not well distributed.

a. To convert to addresses between 1 and 20 suppose we take the fourth digit of the key as the low order digit of the result. Then let the high order digit of the relative address be 0 if the third digit of the key is odd and 1 if the third digit is even. This gives us a fairly random set of addresses between 00 and 19. Adding 1 will give addresses between 01 and 20.

For example,

key 13607 converts to address 10 + 1 = 11
key 13185 converts to address 08 + 1 = 09
key 12474 converts to address 17 + 1 = 18
etc.

Digit Position →	1st Ten Thousands	2nd Thousands	3rd Hundreds	4th Tens	5th Units
Digit ↓	Number of Keys with Digit (Row) in the Position (Column)				
0			1	1	
1	12		1	1	
2		6	1	1	
3		6	1	1	
4			2	1	5
5			1	1	3
6			1	2	
7			1	2	2
8			1	1	
9			2	1	2

FIGURE 10–2. A Digit Analysis

b. To convert to addresses between 1 and 200, we might take the third and fourth digits in the key as the low order two digits of the address. To assign the high order digit we can use the second digit of the key. For example, let the high order digit of the address be 0 if the second digit of the key is 2 and 1 if the second digit of the key is 3. Adding 1 will give addresses between 1 and 200.

   For example,

   key 13*60*7 converts to address 1 60 + 1 = 161
   key 13*18*5 converts to address 1 18 + 1 = 119
   key 12*47*4 converts to address 0 47 + 1 = 048
   etc.

c. Digit analysis is probably *not* a reasonable way to convert these keys to relative addresses between 1 and 2000. In order to minimize the number of synonyms, we would need at least three digits of the key which were fairly evenly distributed. Why? We do not have that condition with the given keys.

Words as Keys

In all of the examples so far, the keys have been numbers. However, many times the keys are not pure numbers. For example, your name may be used as a key in many files which contain information about you. A typical inventory of parts may have keys containing mixed digits and letters, such as F37BA2 or ZXA385. How can these keys be converted to addresses? The answer is simple in theory but sometimes messy in practice. Convert the symbol to a number and then use a hash function suitable for numbers to convert it to an address. Here are some suggestions for converting symbolic keys to numbers. The programs in Figures 15–16 and 15–18, Chapter 15, illustrate the creation of and access to a hashed random file.

Add or Multiply the Values of a Code

A code, such as ASCII or EBCDIC, may be used to convert symbols to numbers by writing the decimal, octal, or hexadecimal values of the code and adding or multiplying those values, depending upon how large a base of numbers is needed.

Example 10–10

Use hexadecimal ASCII values for the characters and convert the following keys to relative addresses between 1 and 100.

FBALT6	SLCTR4	PZFML7
CZYNT2	BOSVA3	LSMRQ5
LAXSS1	LTDNB9	

Solution:

The ASCII for FBALT6, from Table 2–3 is
100 0110 100 0010 100 0001 100 1100 101 0100 011 0110.
In groups of four, adding a leading zero to each character and converting to hexadecimal (see Table 2–1, Chapter 2), the codes are

Character	*Binary*	*Hexadecimal*
F	0100 0110	46
B	0100 0010	42
A	0100 0001	41
L	0100 1100	4C
T	0101 0100	54
6	0011 0110	36

Now let's add the hexadecimal numbers. Each time the sum equals 16 (not 10) we carry one to the next column.

(hexadecimal) $46+42+41+4C+54+36=19F_{16}$

Using radix conversion (this time the key really *is* in base 16)

$$19F_{16}=F\times 16^0+9\times 16^1+1\times 16^2$$
$$=15\times 1+9\times 16+1\times 256=415_{10}$$

Now convert this to a relative address between 1 and 100 by the quotient/remainder method

415/100 = 4 Remainder 15

Thus FBALT6 will be stored at relative address $15+1=16$.

You may note that we have done this problem the hard way. We could have obtained the same result by adding the decimal representation of the ASCII for FBALT6; namely, from Table 2–3,

$70+66+65+76+84+54=415_{10}$

Why?
Converting the key PZFML7, we obtain

Character	*Binary*	*Hexadecimal*
P	0101 0000	50
Z	0101 1010	5A
F	0100 0110	46
M	0100 1101	4D
L	0100 1100	4C
7	0011 0111	37

Adding,

(hexadecimal) $50+5A+46+4D+4C+37=1CO_{16}$

Transforming the radix,

$$1CO_{16}=0\times 16^0+C\times 16^1+1\times 16^2$$
$$=0\times 1+12\times 16+1\times 256=448_{10}$$

Using the quotient/remainder function,

448 / 100 = 4 Remainder 48.

Thus PZFML7 will be stored at relative location $48+1=49$.
Again, using decimal ASCII you would obtain directly from Table 2–3 the result

$80+90+70+77+76+55=448_{10}$

Use the Position of the Letter in the Alphabet

Perhaps the simplest way of converting words or strings of symbols to numbers is to use the position of the letters in the alphabet. When you are having trouble falling asleep at night, try memorizing Table 10–1.

TABLE 10–1. Relative Positions of the Letters in the Alphabet.

Letter	*Position*	*Letter*	*Position*	*Letter*	*Position*
A	1	J	10	S	19
B	2	K	11	T	20
C	3	L	12	U	21
D	4	M	13	V	22
E	5	N	14	W	23
F	6	O	15	X	24
G	7	P	16	Y	25
H	8	Q	17	Z	26
I	9	R	18		

Example 10–11

Use the positions of the letters of the alphabet to convert the following keys to relative addresses between 1 and 1200.

FBALT6	SLCTR4	PZFML7
CZYNT2	BOSVA3	LSMRQ5
LAXSS1	LTDNB9	

Solution:

For simplicity we will use the value of each digit as it appears. From Table 10–1.

Character	*Position or Value*
F	6
B	2
A	1
L	12
T	20
6	6

If we were to add these values, the result would be 47, much too small to convert efficiently to a relative address between 1 and 1200. Thus we will *multiply*

$6 \times 2 \times 1 \times 12 \times 20 \times 6 = 17280$

Since the *product almost always turns out to be an even number* (at least one of the character positions will usually be even), we will not use the units digit. Instead, we will use the next four digits (1728 in this case) to convert to a relative address between 1 and 1200. Using the quotient/remainder method,

$1728 \ / \ 1200 = 1$ remainder 528.

So the relative address of FBALT6 is $528 + 1 = 529$.

Similarly, PZFML7 becomes

$16 \times 26 \times 6 \times 13 \times 12 \times 7 = 2725632$.

Taking the four digits before the low order digit, namely 2563, and applying the quotient/remainder method

$2563 \ / \ 1200 = 2$ remainder 163,

we find that the relative address of PZFML7 is $163 + 1 = 164$.

Hash in a Bucket

Example 10–3 illustrated how to place records in buckets. In that example, however, the bucket was an entire track, and the relative record addresses were converted to absolute addresses such that the buckets were always filled. Example 10–12 illustrates a slightly different situation.

Example 10–12

It is desired to place 5000 records, whose keys have been converted already to relative record numbers between 1 and 7500, into buckets. The buckets are to be numbered consecutively beginning with 1. Each bucket will be able to contain 10 records, but only eight spaces in the bucket will be filled by records with different keys, so that if there are collisions among the relative record numbers the synonyms can also be placed in the bucket.

a. How many buckets will be needed for the file?
b. Into which bucket would you place records with relative numbers
   0005 7113 4261 3618 ?
c. What would happen to a second record whose relative record number is 4261 ?
d. What would happen if four records had relative record number 4261 ?
e. What is the packing factor for the file?

Solution:

a. We need space for 7500 records with eight spaces used per bucket.

   7500 / 8 = 937.5

   Thus 938 buckets are needed.

b. To find the bucket into which a given record belongs, we subtract 1 from the relative record number and divide by the number of records per bucket. The quotient plus 1 is the bucket number.

Rel. Rec. Number	*Rec. No. Minus 1*	*Quotient*	*Remainder*	*Bucket No.(add 1)*
		(divide by 8 rec./bucket)		
0005	0004	0	4	1
7113	7112	889	0	890
4261	4260	532	4	533
3618	3617	452	1	453

c. A second record whose relative record number is 4261 would also go into bucket number 533 (along with records 4257 through 4264), since space is reserved in each bucket for two synonyms.

d. If four records had relative record number 4261, not all of them could be placed into bucket 533. Even if there were only one each of the other records from 4257 through 4264, the first two synonyms of 4261 would fill up bucket 533. The fourth relative record 4261 would have to be placed somewhere else. This might be in bucket 534 or the next bucket in which there were an empty space. Otherwise it could be in a separate overflow bucket, with the last record in bucket 533 containing a pointer to the overflow bucket.

e. The packing factor is

5000 records / (10 spaces per bucket $\times$ 938 buckets)
= 5000 / 9380 = 53.3%.

A Scatter Table (Hash on the Table?)

At the beginning of this chapter it was stated that one way of reading a random file in sequential order is to keep a "tickler" file of the keys in order, read the tickler file, and look up the records in order. This is slow at best. The other way that was mentioned to read the file in order is to sort the file before printing it, which my be even slower.

Suppose, however, that the records are stored physically in the file in sequential order or in a linked list. Then an extra table, called a *scatter table,* could be created, such that the hash function converts the record key to its position in the scatter table. The scatter table would contain pointers to the records in the primary data area so that the records can be found directly, as illustrated by the programs in Figures 15–20 and 15–22, Chapter 15.

One disadvantage of the scatter table is that extra space is required for the table. Another is that two operations must be performed in order to find a random record; i. e., (1) apply the hash function to find a record's position in the scatter table, then (2) follow the pointer in the table to the record location. The advantage of this method, of course, is that reading the prime data area from the beginning results in a sequential read of the file.

Example 10–13

Demographic information about a number of towns in Georgia is stored in alphabetical, sequential order as shown in Table 10–2.

a. Find a hash function and make a scatter table with spaces for 19 records (11 / 19 = approx. 58% loading in the hash table) to allow rapid access to any record in the file.
b. Use the scatter table to find the record for Savannah and the record for Thunderbolt.

TABLE 10–2. A Small File.

Data Location	*Key*	*Data Location*	*Key*
R1	Americus	R7	Gainesville
R2	Athens	R8	Macon
R3	Atlanta	R9	Savannah
R4	Augusta	R10	Thunderbolt
R5	Brunswick	R11	Zebulon
R6	Columbus		

Solution:

a. Note that we chose a scatter table length of 19 (rather than 18 or 20, for example) mainly to try to reduce the number of collisions. For simplicity, let's convert the names to numbers by adding the relative positions of the characters in the alphabet. Then use the quotient / remainder method to convert the numbers to relative addresses in the scatter table.
For example,

Americus = 1 + 13 + 5 + 18 + 9 + 3 + 21 + 19 = 89
89 / 19 = 4 Remainder 13

The position of Americus in the scatter table is 13 + 1 = 14. The remaining keys convert as follows:

Key	converts to *Number* (by adding character positions in alphabet)	converts to *Scatter Table Address* (by quotient/ remainder method)
Americus	89	14
Athens	67	11
Atlanta	69	13
Augusta	90	15
Brunswick	120	7
Columbus	106	12
Gainesville	115	2
Macon	46	9
Savannah	80	5
Thunderbolt	139	7
Zebulon	95	1

You should note that there is one collision, which is not unreasonable, but it does give us the added problem of deciding what to do with it. In order to keep the problem as simple as possible, let's put the synonym in the next available location. The scatter table then appears as shown in Table 10–3.

Note that the key column may not be needed in the scatter table. However, it might be convenient in searching the table to have the keys recorded.

b. To find Savannah in the file, first convert the key Savannah to its position in the scatter table

Savannah = 19 + 1 + 22 + 1 + 14 + 14 + 1 + 8 = 80
80 / 19 = 4 Remainder 4.

The position of Savannah in the scatter table is 4 + 1 = 5.

TABLE 10–3. A Scatter Table for the File in Table 10–2.

Position	*Key*	*Record Pointer*
1	Zebulon	R11
2	Gainesville	R7
3		
4		
5	Savannah	R9
6		
7	Brunswick	R5
8	Thunderbolt	R10
9	Macon	R8
10		
11	Athens	R2
12	Columbus	R6
13	Atlanta	R3
14	Americus	R1
15	Augusta	R4
16		
17		
18		
19		

Position 5 in the scatter table (Table 10–3) points to record R9 in the prime data area (Table 10–2). Examination of record R9 does indeed give us the information for Savannah.

To find Thunderbolt, convert the key Thunderbolt to a position in the scatter table

Thunderbolt = 20 + 8 + 21 + 14 + 4 + 5 + 18 + 2 + 15 + 12 + 20 = 139
139 / 19 = 7 Remainder 6

The position of Thunderbolt in the scatter table should be 6 + 1 = 7.

Position 7 in the scatter table points to record R5 in the prime data area. But examination of record R5 gives us information for Brunswick, not Thunderbolt. So we go to the next entry in the scatter table (since our algorithm placed synonyms in the closet available location), position 8. Position 8 in the scatter table points to record R10 in the prime data area. Examination of record R10 does give us the information for Thunderbolt.

MANAGING RANDOM FILES

Creating Random Files

The methods used for creating and maintaining a random file have considerable bearing on whether access to the file will be efficient. It probably is not a good idea to begin a random file with one record and add all other records later. Small files are most easily organized and rapidly searched in a sequential organization. So as a file grows, you may wish to collect data and write records sequentially until the file reaches a good size. At that time you will have enough records that you can choose a hash function and try it to see if it leads to an efficient organization with few synonyms and a reasonable number of reads to find the average record.

The number of reads per record as well as the number of synonyms will be determined by the hash function you choose. Whether your hash code really works depends as much upon the average number of reads per record (how long will it take you to access the file?) as upon the number of synonyms. Example 10–14 illustrates that the two concepts are intimately related.

Example 10–14

Suppose you have two different hash functions operating on the same 10 keys, as shown in Table 10–4. We will load the records into the storage area in order at the closest empty higher numbered location. A search for a record will begin at the address to which its key converts and proceed to successive locations until it is found.

Note that there are two synonyms in each case; both hash functions produce 20 percent collisions. However, the average number of reads to find the records in the file will be different. In both cases, records A, B, C, D, E, F, and G will be found with one read. Once the key has been converted, we look at the appropriate location and find the record. Record H in one case and record J in the other are likely to take two reads to find. We would look for them at relative addresses 7 and 8 respectively; not finding them there we would look at the next address, and it would require two reads to find those records.

TABLE 10–4. Keys Converted to Relative Addresses by Two Different Hash Functions.

Hash Code I

Key	*A*	*B*	*C*	*D*	*E*	*F*	*G*	*H*	*J*	*K*
Relative Address	1	2	3	4	5	6	7	7	9	9
Loaded at	1	2	3	4	5	6	7	8	9	10
Reads per Record	1	1	1	1	1	1	1	2	1	2

Hash Code II

Key	*A*	*B*	*C*	*D*	*E*	*F*	*G*	*H*	*J*	*K*
Relative Address	1	2	3	4	5	6	7	8	8	8
Loaded at	1	2	3	4	5	6	7	8	9	10
Reads per Record	1	1	1	1	1	1	1	1	2	3

Finding record K in the case of the first hash function involves looking at record 9. K is not there, so we look at record 10, where we find it. Two reads were required. In the case of the second hash function, we look for record K at address 8. It is not there, so we look at address 9. Still not having found record K, we continue our search at record 10, where it is finally found. It has required three reads to find it.

Thus, using Hash Code I, it takes a total of 12 reads to find 10 records. The average number of reads per record in this case is 1.2. Using Hash Code II, it takes 13 reads to find the same 10 records, so that the average number of reads per record is 1.3. Since the number of synonyms is the same in each situation, we would choose Hash Code I to organize this file, providing all other considerations (such as how difficult and time consuming it is to apply the code) are the same.

You should be aware that you would have no basis for choosing between hash functions in Example 10–14 above if you did not have a significant number of records. Had you tried to choose which hash code to use, given only records with keys A, B, C, D, and E, there would have been absolutely no basis for choice. You must have more than a few records before you create a directly organized file if you expect to choose a hash function intelligently and avoid excessive reorganization at a later date.

There is a tradeoff. The time you spend trying to find a hash function which produces a minimum number of synonyms and reads per record, and the time you spend ultimately searching the file are all expensive. Is it worth the effort and time to find a "better" hash function which increases access speed slightly? That is a decision which you must make as you organize your file. An analyst becomes most valuable to an employer as she or he learns to make such decisions wisely.

Loading and Maintaining Random Files

Generally, when loading random files, storage space should be cleared for the file in advance, so that the user and the computer both know how much storage area will be required. Remember that space must be reserved for pointers if they are to be used, and at least one easily accessible record space must be available for storing the hashing algorithm. If it is desired to have the records in sequential order and use a scatter table, as in Example 10–13, the records will also have to be sorted before they are written to the file, and additional space must be reserved for the scatter table. Generally, records in a random file are formatted with keys and unblocked. A blocked format really makes sense only if the records are sorted sequentially and a scatter table is used, or in the rare case where hashing leads to direct addressing.

Of course additions to the file are made by converting record keys to addresses and storing the records in those addresses if available. If collisions result, the user must determine where to store the synonyms, whether there is space available in a bucket, whether the synonyms should go at the next available higher address, or whether synonyms should go in an overflow area and pointers provided in the prime area so that they can be found. Note that if the records are in sequential order, adding records to the file does present problems. If sequential order is to be maintained, the entire file and the scatter table would have to be rewritten.

Deletions from a direct access file are most easily made logically rather than physically. The area occupied by a record is simply flagged as deleted and reusable. Generally, this is done by writing over the first two bytes of the area with all 1's or some similar code. Then when records are added, if the key happens to convert to an address containing a deleted record, the new record is written into that address. There may be problems with security, however, anytime a record is deleted logically rather than physically. Most of the data is still on the storage device, and could be accessed by someone who was determined to do so. If security is a problem, a logical deletion might still be performed by writing over the entire record with 1's or 0's or some random pattern.

The following examples all refer to a hypothetical file of children's books illustrated in Table 10–5. Although it is irrelevant to the examples, the hash code used to convert to relative addresses between 1 and 10 was to add up all the bits in the no-parity seven-bit ASCII for the alphabetical characters, then use the quotient remainder method. Admittedly, this is a poor hash function, but it gives lots of synonyms, which we need to better illustrate the point here. The examples illustrate different methods of loading, maintaining,

TABLE 10–5. A Short File of Children's Books.

Key	*Relative Address*	*Frequency of Reference*	*Key*	*Relative Address*	*Frequency of Reference*
Ferdinand the Bull	1	4%	Fly Went By	8	7%
Bears on Wheels	5	7%	Blue-Nosed Witch	8	20%
Pegleg Willy	7	2%	Twig	9	7%
Matti	10	7%	Huge Harold	9	10%
Little Prince	7	20%	Mister Blue	1	16%

adding to, and deleting from a random file. Please be aware that these are not the only methods, but they are perhaps the most popular.

Progressive Read Load

One way of loading the records is to place them into the file in the order in which they occur, placing records at the next larger available address if the address where they should be is already filled. Then the search for a record begins at the address to which its key converts and proceeds through successive addresses, if necessary, until the record is found. This is called a *progressive read load.* This is illustrated in Example 10–15 for the file in Table 10–5. The *Frequency of Reference* column in Table 10–5 refers to the percentage of the time that record is referenced when we look at the file. This will be used in Example 10–19, which illustrates activity loading.

Example 10–15

Perform a progressive read load on the file in Table 10–5 and determine the average number of reads per record.

Solution:

The records are loaded into the file in the order in which they occur, resulting in Table 10–6.

Note that each record is loaded as close as it can be at or following the storage address to which its key converts. Also note that 13 spaces are needed in which to store these 10 records. Hence the loading factor is about 77 percent. If you wished to have 100% loading, you could define a circular storage area such that the next address logically following 10 is 1. This is an exercise for the student at the end of the chapter.

The Number of Reads column may require some explanation. For records which are stored at the address to which their keys convert, such as Pegleg Willy at address 7, it requires only one read to find the record. For Mister Blue, however, we begin by looking at address 1, because that is the address to which the key converts. But Mister Blue is not in location 1, Ferdinand is there. So in the progressive read method, we look at the next successive record in the file, namely record 2. Mister Blue is found there, so it took two reads to find this record. To find Blue-Nosed Witch, we look first at location 8, to which the key converts. Not finding the record there we proceed to search through addresses 9, 10, and 11 before we find it. Thus, it takes four reads to find the Blue-Nosed Witch.

TABLE 10–6. One Pass, Progressive Read Load of the File in Table 10–5.

Record	*Relative Address*	*Where Loaded*	*Number of Reads*
Ferdinand the Bull	1	1	1
Bears on Wheels	5	5	1
Pegleg Willy	7	7	1
Matti	10	10	1
Little Prince	7	8	2
Fly Went By	8	9	2
Blue-Nosed Witch	8	11	4
Twig	9	12	4
Huge Harold	9	13	5
Mister Blue	1	2	2
			Total 23

The average number of reads per record is found simply by adding up the total number of reads for each record and dividing by the total number of records. Thus the average number of reads per record for the file loaded in this manner is

23 / 10 = 2.3 reads per record.

This is not an efficient number. A reasonable number is 1.2 reads per record or fewer. Thus, this would give us more cause for trying to find a different hash function and/or a different method of loading the file.

Linked Load

Another way of providing for reading synonyms after having loaded a file in one pass as illustrated in Example 10–15, is to provide a pointer in each record which has a synonym, and to search for the synonyms by following the chain of pointers. Such a method is called a *linked load.*

Example 10–16

Load the file of Table 10–5 using a linked load and calculate the average number of reads per record.

The solution is shown in Table 10–7.

There is then an average of 20 reads / 10 records = 2.0 reads per record, an improvement over the progressive read method.

Note that the file is loaded in the same order and in the same manner as described in Example 10–16. The link pointers and the number of reads per record (where greater than 1) are calculated and inserted *as the synonyms are loaded*. For example, when Little Prince is loaded, it is discovered that it cannot be loaded at location 7, to which its key converts. It is loaded at 8, the closest location. The record at 7 is examined; after it is determined that no pointer already exists in this record, a pointer is written to the first synonym of 7, namely Little Prince, at location 8. In order to find this record, we convert its key to address 7, look at 7, discover it is not there, so follow the pointer in 7 to address 8, where we find Little Prince. Thus it requires two reads to find Little Prince. Similarly, when Fly Went By must be loaded at address 9 instead of 8, a pointer is provided at 8, telling where the first synonym of address 8 is, namely Fly Went By at address 9. When we try to add Blue-Nosed Witch at location 8, we find 8, 9, and 10 are filled. Thus we load Blue-Nosed Witch into location 11. We would like to put a pointer to Blue-Nosed Witch (11) at location 8, but 8 already points to 9. Hence we must go to 9 which does not already have a pointer and place the new pointer there. It will then require reading records at addresses 8, 9, and 11 (three reads) to find Blue-Nosed Witch. We have begun a *chain* of pointers which eventually requires us to perform four reads in order to find Huge Harold. Why doesn't Mister Blue get added to this chain and require five reads?

TABLE 10–7. One Pass, Link Load of the File in Table 10–5.

Record	*Relative Address*	*Where Loaded*	*Link Pointer*	*Number of Reads*
Ferdinand the Bull	1	1	2	1
Bears on Wheels	5	5		1
Pegleg Willy	7	7	8	1
Matti	10	10		1
Little Prince	7	8	9	2
Fly Went By	8	9	11	2
Blue-Nosed Witch	8	11	12	3
Twig	9	12	13	3
Huge Harold	9	13		4
Mister Blue	1	2		2
				Total 20

Two-Pass Load

We may be able to improve our read efficiency by a *two-pass load.* In this case, rather than load all of the records in order, we load all of the records we can, in the order they appear, in the location to which their keys convert. Then we begin again at the top and load all of the synonyms.

Example 10–17

Perform a two-pass link load on the file of Table 10–5 and determine the average number of reads per record.

The solution is shown in Table 10–8.

In this case there are only 14 reads / 10 records = 1.4 reads per record average. We are progressively improving the situation.

Notice that all of the records which did not produce collisions were loaded on the first pass. Then we began again from the top and loaded those which were synonyms (such as Little Prince, whose key converts to address 7) in the next higher available location (11 in the case of Little Prince). A link pointer is placed at the appropriate place to establish a chain of pointers to the synonyms (a pointer is provided at address 7, pointing to the synonym at 11).

TABLE 10–8. Two Pass, Link Load of the File in Table 10–5.

Record	*Relative Address*	*Where Loaded 1st Pass*	*Where Loaded 2nd Pass*	*Link Pointer*	*Number of Reads*
Ferdinand the Bull	1	1		2	1
Bears on Wheels	5	5			1
Pegleg Willy	7	7		11	1
Matti	10	10			1
Little Prince	7		11		2
Fly Went By	8	8		12	1
Blue-Nosed Witch	8		12		2
Twig	9	9		13	1
Huge Harold	9		13		2
Mister Blue	1		2		2
					Total 14

Link Loading with Synonyms in a Separate Area

We can examine what will happen if we load all the synonyms in the file in a separate area and provide link pointers to them in the main area.

Example 10–18

Load the file in Table 10–5, placing all of the synonyms in a separate area beginning at address 20. The solution is shown in Table 10–9.

We have not improved the situation over the two-pass, link-load method. The average number of reads per record is still 14 reads / 10 records = 1.4 reads per record. This will be true in general. Perhaps we have made the file a bit less confusing, but we have required more space and have not reduced the average number of reads per record.

Activity Load

As you use your direct access files you may wish to keep statistics about how often the records are accessed. If you can determine that some records are accessed a large fraction of the time, you may be able to reorganize the file to speed up the average access time by greatly reducing the average number of

TABLE 10–9. Link Loading the Synonyms into a Separate Area.

Record	*Relative Address*	*Where Loaded*	*Link Pointer*	*Number of Reads*
Ferdinand the Bull	1	1	23	1
Bears on Wheels	5	5		1
Pegleg Willy	7	7	20	1
Matti	10	10		1
Little Prince	7	20		2
Fly Went By	8	8	21	1
Blue-Nosed Witch	8	21		2
Twig	9	9	22	1
Huge Harold	9	22		2
Mister Blue	1	23		2
				Total 14

reads per record. This is especially true if some of the records which are sought most often happen to be synonyms when the file is loaded in some other order. Of course, you will not be able to organize the file and perform an *activity load* until you have used it for a while and have gathered the statistics, unless it is an unusual situation where you know the activity in advance. An activity load may be performed on one pass or two passes, with link pointers or using progressive read.

Example 10–19

The records in the file in Table 10–5 have been determined, after some use of the file, to be referenced with the frequency shown in the figure. Reload the file in order of decreasing frequency of reference, with a two-pass link load; determine the average number of reads per record.

Solution:

Rewrite the file in order of decreasing frequency of reference and load the records which do not produce collisions first; then on a second pass load the synonyms, find the link pointers, and calculate the number of reads. The average number of reads per record is the total of the reads per record × frequency of reference column, as shown in Table 10–10.

Finally, we have the number of reads per record down to 1.20, which is a reasonable number, in spite of the fact that we still have 40% synonyms in the file with the hash function which we used.

Reorganization

If a file is volatile it may be necessary to reorganize the file frequently in order to keep a large number of records from producing collisions and requiring an inordinate amount of read time. Reorganization can be done in place, by unloading into another area, incrementally, or while still in use, as described in Chapter 7 for Sequential Files.

On most computer systems only a basic direct access method (BDAM) is provided for random files by the system. Thus the user will have to perform blocking if desired, all of the hashing, and most of the organization details.

TABLE 10–10. A Two Pass, Activity, Link Load of the File in Table 10–5.

Key	*Relative Address*	*Loaded at 1st Pass*	*Loaded at 2nd Pass*	*Link Pntr*	*Refer. Freq.*	*Number of Reads*	*Reads × Frequency*
Little Prince	7	7		13	20%	1	0.20
Blue-Nosed Witch	8	8		11	20%	1	0.20
Mister Blue	1	1		2	16%	1	0.16
Huge Harold	9	9		12	10%	1	0.10
Bears on Wheels	5	5			7%	1	0.07
Matti	10	10			7%	1	0.07
Fly Went By	8		11		7%	2	0.14
Twig	9		12		7%	2	0.14
Ferdinand the Bull	1		2		4%	2	0.08
Pegleg Willy	7		13		2%	2	0.04
						Total	1.20

QUESTIONS

1. Isn't it true that each record in Figure 10–1 has its own address by which it can be located? So why is blocking of random records so bad? What difference does it make?
2. a. A file with 5000 records is to be loaded into an area containing space for 6250 records. What is the packing factor?

   b. A file contains 3000 records. It is to be loaded with a loading factor of 75 percent. How many locations must be reserved for the file?
3. In Example 10–2, how could you handle the addition of the 50 cars with keys BLT007 through BLT056 to your file and still maintain direct addressing? (HINT: consider the first letter of the plate number in your hash function.)
4. a. The key of a record is called its ______ identifier.

   b. The storage address of a record is called its ______ identifier.
5. What does a hash function, or hashing, do?

6. Your company has 300 employees. Each has been assigned an employee identification number. The employee numbers are EN-001-81, EN-002-78, EN-003-82, EN-004-76, . . . ,EN-263-72, . . . ,EN-300-83, where the last two digits indicate the date of hire, and the other digits run consecutively from 1 to 300.

   a. What is a simple function for changing employee ID's to storage addresses?

   b. Would this be called direct or indirect addressing?

7. a. Wht is a synonym?

   b. What is a collision?

8. A file with 20,000 records is loaded onto a DASD.

   a. If the packing factor is 80%, space for how many records must be allowed for this file?

   b. If the packing factor is 75 percent, space for how many records must be allowed for this file?

   c. If the keys of the file convert to addresses with 20 percent synonyms, how many collisions are likely to occur when the 20,000 keys are converted?

9. The records in problem 6 are each 1064 bytes long plus a 28-byte key. The file will be stored on one contiguous extent on DASD Device II, described in Figure 5–7, Chapter 5. The storage addresses begin with record 1 on a set of tracks numbered consecutively from 302. What are the absolute track and record address of the records with keys.

   a. EN-300-83 b. EN-263-72 c. EN-112-79?

10. The records in Example 10–4 are to be unblocked, formatted with keys, and stored on DASD Device II, described in Figure 5–7, Chapter 5. Each record is 329 bytes in length plus a four-byte key. The file begins on track 3 of cylinder 183. On which track is the record for October 15? Which record on that track is October 15?

11. What if, in Example 10–5, you divide the entire Social Security Number, 468397482, by the number of record spaces, 250?

    a. What is the quotient?

    b. What does it mean?

    c. What is the remainder?

d. Will the remainder always be the same when we divide a number of record spaces into any number of digits of the key? Why or why not?

e. What happens when we divide by the prime number 241 of Example 10–6 instead of by 250?

12. Why is the quotient significant in Example 10–3 but not in Example 10–5?

13. In Example 10–5 assume that the records are 388 bytes long including the key. They are to be unblocked, formatted with keys on DASD Device II (described in Figure 5–7, Chapter 5). The records will be stored in one contiguous extent beginning at record 1, track 9, cylinder 203. What will be the absolute track and record address of the record for the employee with Social Security number 468-39-7482?

14. 8000 records are unblocked and formatted with keys on a DASD with 30 tracks per cylinder, 19,250 bytes per track. Blocks per track = (bytes per track)/(180 + C + D), where C = 0 when formatted without keys, C = 80 when formatted with keys, and D = length of key area plus data area for the block. The records have length = 496 bytes plus a 16-byte key. Keys have been converted to relative addresses 1 through 8000. Find

    a. the number of records per track.

    b. the total number of tracks required.

    c. the relative track and relative record location of the record with relative address 1213.

    d. the relative track and relative record location of the record with relative address 6820.

    If the first record is stored at the beginning of track 5, cylinder 104, what are the absolute track and record addresses of

    e. the record with relative address 1213?

    f. the record with relative address 6820?

15. 5000 records are formatted with keys and stored unblocked on DASD Device I, described in Figure 5–7, Chapter 5. The record length is 200 bytes plus a 32-byte key. The keys have been converted to relative addresses from 1 to 5000. Find

a. the number of records per track.

b. the total number of tracks required.

c. the relative track and relative record location of the record with relative address 1932.

d. the relative track and relative record location of the record with relative address 3749.

If the first record is stored at the beginning of track 1, cylinder 305, what are the absolute track and record addresses of

e. the record with relative address 1932?

f. the record with relative address 3749?

16. Use folding, dividing into halves, to convert the following keys

1 0 6 4 9 6 1 7 5 2	7 2 9 2 9 7 4 1 6 3
2 1 3 4 6 8 5 6 4 3	0 2 8 4 6 5 7 6 1 4
8 9 2 1 6 3 3 0 4 6	1 1 1 2 3 4 6 7 5 2

a. to relative addresses between 1 and 1000.

b. to relative addresses between 1 and 400.

c. Use folding, dividing into three digit segments, beginning from the right, to convert the keys into relative addresses between 1 and 100.

17. 750 records are to be loaded with a packing factor of 75 percent. Given the keys

1752 5643 3046 4163 7614 and 6753,

convert them to relative addresses in the appropriate range using radix transformation, assuming

a. the keys are written in base 8.

b. the keys are written in base 13.

18. In Example 10–9, complete converting all of the keys to relative addresses

a. between 1 and 20 b. between 1 and 200.

How many collisions occur in each case?

19. Perform a digit analysis on the keys

02010	08832	05628
14122	10914	17734
06234	02028	09814
18316	14136	11922
00424	06210	03036
12538	18322	15114
04614	01432	07224
16722	13516	19330

and convert them to a set of relative addresses between 1 and 30.

20. A file of your buddies is organized using the nicknames as keys. Use binary ASCII with no parity and add up the ones to convert the following nicknames to relative addresses between 1 and 20. How many collisions do you get?

Buzz	Liz	Snippets
Noodley	Highpockets	Trudgeon
Skinny	Grumbly	
Misty	Red	

21. Complete the conversion of the keys in Example 10–10 to relative addresses between 1 and 100.
    a. Perform at least one of the conversions by writing the hexadecimal equivalents and converting as the example shows for FBALT6 and PZFML7.
    b. Can you think of a hash method which you could use such that writing the code in hexadecimal form would give different results from writing the code in decimal? (HINT: what if you add a parity bit? or what if you do not use radix transformation?). Illustrate your method on one of the keys in Example 10–11, and show that it does give different results for hexadecimal and decimal form of the code.

22. Use decimal ASCII values for the characters and multiply them together to convert the following keys to relative addresses between 1 and 2000. Note that the product of the multiplication will nearly al-

ways be an even number. Why? You may wish not to use the low order digit of the product.

BROWN	YELLOW	PURPLE	WHITE
GREEN	RED	GOLD	GRAY
BLUE	VIOLET	BLACK	

How many collisions do you get?

23. Use the positions of the letters in the alphabet to convert the following keys to addresses between 1 and 25

HARRY TRUMAN	ABRAHAM LINCOLN
THOMAS JEFFERSON	GEORGE WASHINGTON
DWIGHT EISENHOWER	LYNDON JOHNSON
JOHN KENNEDY	

How many synonyms did you have?

24. Suppose none of the hash functions described in the chapter work acceptably for a file of major train stations in Germany. The keys of the file are the names of the cities where the stations are, such as

BONN	DARMSTADT	LUDWIGSHAFEN
FRANKFURT	MAINZ	WUPPERTAL
KOBLENZ	MUNCHEN	HEIDELBERG etc.

Create a *new* (different from any in the text) hash function which might work for this file.

25. The keys of 3000 records have already been converted to relative record numbers between 1 and 3600. The records are to be placed into buckets which are numbered consecutively beginning with 1. Each bucket can contain five records, but only four spaces in the bucket will be filled by records with different keys, so that if collisions occur among the relative record numbers, a synonym can also be placed in the bucket.

    a. How many buckets will be needed for the file?

    b. If 320 bytes (including key and overhead) must be reserved for each record, how much space is needed in the prime data area for this file?

c. What is the packing factor for the file?

d. Into which buckets would you place records with the following relative numbers: 1222 0019 1984 3133 0125?

e. Where would you put the second record whose key converts to relative address 1984?

f. Where would you put the third record whose key converts to relative address 1984?

g. What are the relative record numbers of the four records which go into bucket number 25?

26. Your activity calendar is stored by month in a prime data area as follows:

Location	*Contents*	*Link Pointer*
R1	Starting Point=	R5
R2	January	
R3	February	
R4	March	
R5	April	R9
R6	May	
R7	June	
R8	July	
R9	August	R13
R10	September	
R11	October	
R12	November	
R13	December	

The first two link pointers for reading the file in alphabetical order by month have been provided.

a. Complete the list of pointers to link the calendar alphabetically by month.

b. Create a scatter table to allow you to find any month's record in the file "immediately."

Make your own decisions about what hash function you wish to use, how long the scatter table will be, whether you wish to include the keys in the scatter table, and how to handle synonyms.

27. The text says "a blocked format [for records in a random file] really only makes sense if the records are sorted sequentially and a scatter table is used. . . ." Why would a blocked format perhaps be more appropriate in this case than for another method of storing random records?

28. Work Example 10–15 using a circular storage area with limits at 1 and 10; i.e., assume that address 1 logically follows address 10.

29. Perform a *two-pass* progressive read load on the file in Table 10–5 and calculate the average number of reads per record.

30. Add

Record	*Relative Address*
Five O'Clock Charlie	9
My Name is Lion	3
Burton and Dudley	1

and calculate the average number of reads per record for

a. the progressive read load of Example 10–15 (Table 10–6).

b. the two-pass link load of Example 10–17 (Table 10–8).

c. the link load with synonyms in a separate area in Example 10–18 (Table 10–9).

d. Add a separate link field to your file in parts a, b, and c above to allow you to read the file in alphabetically sequential order.

31. Assume you have the following records in a random file:

Key converts to	*Relative Address*	*Frequency of Reference*
Adams	1	2.5%
Baker	2	2.5%
Charlie	1	40%
Dog	3	2.5%
Elmer	4	2.5%
Fred	5	10%
George	3	2.5%
Henry	6	2.5%
Ida	3	20%
James	4	15%

Using Tables 10–6 through 10–9 in the text as examples, show where the records are loaded, what the link pointers are (if applicable), the number of reads to locate the records, and the average number of reads per record for

a. a one-pass link load of the file.

b. a two-pass link load of the file.

c. a one-pass progressive read load of the file.

d. an activity-sequence progressive read load of the file.

32. For the following cookie recipe file, which is stored in alphabetical order,

Key	*Frequency of Reference*	*Key*	*Frequency of Reference*
Applesauce	4%	Lemon	4%
Butter	5%	Macaroon	4%
Chocolate Chip	25%	Molasses	4%
Date	4%	Oatmeal	8%
Fig	4%	Peanut Butter	8%
Ginger Snap	20%	Sugar	10%

perform each of the following and calculate the average number of reads per record in each case (see below for a description of the hash code)

a. progressive read load.

b. a one-pass link load.

c., d. a two pass link load; and write a scatter table.

e. an activity load with progressive read.

f. an activity, two pass, link load.

For your *hash code* add up the *decimal* value of ASCII (with no parity) for the letters (not spaces) and use the quotient/remainder function to convert to addresses between 1 and *13*. For example,

Key	*Relative Address*
Ginger Snap	6
Molasses	8

Ginger Snap

$\rightarrow 71 + 105 + 110 + 103 + 101 + 114 + 83 + 110 + 97 + 112 = 1006$

$1006 / 13 = 77$ Remainder 5 Address $= 5 + 1 = 6$.

Molasses $\rightarrow 77 + 111 + 108 + 97 + 115 + 115 + 101 + 115 = 839$

$839 / 13 = 64$ Remainder 7 Address $= 7 + 1 = 8$.

CHAPTER 11

PARTITIONED AND INDEXED ORGANIZATIONS

Often we need to be able to read a file sequentially *and* find individual records quickly. One way of doing this is to organize the data sequentially and use a scatter table as shown in the last chapter. Indeed, this is very much like the *indexed sequential* file organization which will be discussed in this chapter, although we will refine and improve upon that method, which poses major difficulties when records must be added to the file.

Another way of organizing files so that large parts of the file can be found rapidly and then read sequentially is called *partitioned organization.* In this case, rather than find an individual record quickly, it is necessary to locate a major portion of the file, which will then be read in sequential order. We will discuss this type of organization before discussing indexed sequential files.

PARTITIONED FILES

Suppose that you have been hired to develop a self-guided walking tour of a small zoo. You have printed a map, such as that sketched in Figure 11–1, which outlines the locations of the different exhibits and suggests a path which can be followed to see everything. At each station, you will provide CRT screens connected to the central computer, which will allow the patron to call up the names of the animals and see a written description of that species. For example, at the tiger area, the visitor could type in "Bengal," and several pages of information about Bengal Tigers would be displayed for the patron to read.

A good way to handle this information in the computer is with a partitioned organization. In a *partitioned file,* the information is divided into members, large blocks of information. Each member is itself a sequential subfile, and a directory is maintained which contains the names and storage addresses of all of the members. When it is desired to access the information for a particular member of the file, the name or key of that member is specified. The computer searches the directory for the name of that member, then reads the subfile sequentially from the indicated location in the storage area.

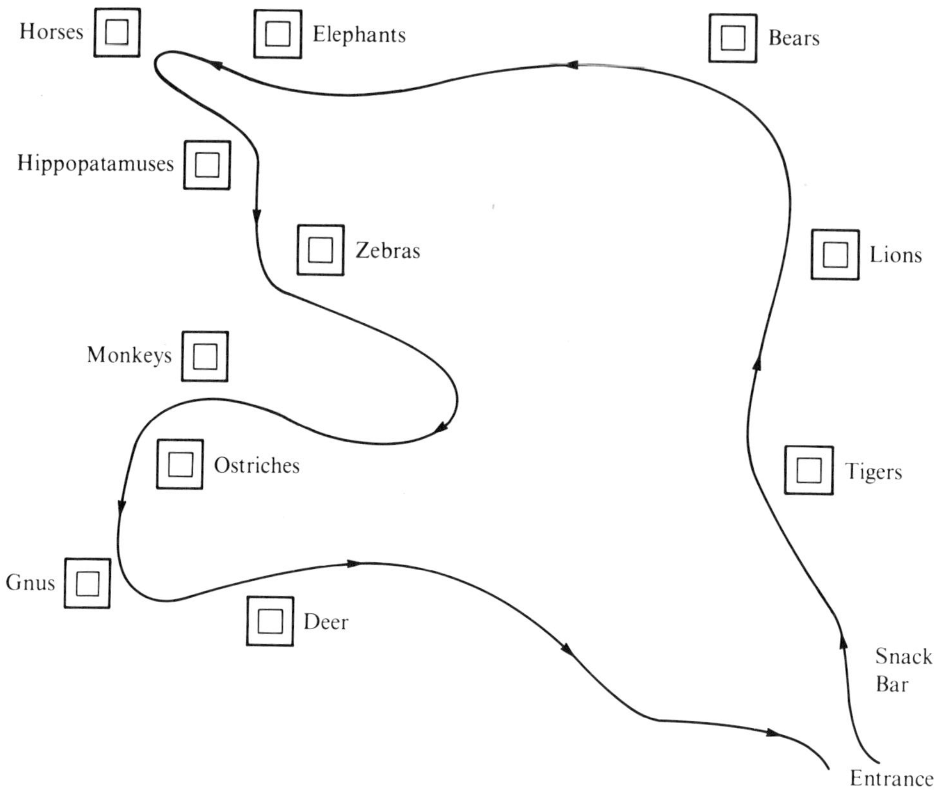

FIGURE 11–1. Touring the Zoo

Obviously, a partitioned file must be stored on a direct access storage device (DASD), since members are located by the address stored in the directory. Records within a member are stored and read in the order in which they were written, i. e., sequentially. In general, member record formats are quite flexible. They may be formatted with or without keys, blocked or unblocked, and with fixed or variable length. However, in order to keep the access method relatively simple, it is suggested that all the records in a given member be of the same format.

Partitioned File Directory

In a partitioned file, the order in which the members are stored in the data area need not be the same as the order in which the member names appear in the directory. That means that the directory can be sorted or reorganized without reorganizing the members. In addition to some non-data information present in every record on a DASD as described in Chapter 5, the directory contains one record for each member of the set. Directory records will generally have a key area, containing the name of the member, and a data area containing the address of the member. For the zoo example, part of the directory might appear as shown in Figure 11–2.

Note that this particular directory appears to have been organized alphabetically, even though the members are not stored in that order on the disk.

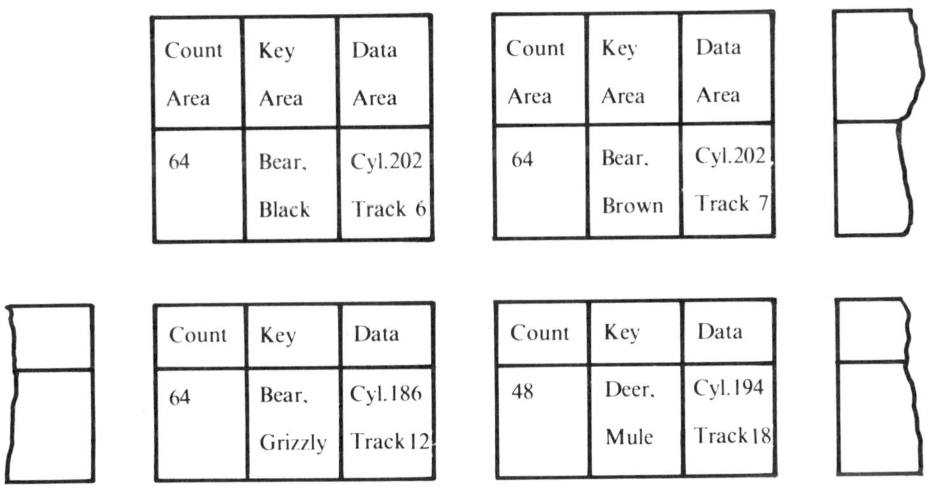

FIGURE 11–2. Excerpt from Directory of Partitioned Zoo File

The count field in a directory record contains information such as the number of bytes required by this directory record. The data area of the directory records must contain the starting address of the member named in the key field. In addition, the directory data area may contain other information which the user desires. If directory records are written in sequential order, they may be blocked with each block preceded by a key area containing, as usual, a repeat of the key of the last entry in the block.

Storage Organization

A partitioned file requires DASD storage space not only for the records of the sequential members but also for the directory. There is usually a major difference between these two areas. In principle, the storage area for the member subfiles is unlimited. Thus, a common access method may not allow reuse of the area where a member has been stored and then logically deleted without complete reorganization of the file. A new member is simply stored in a new extent. If the area originally designated for the members of the file is filled, new space is allocated automatically. On the other hand, the size of the directory area must be specified in advance on most systems and will be fixed, both in the number of bytes it can occupy and in the number of entries it can hold. When the directory is "full," no more records can be added to the file. For this reason the access methods are usually written to allow the user to reuse the area in a directory from which an entry has been logically deleted.

Partitioned File Uses

Partitioned organization is useful whenever a predetermined quantity of information is to be retrieved sequentially without having to read all of the data from a large file. Common applications will be in situations similar to the zoo example illustrated in Figures 11–1 and 11–2.

The most familiar application is the storage of user data files or programs on a floppy disk in a small system or on a reserved disk area in a large, multi-user system. The programs or files are members of an entire set of files defined by the areas assigned on the disk. The directory contains information about the name, size, location, and status of the members and can be examined by commands such as DIR, CATALOG, MAP, etc. (depending upon the job control language of the system). The members can be called up, read, and examined sequentially by commands such as LIST, COPY, OLD Name, etc.

The directory will have a limited size, normally about 64 record entries or so. It will be stored on a designated track or tracks on a floppy disk or in a designated area on a large disk system. When members are deleted from the file, the directory entries may be reused; but when the directory is full, no more programs or subfiles may be added to the area, even if the allocated area is not filled, until some directory entry has been deleted. The user may never become aware that member areas are not reused when deletions are made, because reorganization occurs automatically on most systems as part of a LOG OFF or LOG ON procedure. However, the problem may become apparent as a disk area fills or as a user's status is changed (perhaps as a larger area is allocated and the user must log off and back on again to obtain use of the larger area).

INDEXED SEQUENTIAL FILES

An organization method similar to that of partitioned files but offering the capability of quick access to a single record or a small range of records is called *indexed sequential* organization. In addition, an indexed sequential file can be read quickly in sequential order by keys.

The indexed sequential file organization has the advantages of direct or random organization (finding individual records quickly) and of sequential organization (reading all of the records in order). Also inherent in this type of file organization is that the user need do only a relatively small amount of advance planning before such a file is created. No concern need be taken over finding an appropriate hash function, how the file is to be loaded, how synonyms will be handled, etc.

Superficially, then, it appears that an indexed sequential file represents the best of all possible worlds. However it does have some problems which keep it from being perfect. First, the access methods written to handle such a file are large and complex. Second, access to individual records takes somewhat longer than in a directly organized file, and access becomes considerably slower as additions are made to the file. Finally, there are problems, which are not trivial, of maintaining accurate indexes and pointers and of reorganizing a volatile file often to prevent unacceptable deterioration in access speed. Thus an indexed sequential file becomes almost unmanageable for large, volatile data bases.

What Does an Indexed Sequential File Look Like?

Just as a partitioned file has a directory of members, an indexed sequential file has an *index* of the records in the file. At this point, most of the similarity between partitioned and indexed sequential files ends. The index of an indexed sequential file is always ordered by keys. Each index entry contains the highest key value in a block (of one or more records) and the address of the block. If the index of records or blocks is itself quite long, there may be a higher level index in which are recorded the largest keys and addresses of blocks of index. For very large files there may be a multilevel hierarchy of indexes.

In addition to the *index area,* there will be a *prime data area* in which the data records themselves are stored in *key sequential order.* The prime data area is as large as is needed to store all of the records. Although records are usually blocked, this is not mandatory. However, it is essential that records be formatted with keys so that the indexes make sense. The prime data area need not be one contiguous extent, but the use of multiple extents will normally be transparent to the user and is generally of little concern except to those who manage the operating system.

Also, every volatile indexed sequential file must have an *overflow area,* where provision is made for addition of records to the file. The overflow area may comprise tracks reserved for this purpose within each prime data cylinder, separate cylinders reserved at the end of the entire file, or some combination of these.

Example 11–1

As an elementary example of an indexed sequential file, consider a file in which the keys are the names of energy sources, such as

Biomass	Diesel
Carbide	Electrochemical
Coal	etc.,

and the data would be the availability, reserves, relative cost, and so forth for each source. In an indexed sequential file, each index entry refers to an entire block of records. For the sake of illustration we assume that three records are written in each block. The file would appear as shown in Figure 11–3.

Some comments should be made about Example 11–1. In the index are recorded the highest keys in each block and the address of each block. The index entries as well as the records in the prime data area are in key sequential order. The entire file may be read in sequential order by starting at the first record on the first track of the prime data area and reading all records in the order in which they are stored.

Notice that the records for Shale Oil and Ocean Currents were added, in that order, after the rest of the file had been created. Figure 11–3 illustrates

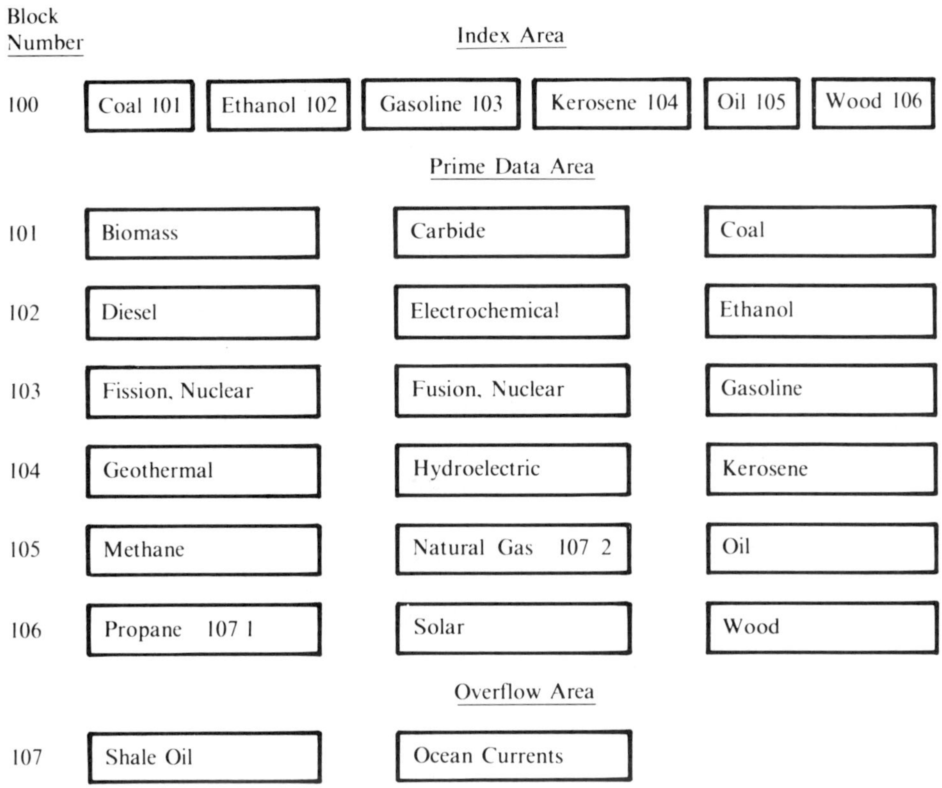

FIGURE 11–3. An Indexed Sequential File of Energy Sources

one method of adding a record—namely, writing it directly to the overflow area and placing a pointer in the record which logically precedes it. This, and other methods of handling additions to an indexed sequential file, will be discussed in detail later.

The Prime Data Area

The records in the prime data area of an indexed sequential file must be formatted *with keys* and written in key sequential order. Each record must have a unique key. To keep the access method as uncomplicated as possible, all keys should be the same number of bytes in length. Also, you will probably wish to make all the records the same format. Records may be unblocked or blocked, with the highest record key in the block recorded in the block key area as shown in Figure 11–4. There will be one index entry for each block. If

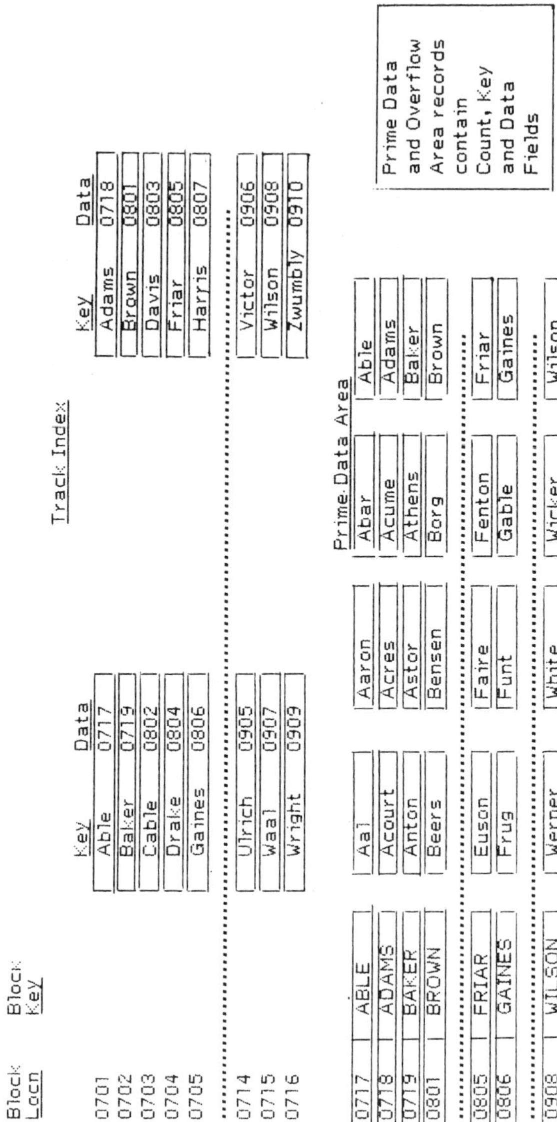

FIGURE 11–4. An Indexed Sequential File of Precinct Voters

the records are unblocked, they can be considered to be blocked with a blocking factor of 1, in which case the index will contain one entry for each record.

The Index Area

Indexes may be sparse or dense. The ultimate *dense index* is one for a file of unblocked records, for which there is one index entry for each record. The ultimate *sparse index* would be a rather useless entity which contained one entry, the key of the last record in the file and the address of the first record in the file; i. e., an index which considered the file as one large block with a blocking factor equal to the total number of records in the file. Obviously, the most useful indexes will lie somewhere between these two extremes.

You should be aware of the tradeoffs between sparse and dense indexes. If an index is sparse it will be relatively short, and you will spend little time searching it to find the address of the block which contains the record you want. But the block will be large, and some time will be required to extract the appropriate record. On the other hand, if the index is dense, most of your time will be spent searching the lengthy index. Then the block to which the index entry points will be small, and the record can be extracted quickly.

The Track Index

On large disk systems it is often convenient to consider each track to be a block of records, and index entries then contain the highest record key and the address of the track. This type of index is called a *track index*. We will use the term track index in our illustrations throughout the chapter, well aware that "track" can be interpreted as a block of any size and that the "track" address is simply the relative or absolute address of the block.

Figure 11–4 shows a file containing records whose keys could be the names of voters on a precinct registration list. In this file, the blocking factor is 4. The locations ("Block Locn") in the figure can be interpreted as relative block numbers or as cylinder and track addresses on a DASD. Note that in the prime data area only the keys have been shown for brevity. Each record of course will have Count, Key, and Data fields containing the information we wish to store in the file.

The access methods are simplest if all track index entries are written in fixed length format. The user may wish to leave room in the data area of the track index entries to record information other than the block address, such as blocking factors, record lengths, or record types (if they differ) in the prime data area.

Example 11–2

Beginning with the track index in Figure 11–4, find the information contained in the file for Faire.

Solution:

Read the track index, beginning at location 0701 (which could be interpreted as block 0701 or as cylinder 07, track 01) until you find the first entry which is not less than Faire, namely, Friar 0805.

This tells you that the record for Faire is in block 0805 or on cylinder 08, track 05. Then read all of the records in this block until you find Faire.

The Cylinder Index

In Figure 11–5 the file of Figure 11–4 has been reproduced, but there are two *"higher" levels of index* shown above the track index. If the track index is large, covering more than three or four tracks itself, it may be blocked. Each block in the track index is then referenced by an entry in a next higher level index. The higher level index entry contains the highest key in a track index block and the address where that block of the track index is found. It is often convenient on a large DASD to block track index entries together so that the entries in one block refer to all of the records on a single cylinder. The index of locations of blocks of track index is then appropriately called a *cylinder index,* and this name is commonly used for the second level index whether or not it is directly related to the contents of a single cylinder.

The cylinder index may be stored in the same extent with the file, as suggested by Figure 11–5, or it may be elsewhere, even on a different disk if desired. Note that the particular cylinder index in Figure 11–5 is rather dense, since the blocking factor for track index records in this case is only 2.

The Master Index

For a very large file or with relatively dense indexes, the cylinder index itself may be too large to search in an acceptable time. In this case a third level of index may be written in the same form as the lower levels of index. The third level is commonly called a *Master Index.* A master index entry contains the highest key in a block of cylinder index records and the address of that cylinder index block. It is conceivable that the master index could be

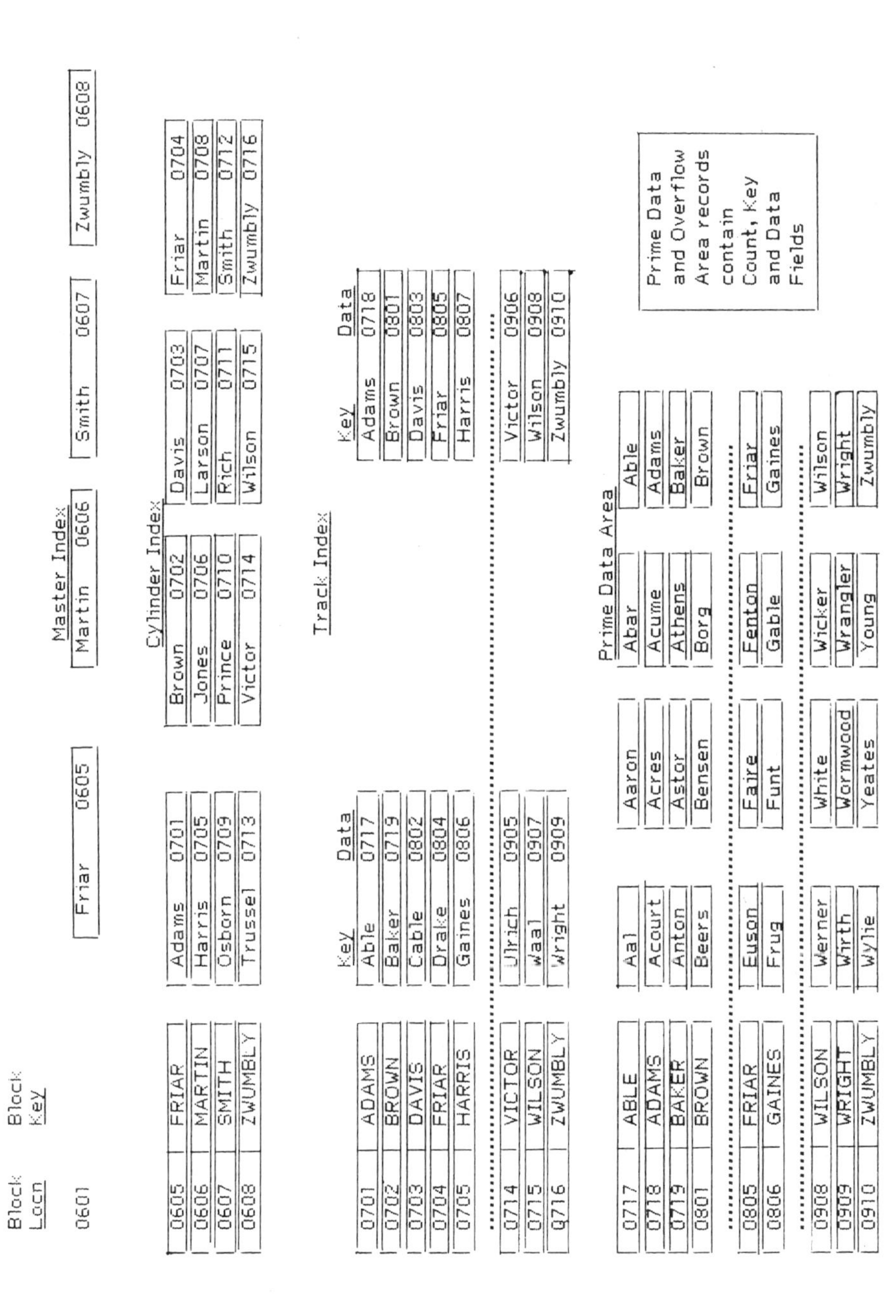

FIGURE 11–5. An Indexed Sequential File of Precinct Voters with Cylinder and Master Indexes

large enough to warrant a higher level master index and so on, ad infinitum. However, most indexed sequential files will require at most three index levels.

Example 11–3

Beginning with the Master Index in Figure 11–5, find the record for Astor.

Solution:

Read the master index until you find an entry with a key not less than Astor namely, Friar 0605.

Proceed to address 0605 (which may be a relative block address or an absolute address, such as cylinder 06, track 05) and read this block of the cylinder index until an entry with a key not larger than Astor is found, namely, Brown 0702.

Find the track index block at address 0702 and read track index entries until one not less than Astor is found, namely, Baker 0719.

Go to address 0719 in the prime data area and read records consecutively until the desired record for Astor is found, the second record in the block.

Some room may be left at the end of each index for *dummy entries*. These are index entries with all l's, a key such as ZZZZZZ, or some other indicator that this entry does not yet refer to an existing part of the file. Dummy entries provide for addition of records with keys higher than any yet recorded in the file, as will be shown later. A search of indexes is usually performed linearly as indicated in Example 11–3 above. However, if indexes are large and the file is relatively static, you could write your access method to perform a binary search of the indexes.

OVERFLOW

The Overflow Area

There are three common methods of adding new records to an indexed sequential file. These are

1. Sparse loading.
2. Placing new records into an overflow area.
3. Placing new records in sequential order in the prime data blocks and bumping from the end of the block into an overflow area.

The last two of these involve setting aside a special *overflow area* where records are placed for which there is no room in the prime data area.

Sparse Loading

One way of handling additions to a file is to load the file sparsely in the first place. Leaving room for extra records in each block accommodates nicely the addition of records. Of course, utilization of storage space is not particularly efficient if up to half of the record spaces are unused initially; however, if memory space is not a problem, the method is easy to apply. Another problem with *sparse loading* is that it is impossible to predict in advance which blocks will need to accommodate the most additions. Eventually some block will require adding one more record than there are free spaces, while other blocks may have no additions at all. At that time the user must decide what to do with the extra records. Usually, a time-consuming reorganization of the file is demanded. The reorganization may be postponed for a time by placing new additions in available slots in other blocks and providing a chain of pointers; however, reorganization is inevitable. It may be better to face up to it sooner than later, as the following example indicates.

Example 11–4

Assume that each prime data block in Figure 11–5 has room for six records, but that only the four shown have been recorded, leaving two spaces free for additions.

a. Show how you would add records Acron, Atters, and Barton to the file.
b. What would happen when you subsequently try to add Acme and Adair?

Solution:

a. To simplify the addition procedure we will set down some rules:
   (1) Keep the records in sequential order by inserting in the proper place and moving subsequent records toward the end of the block.

(2) Never insert a record into a block unless the key of that record is less than the largest key already in the block. *This prevents us from having to change any index entries.* Why?

Thus Acron will go between Acres and Acume in block 0718, Atters will go between Athens and Baker in block 0719, and Barton will be placed before record Beers in block 0801 (*not* after Baker in block 0719).

After adding these records, blocks 0717 through 0801 will appear as shown in Figure 11–6. No changes will have been made in the indexes.

b. We now add Acme to the beginning of block 0718 (*not* to the end of block 0717) so that block 0718 is now full and appears as

Block Locn	*Block Key*						
0718	ADAMS	*Acme*	Acourt	Acres	Acron	Acume	Adams

An attempt to add Adair (between Acume and Adams in block 0718) leads to an overflow from the block. The questions arise of where to place the overflow record and whether Adair or Adams should overflow. One temporary way of handling the situation is to place Adams in the next available location (at the end of block 0719) and place a pointer (0719, record 6) to it in the last record of block 0718, as shown in Figure 11–7. But this only postpones the permanent solution of creating more

Block Locn	Block Key						
0717	ABLE	Aal	Aaron	Abar	Able		
0718	ADAMS	Acourt	Acres	Acron	Acume	Adams	
0719	BAKER	Anton	Astor	Athens	Atters	Baker	
0801	BROWN	Barton	Beers	Bensen	Borg	Brown	

FIGURE 11–6. Sparsely Loaded Blocks 0717–0801 of the Precinct Voters Files after Addition of Acron, Atters, and Barton

FIGURE 11–7. Sparsely Loaded Blocks 0717–0801 of the Precinct Voters File after Addition of Acme and Adair

space, rewriting the file, and updating the indexes—in short, reorganizing. You can see that adding more records to blocks 0718 or 0719 can be accomplished only with considerable effort.

Cylinder Overflow Areas and Separate Overflow Cylinders

Other than sparse loading, the handling of additions to an indexed sequential file requires that some records be written into an overflow area reserved for this purpose. Reading a block to which additions have been made generally means jumping back and forth between the prime data and overflow areas. This can degrade access time significantly; exactly how much depends upon where the overflow area is physically located.

If the tracks on which overflow records are written are on the same cylinder with the corresponding prime data records, switching back and forth between prime data blocks and overflow areas is a matter of electronic head selection and is done in microseconds. Tracks reserved for overflow at the end of a cylinder containing prime data are called a *cylinder overflow area.* Alternatively, if the overflow records are stored on a cylinder separate from the prime data area, then reading prime data blocks and overflow records requires motion of the access arm. Use of such a *separate overflow cylinder* will slow down record access considerably.

A cylinder overflow area, although it allows much faster access, shares some of the same problems with sparse loading. It is difficult to predict which blocks will have the most record additions and how many tracks to reserve for overflow on each cylinder. Inevitably, some cylinders will have many additions, and the cylinder overflow area will fill quickly, while other cylinders have mostly empty cylinder overflow areas. There inevitably comes a time when the user has to decide what to do with one more record than can fit in the cylinder overflow area. A temporary solution could be to place the record at some other available location and provide a pointer. The permanent solution, of course, is a reorganization of the file.

Many systems use a combination of cylinder overflow areas and separate overflow cylinders. When the cylinder overflow area is filled, additional records can be written into the separate cylinder. Choosing the right balance, how much space to reserve on each cylinder so that a minimum of space is wasted and yet a minimum amount of overflow occurs into a separate cylinder, is a task the wise performance of which makes a senior programmer valuable.

Placing New Records into an Overflow Area

A second method of handling new records, other than sparse loading, is to place them directly into an overflow area. Pointers must be provided in the prime data and in the overflow records so that the records can be found. With this method, no space for additions need be provided within prime data blocks, and changes usually need not be made in indexes when records are added. Because none of the prime data records are moved, data integrity is not compromised. However, space must be reserved in each prime data record for the possible addition of pointers. Also, reading a block to which additions have been made means jumping between prime data and overflow areas. The amount by which this degrades access time depends upon whether the records are in a cylinder overflow area or on a separate cylinder.

Example 11–5

a. Add records for Asner, Acron, Atters, and Adair to the file of Figure 11–5 by placing the added records directly into an overflow area and providing pointers as needed. Assume that each block in the overflow area can contain three records.

b. Add records Acrid and Afton to the file in the same manner.

Solution:

a. Figure 11–8 shows the file after adding Asner, Acron, Atters, and Adair.

Notice that the pointers in the prime data and overflow records refer to block and relative record number; for example,

1008/2 means record 2 in block 1008.

Also be aware that we have not had to change any index entries because the last records in each prime data block have remained the same. The records in the prime data area are still in sequential order by key. Records in the overflow area are not necessarily in key sequential order but are linked to the appropriate prime data blocks by pointers. If the block locations are interpreted as cylinder and track numbers (i. e., 1008 is cylinder 10, track 08), then the overflow area shown in the figure is a separate overflow cylinder.

b. Adding Acrid to the file (at block 1009, record 2) involves following the standard procedure for adding a record to a linked list. The record which precedes Acrid (namely Acres) is changed to point to Acrid, and the pointer assigned to Acrid is that previously assigned to Acres, as shown in Figure 11–9.

Adding Afton presents a serious problem, however, and requires a decision. Does Afton belong logically at the end of block 0718 or at the beginning of block 0719? Our inclination would be to put it at the beginning of block 0719 so that the index entries for 0718 and 0719 need not be changed. If we do that, however, there is no place to put a pointer (before the first record, Anton, in block 0719) which indicates that Afton is there. If we place Afton logically at the end of track 0718, the block 0718 has Afton (not Adams) as its highest key; and the track index entry (record 2 of block 0701) must be changed. Also, this requires a change (from Adams to Afton) in record 1 of block 0605 of the cylinder index; if the conditions were right (or wrong?) it could require changing the master index also (although that is not necessary in this case).

In our example we will choose to add Afton logically to the end of block 0718 and change the indexes as necessary, fully aware that we would have to write tests and procedures in our access method to handle the special situation of adding a record whose key lies between existing blocks. Physically, of course, Afton goes in the first available location in the overflow area (record 3 of block 1009), and a pointer to Afton is provided in record Adams. The pointer in Afton will have to be some special code indicating that Afton is the logical end of the block. A common way of doing this is to use a byte of 1's, decimal 255, as the "pointer to nowhere", which we have done.

Figure 11–9 shows the file after adding Acrid and Afton.

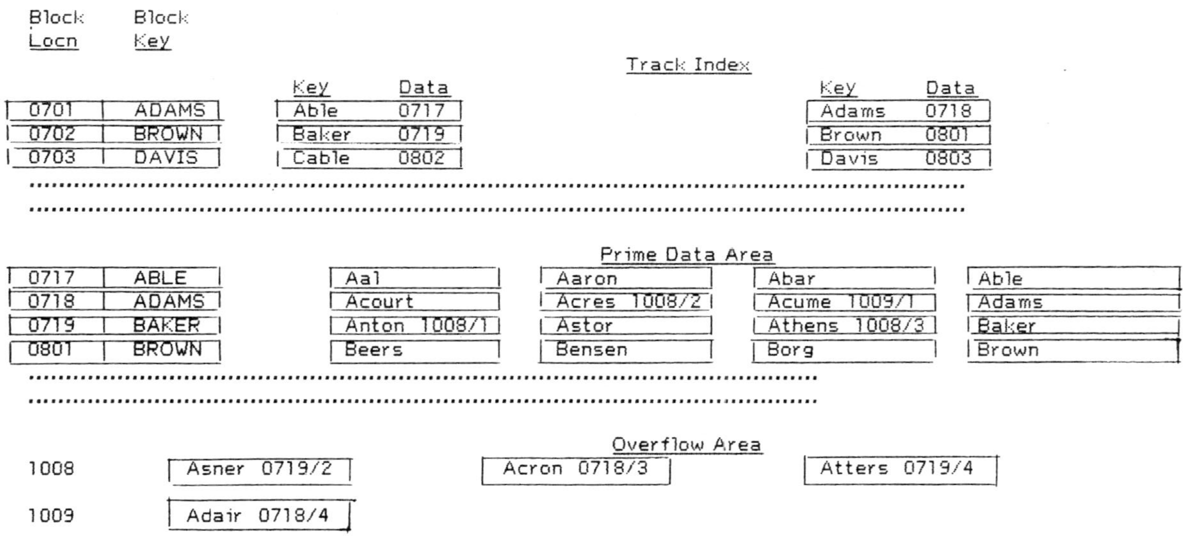

FIGURE 11–8. The File of Precinct Voters with Asner, Acron, Atters, and Adair Added in an Overflow Area

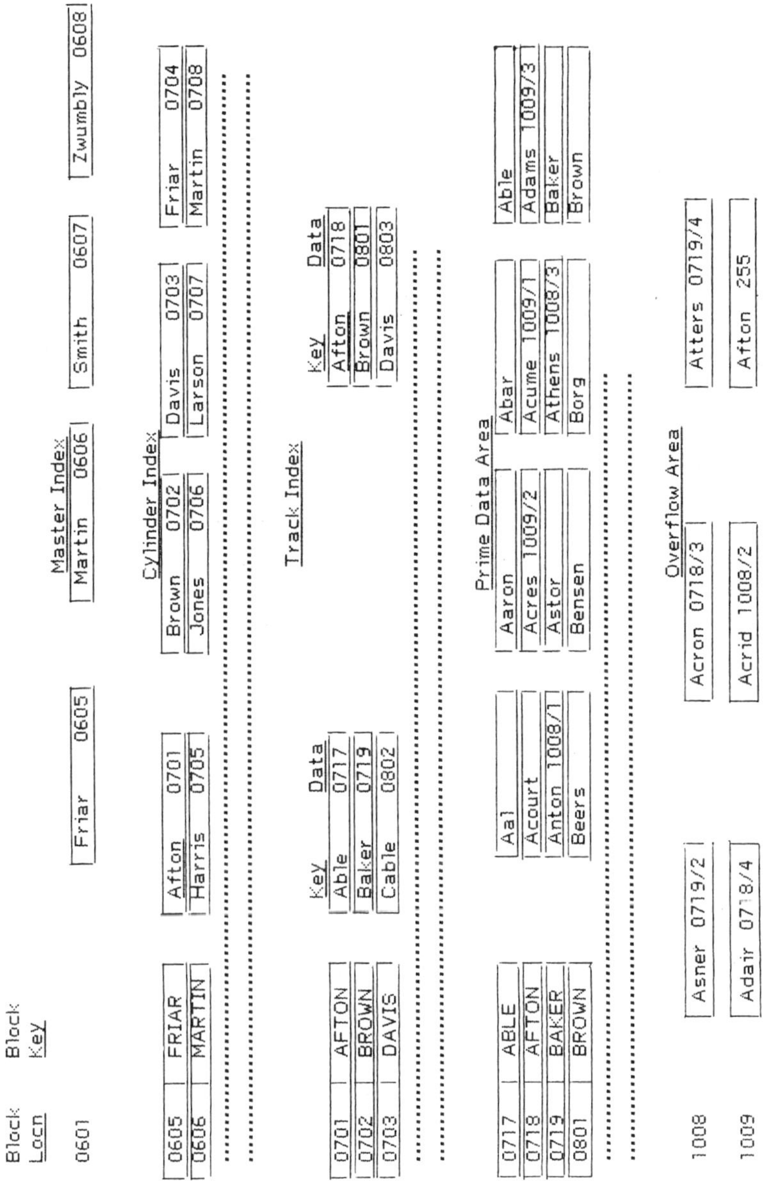

FIGURE 11–9. The File Precinct Voters after Adding Asner, Acron, Atters, Adair, Acrid, and Afton to an Overflow Area

Inserting Additions in Sequential Order into Prime Data Blocks

Still another method of adding records to an indexed sequential file is to insert the records to be added in proper sequential order into the appropriate block in the prime data area, move all of the succeeding records in the block one record space toward the end of the block, and bump the last record in the block into the overflow area. With this method, no pointers need be provided within prime data records. All records in the prime data area are in sequential order, so that when reading a block there is no need to jump back and forth between prime data tracks and overflow tracks. The keys of the overflow records fall between the last record key physically in the prime data block and the originally highest key in that block. Overflow records are in no predictable order and must be linked together with pointers. No space is necessary in the prime data records for pointers; however, the number of track index records is doubled.

For each block of data there are now two track index records, normal and overflow. For a block to which no additions have been made, the track index records appear as shown in Figure 11–10.

When additions are made to a block, the Normal-Key and Overflow-Data areas of the index are changed. The Normal-Key area is changed to contain the new highest key physically in the block (remember, the previously highest key record has been bumped into the overflow area). The Overflow-Data area originally contains a byte of 1's, decimal 255, or some similar "pointer to nowhere," indicating that there is no overflow from this block. When additions are made, the Overflow-Data area is changed to point to the location of the latest overflow record from the block. The latest overflow record will in turn have a pointer to the previous record which overflowed. Of course, if the latest overflow record is the only overflow record from the block, then it will contain the 255 pointer to nowhere indicating the end of the chain of overflow records from the block.

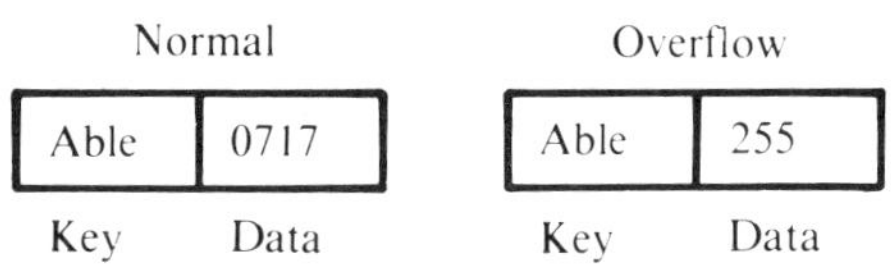

FIGURE 11–10. Normal and Overflow Track Index Records for a Prime Data Block at Address 0717 to Which No Additions Have Been Made

It is important that the Normal-Data area of the track index record never get changed; it always points to the original block address. Neither does the Overflow-Key area change. The latter always contains the original permanent highest key in the block, which will always be the end of the chain of overflow records from the block. No record may ever be added to the block or its chain of overflow records which has a key higher than the original highest key.

Often with this method of handling additions, *dummy records,* unused spaces are provided at the end of each index level in case a record with key higher than any original key in the file is added. This is the only situation which would require a new index entry to be created.

Example 11–6

a. Add records for Asner, Acron, Atters, and Acquit to the file of Figure 11–5 by placing the added records into the appropriate prime data blocks, moving records from the ends of the blocks into an overflow area, and providing overflow records in the track index. Assume that each block in the overflow area can contain three records.

b. Add records Acrid and Afton to the file in the same manner. Also add a record with key Zygurgy.

Solution:

a. Figure 11–11 shows the file after adding Asner, Acron, Atters, and Acquit.

   Notice that pointers in the overflow track index records and in the overflow area refer to block and relative record number, for example:

   1008/2 means record 2 in block 1008.

   Overflow track index records have been provided even for those blocks which have no overflow, so that they can be compared with those which do have overflow. Cylinder and Master Indexes have not changed from Figure 11–5.

   The changes made in track indexes are as follows: Track Index Normal-Key area always is the highest key physically in the block, and

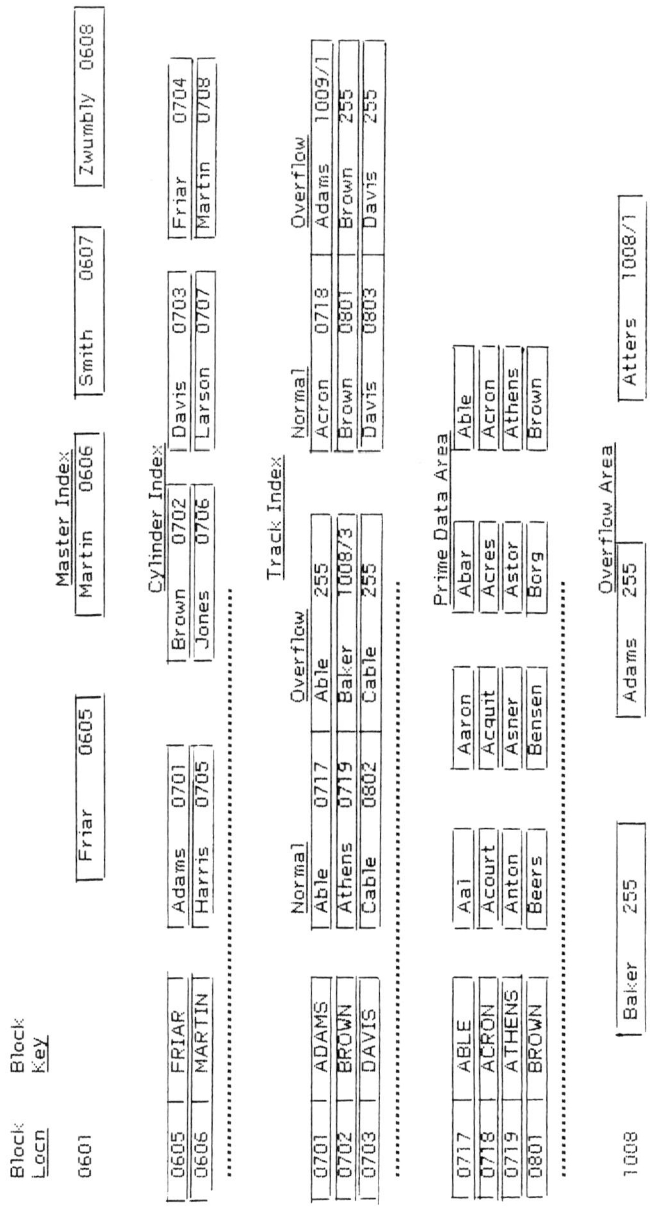

FIGURE 11–11. The File of Precinct Voters after Adding Asner, Acron, Atters, and Acquit in Prime Data Blocks

Track Index Overflow-Data area always points to the latest record bumped into the overflow area from the prime data block.

Records in the prime data blocks are always in key sequential order. Records in the overflow area have unpredictable order and must be linked together by pointers.

You should follow through the procedure of adding Asner, Acron, Atter, and Acquit, one at a time, in that order, to show yourself how the overflow records, pointers, and index changes occurred.

b. Adding Acrid simply requires placing Acrid after Acres in block 0718, moving Acron to the overflow area, and changing the track index Normal-Key and Overflow-Data entries accordingly.

Afton is added *at the beginning* of block 0719, since its key is larger than the highest key (Adams) allowed in block 0718 and smaller than the first key (Anton) in block 0719. This bumps Athens into the overflow area and requires changing track index entries.

Zygurgy is larger than any other entry in the file. Thus, if we have allowed room, in the form of dummy entries in the index areas, Zygurgy is added in a new block; new index entries are created to accommodate that block.

The final form of the file is shown in Figure 11–12.

Example 11–7

Illustrate how the record Acume is found in Figure 11–12.

Solution:

Beginning with the master index, find the first entry not larger than Acume, namely Friar 0605.

In block 0605 of the cylinder index, find the first entry not larger than Acume, namely Adams 0701.

In block 0701 of the track index, find the first entry not larger than Acume. This is the overflow entry associated with block 0718 of the prime data area, namely Adams 1009/2.

In block 1009 of the overflow area look at record 2. Is this Acume? No—it is Acron and has a pointer 1009/1. Look at the record indicated by the pointer, the first record in block 1009. Is this Acume? Yes, you have found the record you were seeking.

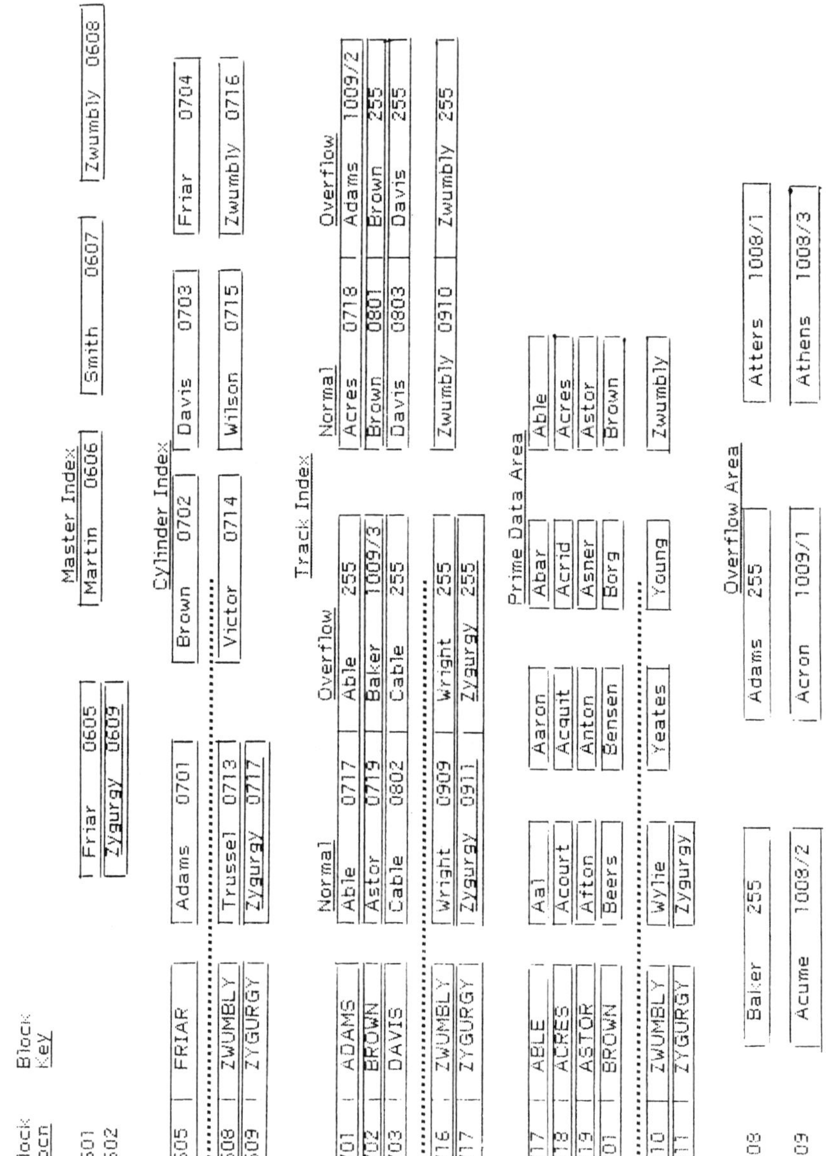

FIGURE 11–12. The File of Precinct Voters after Adding Asner, Acron, Atters, Acquit, Acrid, Afton, and Zygurgy in Prime Data Blocks

DELETIONS FROM AN INDEXED SEQUENTIAL FILE

Logical deletions from an indexed sequential file are reasonably straightforward. They are performed, as in most other types of file organization, by flagging a record to be deleted with some signal, such as two bytes of 1's. No matter how an indexed sequential file was loaded or how additions are made, the access method is generally written so that the logically deleted space becomes available for addition of records.

Deleting from a Sparsely Loaded File

In a sparsely loaded file, *physical* deletions can also be accomplished, if desired, without reorganizing the entire file. This is done by moving records in the block back to the left to fill in the deleted record spaces and to leave the blank spaces at the end of the block. (See Example 11–8.)

Deleting Records from a File Where Additions Have Been Placed Directly in the Overflow Area

Possibly the simplest way to delete records from a file where records are added directly to an overflow area is logically. In this case the deleted record should be flagged by a "deleted" indicator (two bytes of 1's or something similar). The pointers in the file are then changed in the same manner as deleting from a linked list. To do this, find the record which logically precedes the record to be deleted and replace its pointer with the one in the record which is deleted. Note that a record which has no explicit pointer implicitly points to the next record in the block. Example 10–9 illustrates a number of situations which can occur.

Deleting Records from a File Where Overflow Occurs from the Ends of the Blocks

In the type of indexed sequential file illustrated in Figure 11–12, additions are made within the primary data blocks so that the records in the prime data area are always in key sequential order. Logical deletions of records from this type of file are performed in the same manner described in the previous section except that pointers need not be provided in the prime data area. (See Example 10–10.)

Example 11–8

a. Delete Acres and Acume from the sparsely loaded file shown in Figure 11–7.

b. Delete Brown from the file.

Solution:

Figure 11–13 illustrates the results of the following steps. Strike-throughs indicate that a record has been flagged as *logically* deleted.

a. Acres and Acume may be physically removed from the file and the following records moved to the left to fill in the empty spaces. This brings Adams back from the arbitrary place where it was located and eliminates the necessity of a pointer in Adair.

b. If we delete Brown (the last record in block 0801) physically, the block key must be changed (to Borg), the corresponding track index entry must be changed, and (in this case) the cylinder index entry must be changed (see Figure 11–5). Certainly, if we are writing our own access method, we have the liberty to do this. However, to preserve the integrity of the divisions between blocks, we may wish only to delete Brown logically by placing a "deleted" flag (such as two bytes of 1's) in the data area. Then we can leave the indexes unchanged until the file is reorganized or until we need Brown's space at the end of block 0801 for future additions.

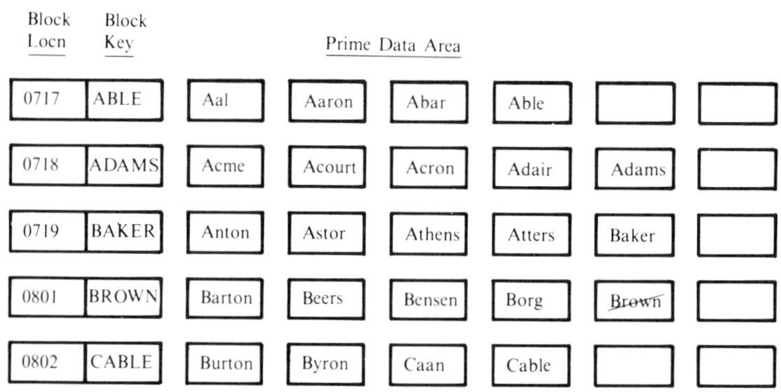

FIGURE 11–13. Sparsely Loaded File of Precinct Voters File of Figure 11–7 after Physically Deleting Acres and Acume and Logically Deleting Brown

The file after these deletions could appear as shown in Figure 11–13.

Example 11–9

Delete the following records from the file of Figure 11–9:

a. Aaron b. Acume c. Atters d. Anton e. Brown

Solution:

The results of the following steps are illustrated in Figure 11–14, where strike-throughs indicate records which have been flagged as logically deleted.

a. Logically deleting Aaron is easy. Simply flag Aaron as deleted, and place a pointer in Aal which points to the position to which Aaron pointed (implicitly) before, namely 0717/3.
b. Deleting Acume is almost as simple. Flag Acume deleted. The record which logically precedes Acume is in the overflow area, record 2 in block 1008, namely Acron 0718/3. Change the pointer in this record to the value which was in Acume, namely 1009/1.
c. Atters is found in the overflow area, but deleting it is no different. Flag Atters as deleted. The record which logically precedes Atters is Athens 1008/3, in record 3, block 0719 of the prime data area. Replace the pointer in Athens by the pointer 0719/4 in Atters.
d. Anton appears at the beginning of block 0719. To delete this record we again flag it as deleted. It is important, however, that there is no record in the block which logically precedes Anton. Thus we cannot point past Anton. There are a number of different ways we could conceive to solve this problem, such as physically deleting Anton and moving all the records in the block. But most such methods introduce significant complications. The most straightforward solution to the problem, which we choose to use here, may be to leave Anton in place with its "deleted" flag and allow the access program to read its pointer even though the record's data is to be ignored.
e. Deletion of Brown (the last record in block 0801) could require changing index entries if we are not careful. A simpler way of handling this problem is to delete Brown logically, put a "pointer to nowhere" (such as a byte of 1's, decimal 255) in the record Borg, which logically precedes Brown, and thus indicate that Borg is at least temporarily the end of the block.

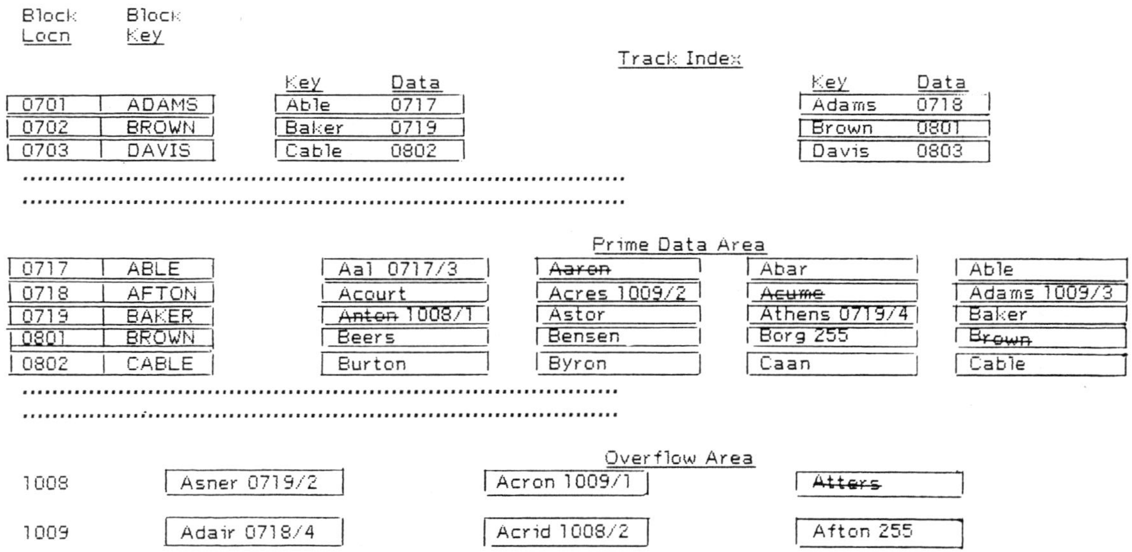

FIGURE 11–14. The File of Precinct Voters Where Added Records Have Been Placed in the Overflow Area (see Figure 11–9) and Aaron, Acume, Atters, Anton, and Brown Have Been Logically Deleted

Example 11–10

Delete the following records from the file of Figure 11–12:

a. Aaron b. Acume c. Adams d. Athens e. Brown

Solution:

The results of the following steps are illustrated in Figure 11–15, where strike-throughs indicate records have been flagged as logically deleted.

a. Deleting Aaron is a matter of flagging Aaron as a deleted record. No pointers need be changed, since the block is read in sequential order, and any record which is flagged is simply skipped.
b. Since Acume is in the overflow area, it is in a linked list. Besides flagging Acume deleted, we may desire to change the pointer in Acron (which logically precedes Acume) to the value which was previously the pointer in Acume, namely 1008/2.
c. Adams is at the end of an overflow chain. We may wish to flag Adams deleted but leave the 255 pointer. In this manner *we need not change the index* entries, and we keep intact the signal that no record greater than Adams is associated with prime data block 0718. Be aware, of course, that until the file is reorganized you probably would not wish to reuse the area (block 1008, record 2) from which Adams was deleted. Why? We could place pointer 255 in Acron and change index entries, but we choose not to do so in this example.
d. Superficially it appears that deleting Athens is just like deleting Acume; i. e., flag it and change the pointer of the logically preceding record. However, Athens is first in the chain of overflow records from block 0719. The pointer (1009/3) which points to Athens is in the first overflow record in *track index* block 0702. We would choose to flag Athens as deleted and leave its pointer. However, changing the pointer in the track index does not lead to a cascade of further changes, so we choose to change Baker 1009/3 in track index block 0702 to Baker 1008/3 and to logically delete Athens and its pointer completely.
e. To avoid a cascade of index changes we will simply flag Brown (the last record physically and logically in prime data block 0801) deleted and keep Brown temporarily as the block key. A future addition to the block with key greater than Borg and less than or equal to Brown can fill the

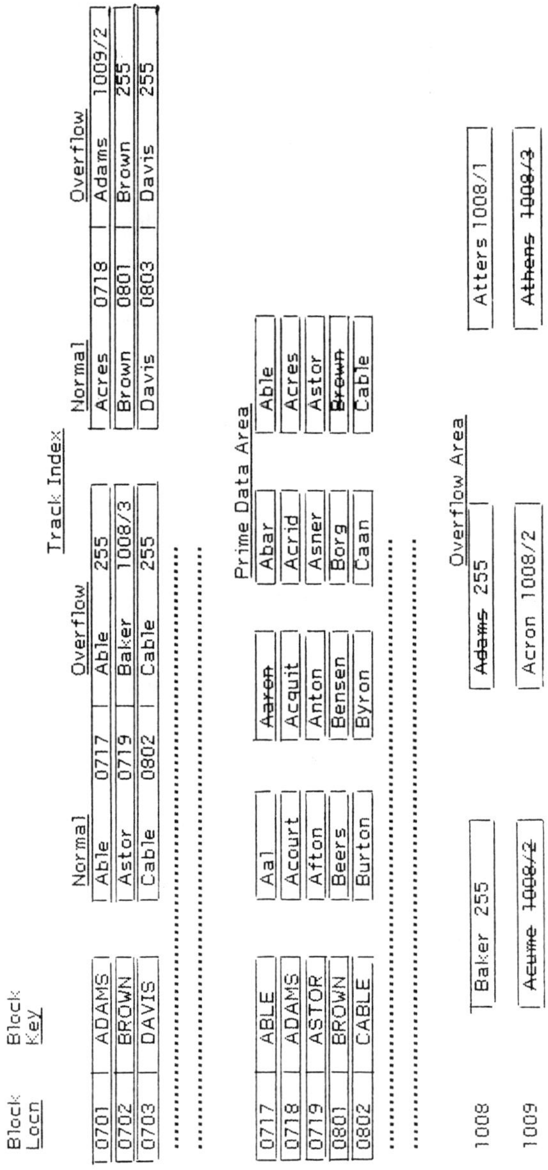

FIGURE 11–15. The File Precinct Voters Where Added Records Are in the Prime Data Area (see Figure 11–12) and Records Aaron, Acume, Adams, Athens, and Brown Have Been Deleted Logically

spot formerly occupied by logically deleted Brown. Then we would change the block key and normal track index entry. Subsequent additions, of course, would begin an overflow chain, the last record of which would have the 255 "pointer to nowhere." The overflow track index entry would point to the beginning of the chain, but until we reorganize the file we would probably choose not to change the key Brown in that entry. This would continue to indicate that Brown is the largest key which can ever be logically associated with prime data block 0801.

MANAGING AN INDEXED SEQUENTIAL FILE

Loading and Maintaining the File

As with directly organized files, it makes little sense to create an indexed sequential file with just a handful of records. There needs to be a sufficient number of records so that a reasonable index can be started and prime data and overflow areas can be reserved intelligently. For a small file, access is rapid even when organized sequentially, and this is the way virtually all files should begin.

Inserting massive numbers of records into an indexed sequential file is also not practical. The records must be inserted one at a time; long linked lists result in the overflow areas, which are slow and cumbersome to read. Massive additions will inevitably cause a complete file reorganization, i. e., rethinking index organization, enlarging and rewriting prime data areas, and cleaning out overflow areas completely.

Thus, sometimes indexed sequential files are indeed the best of worlds, allowing both sequential and random access. But if the file is extremely large, the indexes become long, complex, and slow to search. If the file is volatile, overflow areas grow, and access time degrades significantly.

Access Methods

You are likely to see, in the literature on indexed sequential files, acronyms such as QISAM and BISAM for the operating system utility programs which handle indexed sequential files.

QISAM, Queued Indexed Sequential Access Methods, are programs written to handle sequential reading of the files, where the programs can anticipate the next record to be found. BISAM, Basic Indexed Sequential Access Methods, would be used when records are to be read randomly or when updating, adding, or deleting of records is to be performed. Most of these programs automatically handle searches of and changes to indexes, moving records, updating pointers, etc. which we have done by hand in the examples in this chapter.

Whether or not your computer has QISAM or BISAM utilities already available, it may be valuable to practice writing your own set of routines for doing the basic operations necessary to handle indexed sequential files.

QUESTIONS

1. What are the two major storage areas required by a partitioned file? How is each organizcd?
2. Suppose the directory records in a partitioned file had to be in the same order as that in which the file members are stored. Would this limit the usefulness of the file? Why or why not?
3. What would be the implications if you were asked to produce a partitioned file in which each member were allowed to contain records with a variety of different formats?
4. A partitioned file contains information about the animals in your zoo. The Gnu dies, and you acquire an Oryx. Without reorganizing the file, is it normally true that you could
   a. put the information for the Oryx where the information for the Gnu was previously? Why?
   b. enter the key and address of Oryx in the file directory in place of the key and address of Gnu? Why?
5. Give two specific examples of files, other than the ones mentioned in this chapter, in which partitioned organization could be particularly useful.
6. How might a partitioned organization be used to store a reference work, such as an encyclopedia, on disks?
7. On a typical, small, floppy disk you may be able to store about 180 kilobytes of data plus a directory. If the average size of a file is to be about three kilobytes, what would be a reasonable number of entries for which a directory area could be formatted?

8. State a major advantage and a major disadvantage of using indexed sequential files as opposed to sequential or direct.

9. What are the three major storage areas associated with an indexed sequential file?

10. In a track index

    a. what goes into the key area?

    b. what goes into the data area?

11. What is the difference between a sparse index and a dense index? Name one advantage of each.

12. In some indexed sequential files, additions go into the file in appropriate sequential order, and the last record of the track is bumped into the overflow area. What are two alternative methods of handling additions?

13. Name an advantage and a disadvantage of cylinder overflow areas as compared with independent overflow areas.

14. An indexed sequential file is illustrated in Figure 11–16. Assume that there is room for at least one more entry in block 0816. Use the method of adding records into the prime data blocks and bumping the last record from the block into the overflow area.

    a. In which block does record with key CRAMER belong?

    b. What are the current contents (key and data) of the normal entry in the track index for the block where CRAMER will be added?

    c. What are the current contents (key and data) of the overflow entry in the track index for the block where CRAMER will be added?

    d. What record will be bumped into the overflow area when CRAMER is added to the file?

    e. What are the contents of the normal entry in the track index after CRAMER has been added?

    f. What are the contents of the overflow entry in the track index after CRAMER has been added?

    g. What is the value in the pointer field in record DAVIS after CRAMER has been added?

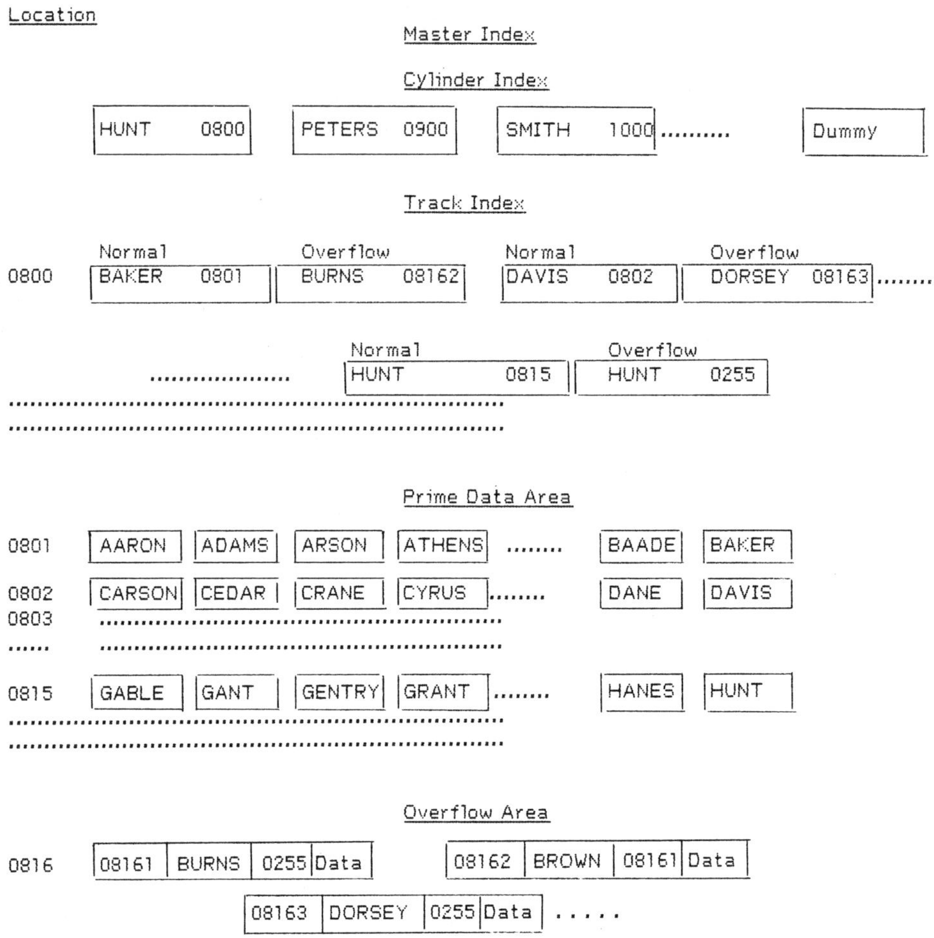

FIGURE 11–16. Indexed Sequential File, Question 11–14

15. Another indexed sequential file is shown in Figure 11–17. In this case the keys are numbers rather than words.

    a. If the file has just been loaded and no additions have yet been made, what should go into the area labeled A in the Track Index?

       Assume now that the record

Key	Data
83	Fargo

is added to the file with the method of keeping data in consecutive order in the blocks.

b. Where would the new record 83 Fargo be located?

c. What would happen to 88 Caspar?

d. After adding 83 Fargo, what should be in locations C and D of the Track Index?

e. Which of the following is a pair of possible values of E and F in the Cylinder Index?
(i) 1135 1130 (ii) 71 1132 (iii) 25 Chicago
(iv) 25 71 (v) 71 1109

f. Which of the following is a pair of possible values of G and H in the Cylinder Index?
(i) 133 1111 (ii) 133 1138 (iii) 12 105
(iv) 133 blank (v) 71 Taos

g. Which of the following is a pair of possible values of P and Q in the Master Index?

(i) 105 Stockton (ii) 105 1131 (iii) 133 1107
(iv) 105 1135 (v)133 1138

16. In the file of Example 1 (Figure 11–3)

a. where would you record the information for a new record on Charcoal? In which record would the pointer to Charcoal be recorded? What would be the value of the pointer?

b. where would you record the information for another new record on Ocean Temperature Gradients? In which record would the pointer to Ocean Temperature Gradients be recorded? What would be the value of the pointer?

17. In Figure 11–5

a. In which block would you find the track index entry which would lead you to record Wicker?

b. What are the contents of the track index entry which would lead you to record Wicker?

c. In which block is the record Wicker actually found?

d. In which block of the cylinder index would you find a record pertaining to record Wicker? What are the contents of that entry? What do they mean?

e. Which entry in the master index pertains to record Wicker?

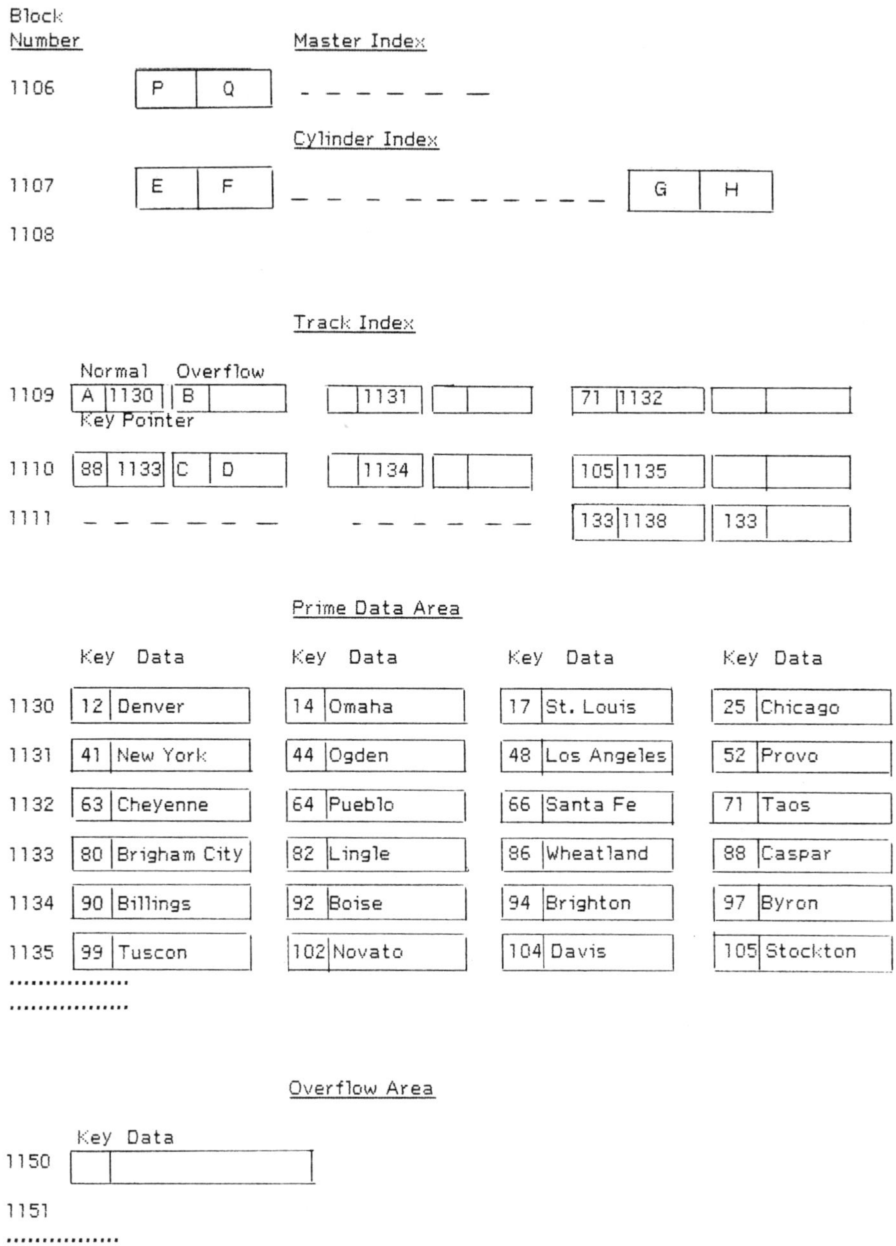

FIGURE 11–17. Indexed Sequential File, Question 11–15

18. Describe the steps you would take to find the record for Mr. Siegfried Wormwood in Figure 11–5. Start by reading the Master Index.

19. In Figure 11–5 assume that sparse loading has left two record spaces empty in each block of the prime data area.

    a. Using Example 11–4 as your guide, show what happens when you add records Whyte, Worth, Wilter, and Wren in that order.

    b. Do you have to change any index entries to add records in this manner?

    c. State at least one advantage and one disadvantage of this type of record addition process.

20. Show a possible way of using pointers to add Acorn and Arbot to the blocks shown in Figure 11–7.

21. a. Add records Witch, Whyte, Worth, and Wren to the file of Figure 11–5 by placing the added records directly into an overflow area and providing pointers as needed. Assume that each overflow block can contain three records.

    b. Add records Wither and Wilter to the file with the procedure given in part a.

22. a. Add records Witch, Whyte, Worth, and Wren to the file of Figure 11–5 by placing the added records into the appropriate prime data blocks, moving records from the ends of the blocks into the overflow area, and providing overflow records in the track index. Assume that each block in the overflow area can contain three records. Provide track index overflow entries as needed.

    b. Add records Wither and Wilter to the file using the procedure of part a. Also add Zzyzx to the file.

23. a. Illustrate how the record Baker is found in Figure 11–11. Begin by reading the master index.

    b. Illustrate how the record Wren is found in the file of problem 22b above. Begin by reading the master index.

24. If the file of Figure 11–5 were sparsely loaded, with room for six records in each prime data block, which of the following records would

you probably delete physically, and which would you delete logically? Why?

Aaron Athens Wilson Young

25. Logically delete records Able, Acres, and Acrid from the file which is shown in Figure 11–9.
26. Logically delete records Anton, Atters, Baker, and Able from the file which is shown in Figure 11–12.

CHAPTER 12

DEVELOPING A DATA BASE

NEW CONCEPTS

The file-handling techniques described so far are by no means an exhaustive list. We have illustrated a few which are fundamental and commonly used. You may be using other techniques already, which you prefer. Hopefully, better and more efficient techniques will be developed. Perhaps you may be involved in that development.

Virtually all methods for handling data in use today involve some combination or modification of the methods we have described. The real breakthroughs may come from radically different thinking about how to organize and access data. Certainly our brains use more sophisticated methods than random or indexed files. The study of human and artificial intelligence may lead to significant improvements in access speed and data integrity. Future methods may indeed be simpler to implement than some of the very complex methods now being proposed.

Writing your own algorithms and making some of the methods described in this text work on the computer will accomplish two very important things. First, these introductory concepts will become part of your repertoire of programming and data-handling techniques, something which will make you more valuable as a computer information systems expert. Second, you will begin to draw conclusions and see relationships which may lead you to significant new discoveries in data management.

Now let's tie together some loose ends, discuss some items we have missed, and look at some extensions of these fundamentals to more sophisticated and complex data management techniques.

VARIABLE LENGTH RECORDS AND TRAILERS

Virtually all of the examples in the preceding chapters have assumed that records are of easy-to-handle, fixed length. How does it change the problems if the record lengths are allowed to vary? Assume that you run a supply house for nuts and bolts. You wish to keep track of monthly orders and billing records for your customers. One customer may order five 1/4-inch nuts. Another may replenish an entire stock of screws, bolts, and nuts from your inventory of 12,000 different items. Obviously, you do not need as much data space in a record for the first customer as you do for the second, so you set up variable length records. How?

One way to handle variable-length records is to estimate the length of a record when it is written and then write into the count field for the record the number of bytes occupied by its data field. Reading the records then involves examining the count field to determine how many data bytes follow. This is simple, efficient, and very useful for files stored on a magnetic tape or other sequential devices. However, changing a record is messy at best, and lengthening a record (as a customer submits a second order this month) is virtually impossible.

Another way of handling variable length records is to assign a minimum fixed length area for each record. Then, as the record length expands, add as many fixed length extensions as are necessary to contain the data. Each extension can be given a slightly different key. For example, customer Williams Department Store might occupy records with keys WDS1, WDS2, WDS3, etc. The extensions (records WDS2, WDS3, etc.) are called *trailer records*. Hopefully it is obvious that, wherever the records are stored, they should be linked together in a chain. Hence, storing variable-length records in this manner becomes a problem like that of handling additions to the prime data and overflow areas of an indexed sequential file. Whether you, the user, wish to use sparse loading, put trailer records directly into an overflow area, or add them to prime data blocks, is your choice. If you have the use of an indexed sequential access method you may already have the programs which you need for handling variable-length records by this method.

VSAM FILES

One of the most flexible data handling techniques is the virtual storage access method (VSAM), which was introduced by IBM Corporation in 1972, and has been emulated by many others since then. The goals of VSAM were to provide a method of handling sequential, random access, and indexed files in a format independent of the storage device.

In VSAM all records are stored in fixed length control intervals (CI's). At the end of each control interval is the non-data information, describing the records within the CI. Each record is assigned a relative byte address (RBA), which is its displacement from the beginning of the file. VSAM treats the file as if it were stored in one contiguous extent beginning at address 0; thus, once the RBA of a record is determined, there is no need for the user to refer to absolute addresses on the storage device. Access depends only upon the characteristics of the file, not of the storage medium.

Records in VSAM files can be stored and accessed in any one of three orders; in key sequence, in entry sequence, or by relative record number.

Key Sequenced VSAM

A key sequenced VSAM file appears similar to an indexed sequential file. Records are loaded into the file in key sequential order, and the index relates keys to the RBA's of the records in the file. The lowest level index is often called the *sequence set;* the collection of higher level indexes, if they are needed, is called the *index set.*

A record in the index set contains the highest key of an index entry at the next lower level and a *vertical pointer* to the address of that entry, just as do the indexes illustrated in Chapter 11. The vertical pointers may be followed through the indexes to find the control interval containing an individual record.

For sequential access to the file, only the sequence set index is used. Each sequence set record may contain vertical pointers to several control intervals. The collection of control intervals referenced by one sequence set entry is called a control area. In addition, there will be a *horizontal pointer* in each sequence set record, which points to the next index entry and defines the logical sequential order in which the control areas will be accessed. Figure 12–1 illustrates the important relationships between the indexes, control areas, control intervals, and records in a key sequenced VSAM file.

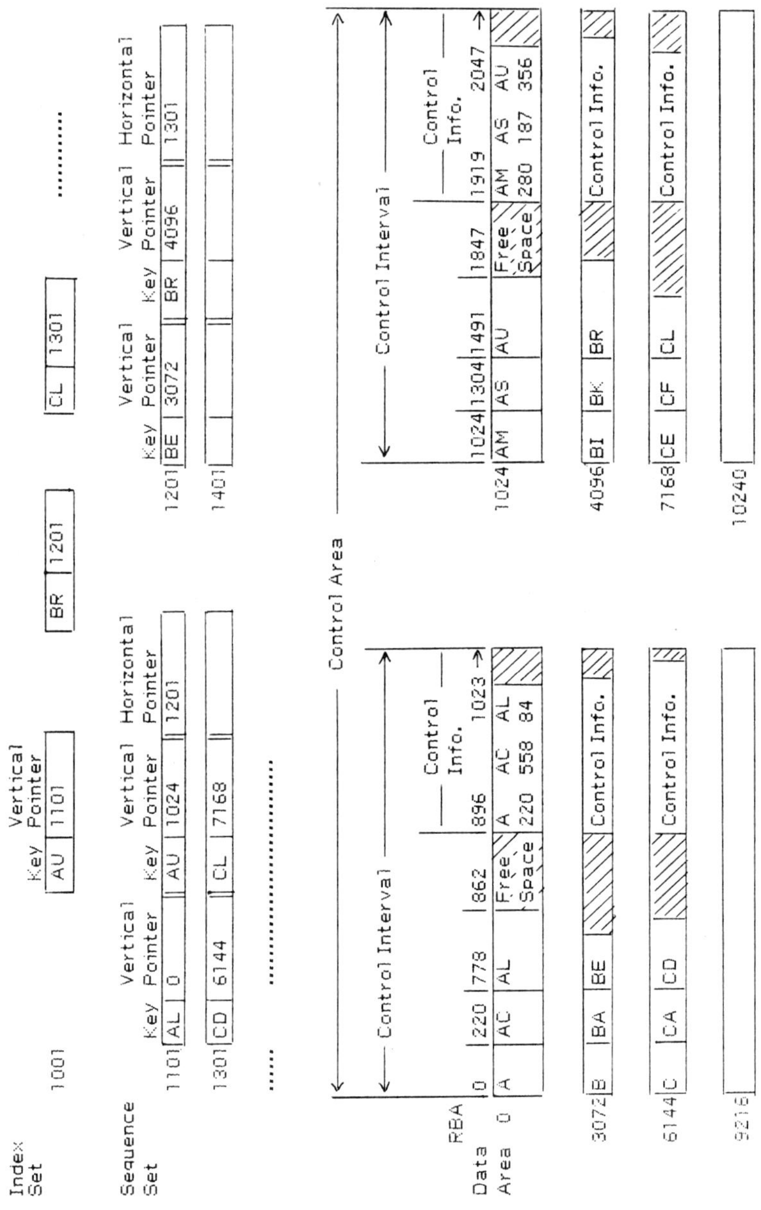

FIGURE 12–1. A Key Sequence VSAM File

Example 12–1

Follow the vertical pointers in Figure 12–1 to find the record for AS (Arsenic).

Solution:

Search the index set for the first key not less than AS, namely AU (Gold). The vertical pointer is to address 1101 in the sequence set.

Search the record at address 1101 in the sequence set to find the first key not less than AS, namely AU. The vertical pointer is to the control interval which begins at relative address 1024.

Examine the CI beginning at RBA 1024 to find record AS, which is a record 187 bytes long beginning at RBA 1304.

In the file illustrated in Figure 12–1 the records are variable length, and there is some unused space in most control intervals. Part of the non-data information in each control interval will be the record lengths, as we have shown in the figure. If all of the records are the same length, then this information may be recorded only once.

When records are deleted from a control interval in a VSAM file, the succeeding records are generally moved to the left and their relative byte addresses are adjusted so that the free space becomes larger. Inserting a new record or lengthening a record causes succeeding records to be moved to the right to fill some of the unused space in the control interval. If the records no longer fit into the control interval, then some of the records are moved to an empty CI in the same control area. If no more control intervals are available, VSAM splits the control area and extends the file. Thus VSAM does not use the separate overflow area required by indexed sequential files, and free areas are used dynamically rather than having to be reclaimed by a complete file reorganization.

Entry Sequenced VSAM

In an entry sequenced VSAM file, the records are loaded in the order in which they occur. New records are added at the end of the file, and no index is maintained. VSAM provides the user with the RBA of each record so that direct access can be accomplished only if the user maintains an independent cross-reference file which relates records to their addresses. This type of file is particularly useful when records are in chronological order, such as a journal or a log of events.

Relative Record VSAM

When a record is added to a relative record file, the user or VSAM assigns it an integer between 1 and *N*, where *N* is the number of the last record in the file. The disk area is formatted as a sequence of fixed length record slots, where each control interval contains a fixed number of records. Access to a record is achieved by using the relative record number as the key. No index is provided for this organization unless the user maintains a separate tickler file of record numbers. However, the user can update records in place, delete records, and insert new records into empty slots.

ALTERNATE KEYS

When data is formatted with keys, only one unique key may be recorded in the key area of a record (or block). However, any field within the data area may be considered a secondary or *alternate record key*. Generally, in order for the keys to be meaningful and easy to find, you would make the related alternate keys the same length and assign them the same relative position within each record.

A set of alternate keys in a file may or may not be *unique*. The primary key must be capable of defining the record precisely, with no ambiguity; hence, it must be unique. On the other hand, you may wish to pick from a student file all of the persons who are 18 years old or from a file of chemical compounds all of the strong acids. These keys (age or acidity) would then not be unique.

Records can be linked together in some fashion by alternate keys, as shown in Example 8–2 and Figure 8–2 (Chapter 8) with multiple pointers. You may even wish to develop hash functions or scatter tables which allow direct access to records by their alternate keys. There are also special secondary access methods, namely multilists and inverted files, which have been developed for handling records with multiple, related keys. These methods are called "secondary" because they allow access to the records through the secondary keys.

Multilists

Data are usually sorted on the primary key but not on the alternate keys. Thus the physical record addresses are generally unrelated to the secondary keys, and secondary search and storage methods must be somewhat different from the primary access methods discussed in previous chapters. A sequential search of alternate keys, for example, could require reading the entire file before the desired records are located.

The *multilist* structure is a combination of linked lists and indexing which allows faster access to a file by secondary keys. Figure 12–2 shows a multilist organization with a two-level index. Of course there may be many

Highest Index Level (Item Types)

	Type	Pointer	Type	Pointer	
600	New Subscription Yr	700	Expiration Month	710	
601	Zipcode	800	Address		....

Lowest Index Level (Item Values)

	Value	Pointer	Value	Pointer	Value	Pointer
700	1962	1101	1963		1964	
......						
708	1982	1102	1983		1984	1103
710	JAN	1101	FEB		MAR	
711	APR		MAY		JUN	
712	JUL	1106	AUG		SEP	
713	OCT		NOV		DEC	
800	01...		02...	1101	03...	
......						
919	97...	1102	98...		99...	

Data Area

	Acct.No. Primary Key	Subscr.Yr. Alt.Key	Pointer	Expir.Mo. Alt.Key	Pointer	Zipcode Alt.Key	Pointer
1101	ADAM3162-04	1962	1104	JAN	1108	02013	1105
1102	BAKE4192-68	1982	1107	JAN	1107	97171	1109
1103	CREN2691-47	1984	1109	JUL	1109	02115	1108
1104	FRED8381-12	1962	1108	JUL	End	97726	End
1105	HENR4443-72	1984	End	JUL	1104	02164	1106
1106	JUST5963-55	1982	End	JUL	1103	02593	1103
1107	MART6871-32	1982	1106	JAN	End	02117	End
1108	RICH5648-82	1962	End	JAN	1102	02447	1107
1109	SMIT9171-68	1984	1105	JUL	1105	97177	1104

FIGURE 12–2. A Multilist File of Periodical Subscribers

index levels, as in an indexed sequential organization, but the two levels here illustrate the method adequately.

Observe in Figure 12–2 that higher level areas always point to areas in the next lower level. The lowest index level points to the first in a chain of Data Area entries containing the desired alternate key. In this limited file there are many index entries which are *null* entries; i. e., there are no records in the file which have those keys. Obviously, if this were a genuine, large subscriber list, there would be considerably fewer null entries.

Each record in the file is a member of a number of linked lists up to the total number of alternate keys specified in the record. Although indexes are usually searched sequentially, they could be sorted and a binary search applied if desired. Records in the data area are generally unblocked.

Adding or updating records may mean changing pointers, removing a record from one list, and inserting it into another, and perhaps even changing an index entry.

Example 12–2

In the multilist of Figure 12–2, make the following changes:

a. The subscriber with primary key BAKE4192-68 has moved from the West Coast (zipcode 97171) to the East Coast (zipcode 02014) and has extended the subscription until March.

b. A new subscriber (at record location 1110) has primary key THOM7246-41, subscription year 1984, expiration date MARch, and zipcode 97119.

Solution:

The following changes are illustrated in Figure 12–3:

a. (1) Record 1102 has been changed to

1102 BAKE4192-68 1982 1107 MAR End 02014 End

(2) Lowest Index Level, Expiration Month Entry for MAR is no longer null. It becomes MAR 1102.

(3) The pointer with key MAR in record 1102 becomes "End" since this is the last (only) record in the chain with this key. (This will be changed again in step b(3) below.)

Highest Index Level (Item Types)

	Type	Pointer	Type	Pointer	
600	New Subscription Yr	700	Expiration Month	710	
601	Zipcode	800	Address		....

Lowest Index Level (Item Values)

	Value	Pointer	Value	Pointer	Value	Pointer
700	1962	1101	1963		1964	
....						
708	1982	1102	1983		1984	1103
710	JAN	1101	FEB		MAR	1102
711	APR		MAY		JUN	
712	JUL	1106	AUG		SEP	
713	OCT		NOV		DEC	
800	01...		02...	1101	03...	
....						
919	97...	1109	98...		99...	

Data Area

	Acct.No. Primary Key	Subscr.Yr. Alt.Key	Pointer	Expir.Mo. Alt.Key	Pointer	Zipcode Alt.Key	Pointer
1101	ADAM3162-04	1962	1104	JAN	1108	02013	1105
1102	BAKE4192-68	1982	1107	MAR	1110	02014	End
1103	CREN2691-47	1984	1109	JUL	1109	02115	1108
1104	FRED8381-12	1962	1108	JUL	End	97726	1110
1105	HENR4443-72	1984	1110	JUL	1104	02164	1106
1106	JUST5963-55	1982	End	JUL	1103	02593	1103
1107	MART6871-32	1982	1106	JAN	End	02117	1102
1108	RICH5648-82	1962	End	JAN	1107	02447	1107
1109	SMIT9171-68	1984	1105	JUL	1105	97177	1104
1110	THOM7246-41	1984	End	MAR	End	97119	End

FIGURE 12–3. The Periodical Subscriber Multilist after Changes of Example 12–2

(4) The month expiration pointer in record 1108

1108 RICH5648-82 1962 End JAN 1107 02447 1107

was changed from 1102 to the previous pointer in record 1102 BAKE4192-68, namely 1107. This removes record 1102 BAKE4192-68 from the chain of JAN expiration dates.

(5) Lowest Index Level, Zipcode Entry 97 . . . 1102 was changed to 97 . . . 1109 where 1109 was the previous zipcode pointer in record 1102 BAKE4192-68. This removes BAKE4192-68 from the 97 . . . zipcode chain.

(6) Record 1102 BAKE4192-68 is placed at the end of the 02. . . zipcode chain by changing the pointer in record

1107 MART6871-32 1982 1106 JAN End 02117 1102
from "End" to 1102.

b. (1) The following record has been added:

1110 THOM7246-41 1984 End MAR End 97119 End

(2) 1110 THOM7246-41 is added to the end of the 1984 subscription year list by changing the pointer in

1105 HENR4443-72 1984 1110 JUL 1104 02164 1106
from "End" to 1110.

(3) 1110 THOM7246-41 is added to the end of the MAR expiration month list by changing the expiration month pointer in 1102 BAKE4192-68 from "End" to 1110.

(4) 1110 THOM7246-41 is added to the end of the 97 . . . zipcode chain by changing the zipcode pointer in 1104 FRED8381-12 from "End" to 1110.

Example 12–3

Search the file of Figure 12–3 to find all of the subscribers with zipcode 02. . . whose subscriptions expire in JAN.

Solution:

We may search through the linked list of records with zipcodes beginning 02. . . and determine which of those have JAN expiration dates; or we may search the list of those with JAN expiration and determine which have zipcodes 02. . . . Glancing at the file, we see that the latter procedure is much shorter, since there are only three records in the JAN expiration chain and seven records in the 02. . . zipcode list. In many multilist files the count of records in each chain is recorded in the lowest level index entry so that the computer can determine which chain is shorter.

The procedure is to search the highest level index for Expiration Month, proceed to record 710 and search the lowest level index from that point for JAN, which may also tell us that there are three entries in the JAN chain. Search the highest level index for zipcode, proceed to record 800 and search the lowest level index from that point for 02. . . . This may tell us there are seven entries in the 02. . . zipcode list. Since the JAN expiration month chain is the shorter, we begin at record 1101 (indicated by the index pointer), read

1101 ADAM3162-04 1962 1104 JAN 1108 02013 1105

discover that it has a 02. . . zipcode, and print it out. Following the JAN pointer, we next read

1108 RICH5648-82 1962 End JAN 1107 02447 1107

which also has a 02. . . zipcode. The JAN pointer leads us to

1107 MART6871-32 1982 1106 JAN End 02117 1102

which we also print because of the 02. . . zipcode. This is the end of the JAN expiration month chain. We have found all of the subscribers with zipcode 02. . . and JAN expiration, namely

1101 ADAM3162-04, 1108 RICH5648-82, and
1107 MART6871-32.

The multilist structured file requires a considerable amount of non-data storage area in the form of indexes and pointers. Whether one gains an advantage from this method of organization depends upon the relative amounts of time needed to search and sort the records. Files can be sorted by alternate key and accessed directly or sequentially; however, a multilist may be justified if the time to sort is significantly greater than the time required to search and maintain the linked list pointers.

Inverted Files

The *inverted file* structure is a modification of the multilist which allows considerably faster access to records based upon inquiries with multiple conditions.

As we saw in the multilist examples, finding a record with more than one condition (such as 1984 subscription date *and* 97. . . zipcode) involves determining from the indexes which is the shorter chain, following the pointers to read every record in the linked list, and examining each record to see if it meets all of the conditions. An inverted file handles this situation more efficiently by inserting into the file an extra level of non-data information, called the *access lists.* All of the chain pointers are recorded in the access lists rather than within the data records themselves. The access lists are sorted by physical addresses because the method of search for multiple conditions is to merge the access lists for the conditions and read all of the records whose addresses appear in the resulting list.

Figure 12–4 shows the file of Figure 12–2 organized as an Inverted File. Of course, in this small file there are still a considerable number of null entries. Updating or adding records to an inverted file involves changing and possibly sorting and rewriting the access lists, but it does not require changing index entries.

Example 12–4

In the inverted file of Figure 12–4, make the following changes:

a. It has been discovered that the subscriber with primary key MART6871-32 really began a subscription in 1962 rather than in 1982 and has renewed the subscription until SEPtember.

b. A new subscriber (at record location 1110) has primary key STEI9141-63 and subscription year 1984, expiration month SEPtember, zipcode 03964.

Highest Index Level (Item Types)

	Type	Pointer	Type	Pointer	
600	New Subscription Yr	700	Expiration Month	710	
601	Zipcode	800	Address		....

Lowest Index Level (Item Values)

	Value	Pointer	Value	Pointer	Value	Pointer
700	1962	1000	1963		1964	
.....	.....					
708	1982	1020	1983		1984	1022
710	JAN	1030	FEB		MAR	1033
.....	.....					
712	JUL	1037	AUG		SEP	1039
713	OCT		NOV		DEC	
800	01...		02...	1044	03...	
.....	.....					
919	97...	1095	98...		99...	

Access Lists

	Key	List
1000	1962	1101 1104 1108
.....	.....	
1020	1982	1102 1106 1107
.....	.....	
1022	1984	1103 1105 1109
1030	JAN	1101 1102 1107 1108
.....	.....	
1033	MAR	
.....	.....	
1037	JUL	1103 1104 1105 1106 1109
.....	.....	
1039	SEP	
1044	02...	1101 1103 1105 1106 1107 1108
.....	.....	
1095	97...	1102 1104 1109

Data Area

	Acct.No. Primary Key	Subscr.Yr. Alt.Key	Expir.Mo. Alt.Key	Zipcode Alt.Key
1101	ADAM3162-04	1962	JAN	02013
1102	BAKE4192-68	1982	JAN	97171
1103	CREN2691-47	1984	JUL	02115
1104	FRED8381-12	1962	JUL	97726
1105	HENR4443-72	1984	JUL	02164
1106	JUST5963-55	1982	JUL	02593
1107	MART6871-32	1982	JAN	02117
1108	RICH5648-82	1962	JAN	02447
1109	SMIT9171-68	1984	JUL	97177

FIGURE 12–4. In Inverted File of Periodical Subscribers

Solution:

The following changes are illustrated in Figure 12–5.

a. (1) Record 1107 has been changed to

1107 MART6871-32 1962 SEP 02117

(2) Record 1107 is removed from the access lists for 1982 and JAN. This can be done by deleting logically or by physically rewriting these access lists as shown in the figure.

(3) Record 1107 is added to the access lists for 1962 and SEP, and those lists are sorted and rewritten, as necessary, to keep them in order of physical addresses.

b. (1) Record 1110 STEI9141-63 1984 SEP 03964 has been added.

(2) Pointer 1110 is added to the access lists for 1984 and SEP.

(3) A new access list is begun at available location 1045 for zipcode 03. . . . The pointer to this location is entered into the lowest index entry for zipcode 03. . . , and the pointer 1110 is entered into the new access list.

Example 12–5

Search the file of Figure 12–5 to find all of the subscribers with zipcode beginning 02. . . who entered subscriptions in the year 1962.

Solution:

Search the highest level index for the zipcode, proceed to the indicated record 800, and search the lowest level index for zipcode entry 02. . . 1044. This tells us that the access list is record

	Key	List
1044	02. . .	1101 1103 1105 1106 1107 1108

which we read and store.

Highest Index Level (Item Types)

	Type	Pointer	Type	Pointer	
600	New Sub-scription Yr	700	Expiration Month	710	
601	Zipcode	800	Address		....

Lowest Index Level (Item Values)

	Value	Pointer	Value	Pointer	Value	Pointer
700	1962	1000	1963		1964	
....						
708	1982	1020	1983		1984	1022

710	JAN	1030	FEB		MAR	1033
....						
712	JUL	1037	AUG		SEP	1039
713	OCT		NOV		DEC	

800	01...		02...	1044	03...	1045
....						
919	97...	1095	98...		99...	

Access Lists

	Key	List
1000	1962	1101 1104 1107 1108
.....	.....	.....
1020	1982	1102 1106
.....	.....	.....
1022	1984	1103 1105 1109 1110

1030	JAN	1101 1102 1108
.....	.....	.....
1033	MAR	
.....	.....	.....
1037	JUL	1103 1104 1105 1106 1109
.....	.....	.....
1039	SEP	1107 1110

1044	02...	1101 1103 1105 1106 1107 1108
1045	03...	1110
.....	.....	.....
1095	97...	1102 1104 1109

Data Area

	Acct.No. Primary Key	Subscr.Yr. Alt.Key	Expir.Mo. Alt.Key	Zipcode Alt.Key
1101	ADAM3162-04	1962	JAN	02013
1102	BAKE4192-68	1982	JAN	97171
1103	CREN2691-47	1984	JUL	02115
1104	FRED8381-12	1962	JUL	97726
1105	HENR4443-72	1984	JUL	02164
1106	JUST5963-55	1982	JUL	02593
1107	MART6871-32	1962	SEP	02117
1108	RICH5648-82	1962	JAN	02447
1109	SMIT9171-68	1984	JUL	97177
1110	STEI9141-63	1984	SEP	03964

FIGURE 12–5. The Inverted File of Periodical Subscribers, after Changes of Example 12–4

Similarly, beginning with the highest level index, we find the New Subscription Year pointer to 700. At address 700 in the lowest level index we discover that the access list for 1962 entries is

```
     Key   List
1000 1962 1101 1104 1107 1108
```

which we read and store.

Now create a new *target list* by finding the intersection (AND) of the pointers in records 1044 and record 1000, namely

```
            Keys             List
Target List 1962 and 02. . . 1101 1107 1108
```

Now read all of the records pointed to by the target list, namely

```
1101 ADAM3162-04  1962  JAN  02013
1107 MART6871-32  1962  SEP  02117
1108 RICH5648-82  1962  JAN  02447
```

which is the desired list of subscribers with zipcode 02. . . and subscription year 1962.

In contrast to the multilist there is no need to record the number of records for each chain of an inverted file. Merging of access lists no longer requires us to pick out the shortest chains. The area required for storage of non-data information must be expanded to include access lists, but some storage space is retrieved because no pointers are needed within the data records. This access method assumes an added burden of sorting and rewriting the sequential access lists whenever an update occurs; however, the inverted file organization may be justified by the much shorter time required to find records with many related conditions.

Files containing records with multiple alternate keys may be *fully inverted* or only *partially inverted.* If searches on some keys are always made alone, rather than with others, there needn't be access lists for those keys, and pointers can be stored in the data records as in a multilist. This can be in the same file in which other chains are organized with access lists, in which case the file is then only partially inverted, i. e., inverted on some keys only.

The indexes and access lists which we have shown have all been *single key indexes,* where each key has its own access list. If a file is to be searched repeatedly for the same particular combination of keys, then you may wish to set up *multiple key indexes* and access lists. For example, in the subscriber file, if you wished to send out renewal notices in any given month to those whose subscriptions expire within that month and to those whose subscriptions expire within six months, you could set up access lists which are the unions of lists for JAN or JUL, FEB or AUG, MAR or SEP, etc. and make those multiple key target lists permanent parts of the file, pointed to by new index entries.

DATA BASES

To discuss data base design and implementation in detail would require another volume. However, we will provide an introduction to data base concepts so that you can see how they relate to the file designs which have been considered already.

Data base processing is a method of handling related data from a number of files by considering the files to be a library of data. A data base management system (DBMS) is a set of programs which acts as the librarian, an intermediary between the user applications programs and the physical storage medium. Thus the user's program may be independent of the data format, and data from many files can be integrated into one coherent unit. When the format of a file is changed, if the user is relying only upon the file handling techniques described so far, all the applications programs which refer to that file must be modified to reflect the format changes. When the data in one file is updated, all related files must be updated also. In a data base management system, records are accessed by their relationships, and changing a record in one file should result in automatic changes of that data in all of the files.

A data base management system requires much more storage area than that required by the data records alone. The management programs as well as relationships between the data, the indexes, and the pointers all require extra storage space. In fact, a data base may take as much as two or three times the total of the space used by the data. Also, the management programs are often quite complex and may require considerable development effort and a fairly sophisticated central processing unit.

In a data base we distinguish between three "views" of the data. The *internal view* is closely related to the storage characteristics; it describes the indexes or lists, the sequence in which records are stored, and the logical record formats, but not the physical blocks, tracks, and cylinders. The *conceptual view* is the description of the data in terms of which records exist, what their properties are, and what set of relationships is defined between them. The conceptual view is the total logical description of the data base, which may be available only to the Data Base Administrator (DBA), the person in charge of defining and maintaining the data base. The user gets an *external view* of the data, the subset of properties and relationships which are needed for a specific application.

There are two fundamental types of relationships between records in a data base. One of these is the *hierarchical* or *tree* relationship, such as that illustrated in Figure 12–6. In a tree all of relationships are *one to many;* that is, a *parent* may have many *children,* but not vice versa. The second type of data relationship is the *network* where any parent may have many children and any child may have many parents. A specific type of network is exemplified by multilists and inverted files such as those shown earlier in Figures 12–2 and 12–4. Observe in those figures that the index record JAN, for example, has several children, namely

```
1101 ADAM3162-04  1962  JAN  02013
1102 BAKE4192-68  1982  JAN  97171
1107 MART6871-32  1982  JAN  02117
1108 RICH5648-82  1962  JAN  02447.
```

Also note that any record may have more than one parent, such as record

```
1107 MART6871-32 1982 JAN 02117
```

which has index records JAN, 1982, and 02. . . as parents.

Some data base management systems are especially good at handling data hierarchies, while others are specially designed to pick out relationships within data networks.

Relational Data Bases

Although the relational approach to management of network data bases is simpler in theory than many other approaches, it was more difficult to implement, and its use appeared somewhat later than hierarchical systems. Many of the older data bases are still handled in hierarchical form because they were initially built that way, and it is difficult and expensive to change.

In most relational data base systems all the records in a file are fixed length and have the same format. The files are viewed as tables or two-dimensional arrays where the records form the rows of the table and the fields within the records define the columns. Consider the files in Table 12–1, for example. In the first file the Division Number is considered to be the primary key. The descriptions of the divisions are the rows of the table; *Division Number, Division Name,* and *Location* are the column headings.

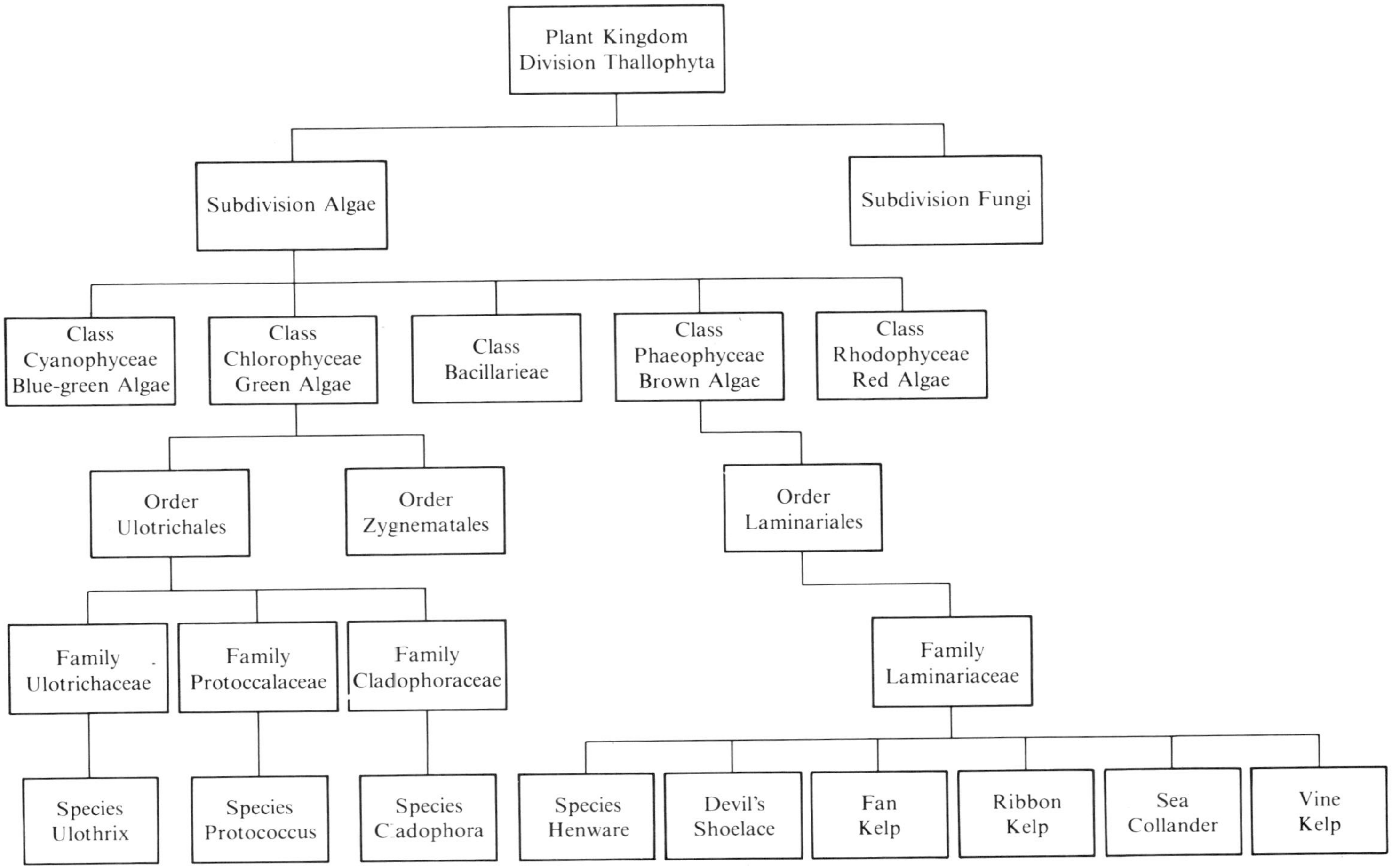

FIGURE 12–6. A Hierarchical Relationship Illustrated by Representatives of the Plant Kingdom

The relationships between entries in the data base tables are not explicitly defined, but they must be specified implicitly by one or more common, connecting fields, such as the Division Number columns in both files of Table 12–1. Information can be retrieved by examining the data in the files and the connecting relationships. A query language built into most management systems allows you to ask questions which would cause the management system to apply file handling techniques such as those discussed in this text to perform the necessary searches.

TABLE 12–1. Related Files in a Relational Data Base.

Divisions

Division Number	*Division Name*	*Location*
D001	Purchasing	ET236
D002	Manufacturing	ET236
D003	Sales	FA117
D004	Warehouse	SG021

Employees

Employee Number	*Employee Name*	*Hourly Wage*	*City Address*	*Division Number*
036522	JONES, SAM	3.85	OGDEN	D003
047694	SMITH, TOM	4.50	LAYTON	D001
093285	WILLS, SUE	8.15	ROY	D002
104478	BURNS, EVA	14.60	LAYTON	D003
119362	SNOW, ABE	5.45	OGDEN	D004
124803	RICH, MARY	7.00	LOGAN	D002
136981	THORN, TED	6.85	OGDEN	D004
147002	WOOD, BILL	9.10	ROY	D002
159983	GRANT, ELLA	12.50	LAYTON	D004
164397	BRICK, GAIL	4.35	ROY	D002
177045	STONE, MARK	6.70	HOOPER	D003

Example 12–6

A query language allows you to make the following requests, based upon Table 12–1:

a. List the employees who work in the Sales Division.

b. Find the average salary of the employees in the Warehouse Division who live in Ogden.

Illustrate how the desired results might be obtained by a relational data base management system.

Solution:

a. Examine the records in the Divisions file to determine that the division number of Sales is D003. Search the Employees file for those records for which the division number is D003. This may be done sequentially. On the other hand, the employee file may have been set up as a multilist or an inverted file on the secondary division number key, in which case finding those with division number D003 would involve following the linked list or reading the access list. In any case, it is discovered that the employees who work in the Sales Division are

036522	JONES, SAM	3.85	OGDEN	D003
104478	BURNS, EVA	14.60	LAYTON	D003
177045	STONE, MARK	6.70	HOOPER	D003

b. Examine the Divisions file to determine that the Warehouse is D004. Search the Employees file for those who work in division D004 and live in OGDEN. This could be done most efficiently if the Employees file were inverted on the division number and address keys. Then the intersection of the access lists for D004 and OGDEN could be merged to find records

119362	SNOW, ABE	5.45	OGDEN	D004
136981	THORN, TED	6.85	OGDEN	D004

The average salary is determined by averaging the salary fields of these records, namely

Average salary of employees in the warehouse division who live in Ogden $=(5.45+6.85)\ /\ 2=\$\ 6.15$ per hour.

Hierarchical Data Base

A record in a hierarchy may have only one parent, while in a network the number of parents is theoretically unlimited. Thus a hierarchy could be viewed as a special network and handled by relational data base techniques. However, some systems are strictly limited to handling data bases with a hierarchical structure. Hierarchical data base management systems have been in use since the late 1960's, and most are constantly being updated and improved.

Within a hierarchical data base the records and files are related in a tree structure such as that illustrated earlier in Figure 12–6. The order of entries in the data base may be defined by assigning to each one a sequence code which defines the level and the order of each record within that level. Then the search for the records can be performed by using the tree search techniques described in Chapter 8.

If the records are physically contiguous within a storage area, they may be organized and accessed in a sequential or indexed sequential form. Otherwise the records may be distributed throughout the storage area and connected by pointers. A vertical pointer in each parent will indicate the first child in a linked list of children. A horizontal pointer in each record will point to the next record in the list of children belonging to the same parent. Each record may also contain a pointer which indicates its parent.

Example 12–7

Illustrate how the following tasks might be solved from the hierarchy of Figure 12–6:

a. Determine how many orders are defined in the file within the Class Green Algae. What are they?

b. Find the record or file containing the information about Ribbon Kelp.

Solution:

a. Read the root record, Plant Kingdom, and follow the vertical pointer to the first child, Subdivision Algae. Read the records at this level.

   Read the records in the third level (Class Blue-green Algae, Green Algae. . .) until Class Green Algae is found.

   Follow the vertical pointer in Class Green Algae to the first child, Order Ulotrichales; and read the other Orders by following horizontal pointers from Order Ulotrichales to Order Zygnematales until the end of list pointer is encountered at Zygnematales.

There are then *two* orders defined in the file within the Class Green Algae, namely Ulotrichales and Zygnematales.

b. Read the file beginning with the root record again. In this case the entire file may need to be read until the Species Ribbon Kelp is found. One method of such a search was illustrated in Example 8–7, Chapter 8. Another method of finding Ribbon Kelp would be to have a sequential index of the species which we could search in order to find the appropriate record directly.

QUESTIONS

1. Outline how you would set up the inventory file of nuts and bolts discussed in the section on VARIABLE LENGTH RECORDS AND TRAILERS. Among other things, indicate
   a. what you would use for record keys
   b. how you would identify the items sold
   c. what kind of data you would want to put into each customer's record
   d. how you would handle the variable length record problems.
   e. Illustrate how you would record the information for a few customers and their orders in sparse loading, *or* adding directly to overflow, *or* recording additions in prime data blocks (your choice).
   f. Indicate whether indexes would be useful
2. Name the three methods by which records may be organized and accessed using VSAM.
3. a. What is the major difference between indexes for key-sequenced VSAM files and indexes for indexed sequential files?
   b. What is a horizontal pointer? What is a vertical pointer?
4. In the VSAM file of Figure 12–1 assume that each control interval is 1024 bytes long as shown and that 128 bytes are needed at the end of each CI for non-data control information. Add the next Control Area to the file, which will contain the records

Key	*Record Length (bytes)*
CM (Curium)	316
CO (Cobalt)	112
CR (Chromium)	392
CS (Cesium)	408
CU (Copper)	224
DY (Dysprosium)	168

Show the new index set and sequence set entries as well as the RBA of each new record.

5. a. In the VASM file of Figure 12–1 we forgot the record for AT (Astatine). Suppose this record were 68 bytes long. Show the changes needed to add this record to the file.

   b. Suppose a new isotope of Actinium (AC) is to be added to the file of Figure 12–1. This record will be given key AI (for Actinium Isotope) and will be 186 bytes long. Describe briefly what will happen to the file if

      (1) another empty control interval is available in the control area which contains the record for AC.

      (2) no more empty control intervals are available in the control area which contains AC, and no more control areas are available in the space allocated for the file.

6. Give examples of files in which you would have alternate keys which are

   a. unique   b. not unique

7. What special provisions would you have to make if you were to be able to find a record by an alternate key if the file were

   a. directly organized

   b. organized by an indexed sequential method?

8. Make the following changes in the multilist in Figure 12–3:

   a. Logically delete record

      1106 JUST5963-55 . . . .

      from the file. (Flag as deleted by giving the Primary Key, Account Number, the value ZZZZ0000-00.)

b. Add a new subscriber (at record location 1111) with

Account Number	WALT1234-56	Subscription Yr.	1984
Expiration Month	AUG	Zipcode	02194

9. In the file of Figure 12–3, illustrate how to find all of the records with 1984 new subscription date and JUL expiration month. (Assume that the length of each chain has been stored in the corresponding lowest level index entry.)
10. Make the following changes in the inverted file of Figure 12–5:

a. Logically delete record

1104 FRED8381-12 . . . .

from the file. (Flag as deleted by giving the Primary Key, Account Number, the value ZZZZ0000-00.)

b. Add a new subscriber to location 1111 with

Account Number	THAL2361-42	Subscription Yr.	1984
Expiration Month	MAR	Zipcode	03614

c. Add a new subscriber to location 1104 with

Account Number	FERN4793-82	Subscription Yr.	1984
Expiration Month	JAN	Zipcode	03990

11. In the file of Figure 12–5 illustrate how to find all of the subscribers with 1984 new subscription year and JULY expiration month and zipcode beginning 02. . . .
12. a. In the file of Figure 12–5 create a new permanent multiple key target access list, with appropriate index entries, for those records with zipcode beginning 02. . . *and* expiration month of (JAN *or* JUL).

b. List the records which are indicated in this multiple key entry.

13. In the Employees file of Table 12–1, what are the column headings?
14. Illustrate how the following queries might be answered from Table 12–1 by a relational data base system:

a. Who are the employees who work in building ET236?

b. How many employees in Sales make more that $6.00 per hour and do not live in Layton?

15. Illustrate how a hierarchical data base management system might accomplish the following tasks from the file described in Figure 12–6:

    a. In which Family, Order, and Class does the Species Devil's Shoelace belong?

    b. How close is the relationship between Ulothrix and Henware?

    c. Find the record for Family Cladophoraceae.

PART III

FILE MANAGEMENT TECHNIQUES

PROLOGUE

JOHN VON NEUMANN

Johann (John) Von Neumann was born in Budapest, Hungary, in 1903. His unusual mathematics ability was fostered in childhood by private tutoring from university professors, and at age 19 he was already recognized as a professional mathematician. He taught at Berlin (1927–1929), at Hamburg (1929–1930), and then at Princeton University (1930–1933) before he was asked to join the Institute for Advanced Study at Princeton, where he was the youngest permanent member of that distinguished faculty. As a professor at the Institute and as a consultant during World War II and thereafter for the U.S. Army, the Navy, and the Atomic Energy Commission, John Von Neumann pursued work in pure and applied mathematics, logic, analysis, mathematical physics, electronics design, statistics, nuclear energy, and computing. He was comfortable in all of these fields and received many awards for his services.

Von Neumann developed numerous methods of computer programming, including the concept of storing both program and data within computer memory. He supervised construction of an early computer at the Institute for Advanced Study and developed many of the devices which are essential to the function of present computing systems. For these accomplishments he is often recognized as "the father of modern computing." Before his death in 1957, he had begun to work on general theories of automation, including how to build self-reproducing machines and computers which could diagnose and compensate for failures within their own components.

CHAPTER 13

SPACE ALLOCATION AND CATALOGS

DEVICE AND SPACE ALLOCATION

The user and/or the computer operating system must determine which I/O or storage device is to be used for a given application. There are two fundamental methods for allocating the device. In one case, *general allocation,* it is assumed that an appropriate device will be available when requested. In this situation complex strategies and job scheduling must be implemented so that no part of the system sits idle for long periods of time, waiting for devices to become available. The other method requires *data staging,* where the user's program accesses only a DASD. As other devices become ready the data is moved from the DASD to the device or vice-versa. In practice, many systems strike some compromise between these two approaches.

General Allocation

If it is assumed that devices must be available when requested, the computer operator or the operating system's job scheduler programs survey the priority, anticipated execution time, primary memory requirements, and

I/O device requests of all jobs known to be waiting in a job queue. Then the scheduler, within its capability, determines the order in which the jobs are to be executed to obtain the most efficient use of the equipment.

To accomplish its task the job scheduler must have access to a *device unit table* in which is listed each piece of peripheral equipment in the system as well as its status; i. e., whether available or not. A device may be unavailable to a user if it is currently in use or if it has been disconnected for repair or some other reason. Also, not every user is permitted access to every unit. Some devices are assigned to specific purposes, such as the operator's console or a DASD on which only the operating system resides.

The job scheduler, whether a human operator or an operating system program, may allocate devices either statically or dynamically. In *static allocation* all of the devices needed for a job are assigned before program execution begins and released at job termination. *Dynamic allocation* assigns devices when requested by the program. Obviously, dynamic allocation has the advantage of reducing the amount of time during which a particular job needs a device. However, it can lead to a deadlock situation, where processes are delayed indefinitely while waiting for another to release a device.

The tasks of job scheduling are made easier, but the efficiency of the system may be reduced, if the user requires one specific device. In this *demand allocation* situation, there are no alternatives; the user demands a specific channel and unit, or the requested data has been mounted already on a particular tape or disk drive. In this case the only decision to be made by the scheduler is whether or not the devices which were requested are available.

A much greater flexibility is achieved when alternatives are available in the way units can be assigned. In *decision allocation* more than one piece of equipment is available on the system which will satisfy the user's needs. Then the scheduler may assign those devices arbitrarily or follow a carefully planned decision algorithm to improve the system efficiency. Possible decision algorithms which could be built into an operating system might include selecting first the devices which cannot fill the requirements of other programs, or selecting devices which already have mounted volumes of data which can be used. In the latter case the scheduler must be capable of *automatic volume recognition,* of searching the device unit table periodically to determine which volumes have been mounted. The process of loading a tape or a disk must cause a system interrupt during which the volume label is read into the unit table.

Data Staging

In a multi-user environment it may not be reasonable to expect a job scheduler to be adept at allocating all devices to all users. The method of staging may then be the best method for allocating devices and space. You may have experienced a time-sharing environment where you were not allowed to write directly to the printer. Instead, you had to write to a file in a printer SPOOL area on the DASD. The printer SPOOL (which stands for Simultaneous Peripheral Operations On Line) acts as a large queue from which the printer accepts data as it can. This is an example of data staging; the user always reads from or writes to a DASD rather than directly from or to an I/O device.

In data staging, the job scheduler need not require all devices to be available before execution of a program. Indeed, one program might produce numerous output reports on only one printer, simply by staging each output to a separate DASD file in the printer SPOOL area. Another advantage of staging lies in the fact that data may be processed again without having to rerun a program, because input or output data which pass through a file on a DASD will be stored there until that area is released for other uses.

Staging uses extra channels, control units, and DASD storage space. It delays the time between a process and the physical I/O operations. It tends to compromise data integrity, just as any other extra handling does. However, the freedom gained by servicing concurrent users generally outweighs these disadvantages.

Allocating Space

Already considered in Chapter 5 was the question of determining the amount of space to be allocated to a file on a DASD. The space required for actual data is simply the number of blocks times the total number of bytes in each block. Included within the block length must be the space for pointers in linked lists and for record overhead, such as count and address areas. If data compression techniques are applied, the block lengths may be reduced in size by the amount of compression achieved. Given the total number of records, the blocking factor, and the total number of bytes per record, it is a straightforward procedure, illustrated in the examples of Chapter 5, to determine the number of tracks and cylinders required to store a data file on a given device.

It has also been emphasized that considerably more storage space must be allocated for files which contain indexes, access lists, tickler files, scatter tables, hash functions, etc. Nevertheless, once the lengths of records in the indexes or tables have been determined, the amount of space allocated for those features is calculated in the same fashion as for the data.

A different problem, however, is to keep track of *where* each piece of information is recorded. This must be accomplished by some system of cataloging.

FILE CATALOGS AND TABLES

A catalog or file table is itself a file, the records of which contain the descriptions and addresses of other files. The catalog must be indexed so that the individual records which it contains may be accessed, updated, inserted, and deleted quickly and easily. Catalogs are generated automatically by most modern operating systems.

A system of file catalogs, or directories, may be considered as a hierarchy in which a master catalog points to subcatalogs in a tree structure similar to the indexes illustrated for indexed files in Chapter 11. The highest level catalog entries point to other catalogs, while the lowest level entries point to files. When a user wishes to locate a file, the catalog levels are searched until a descriptor of the desired file is found.

A file descriptor may be contained within the catalog itself, or all of the descriptors for the files on a given medium may be stored in a specific contiguous extent on that medium, in which case the descriptors are pointed to by the lowest level catalog entries. The file descriptor index on a disk pack is commonly called the *Volume Table of Contents,* VTOC. Within the VTOC, for each file you may find its physical address, the dates when the file was created and when the latest changes were made, who owns it, the access level authorized, how the file is organized and the records formatted, and perhaps even the date when it can be released or deleted.

When a program requests access to a file it may use a set of three catalogs called file tables. The first of these, the *file control table,* FCT, will be directly accessible within a user's program area. An FCT is generated whenever a program is compiled. It will contain separate entries for each file defined or requested by the program. When a file is opened and activity occurs within the file the information in the file control table is updated, and any changes in information regarding the file are transmitted to the VTOC when the file is closed.

A second catalog, called the *active file table,* AFT, is maintained by most systems to keep track of all of the active files in the system. This table is kept within the storage area assigned to the operating system. The AFT contains an entry for every open file in the system. Within an AFT entry will be found such information as the name of the file, the names of the programs which are to use the file, and the address of the file itself. When a file is closed, the AFT entry which refers to it is removed.

The third catalog needed to run a program is the *device unit table,* DUT, which also resides within the operating system storage area. In this table are listed all of the I/O devices for the system, with type, status, currently assigned identifier, and address for each device. When a user's program is compiled it creates the File Control Table within the user area. Opening a file or requesting use of an I/O device during program execution creates entries in the Active File Table and relates AFT, FCT, and DUT entries for allocation of space and I/O equipment.

Still another set of directories is needed to keep track of space on a storage device. One of these, the *Device Block Space Table,* DBST, is provided for each device on the system and contains information about whether each block (track, cylinder, or other physical unit) on the device is available for use. The DBST normally will be stored on the storage medium itself, but it must be available to the operating system when the device is in use and may be moved temporarily to special supervisory memory locations for that purpose. A *File Block Table,* FBT, is stored on the secondary storage medium to keep track of which blocks are assigned to each file. If the device architecture requires fixed length blocks, the DBST and the FBT may be in the form of a "bit map," a few bytes containing one bit for each block. The system protocol would dictate whether a "0" or a "1" in the bit map signifies that the block is available. When block lengths are variable, such as on a "conventional" DASD, the DBST and FBT may be simple indexes or catalogs of block lengths and addresses.

FILE CONTROL SYSTEMS

Programs for handling the reading and writing of files are part of the *file control system.* Also included within every such system are the programs for generating, accessing, and maintaining the file catalogs, directories, and tables. Most of these operations occur automatically without user intervention; however, there must be functions which allow the user to have some control over the operating system. The commands and programs within an operating system which are directly accessible to the programmer form the job control language of any computer system.

Commands

The individual commands most familiar to users of large machines are those which allow simple creation, examination, relocation, and deletion of files. Indeed, you may be familiar already with such JCL commands as GENERATE or CREATE for creating a new file or allocating space to be used by a file, LIST for examining the contents of a file, COPY, MOVE, or RELOCATE for moving the contents of a file to another area, NAME or RENAME for changing a file description, or KILL, ERASE, ELIMINATE, or DELETE for erasing a file and freeing the area for future reuse. In most job control languages these commands may be used with a number of options such as requiring contiguous space for a new file, defining the extent of an area, specifying the size of a buffer or the record length to be used for reading from or writing to the file, naming the source and destination for examination or relocation, defining the access authorization to the file, etc.

Another set of commands, which may be available directly within the job control language or called from higher level languages, includes the FIELD, PUT, and GET type of instructions which control reading from and writing to a file. The FIELD command defines an I/O buffer, namely which variables are to occupy which bytes within the buffer. PUT moves the contents of the buffer to the output medium, and GET moves a record from the input device to the buffer. In some languages, such as BASIC, the programmer gets very close to these commands. Their use is illustrated in Chapter 15. In other languages, such as FORTRAN or COBOL, the file handling commands will be contained within operating system routines which are called by READ and WRITE statements.

Utilities

In addition to simple commands, most file control systems have system utilities, which are entire programs available to the user. These include the system editors, as well as special functions such as indexed or random file handling programs, language compilers and interpreters, and routines which have been added to the system library by users and operators. To call a system editor, for example, the user issues an edit command. Numerous options may be available, such as specifying the name and characteristics of the file to be edited. Once the editor has been invoked the user is actually running an operating system program which itself recognizes a variety of commands for inserting, deleting, and changing records. In another situation, after issuing a command to call an indexed file utility the user may have instructions available for manipulating and searching for records on multiple keys without ever being concerned about the file structure at all.

Newer operating systems will appear to the user as a set of utility programs from which larger sets of utilities may be built. The direction of development is an attempt to make the computer more friendly to the user and the file handling more powerful.

QUESTIONS

1. All computer systems keep track of I/O and storage devices by specifying the device status to be READY (or AVAILABLE) or NOT READY. When would it be valuable to have a third status state, namely SCHEDULED TO BECOME AVAILABLE?

2. Describe at least one other decision algorithm, not discussed in this chapter, which might make decision allocation more efficient than simple arbitrary assignment.
3. Suppose one user's program has a demand allocation of devices requirement. In what circumstances could this cause a second user's decision allocation to become a demand allocation?
4. Aside from deadlock or delay while waiting for devices to be released, what other problems could result from excessive use of dynamic allocation?
5. a. How does the concept of staging discussed in this chapter relate to the data staging concept discussed in conjunction with mass storage systems in Chapter 3?

   b. What does staging have to do with virtual memory?
6. What would be wrong with using a magnetic tape as a staging medium?
7. a. If staging of data and programs through a DASD can be so efficient, why not build computers with very small primary memories which handle everything with staging?

   b. Why not build huge primary memories and elimate staging altogether?
8. Distinguish between each of the following file tables or catalogs and indicate where each is most efficiently located:

   VTOC FCT AFT DUT DBST FBT
9. In which file table(s) would you most likely find passwords or access permission information? Why?
10. Which of the following would be preferable during creation of a file? Why?

    a. to allocate too much space initially and then release unused areas.

    b. to allocate a small amount of space and then extend it as needed.
11. What is the difference in JCL between a command and a utility? Give at least one example of each.

CHAPTER 14

ALGORITHMS FOR LINEAR DATA STRUCTURES

INTRODUCTION

In this chapter and the next you will find algorithms illustrating some of the file handling techniques which have been discussed in the text. There are also a number of exercises which will encourage you to practice those techniques.

The programs are written in BASIC, structured as well as is feasible in that language. Subprograms for different functions are numbered consistently so that they can be used in many programs with only slight modifications. A list of the subprograms and of the programs in which they appear is given in Table 15–1 at the end of Chapter 15. The version of BASIC used is Microsoft*; however, an attempt has been made to keep the commands as fundamental as possible so that the language will be common to most machines. You may have to modify the commands for opening files so that the programs will run on your computer, but most other instructions should be executable without significant changes.

Given the fact that many other languages are better suited for file handling and structured programming, it may seem incongruous to use BASIC

*Microsoft BASIC is copyrighted by Microsoft Corporation.

for illustrating those techniques. However, there are two very good reasons for doing so. First, nearly every reader of this book who has use of a computer should have access to BASIC language. No other language is so universally available. If the student has learned another language, it should not be difficult to become familiar quickly with enough BASIC so that the programs can be read and understood.

The second reason for choosing BASIC is precisely that file handling is not particularly simple in this language. There are few sophisticated, built-in access routines. Thus the programmer must handle many of the details which are hidden within special commands in other languages. This forces us to lay out precisely what is needed to code each algorithm. If the reader can understand file handling in BASIC, translating those techniques to other languages should be straightforward.

Methods of handling sequential files and other linear organizations are illustrated first. Then in Chapter 15 some random or direct access file techniques and nonlinear methods are shown. No attempt has been made to present an exhaustive software package, but enough examples are given that you will have a foundation upon which to build more elegant data structures. The programs build upon each other, with later algorithms using some of the routines developed early. Each procedure is diagrammed and explained as it occurs the first time.

Remember that these programs are designed to *illustrate* the methods. In the sample runs, you will see much printed information which you would not need if you were going to use the procedures efficiently as part of another programming package. These extra illustrative steps can be removed easily by deleting appropriate PRINT statements and GOSUB commands which refer to printing subroutines. In addition, the subprograms are shown in the program listings in as logical an order as possible, with branches generally in the forward direction. The order in which you see them listed here, therefore, may not be the same as the numerical order (by line number) which you would see when you list the programs on your computer.

WRITING TO A SEQUENTIAL FILE

On most systems, writing to a sequential file is a matter of opening the file by name, specifying a logical file number by which the file is referenced while it is open, writing variables into the file, and closing the file when finished.

In the program CREATE, in Figure 14–1, those steps are followed. The OPEN command in this version of BASIC requires that the file be opened for Output ("O") from the computer to the disk. The OPEN command on your

```
Clear space for strings
What are the name and number of the file?
Open the file for output (write)

┌──────────────────────────────────────────┐
│       Request a record                   │
│       Write the record into the file     │
└─────────────── Repeat unless the record is STOP┘

Close the file
Stop
```

FIGURE 14–1(a). Create a Sequential File—Pseudocode

```
1000 REM********** CREATE A SEQUENTIAL FILE *****************
1005 REM CLEAR SPACE FOR STRING VARIABLES,
1010 REM OPEN A FILE FOR OUTPUT OF DATA INTO THE FILE
1020 REM THEN OUTPUT STRINGS TO THE FILE
1025 CLEAR 2000
1027 INPUT "WHAT IS THE NAME OF YOUR FILE";NM$
1028 INPUT "BY WHAT NUMBER SHOULD I REFER TO THE FILE";NO
1030 OPEN "O",NO,NM$
1040 PRINT "GIVE ME STRINGS A$,B$,C$ (TERMINATE WITH A$=STOP)"
1045 INPUT A$,B$,C$
1050 IF A$="STOP" GOTO 1090
1060      PRINT #NO,A$,CHR$(44),B$,CHR$(44),C$
1070      GOTO 1040
1090 CLOSE NO
1099 END
```

FIGURE 14–1(b). Create a Sequential File—The Program

computer should be similar to this but may differ slightly. A sequential file is opened either for Output (write) or Input (read). Most small systems will not allow you to read from and write into a sequential file at the same time. This is consistent with the description in Chapter 7 of how sequential files are handled.

The program in Figure 14–1 creates a sequential file with three strings (sequences of characters) on each line. After each new statement, such as *PRINT #1,A$,CHR$(44),B$,CHR$(44),C$* is executed, a nonprinting, end-of-line character is inserted into the file automatically. Thus each line of the file is a separate record containing three fields, as shown by the sample run and listing of the file in Figure 14–2. It is important that the program had to print the separators between fields (commas in this case), which is done by PRINT CHR$(44), since ASCII for the comma is 44. If you do not print field separators into the file, each record may be assumed to be one long field and would be read as one variable.

```
WHAT IS THE NAME OF YOUR FILE? DATA
BY WHAT NUMBER SHOULD I REFER TO THE FILE? 1
GIVE ME STRINGS A$,B$,C$ (TERMINATE WITH A$=STOP)
? BUZZ, UZRA*BILL, 1968
? NOODLEY, HOLMES*NORRIS, 1975
? SKINNY, WILSON*TOM, 1982
? MISTY, JONES*SALLY, 1980
? LIZ, SMITH*ELIZABETH, 1974
? HIGHPOCKETS, RICH*HOWARD, 1980
? GRUMBLY, SMITH*TED, 1983
? RED, BARTON*FRITZ, 1978
? SNIPPETS, WILKINS*MARY, 1982
? TRUDGEON, FISH*ARNOLD, 1980
? TOPPER, PEARSON*TOM, 1975
? STOP
??
```

FIGURE 14–2(a). Running the Program to Create a Sequential File

```
BUZZ          ,   UZRA*BILL          ,   1968
NOODLEY       ,   HOLMES*NORRIS      ,   1975
SKINNY        ,   WILSON*TOM         ,   1982
MISTY         ,   JONES*SALLY        ,   1980
LIZ           ,   SMITH*ELIZABETH    ,   1974
HIGHPOCKETS   ,   RICH*HOWARD        ,   1980
GRUMBLY       ,   SMITH*TED          ,   1983
RED           ,   BARTON*FRITZ       ,   1978
SNIPPETS      ,   WILKINS*MARY       ,   1982
TRUDGEON      ,   FISH*ARNOLD        ,   1980
TOPPER        ,   PEARSON*TOM        ,   1975
```

FIGURE 14–2(b). The Resulting File

Some computers allow you to write only strings into a file. Others will let you write numbers, either directly (by using variable name A, instead of A$, in this case) or by conversion functions which convert numbers to strings and vice versa. In this chapter we will begin by writing only strings into our files. Following the discussion of the List Linker program (Figure 14–15), an algorithm is given for converting integers to strings. This algorithm is used in subsequent programs for storing integers (in the form of character strings) in some files.

READING FROM A SEQUENTIAL FILE

The program RECALL, in Figure 14–3, reads the records from a sequential file and prints them so that they can be examined. The file is first opened

```
Clear and dimension string space
What are the name and number of the file?
How many records are to be read from the file? (N)
Open the file for input (read)

        Read a record from the file
                    Repeat N times

Print the N records
Close the file
Stop
```

FIGURE 14–3(a). Recall Records from a Sequential File—Pseudocode

```
1100 REM********** RECALL A SEQUENTIAL FILE ************
1110 REM DIMENSION VARIABLES, CLEAR SPACE FOR STRINGS
1120 REM OPEN THE FILE FOR INPUT FROM THE DISK
1130 REM INPUT THE DATA FROM THE FILE
1140 CLEAR 2000
1145 DIM A$(20),B$(20),C$(20)
1147 INPUT "WHAT IS THE NAME OF YOUR FILE";NM$
1148 INPUT "BY WHAT NUMBER SHOULD I REFER TO THE FILE";NO
1150 INPUT "HOW MANY STRINGS (<=20) TO READ FROM FILE";N
1160 IF N<=0 GOTO 1240
1170      OPEN "I",NO,NM$
1180      FOR I=1 TO N
1190           INPUT #NO,A$(I),B$(I),C$(I)
1200      NEXT I
1210      FOR I=1 TO N
1220           PRINT A$(I),B$(I),C$(I)
1230      NEXT I
1240 CLOSE NO
1249 END
```

FIGURE 14–3(b). Recall Records from a Sequential File—The Program

for Input ("I") from the disk to the computer. It is important that OPEN "I" sets the read pointer to the first record. Because the file is sequential, if you wish to find the fifth record, for example, you will have to read and discard the first four records.

The records are read one at a time from the file by a command such as *INPUT #1,A$,B$,C$,* where A$, B$, C$ are variable names given to the three fields in one record. If you had forgotten to write field separators (commas) into the file, the command *INPUT #1,A$,B$,C$,* would try to read three records. Figure 14–4 shows what happens when program RECALL, Figure 14–3, is executed to read the file created in Figure 14–2.

```
WHAT IS THE NAME OF YOUR FILE? DATA
BY WHAT NUMBER SHOULD I REFER TO THE FILE? 1
HOW MANY STRINGS (<=20) TO READ FROM FILE? 11
BUZZ                UZRA*BILL               1968
NOODLEY             HOLMES*NORRIS           1975
SKINNY              WILSON*TOM              1982
MISTY               JONES*SALLY             1980
LIZ                 SMITH*ELIZABETH         1974
HIGHPOCKETS         RICH*HOWARD             1980
GRUMBLY             SMITH*TED               1983
RED                 BARTON*FRITZ            1978
SNIPPETS            WILKINS*MARY            1982
TRUDGEON            FISH*ARNOLD             1980
TOPPER              PEARSON*TOM             1975
```

FIGURE 14–4. Running the Program to Recall Records from a Sequential File

SORTING

Bubble Sort

A program to perform a Bubble sort on a list of strings A$(I) is shown in Figure 14–5. You may use the bubble sort subroutine (lines 1300–1399) to sort any list of *N* strings, whether you enter them with INPUT or READ statements or whether you read them from a file as we have done using the RECALL routine (lines 1100–1249). Note that we chose only to remember and sort on the first field of each record. Line 1190 reads all three fields in the record, but B$ and C$ are ignored in the rest of the program.

```
Clear and dimension string space
Read the data (See Figure 14-3)

┌──── Sort the data ───────────────────────────────┐
│         Let the length of list = N                │
│                                                   │
│   ┌──────────────────────────────────────────────┐│
│   │      ┌──────────────────────────────────────┐ ││
│   │      │   Compare adjacent elements           │ ││
│   │      │   Interchange when an element is larger│ ││
│   │      │        than its successor             │ ││
│   │      └──────────────── Repeat N-1 times ─────┘ ││
│   │                                               ││
│   │     Reduce the length of the list by 1        ││
│   └─────────────────── Repeat until list length = 2┘│
└───────────────────────────────────────────────────┘

Print the sorted list
Stop
```

FIGURE 14–5(a). Perform a Bubble Sort—Pseudocode

```
100 REM *********** PERFORM A BUBBLE SORT *************
105 CLEAR 2000
106 DIM A$(20)
110 REM READ THE DATA TO BE SORTED
120 GOSUB 1100
130 REM SORT THE DATA
140 GOSUB 1300
150 REM PRINT THE SORTED RESULTS
155 PRINT "COMPLETELY SORTED, THE DATA LOOKS LIKE:"
160 GOSUB 1400
170 REM END OF PROGRAM
180 GOTO 9999


1100 REM********* RECALL A SEQUENTIAL FILE ************
1120 REM OPEN THE FILE FOR INPUT FROM THE DISK
1130 REM INPUT THE DATA FROM THE FILE
1147 INPUT "WHAT IS THE NAME OF YOUR FILE";NM$
1148 INPUT "BY WHAT NUMBER SHOULD I REFER TO THE FILE";NO
1150 INPUT "HOW MANY STRINGS (<=20) TO READ FROM FILE";N
1160 IF N<=0 GOTO 1240
1170      OPEN "I",NO,NM$
1180      FOR I=1 TO N
1190           INPUT #NO,A$(I),B$,C$
1200      NEXT I
1205      PRINT "UNSORTED, YOUR DATA LOOKS LIKE:"
1210      FOR I=1 TO N
1220           PRINT A$(I)
1230      NEXT I
1235    PRINT
1240 CLOSE NO
1249 RETURN


1300 REM *********** BUBBLE SORT ROUTINE ***********
1310 FOR K=2 TO N-1
1315      REM LL=LENGTH OF LIST GOES FROM N-1 DOWN TO 2
1320      LL=N-K+1
1330      FOR X=1 TO LL
1335         REM COMPARE ADJACENT ELEMENTS A$(X) AND A$(X+1)
1340         IF A$(X) <= A$(X+1) GOTO 1380
1345              REM WHENEVER A$(X) > A$(X+1) INTERCHANGE THEM
1350              T$=A$(X)
1360              A$(X)=A$(X+1)
1370              A$(X+1)=T$
1380      NEXT X
1385      REM PRINT THE DATA AFTER EACH PASS
1386      PRINT "AFTER PASS ";K-1;" THE DATA LOOKS LIKE:"
1387      GOSUB 1400
1390 NEXT K
1399 RETURN
```

FIGURE 14–5(b). Perform a Bubble Sort—The Program

```
1400 REM *********** PRINT THE RESULTS ***********
1420 FOR I=1 TO N
1430      PRINT A$(I)
1440 NEXT I
1445 PRINT
1449 RETURN


9999 END
```

FIGURE 14–5(b). Continued

The actual procedure for the bubble sort is the subroutine in lines 1300 through 1399. If you follow this through carefully, you will see that the length of the list (LL) starts with the total number of elements (actually $N-1$, because, in the last comparison, the next element to be compared with the N 1st is the Nth). Then for the entire list, each element A$(X) is compared with the next element A$(X+1). Whenever any element is larger than the next, they are interchanged (lines 1350–1370). A little reflection should convince you that the interchange involves storing one of the elements in a temporary location (T$) so that it is not lost.

At the end of the first pass, the largest element is at the end of the list. The subroutine call at lines 1385–1387 prints the data after each pass. These lines may be deleted if you wish just to see the final results. The length of the list (LL) is then reduced by 1, and all the remaining elements are compared again, with interchanges made as appropriate. After the length of the list has been reduced to 2, the sort is complete, and the elements are printed out in final order by the subroutine at lines 1400–1499. Figure 14–6 shows a sample run of the program, where we chose to read and sort the first five records from the file.

Selection Sort

A Selection Sort program is shown in Figure 14–7. The program appears similar to the bubble sort program, but there are two important differences:

1. In this program we chose to keep all three fields of each record but to sort on field A$. Therefore, when an interchange is made (lines 1580–1587), all three field variables, A$(I), B$(I), and C$(I), are interchanged.

```
WHAT IS THE NAME OF YOUR FILE? DATA
BY WHAT NUMBER SHOULD I REFER TO THE FILE? 1
HOW MANY STRINGS (<=20) TO READ FROM FILE? 5
UNSORTED, YOUR DATA LOOKS LIKE:
BUZZ
NOODLEY
SKINNY
MISTY
LIZ

AFTER PASS  1   THE DATA LOOKS LIKE:
BUZZ
NOODLEY
MISTY
LIZ
SKINNY

AFTER PASS  2   THE DATA LOOKS LIKE:
BUZZ
MISTY
LIZ
NOODLEY
SKINNY

AFTER PASS  3   THE DATA LOOKS LIKE:
BUZZ
LIZ
MISTY
NOODLEY
SKINNY

COMPLETELY SORTED, THE DATA LOOKS LIKE:
BUZZ
LIZ
MISTY
NOODLEY
SKINNY
```

FIGURE 14–6. Running the Program to Perform a Bubble Sort

2. The selection sort subroutine (lines 1500–1599) is used instead of a bubble sort routine.

In the selection sort routine, the length of the list (L) begins at *N* and is reduced by 1 after each pass until the sort is completed when the list has a length of 2. At the beginning of each pass, the maximum value (MX$) is assumed to be the first element in the list. Each element A$(X) is read, and

```
Clear and dimension string space
Read the data (See Figure 14-3)

-------Sort the data-------------------------------
        Let the length of list = N

        Read the list
        Find maximum element and its subscript
        Interchange maximum with end of list
        Reduce length of list by 1
        ----------------Repeat until length of list = 2

Print the sorted list
Stop
```

FIGURE 14–7(a). Perform a Selection Sort—Pseudocode

```
100 REM *********** PERFORM A SELECTION SORT ************
105 CLEAR 2000
106 DIM A$(20),B$(20),C$(20)
110 REM READ THE DATA TO BE SORTED
120 GOSUB 1100
130 REM SORT THE DATA
140 GOSUB 1500
150 REM PRINT THE SORTED RESULTS
155 PRINT "COMPLETELY SORTED, THE DATA LOOKS LIKE:"
160 GOSUB 1400
170 REM END OF PROGRAM
180 GOTO 9999


1100 REM********** RECALL A SEQUENTIAL FILE ***********
1120 REM OPEN THE FILE FOR INPUT FROM THE DISK
1130 REM INPUT THE DATA FROM THE FILE
1147 INPUT "WHAT IS THE NAME OF YOUR FILE";NM$
1148 INPUT "BY WHAT NUMBER SHOULD I REFER TO THE FILE";NO
1150 INPUT "HOW MANY STRINGS (<=20) TO READ FROM FILE";N
1160 IF N<=0 GOTO 1240
1170      OPEN "I",NO,NM$
1180      FOR I=1 TO N
1190           INPUT #NO,A$(I),B$(I),C$(I)
1200      NEXT I
1205      PRINT "UNSORTED, YOUR DATA LOOKS LIKE:"
1210      FOR I=1 TO N
1220           PRINT A$(I);B$(I);C$(I)
1230      NEXT I
1235    PRINT
1240 CLOSE NO
1249 RETURN
```

FIGURE 14–7(b). Perform a Selection Sort—The Program

```
1500 REM *********** SELECTION SORT ***********
1510 FOR K=2 TO N
1515      REM L=LENGTH OF LIST GOES FROM N DOWN TO 2
1520      L=N-K+2
1535      REM BEGIN WITH MAXIMUM, MX$, EQUALS A$(1)
1536      REM AND MAXIMUM COUNTER, MC, AT 1
1540      MX$=A$(1)
1545      MC=1
1550      FOR X=2 TO L
1555           REM COMPARE EACH ELEMENT TO MAXIMUM,
1556           REM AND SET ELEMENT TO MAXIMUM IF LARGER
1560           IF A$(X) <= MX$ GOTO 1570
1565                MX$=A$(X)
1566                MC=X
1570      NEXT X
1580      T$=A$(L): U$=B$(L): V$=C$(L)
1585      A$(L)=A$(MC): B$(L)=B$(MC): C$(L)=C$(MC)
1587      A$(MC)=T$: B$(MC)=U$: C$(MC)=V$
1590      REM PRINT THE DATA AFTER EACH PASS
1591      PRINT "AFTER PASS ";K-1;" THE DATA LOOKS LIKE:"
1592      GOSUB 1400
1595 NEXT K
1599 RETURN


1400 REM *********** PRINT THE RESULTS ***********
1420 FOR I=1 TO N
1430      PRINT A$(I);B$(I);C$(I)
1440 NEXT I
1445 PRINT
1449 RETURN


9999 END
```

FIGURE 14–7(b). Continued

when one larger than the maximum (MX$) is found, it becomes the maximum (MX$), and its subscript (X) is remembered as the position of the maximum (MC). At the end of the pass, the fields of the last record in the list (A$(L), B$(L), C$(L)) are interchanged with the fields of the record at the maximum position (A$(MC), B$(MC), C$(MC)), using T$, U$, and V$ as temporary storage locations.

Lines 1590–1592 call the routine to print the data after each pass. These lines may be deleted if you desire to see only the final results.

Figure 14–8 shows a sample run of the selection sort program, where we chose to read and sort the first five records of the file.

```
WHAT IS THE NAME OF YOUR FILE? DATA
BY WHAT NUMBER SHOULD I REFER TO THE FILE? 1
HOW MANY STRINGS (<=20) TO READ FROM FILE? 5
UNSORTED, YOUR DATA LOOKS LIKE:
BUZZ            UZRA*BILL         1968
NOODLEY         HOLMES*NORRIS     1975
SKINNY          WILSON*TOM        1982
MISTY           JONES*SALLY       1980
LIZ             SMITH*ELIZABETH   1974


AFTER PASS  1   THE DATA LOOKS LIKE:
BUZZ            UZRA*BILL         1968
NOODLEY         HOLMES*NORRIS     1975
LIZ             SMITH*ELIZABETH   1974
MISTY           JONES*SALLY       1980
SKINNY          WILSON*TOM        1982


AFTER PASS  2   THE DATA LOOKS LIKE:
BUZZ            UZRA*BILL         1968
MISTY           JONES*SALLY       1980
LIZ             SMITH*ELIZABETH   1974
NOODLEY         HOLMES*NORRIS     1975
SKINNY          WILSON*TOM        1982


AFTER PASS  3   THE DATA LOOKS LIKE:
BUZZ            UZRA*BILL         1968
LIZ             SMITH*ELIZABETH   1974
MISTY           JONES*SALLY       1980
NOODLEY         HOLMES*NORRIS     1975
SKINNY          WILSON*TOM        1982


AFTER PASS  4   THE DATA LOOKS LIKE:
BUZZ            UZRA*BILL         1968
LIZ             SMITH*ELIZABETH   1974
MISTY           JONES*SALLY       1980
NOODLEY         HOLMES*NORRIS     1975
SKINNY          WILSON*TOM        1982


COMPLETELY SORTED, THE DATA LOOKS LIKE:
BUZZ            UZRA*BILL         1968
LIZ             SMITH*ELIZABETH   1974
MISTY           JONES*SALLY       1980
NOODLEY         HOLMES*NORRIS     1975
SKINNY          WILSON*TOM        1982
```

FIGURE 14–8. Running the Program to Perform a Selection Sort

STACKS

A Simple Stack Handler

Before we can illustrate the quick sort we must be able to write fields to a stack. Since a stack is generally temporary, we will not worry (until we can access random files) about writing it to a disk; instead we will use subscripted variables to contain the stack records.

In the Stack Handler program of Figure 14–9, we have chosen to represent the top of stack pointer by SP. This particular program will write three fields in each record on the stack. Thus, for example, ST$(5,1), ST$(5,2), and ST$(5,3) would be the three fields in record 5 on the stack.

A flag (FL) is set by the PUSH, POP, and STOP routines in the program so that (in line 960) if FL is negative the program returns to the menu, and if FL is positive the program stops.

```
Clear and dimension string space
Initialize stack pointer (SP=0)

┌──── Menu ──────────────────────────────────────────────────┐
│                                                            │
│   ┌──── PUSH ──────────────────────────────────────────┐   │
│   │          Increment stack pointer (SP)              │   │
│   │          What is to be pushed onto the stack? (P)  │   │
│   │          Set top of stack = P                      │   │
│   │                                                    │   │
│   │          Print the stack                           │   │
│   │                 If SP=0, print "empty"             │   │
│   │                 Otherwise                          │   │
│   │                                                    │   │
│   │                   ┌── Print an element ───────┐    │   │
│   │                   └──── Repeat for I=1 to SP──┘    │   │
│   │                                                    │   │
│   └──────────────────────── Return to Menu ────────────┘   │
│                                                            │
│   ┌──── POP ───────────────────────────────────────────┐   │
│   │          If SP=0, print "you can't POP from an empty stack"
│   │          Otherwise                                 │   │
│   │                 Set top of stack to temporary T$   │   │
│   │                 Decrement the stack pointer        │   │
│   │                 Print the stack (See PUSH above)   │   │
│   │                                                    │   │
│   └──────────────────────── Return to Menu ────────────┘   │
└────────────────────────────────────────────────────────────┘
Print the stack (See PUSH above)
Stop
```

FIGURE 14–9(a). A Stack Handler—Pseudocode

```
900 REM *********** STACK HANDLER ***********
905 CLEAR 2000
906 DIM ST$(20,3)
910 REM SET STACK POINTER TO ZERO (STACK IS INITIALLY EMPTY)
912 SP=0
920 REM PUSH OR POP MENU
925 PRINT "SPECIFY BY NUMBER, WOULD YOU LIKE TO"
927 PRINT "      1. PUSH ?"
928 PRINT "      2. POP  ?"
929 PRINT "      3. STOP ?"
930 INPUT "WHAT IS YOUR CHOICE";CH
932 PRINT
940 ON CH GOSUB 1600, 1650, 980
950 PRINT
960 IF FL > 0  GOTO 9999  ELSE  GOTO 925


1600 REM *********** PUSH ONTO THE STACK ***********
1602 REM AFTER INCREMENTING THE STACK POINTER (SP)
1605 SP=SP+1
1610 PRINT "WHAT THREE FIELDS WOULD YOU LIKE TO PUSH"
1612 PRINT "INTO THE TOP RECORD OF THE STACK"
1614 INPUT P1$,P2$,P3$
1620 ST$(SP,1)=P1$
1622 ST$(SP,2)=P2$
1624 ST$(SP,3)=P3$
1630 REM PRINT THE STACK
1632 PRINT
1635 PRINT "THE STACK NOW LOOKS LIKE:"
1637 GOSUB 1250
1640 FL = -1
1649 RETURN


1650 REM *********** POP FROM THE STACK ***********
1652 REM AND DECREMENT THE STACK POINTER (SP)
1655 IF SP <> 0 GOTO 1670
1660      PRINT "YOU CANNOT POP FROM AN EMPTY STACK"
1662      GOTO 1699
1670 PRINT
1672 PRINT "FROM THE TOP OF THE STACK AT POSITION ";SP
1674 PRINT "I AM REMOVING   ";ST$(SP,1),ST$(SP,2),ST$(SP,3)
1676 PRINT "AND STORING THEM FOR NOW IN T1$, T2$, AND T3$"
1680 T1$=ST$(SP,1): T2$=ST$(SP,2): T3$=ST$(SP,3)
1682 SP = SP - 1
1685 REM PRINT THE STACK CONTENTS
1687 PRINT
1689 PRINT "THE STACK NOW LOOKS LIKE:"
1690 GOSUB 1250
1694 FL = -1
1699 RETURN
```

FIGURE 14–9(b). A Stack Handler—The Program

```
980 REM *********** STOP ROUTINE ***********
982 REM FIRST PRINT THE STACK CONTENTS, THEN STOP
984 PRINT
985 PRINT "THE FINAL STACK LOOKS LIKE:"
986 GOSUB 1250
990 FL = 1
999 RETURN


1250 REM *********** PRINT THE STACK ***********
1255 IF SP <> 0  GOTO 1270
1260        PRINT "THE STACK IS EMPTY."
1265        GOTO 1299
1270 FOR I = 1 TO SP
1271      CT = SP-I+1
1272      PRINT CT,ST$(CT,1),ST$(CT,2),ST$(CT,3)
1274 NEXT I
1276 PRINT "THE TOP OF THE STACK IS AT POSITION ";SP
1280 PRINT
1299 RETURN


9999 END
```

FIGURE 14–9(b). Continued

Procedure PUSH onto the stack (lines 1600 through 1649) increments the stack pointer by 1 and places the three fields indicated by the user on the top of the stack. Subroutine POP from the stack (lines 1650 through 1699) assigns the three fields on the top of the stack to temporary variables T1$, T2$, and T3$ and decrements the stack pointer by 1. The POP subroutine will not allow you to POP from an empty stack. All three subroutines (PUSH, POP, STOP) make use of the procedure at lines 1250 through 1299 to print the current contents of the stack.

Figure 14–10 illustrates the program performing the stack operations of Figure 8–6, Chapter 8, where the stack locations are 1 through 5 (rather than 32740 through 32744).

Stack Arithmetic

Figure 14–11 is a stack arithmetic simulator. We have used the routines of the stack handler program (Figure 14–9) with some modifications. First, the variables are numeric rather than string. Second, only one field (numeric) is

```
SPECIFY BY NUMBER, WOULD YOU LIKE TO
     1. PUSH ?
     2. POP  ?
     3. STOP  ?
WHAT IS YOUR CHOICE?  1

WHAT THREE FIELDS WOULD YOU LIKE TO PUSH
INTO THE TOP RECORD OF THE STACK
? QUARTZ, 12115, DEC. 22

THE STACK NOW LOOKS LIKE:
 1             QUARTZ                12115          DEC. 22
THE TOP OF THE STACK IS AT POSITION  1

? BARITE, 12116, JAN. 5

? GALENA, 12117, MAR. 17

? HALITE, 12118, APR. 12

? ARGENITE, 12119, JUN. 18

THE STACK NOW LOOKS LIKE:
 5             ARGENITE              12119          JUN. 18
 4             HALITE                12118          APR. 12
 3             GALENA                12117          MAR. 17
 2             BARITE                12116          JAN. 5
 1             QUARTZ                12115          DEC. 22
THE TOP OF THE STACK IS AT POSITION  5

SPECIFY BY NUMBER, WOULD YOU LIKE TO
     1. PUSH ?
     2. POP  ?
     3. STOP ?
WHAT IS YOUR CHOICE? 2

FROM THE TOP OF THE STACK AT POSITION  5
I AM REMOVING     ARGENITE           12119          JUN. 18
AND STORING THEM FOR NOW IN T1$, T2$, AND T3$

THE STACK NOW LOOKS LIKE:
 4             HALITE              12118            APR. 12
 3             GALENA              12117            MAR. 17
 2             BARITE              12116            JAN. 5
 1             QUARTZ              12115            DEC. 22
THE TOP OF THE STACK IS AT POSITION  4
```

FIGURE 14–10. Running the Stack Handler Program

```
Dimension stack variable array (ST(20))
Initialize stack pointer (SP=0)

Menu 1
    Set arithmetic operation flag off (F2=-1)
    Set print flag on (PF=1)
  PUSH
        See stack handler PUSH routine (Figure 14-9)
        Return to Menu 1
  POP
        See stack handler POP routine
        Return to Menu 1
  Arithmetic Operation
    Set arithmetic operation flag on (F2=1)
    Print the stack

    Menu2
      Add
        1. Set print flag off
        2. POP, A1=record POPped
        3. POP, add A1 to record POPped
        4. Turn print flag on
        4. PUSH and print stack
            Return to Menu 1
      Subtract
        Same as Add except
        3. POP, subtract A1 from record POPped
            Return to Menu 1
      Multiply
        Same as Add except
        3. POP, multiply A1 by record POPped
            Return to Menu 1
      Divide
        Same as Add except
        3. POP, divide record POPped by A1
            Return to Menu 1
      Interchange
        1. Set print flag off
        2. POP, A1=record POPped
        3. POP, A2=record POPped
        4. PUSH A1 onto stack, then PUSH A2
        5. Turn print flag on and print stack
            Return to Menu 1
      None of these
            Print the stack
            Return to Menu 1
  Print and Halt
        Print the stack
        Stop
```

FIGURE 14–11(a). Stack Arithmetic—Pseudocode

```
900 REM *********** STACK ARITHMETIC ***********
905 DIM ST(20)
910 REM SET STACK POINTER TO ZERO (STACK IS INITIALLY EMPTY)
911 REM AND CLEAR THE ACCUMULATOR (AC)
912 SP=0: AC=0
920 REM MENU OF OPERATIONS
922 REM INITIALIZE ARITHMETIC FLAG (F2) AND PRINT FLAG (PF)
923 F2 = -1: PF = 1
925 PRINT "SPECIFY BY NUMBER, WOULD YOU LIKE TO"
927 PRINT "      1. PUSH SOMETHING ONTO THE STACK ?"
928 PRINT "      2. POP THE TOP NUMBER FROM THE STACK ?"
929 PRINT "      3. PERFORM AN ARITHMETIC OPERATION (+ - X /)"
930 PRINT "              OR EXCHANGE THE TOP 2 ELEMENTS ?"
931 PRINT "      4. PRINT THE STACK CONTENTS AND HALT ?"
932 INPUT "WHAT IS YOUR CHOICE";CH
933 PRINT
940 ON CH GOSUB 1600,1650,1700,980
950 PRINT
960 IF FL > 0 GOTO 9999 ELSE GOTO 920


1600 REM *********** PUSH ONTO THE STACK ***********
1602 REM AFTER INCREMENTING THE STACK POINTER (SP)
1605 SP = SP+1
1610 IF F2 < 0 GOTO 1616
1612      P = AC: GOTO 1620
1616 INPUT "WHAT NUMBER SHOULD I PUSH ONTO THE STACK";P
1620 ST(SP)=P
1630 REM PRINT THE STACK
1632 PRINT
1637 IF PF > 0 THEN GOSUB 1250
1640 FL = -1
1649 RETURN


1650 REM *********** POP FROM THE STACK ***********
1652 REM AND DECREMENT THE STACK POINTER (SP)
1655 IF SP <> 0 GOTO 1670
1660      PRINT "YOU CANNOT POP FROM AN EMPTY STACK"
1662      GOTO 1699
1670 PRINT
1675 AC = ST(SP)
1682 SP = SP - 1
1685 REM PRINT THE STACK CONTENTS
1690 IF PF > 0 THEN GOSUB 1250
1694 FL = -1
1699 RETURN


1700 REM *********** ARITHMETIC OR EXCHANGE ***********
1702 REM SET ARITHMETIC FLAG (F2), PRINT THE STACK,
1703 REM THEN GIVE AN ARITHMETIC MENU
```

FIGURE 14–11(b). Stack Arithmetic—The Program

```
1705 F2 = 1: GOSUB 1250
1707 PRINT
1709 PRINT "SPECIFY BY NUMBER, WOULD YOU LIKE TO"
1710 PRINT "      1. ADD THE TOP 2 ELEMENTS ?"
1712 PRINT "      2. SUBTRACT THE TOP ELEMENT FROM THE 2ND ?"
1714 PRINT "      3. MULTIPLY THE TOP 2 ELEMENTS ?"
1716 PRINT "      4. DIVIDE THE 2ND ELEMENT BY THE TOP ?"
1718 PRINT "      5. INTERCHANGE THE TOP 2 ELEMENTS ?"
1720 PRINT "      6. NONE OF THESE."
1725 INPUT "WHAT IS YOUR CHOICE";CH
1727 PRINT
1740 ON CH GOSUB 1800,1820,1840,1860,1880,1780
1745 PRINT
1747 FL = -1
1749 RETURN


1800 REM *********** ADD THE TOP 2 ELEMENTS ***********
1802 REM POP TWICE, THEN ADD, THEN PUSH
1805 PF=-1: GOSUB 1650: A1=AC
1810 GOSUB 1650: AC=AC+A1: PF=1
1815 GOSUB 1600
1819 RETURN


1820 REM *********** SUBTRACT TOP FROM 2ND ELEMENT ***********
1822 REM POP TWICE, THEN SUBTRACT, THEN PUSH
1825 PF=-1: GOSUB 1650: A1=AC
1830 GOSUB 1650: AC=AC-A1: PF=1
1835 GOSUB 1600
1839 RETURN


1840 REM *********** MULTIPLY THE TOP 2 ELEMENTS ***********
1842 REM POP TWICE, THEN MULTIPLY, THEN PUSH
1845 PF=-1: GOSUB 1650: A1=AC
1850 GOSUB 1650: AC=AC*A1: PF=1
1855 GOSUB 1600
1859 RETURN


1860 REM *********** DIVIDE 2ND ELEMENT BY TOP ***********
1862 REM POP TWICE, THEN DIVIDE, THEN PUSH
1865 PF=-1: GOSUB 1650: A1=AC
1870 GOSUB 1650: AC=AC/A1: PF=1
1875 GOSUB 1600
1879 RETURN


1880 REM *********** EXCHANGE TOP 2 ELEMENTS ***********
1882 REM POP TWICE, THEN PUSH TWICE
1884 PF=-1: GOSUB 1650: A1=AC
```

FIGURE 14–11(b). Continued

```
1888 GOSUB 1650: A2=AC
1890 REM SET PRINT FLAG (PF) OFF, PUSH, THEN SET FLAG ON
1894 AC=A1: GOSUB 1600: PF=1
1896 AC=A2: GOSUB 1600
1899 RETURN


1780 REM PRINT THE STACK AND RETURN TO MAIN MENU
1782 GOSUB 1250
1799 RETURN


980 REM *********** STOP ROUTINE ***********
982 REM FIRST PRINT THE STACK CONTENTS, THEN STOP
985 GOSUB 1250
986 FL=1
999 RETURN


1250 REM *********** PRINT THE STACK ***********
1254 PRINT "STACK:   TOP-->";
1255 IF SP <> 0 GOTO 1270
1260      PRINT "THE STACK IS EMPTY."
1265      GOTO 1299
1270 FOR I = 1 TO SP
1271      CT = SP-I+1
1272      PRINT ST(CT);
1274 NEXT I
1275 PRINT: PRINT
1299 RETURN


9999 END
```

FIGURE 14–11(b). Continued

PUSHed onto the stack at once. Third, a second menu is provided in a new ARITHMETIC subroutine (lines 1700–1799).

The short subroutines beginning at 1800, 1820, 1840, etc. perform arithmetic operations on the top two elements of the stack. The procedure is the same in each of these routines; namely, POP the top of the stack, remember it as A1, POP the second element, which is variable AC, perform the arithmetic between A1 and AC, and PUSH the result back onto the top of the stack.

The flags in the program are indicators to allow the PUSH, POP, and PRINT the stack subroutines to perform the appropriate operations and call the printout procedure:

FL = 1 indicates the end of the program

FL = −1 indicates return to the main menu

F2 = 1 indicates an arithmetic operation is being performed, and the value of AC is to be PUSHed onto the stack

F2 = −1 indicates that the user is to be asked which value (P) should be PUSHed onto the stack

PF = 1 indicates that the contents of the stack should be printed

PF = −1 suppresses printing of the stack contents

Figure 14–12 illustrates using the program of Figure 14–11 to perform the calculation [76 − (4 × 9)] with stack arithmetic and Reverse Polish Notation.

```
SPECIFY BY NUMBER, WOULD YOU LIKE TO
      1. PUSH SOMETHING ONTO THE STACK ?
      2. POP THE TOP NUMBER FROM THE STACK ?
      3. PERFORM AN ARITHMETIC OPERATION (+ - X /)
              OR EXCHANGE THE TOP 2 ELEMENTS ?
      4. PRINT THE STACK CONTENTS AND HALT ?
WHAT IS YOUR CHOICE? 1

WHAT NUMBER SHOULD I PUSH ONTO THE STACK? 76

STACK:    TOP--> 76


SPECIFY BY NUMBER, WOULD YOU LIKE TO
      1. PUSH SOMETHING ONTO THE STACK ?
      2. POP THE TOP NUMBER FROM THE STACK ?
      3. PERFORM AN ARITHMETIC OPERATION (+ - X /)
              OR EXCHANGE THE TOP 2 ELEMENTS ?
      4. PRINT THE STACK CONTENTS AND HALT ?
WHAT IS YOUR CHOICE? 1

WHAT NUMBER SHOULD I PUSH ONTO THE STACK? 4

STACK:    TOP--> 4   76


SPECIFY BY NUMBER, WOULD YOU LIKE TO
      1. PUSH SOMETHING ONTO THE STACK ?
      2. POP THE TOP NUMBER FROM THE STACK ?
      3. PERFORM AN ARITHMETIC OPERATION (+ - X /)
              OR EXCHANGE THE TOP 2 ELEMENTS ?
      4. PRINT THE STACK CONTENTS AND HALT ?
WHAT IS YOUR CHOICE? 1

WHAT NUMBER SHOULD I PUSH ONTO THE STACK? 9

STACK:    TOP--> 9   4   76
```

FIGURE 14–12. Running the Stack Arithmetic Program

```
SPECIFY BY NUMBER, WOULD YOU LIKE TO
     1. PUSH SOMETHING ONTO THE STACK ?
     2. POP THE TOP NUMBER FROM THE STACK ?
     3. PERFORM AN ARITHMETIC OPERATION (+ - X /)
            OR EXCHANGE THE TOP 2 ELEMENTS ?
     4. PRINT THE STACK CONTENTS AND HALT ?
WHAT IS YOUR CHOICE? 3


STACK:    TOP--> 9  4  76


SPECIFY BY NUMBER, WOULD YOU LIKE TO
     1. ADD THE TOP 2 ELEMENTS ?
     2. SUBTRACT THE TOP ELEMENT FROM THE 2ND ?
     3. MULTIPLY THE TOP 2 ELEMENTS ?
     4. DIVIDE THE 2ND ELEMENT BY THE TOP ?
     5. INTERCHANGE THE TOP 2 ELEMENTS ?
     6. NONE OF THESE.
WHAT IS YOUR CHOICE? 3



STACK:    TOP--> 36  76


SPECIFY BY NUMBER, WOULD YOU LIKE TO
     1. PUSH SOMETHING ONTO THE STACK ?
     2. POP THE TOP NUMBER FROM THE STACK ?
     3. PERFORM AN ARITHMETIC OPERATION (+ - X /)
            OR EXCHANGE THE TOP 2 ELEMENTS ?
     4. PRINT THE STACK CONTENTS AND HALT ?
WHAT IS YOUR CHOICE? 3

STACK:    TOP--> 36  76


SPECIFY BY NUMBER, WOULD YOU LIKE TO
     1. ADD THE TOP 2 ELEMENTS ?
     2. SUBTRACT THE TOP ELEMENT FROM THE 2ND ?
     3. MULTIPLY THE TOP 2 ELEMENTS ?
     4. DIVIDE THE 2ND ELEMENT BY THE TOP ?
     5. INTERCHANGE THE TOP 2 ELEMENTS ?
     6. NONE OF THESE.
WHAT IS YOUR CHOICE? 2



STACK:    TOP--> 40
```

FIGURE 14–12. Continued

MORE SORTING

Quick Sort

Now that we can handle stacks, we are ready to perform a quick sort.

The quick sort program of Figure 14–13 makes use of the routines developed earlier to read a list of elements from a file and to PUSH, POP, and PRINT a stack. The sort routine itself is the subroutine between lines 1900

```
Clear and dimension string space
Read the data (See Figure 14-3)
Print the list of data
Set LO and HI pointers to ends of list
Set I and J pointers to end of list

Perform the quick sort
  Sort the list
          Set J-decrement flag to on (JF=1)
          Compare and interchange
                  Compare A$(I) with A$(J)
                  Interchange if A$(I)>A$(J) and set J-decrement
                          flag = (-1)x(J-decrement flag)
                  If J-decrement flag = 1, decrement J
                          Otherwise, increment I
                                  Repeat until I = J
          Restore I or J, so that I = J-1

  Print the list, point to Ith and Jth elements

  PUSH
          PUSH LO and I (limits of lower part of list) onto stack
          Set limits I and J (upper part of list) so that LO=J, I=J, J=HI
          Sort from I to J (See Sort the list above)
          Print the list
                  Repeat until at top of list (J=HI)

  POP
          POP limits of new list to be sorted from the stack
          If limits are equal, POP again
          Sort the list (See Sort the list above)
          Print the list
          PUSH
                  See PUSH above
                  Repeat until at top of list (J=HI)
                          Repeat until upper and lower limits both 1

  Print the final list

Stop
```

FIGURE 14–13(a). Perform a Quick Sort—Pseudocode

```
800 REM *********** QUICK SORT ***********
802 REM CLEAR STRING SPACE, DIMENSION STACK (ST) AND VARIABLES
805 CLEAR 2000
807 DIM ST(10,2), A$(20)
810 REM RECALL LIST OF ELEMENTS (A$)
812 GOSUB 1100
820 REM PRINT THE LIST OF ELEMENTS
822 I=0: J=0: LO=1: HI=N
824 PRINT: PRINT "THE ORIGINAL LIST IS"
826 GOSUB 1400
830 REM INITIALIZE I AND J POINTERS
832 I=1: J=N: LO=1: HI=J
840 REM PERFORM THE QUICK SORT
842 GOSUB 1900
845 REM END OF PROGRAM
849 GOTO 9999

1100 REM *********** RECALL THE ELEMENTS ***********
1147 INPUT "WHAT IS THE NAME OF YOUR FILE";NM$
1148 INPUT "BY WHAT NUMBER SHOULD I REFER TO THE FILE";NO
1150 INPUT "HOW MANY STRINGS (<=20) TO READ FROM FILE";N
1160 IF N<=0 GOTO 1240
1170      OPEN "I",NO,NM$
1180      FOR I=1 TO N
1190           INPUT #NO,A$(I),B$,C$
1200      NEXT I
1240 CLOSE NO
1249 RETURN

1900 REM *********** PERFORM THE QUICK SORT ***********
1902 REM INITIALIZE STACK POINTER (STACK INITIALLY EMPTY)
1905 SP=0
1910 REM INITIALIZE LIMITS
1925 REM SET J-FLAG TO DECREMENT J (JF=1)
1927 JF=1
1930 REM COMPARE, IF A$(I)>A$(J) EXCHANGE & RESET J-FLAG
1932 IF A$(I)<=A$(J) GOTO 1940
1935      T$=A$(I)
1936      A$(I)=A$(J)
1937      A$(J)=T$
1938      JF = (-1)*JF
1940 IF JF=1 THEN J=J-1 ELSE I=I+1
1950 IF J>I GOTO 1930
1960 IF JF=1 THEN J=J+1 ELSE I=I-1
1970 REM PRINT THE LIST, INDICATE A$(I) AND A$(J)
1972 PRINT "THE LIST JUST SORTED LOOKS LIKE"
1974 GOSUB 1400
2000 REM PUSH LO AND I AND PRINT THE STACK
2004      P=LO: Q=I: GOSUB 1600
2010 REM SORT LIST FROM J TO HI UNLESS J=HI
2012 IF J>=HI GOTO 2020
2014      LO=J: I=J: J=HI
```

FIGURE 14–13(b). Perform a Quick Sort—The Program

```
2016      GOTO 1925
2020 REM POP NEXT LOWER LIST LIMITS FROM THE STACK
2022 GOSUB 1650
2024 REM STOP WHEN HI = LO = 1
2026 IF LO=1 AND HI=1 GOTO 2040
2030      I=LO: J=HI
2032 REM IF I<>J SORT FROM I TO J, OTHERWISE POP FROM STACK
2034 IF I=J GOTO 2020
2036      GOTO 1925
2040 REM PRINT THE FINAL LIST AND END SORTING
2041 PRINT
2042 PRINT "THE FINAL SORTED LIST LOOKS LIKE"
2043 LO=1: HI=N: I=0: J=0
2045 GOSUB 1400
2049 RETURN


1250 REM *********** PRINT THE STACK ***********
1255 IF SP<>0 GOTO 1270
1260      PRINT "THE STACK IS EMPTY"
1265      GOTO 1299
1270 FOR X = 1 TO SP
1271      CT = SP-X+1
1272      PRINT CT;".",ST(CT,1);ST(CT,2);
1274      IF CT=SP THEN PRINT "<--- TOP OF STACK" ELSE PRINT
1276 NEXT X
1280 PRINT
1299 RETURN


1400 REM *********** PRINT THE LIST ***********
1420 FOR CT=LO TO HI
1430      PRINT A$(CT);
1432      IF CT=I THEN PRINT "<--- I=";I
1433      IF CT=J THEN PRINT "<--- J=";J ELSE PRINT
1440 NEXT CT
1445 PRINT
1449 RETURN


1600 REM *********** PUSH P AND Q ONTO THE STACK ***********
1605 SP=SP+1
1620 ST(SP,1)=P: ST(SP,2)=Q
1630 PRINT "AFTER A PUSH, THE STACK APPEARS:" : GOSUB 1250
1649 RETURN


1650 REM *********** POP LO AND HI FROM THE STACK ***********
1680 LO=ST(SP,1): HI=ST(SP,2)
1682 SP=SP-1
1690 PRINT "AFTER A POP, THE STACK APPEARS:" : GOSUB 1250
1699 RETURN

9999 END
```

FIGURE 14–13(b). Continued

and 2049. Lines 1900 to 1974 perform a quick sort of the list between limits A$(LO) and A$(HI). Lines 2000 through 2049 take care of the stack and of the tests to determine when to PUSH, when to POP, and when to STOP.

Figure 14–14 is a sample run of the quick sort program. The file used, CH9FIG4, was created to contain the list of names in Figure 9–4, Chapter 9, and is shown here:

```
FRED    ,  10  ,  FIRST
DAN     ,   9  ,  SECOND
BILL    ,   8  ,  THIRD
TOM     ,   7  ,  FOURTH
SUE     ,   6  ,  FIFTH
BET     ,   5  ,  SIXTH
GREG    ,   4  ,  SEVENTH
ADAM    ,   3  ,  EIGHTH
SAM     ,   2  ,  NINTH
MARY    ,   1  ,  TENTH
```

Fields 2 and 3 of each record in this file are dummy fields, containing nonsense. We will use one of these fields later to create a linked list. Thus, the sample run, in Figure 14–14, is the same as Example 9–3 (Figure 9–4). You may wish to compare them.

Logical Sorting, Linking a List

Figure 14–15 is a List Linker program, which reads a file (with three fields in each record) from the disk, puts the link pointers in field 2 of the records, and writes the linked list into a new file. The original file, linked file, and the list in linked order are all printed out by the program for the user to examine.

The linking routine itself is in lines 1300 through 1399, which in turn calls a routine (in lines 2200 through 2249) to find the smallest element remaining in the list at each step. The latter procedure uses a stack on which to remember the numbers of the elements which have already been linked. The top of the stack is always the number of the latest element to which a pointer must be assigned.

There are some important limitations to this program. First, in this and the other sort routines we have written so far, the entire file is read into memory and then linked or sorted. Here the linked array is then written back

```
WHAT IS THE NAME OF YOUR FILE? CH9FIG4
BY WHAT NUMBER SHOULD I REFER TO THE FILE? 2
HOW MANY STRINGS (<=20) TO READ FROM FILE? 10

THE ORIGINAL LIST IS
FRED
DAN
BILL
TOM
SUE
BET
GREG
ADAM
SAM
MARY

THE LIST JUST SORTED LOOKS LIKE
ADAM
DAN
BILL
BET
FRED             <--- I= 5

SUE              <--- J= 6
GREG
TOM
SAM
MARY

AFTER A PUSH, THE STACK APPEARS:
 1 .              1  5 <--- TOP OF STACK

THE LIST JUST SORTED LOOKS LIKE
MARY
GREG
SAM              <--- I= 8

SUE              <--- J= 9
TOM

AFTER A PUSH, THE STACK APPEARS:
 2 .              6  8 <--- TOP OF STACK
 1 .              1  5

THE LIST JUST SORTED LOOKS LIKE
SUE              <--- I= 9

TOM              <--- J= 10
```

FIGURE 14–14. Running the Program to Perform a Quick Sort

```
THE LIST JUST SORTED LOOKS LIKE
DAN              <--- I= 4

FRED             <--- J= 5


AFTER A PUSH, THE STACK APPEARS:
 3 .              4  4 <--- TOP OF STACK
 2 .              2  3
 1 .              1  1


AFTER A POP, THE STACK APPEARS:
 2 .              2  3 <--- TOP OF STACK
 1 .              1  1


AFTER A POP, THE STACK APPEARS:
 1 .              1  1 <--- TOP OF STACK


THE LIST JUST SORTED LOOKS LIKE
BET              <--- I= 2

BILL             <--- J= 3


AFTER A PUSH, THE STACK APPEARS:
 2 .              2  2 <--- TOP OF STACK
 1 .              1  1


AFTER A POP, THE STACK APPEARS:
 1 .              1  1 <--- TOP OF STACK


AFTER A POP, THE STACK APPEARS:
THE STACK IS EMPTY


THE FINAL SORTED LIST LOOKS LIKE
ADAM
BET
BILL
DAN
FRED
GREG
MARY
SAM
SUE
TOM
```

FIGURE 14–14. Continued

```
Clear string space and dimension arrays

Read the file into memory
        Ask the name and number of the file and how many records (N)
        Open the file for input (read)
        Read a record
                Input A$(I), B(I), C$(I)
        Repeat for I = 1 to N
        Print the file
                Print A$(I), B(I), C$(I)
        Repeat for I = 1 to N

Link the file in memory with the pointers in field 2
        Set stack pointer (SP=0) and counter (CT=1)
        Find smallest record
                Set minimum (MN$) to "ZZZZZZ"
                Search for smallest
                Set "On Stack" flag to "No" (OS=0)
                IF A$(I)<=MN$, check to see if on stack
                        If element J of stack = record counter I
                                Set "On Stack" flag to "Yes" (OS=1)
                Repeat for J=1 to no. of elements on stack (SP)

                        If I is not on stack
                                Set MN$=A$(I) and smallest element no.(SN) to I
                Repeat for I = 1 to N
        Set Begin Pointer (BP) to smallest element number (SN)
        PUSH smallest element number onto stack
                PUSH element (P)=SMALLEST NUMBER (SN)
                Add 1 to stack pointer (SP)
                Set element SP of stack (ST(SP)) to P

        Link the rest of the list
                Find smallest record (See Find smallest record above)
                Put pointer in field 2 of previously smallest record
                        Set subscript (SS) to element on top of stack (ST(SP))
                        Set field 2 of element SS (B(SS)) to most recent smallest
                                element number (SN)

                PUSH smallest element number onto stack (See PUSH above)
        Repeat for Counter (CT) = 2 to N

        Place an end pointer (=0) in the last element
                Set subscript (SS) to element on top of stack (ST(SP))
                Set field 2 of element SS (B(SS)) to 0
```

FIGURE 14–15(a). Link a List—Pseudocode

```
Write the linked file to the disk and print its contents
        Ask for the name and number of the file to contain linked list
        Open the file for output (write)
        Print "START POINTER", Beginning Pointer, "DUMMY" in 1st record
        Print remaining records
                Print A$(I), B(I)=Pointer, C$(I) into the file
                Repeat for I = 1 to N

        Close the file

        Open the file for input (read)
        Read and print
                Read record I from the file
                Print record I (call it I-1, so START POINTER looks like record 0)
                Repeat for I = 1 to N+1
        Close the file

Read and print the file in linked order
        State the name of the linked file and ask for number
        Open the file for input (read)
        Read the records
                Input A$(I), B(I)=Pointer, C$(I)
                Repeat for I = 1 to N+1

        Print record 1
                (Remember pointers will be one less than record numbers
                        because the original record 1 is now record 2 -
                        START POINTER was stored in record 1.)
                Set subscript (SS) = Start Pointer (B(1) + 1)
                Print record SS

        Print remaining records
                Set subscript (SS) = pointer in previous record (B(SS) + 1)
                Print record SS
                Repeat for I = 2 to N

Stop
```

FIGURE 14–15(a). Continued

```
700 REM *********** LIST LINKER ***********
702 CLEAR 2000
705 DIM A$(20), B(20), C$(20), ST(20)
710 REM READ THE FILE INTO MEMORY
715 GOSUB 1100
720 REM PUT LINK POINTERS IN FIELD 2 OF EACH RECORD
722 PRINT:PRINT "PLEASE BE PATIENT. I'M LINKING.": PRINT
725 GOSUB 1300
730 REM WRITE THE LINKED FILE ON DISK AND PRINT CONTENTS
735 GOSUB 1000
```

FIGURE 14–15(b). Link a List—The Program

```
740 REM READ AND PRINT THE FILE IN LINK ORDER
745 GOSUB 2100
747 REM STOP
749 GOTO 9999


1100 REM *********** READ THE FILE ***********
1110 INPUT "WHAT IS THE NAME OF YOUR FILE";NM$
1115 INPUT "BY WHAT NUMBER SHOULD I REFER TO THE FILE";NO
1120 INPUT "HOW MANY RECORDS (<=20) TO READ FROM THE FILE";N
1125 IF N <= 0 GOTO 1160
1130      OPEN "I",NO,NM$
1140      FOR I=1 TO N
1145            INPUT #NO,A$(I),B(I),C$(I)
1150      NEXT I
1160 CLOSE NO
1170 REM PRINT THE FILE
1172 PRINT:PRINT "THE FILE ";NM$;" TO BE LINKED IS:"
1176 FOR I=1 TO N
1178      PRINT A$(I),B(I),C$(I)
1180 NEXT I
1199 RETURN

1300 REM *********** LINK THE LIST ***********
1310 REM FIND THE FIRST ELEMENT
1315 SP=0: CT=1
1320 REM FIND THE SMALLEST
1325 GOSUB 2200
1330 REM SET BEGIN POINTER (BP) TO SMALLEST ELEMENT NUMBER
1335 BP = SN
1340 REM PUSH THE SMALLEST ELEMENT NUMBER ONTO THE STACK
1345 P=SN: GOSUB 1600
1350 REM LINK THE REST OF THE LIST
1360 FOR CT=2 TO N
1365      REM FIND SMALLEST REMAINING ELEMENT
1367      GOSUB 2200
1370      REM PUT POINTER IN FIELD 2 OF PREVIOUSLY SMALLEST
1372      SS = ST(SP): B(SS) = SN
1375      REM PUSH THE NUMBER OF THE SMALLEST ONTO THE STACK
1377      P=SN: GOSUB 1600
1379 NEXT CT
1380 REM PLACE AN END POINTER (0) IN THE LAST ELEMENT
1382      SS=ST(SP): B(SS)=0
1399 RETURN


2200 REM *********** FIND SMALLEST IN THE LIST ***********
2202 REM INITIALIZE MINIMUM (MN$) LARGER THAN ANY ELEMENT ON THE LIST
2205 MN$="ZZZZZZ"
2210 FOR I=1 TO N
2212      REM SET "ON STACK" FLAG TO "NO" (OS=0)
2213      OS = 0
```

FIGURE 14–15(b). Continued

```
2215      IF A$(I) > MN$ GOTO 2240
2220           IF SP=0 GOTO 2235
2225           FOR J=1 TO SP
2227                IF ST(J) = I THEN OS=1
2230           NEXT J
2232           IF OS=1 GOTO 2240
2233           REM SET MINIMUM TO SMALLEST ELEMENT SO FAR
2234           REM AND SMALLEST NUMBER (SN) TO ITS SUBSCRIPT
2235           MN$=A$(I): SN=I
2240 NEXT I
2249 RETURN


1600 REM *********** PUSH ONTO THE STACK ***********
1610 SP = SP + 1
1615 ST(SP) = P
1649 RETURN


1000 REM *********** REWRITE THE FILE ***********
1005 REM OPEN A FILE, THEN PUT DATA INTO THE FILE
1007 PRINT
1010 INPUT "WHAT IS TO BE THE NAME OF THE LINKED FILE";NM$
1015 INPUT "BY WHAT NUMBER SHOULD I REFER TO THIS FILE";NO
1020 OPEN "O",NO,NM$
1025 REM MAKE THE FIRST RECORD THE START POINTER
1027 REM RECORD IT AND ALL OF THE OTHERS
1030 PRINT #NO,"START POINTER",CHR$(44),BP;CHR$(44),"DUMMY"
1032 FOR I=1 TO N
1035      PRINT #NO,A$(I);CHR$(44),B(I);CHR$(44),C$(I)
1039 NEXT I
1045 CLOSE NO
1050 REM PRINT THE FILE
1052 OPEN "I",NO,NM$
1054 PRINT: PRINT "THE CONTENTS OF LINKED FILE ";NM$;" ARE:"
1056 PRINT "(RECORD NO., AND THREE FIELDS, FIELD 2 = POINTER)"
1058 FOR I=1 TO N+1
1060      INPUT #NO,A$,B,C$
1062      PRINT I-1;A$,B,C$
1064 NEXT I
1066 CLOSE NO
1099 RETURN


2100 REM *********** READ AND PRINT IN LINK ORDER ***********
2105 PRINT: PRINT "THE LINKED FILE IS ";NM$
2107 INPUT "BY WHAT NUMBER SHOULD I REFER TO THE FILE";NO
2110 OPEN "I",NO,NM$
2115 REM READ THE FILE
2120 FOR I=1 TO N+1
2125      INPUT #NO,A$(I),B(I),C$(I)
```

FIGURE 14–15(b). Continued

```
2129 NEXT I
2130 REM BEGIN WITH START POINTER (B(1)) AND PRINT IN ORDER
2131 PRINT: PRINT "THE FILE IN LINKED ORDER IS:"
2132 I=1: SS = B(1) + 1
2134 PRINT I;A$(SS),B(SS),C$(SS)
2140 FOR I=2 TO N
2142      SS = B(SS) + 1
2144      PRINT I;A$(SS),B(SS),C$(SS)
2146 NEXT I
2149 RETURN


9999 END
```

FIGURE 14–15(b). Continued

to the disk as a new file. If your file is very long, it may not all fit in memory, and this program would not work. However, this is the only reasonable way to handle the problem if we insist on using sequential files. Later you will see how to use random files which can be used to link or sort a list which is too long for memory. Also, this program runs rather slowly. Using random files and writing the stack handlers in assembly language would speed it up considerably.

CONVERTING AN INTEGER TO A STRING

You may have observed in the List Linker program (Figure 14–15) that the second field (B(I)) of each record was read and written as a number, not as a string. If your computer allows files in which only strings may be written, you will have to do some conversions. Some BASIC languages have special functions which will do this for you; however, nearly all BASIC languages have two functions which you may use. One of these is VAL(A$), which returns to you the numerical value of a string which looks like an integer. The other is CHR$(A), which gives you the string whose ASCII is A. Since ASCII for 0 is 48 (see Table 2–3), if you wished to write a single digit 5, for example, into a sequential file (which we shall call logical file #1 for now) which allows only strings, you could use the following commands:

```
LET M=5
LET B$=CHR$(M+48)
PRINT #1,B$.
```

```
WHAT IS THE NAME OF YOUR FILE? CH9FIG4
BY WHAT NUMBER SHOULD I REFER TO THE FILE? 1
HOW MANY RECORDS (<=20) TO READ FROM THE FILE? 10

THE FILE CH9FIG4 TO BE LINKED IS:
FRED                         10             FIRST
DAN                          9              SECOND
BILL                         8              THIRD
TOM                          7              FOURTH
SUE                          6              FIFTH
BET                          5              SIXTH
GREG                         4              SEVENTH
ADAM                         3              EIGHTH
SAM                          2              NINTH
MARY                         1              TENTH

PLEASE BE PATIENT. I'M LINKING.


WHAT IS TO BE THE NAME OF THE LINKED FILE? LINKFIG4
BY WHAT NUMBER SHOULD I REFER TO THIS FILE? 2

THE CONTENTS OF LINKED FILE LINKFIG4 ARE:
(RECORD NO., AND THREE FIELDS, FIELD 2 = POINTER)
 0 START POINTER             8              DUMMY
 1 FRED                      7              FIRST
 2 DAN                       1              SECOND
 3 BILL                      2              THIRD
 4 TOM                       0              FOURTH
 5 SUE                       4              FIFTH
 6 BET                       3              SIXTH
 7 GREG                      10             SEVENTH
 8 ADAM                      6              EIGHTH
 9 SAM                       5              NINTH
 10 MARY                     9              TENTH

THE LINKED FILE IS LINKFIG4
BY WHAT NUMBER SHOULD I REFER TO THE FILE? 2

THE FILE IN LINKED ORDER IS:
 1 ADAM                      6              EIGHTH
 2 BET                       3              SIXTH
 3 BILL                      2              THIRD
 4 DAN                       1              SECOND
 5 FRED                      7              FIRST
 6 GREG                      10             SEVENTH
 7 MARY                      9              TENTH
 8 SAM                       5              NINTH
 9 SUE                       4              FIFTH
 10 TOM                      0              FOURTH
```

FIGURE 14–16. Running the Program to Link a List

You can also read the number from the file by the commands

```
INPUT #1,B$
LET M=VAL(B$).
```

Figure 14–17 illustrates a very short procedure to separate the digits of an integer up to six digits long, convert the digits to strings, and concatenate to obtain a string which looks like the original integer. The string is changed back to an integer by the VAL(B$) instruction, of course. Thus, if you are stuck with storing only strings, it is easy to modify the List Linker program to use these procedures wherever a number B(I) is to be written or read.

```
850 REM *********** CHANGE AN INTEGER TO A STRING ***********
855 INPUT "WHAT IS YOUR INTEGER (6 DIGITS OR FEWER)";NU
860 REM INITIALIZE STRING TO EMPTY
862 B$="": I=0
865 I = I + 1
870 REM D IS THE RIGHTMOST DIGIT OF NU
872 D(I) = INT((NU/10 - INT(NU/10))*10 + 0.1)
874 REM CHANGE NU TO WHAT IS LEFT AFTER A DIGIT IS REMOVED
875 NU = INT(NU/10)
879 IF NOT(NU < 1) GOTO 865
880 REM CONCATENATE THE STRINGS FOR THE DIGITS
882 FOR J = 1 TO I
884     CT = I - J + 1
886     B$ = B$ + CHR$(D(CT) + 48)
888 NEXT J
890 REM PRINT THE RESULTS
892 PRINT "B$ = ";B$
895 PRINT "VAL(B$) = ";VAL(B$)
899 END
```

FIGURE 14–17(a). Convert an Integer to a String

```
WHAT IS YOUR INTEGER (6 DIGITS OR FEWER)? 34
B$ = 34
VAL(B$) =  34


WHAT IS YOUR INTEGER (6 DIGITS OR FEWER)? 56789
B$ = 56789
VAL(B$) =  56789
```

FIGURE 14–17(b). Running the Program to Convert an Integer to a String

QUEUES

A Circular Queue

A program to handle a circular queue is almost a copy of the stack handler program (Figure 14–9). The circular queue program in Figure 14–18 asks for the maximum number of records *(N)* of the queue and allows the user to add records to or remove them from the queue. To facilitate testing for an empty or a full queue, the queue in this program is initially filled with blanks (indicated by -----), and positions from which records have been removed are also filled with blanks. FIRST (LL) and LIMIT (UL) are set. IN (the next position at which a record will be inserted) and OUT (OT) (the next position from which a record is to be removed) are incremented when a record is added or removed, respectively. When IN or OUT (OT) exceed LIMIT (UL), they are

```
Clear and dimension string space
Ask how large the queue can be (N)
Initialize pointers and the "queue empty" flag
        FIRST (LL) = 1,  LIMIT (UL) = N,  IN = 1,   OUT (OT) = 0
        Set "queue empty" flag to empty (EM=1)

Fill the queue with blanks (-----)

Menu
    Add to the queue
        If the queue is full, jump to Print the queue

        Put into queue
        Ask what is to be put into the queue
        Put it into the queue
        Turn the empty flag off (EM=0)
        Increment IN
                reset IN to FIRST (LL) if larger than LIMIT (UL)

        Print the queue
        If the queue is empty (EM=1)
                print "the queue is empty" and skip the rest of
                        the Print the queue routine
        If the queue is full (IN=OUT)
                print the queue is full and continue
                Print
                Print I and record I of the queue
                        indicate IN, OUT, FIRST, and LIMIT
                        Repeat for I=FIRST(LL) to LIMIT(UL)
                        Return to Menu
```

FIGURE 14–18(a). A Circular Queue—Pseudocode

```
    Remove from the queue
        If the queue is empty, print "there is nothing to remove"
            and jump to the end of Remove from the queue routine
        Print the record being removed at location OUT(OT)
        Assign fields of record at location OUT to T1$ and T2$
        Set record at location OUT to blank (-----)
        Increment OUT (OT=OT+1)
            reset OUT to FIRST(LL) if larger than LIMIT(UL)
        Check to see if queue is empty
            If record I is not blank, set empty flag off (EM=0)
                Repeat for I=FIRST(LL) to LIMIT(UL)

        If the queue is empty (EM=1), set OUT(OT) to 0
        Print the queue (See Print the queue above)
                Return to Menu

Print the queue
Stop
```

FIGURE 14–18(a). Continued

```
600 REM *********** CIRCULAR QUEUE ***********
605 CLEAR 2000
606 DIM QU$(20,2)
610 REM INITIALIZE POINTERS AND FILL QUEUE WITH BLANKS "-----"
612 INPUT "HOW LARGE (<=20) DO YOU WISH THE QUEUE TO BE";N
614 LL=1: UL=N: IN=1: OT=0: EM=1
616 FOR I=LL TO UL
617     QU$(I,1)="-----": QU$(I,2)="-----"
618 NEXT I
620 REM MENU FOR ADD OR REMOVE
625 PRINT "SPECIFY BY NUMBER, WOULD YOU LIKE TO"
627 PRINT "            1. ADD TO THE QUEUE ?"
628 PRINT "            2. REMOVE FROM THE QUEUE ?"
629 PRINT "            3. STOP ?"
630 INPUT "WHAT IS YOUR CHOICE";CH
632 PRINT
640 ON CH GOSUB 2300, 2350, 680
650 PRINT
660 IF FL>0 GOTO 9999 ELSE GOTO 625


2300 REM *********** ADD TO THE QUEUE ***********
2305 IF EM=1 GOTO 2310
2307     IF IN<>OT OR QU$(IN,1)="-----" GOTO 2310
2308         PRINT "THE QUEUE IS FULL !": GOTO 2330
2310 INPUT "WHAT TWO FIELDS SHOULD GO INTO THE QUEUE";P1$,P2$
2320 QU$(IN,1)=P1$: QU$(IN,2)=P2$: EM=0
2322 IF OT=0 THEN OT=1
2325 IN = IN + 1
```

FIGURE 14–18(b). A Circular Queue—The Program

```
2326 IF IN > UL THEN IN=LL
2330 REM PRINT THE QUEUE
2332 PRINT
2335 PRINT "THE QUEUE NOW LOOKS LIKE:"
2337 GOSUB 1450
2340 FL=-1
2349 RETURN


2350 REM *********** REMOVE FROM THE QUEUE ***********
2355 IF EM=0 GOTO 2370
2360     PRINT "QUEUE IS EMPTY, THERE IS NOTHING TO REMOVE"
2362     GOTO 2399
2370 PRINT
2372 PRINT "FROM POSITION ";OT;" I AM REMOVING"
2374 PRINT QU$(OT,1);" AND ";QU$(OT,2)
2376 PRINT "AND STORING THEM FOR NOW IN T1$ AND T2$."
2380 T1$ = QU$(OT,1): T2$ = QU$(OT,2)
2381 QU$(OT,1) = "-----": QU$(OT,2) = "-----"
2382 OT = OT + 1
2383 IF OT>UL THEN OT=LL
2384 REM CHECK TO SEE IF THE QUEUE IS EMPTY
2385 EM = 1
2386 FOR I=LL TO UL
2388     IF QU$(I,1)<>"-----" THEN EM=0
2389 NEXT I
2390 IF EM=1 THEN OT=0
2394 REM PRINT THE QUEUE
2395 PRINT "THE QUEUE NOW LOOKS LIKE:"
2396 GOSUB 1450
2397 FL=-1
2399 RETURN


680 REM *********** STOP ROUTINE ***********
682 REM FIRST PRINT THE QUEUE, THEN STOP
684 PRINT
685 PRINT "THE FINAL QUEUE LOOKS LIKE:"
686 GOSUB 1450
690 FL=1
699 RETURN


1450 REM *********** PRINT THE QUEUE ***********
1452 IF EM=0 GOTO 1470
1454     PRINT "THE QUEUE IS EMPTY"
1456     GOTO 1490
1460 IF IN<>OT GOTO 1470
1462     PRINT "THE QUEUE IS FULL"
1470 FOR I=LL TO UL
1472     PRINT I;QU$(I,1),QU$(I,2);
```

FIGURE 14–18(b). Continued

```
1474      IF I=IN THEN PRINT " <--IN ";
1476      IF I=OT THEN PRINT " <--OUT ";
1478      IF I=LL THEN PRINT " <--FIRST ";
1480      IF I=UL THEN PRINT " <--LIMIT ";
1482      PRINT
1485 NEXT I
1490 PRINT
1499 RETURN

9999 END
```

FIGURE 14–18(b). Continued

reset to FIRST (LL) to make the queue circular. This particular program assumes that each record in the queue will have two fields.

In the sample run of the program (Figure 14–19) the queue is given a length of three records. From this run you can observe that when IN = OUT the queue is full and you cannot add another record until something is removed.

```
HOW LARGE (<=20) DO YOU WISH THE QUEUE TO BE? 3
SPECIFY BY NUMBER, WOULD YOU LIKE TO
          1. ADD TO THE QUEUE ?
          2. REMOVE FROM THE QUEUE ?
          3. STOP ?
WHAT IS YOUR CHOICE? 1

WHAT TWO FIELDS SHOULD GO INTO THE QUEUE? BROWN, 3218

THE QUEUE NOW LOOKS LIKE:
 1 BROWN         3218 <--OUT  <--FIRST
 2 -----         ----- <--IN
 3 -----         ----- <--LIMIT


SPECIFY BY NUMBER, WOULD YOU LIKE TO
          1. ADD TO THE QUEUE ?
          2. REMOVE FROM THE QUEUE ?
          3. STOP ?
WHAT IS YOUR CHOICE? 1

WHAT TWO FIELDS SHOULD GO INTO THE QUEUE? THOMAS, 2963

THE QUEUE NOW LOOKS LIKE:
 1 BROWN         3218 <--OUT  <--FIRST
 2 THOMAS        2963
 3 -----         ----- <--IN  <--LIMIT
```

FIGURE 14–19. Running the Circular Queue Program

```
SPECIFY BY NUMBER, WOULD YOU LIKE TO
          1. ADD TO THE QUEUE ?
          2. REMOVE FROM THE QUEUE ?
          3. STOP ?
WHAT IS YOUR CHOICE? 2


FROM POSITION  1  I AM REMOVING
BROWN AND 3218
AND STORING THEM FOR NOW IN T1$ AND T2$.
THE QUEUE NOW LOOKS LIKE:
 1 -----         ----- <--FIRST
 2 THOMAS        2963 <--OUT
 3 -----         ----- <--IN  <--LIMIT

SPECIFY BY NUMBER, WOULD YOU LIKE TO
          1. ADD TO THE QUEUE ?
          2. REMOVE FROM THE QUEUE ?
          3. STOP ?
WHAT IS YOUR CHOICE? 1


WHAT TWO FIELDS SHOULD GO INTO THE QUEUE? RICHARDS, 6543

THE QUEUE NOW LOOKS LIKE:
 1 -----         ----- <--IN  <--FIRST
 2 THOMAS        2963 <--OUT
 3 RICHARDS      6543 <--LIMIT


SPECIFY BY NUMBER, WOULD YOU LIKE TO
          1. ADD TO THE QUEUE ?
          2. REMOVE FROM THE QUEUE ?
          3. STOP ?
WHAT IS YOUR CHOICE? 1

WHAT TWO FIELDS SHOULD GO INTO THE QUEUE? ROBERTS, 9742

THE QUEUE NOW LOOKS LIKE:
 1 ROBERTS       9742 <--FIRST
 2 THOMAS        2963 <--IN  <--OUT
 3 RICHARDS      6543 <--LIMIT


SPECIFY BY NUMBER, WOULD YOU LIKE TO
          1. ADD TO THE QUEUE ?
          2. REMOVE FROM THE QUEUE ?
          3. STOP ?
WHAT IS YOUR CHOICE? 1
```

FIGURE 14–19. Continued

```
THE QUEUE IS FULL !

THE QUEUE NOW LOOKS LIKE:
 1 ROBERTS        9742 <--FIRST
 2 THOMAS         2963 <--IN   <--OUT
 3 RICHARDS       6543 <--LIMIT


SPECIFY BY NUMBER, WOULD YOU LIKE TO
          1. ADD TO THE QUEUE ?
          2. REMOVE FROM THE QUEUE ?
          3. STOP ?
WHAT IS YOUR CHOICE? 3


THE FINAL QUEUE LOOKS LIKE:
 1 ROBERTS        9742 <--FIRST
 2 THOMAS         2963 <--IN   <--OUT
 3 RICHARDS       6543 <--LIMIT
```

FIGURE 14–19. Continued

QUESTIONS

1. Modify the programs of Figures 14–1 and 14–3 as necessary to create and read the file shown in Figure 14–2 on *your* computer.
2. Change the bubble sort program in Figure 14–5, so that the smallest element bubbles to the top in each pass rather than having the largest element sink to the bottom.
3. Change the selection sort program in Figure 14–7, so that it sorts on the *second* field (B$) of each record.
4. Change the selection sort program in Figure 14–7, so that the two records, which were interchanged after each pass, are flagged in the printout with an asterisk (*).
5. Modify the program of Figure 14–9 so that it prints locations 32740 through 32744 (instead of 1 through 5) and so that the top of the stack is at the bottom of the list as in Figure 8–6.
6. Modify the program of Figure 14–9 so that the bottom of the stack is array element 10 (rather than 1) and records are pushed into successively lower-numbered array elements as the stack is filled. The program should tell you that the stack is full when record location number 1 is filled and not allow you to PUSH any more records onto the stack until something has been POPped from the stack.

7. Add to the program of Figure 14–11 a function which POPs the top of stack, takes the square root, and PUSHes the root back onto the stack. Then use your new program to perform the calculation

   ```
   (50+SQR(8+17)) / (7+4)
   ```

   in postfix (Reverse Polish) notation.
8. Use the Quick Sort program of Figure 14–13 to sort the DATA file of Figure 14–2.
9. Modify the Quick Sort program of Figure 14–13 to sort the DATA file of Figure 14–2 on the second field (the full name, as shown). Show all three fields in the results.
10. Write a program which opens the new sorted file (resulting from Problem 9) for Input, and another new sequential file for Output. Read from the "Input" file and write to the "Output" file. Insert records

    ```
    DRAGON     DRAKE*RICHARD  1979
    POPPER     MARKS*BRENDA   1980
    ```

    into the appropriate position in the "Output" file, delete the record for HIGHPOCKETS, and change the date for RED to 1977. Print out the new file.
11. Rewrite the List Linker program of Figure 14–15 so that it also puts backwards pointers in field 3 of each record and lists the file for you either in forward or in reverse order.
12. Change the List Linker program so that you can also *delete,* logically, a record from a linked list file. (Remember, all you really have to do to delete a record is to change the pointer of the record which logically precedes it.)
13. Write a queue handler which assumes a linear queue. Show how the queue "walks" through available space as records are added and removed. Set an upper limit on the queue space and allow no more additions after the upper limit is reached.

CHAPTER 15

ALGORITHMS FOR NONLINEAR DATA STRUCTURES

WRITING TO A RANDOM ACCESS FILE

Writing records to a random access file is similar to writing to a sequential file, as illustrated by the program in Figure 15–1 and by the sample run and file in Figure 15–2. However, there are some differences both in theory and in practice.

The first difference which we observe appears in the OPEN file statement. Here the file must be OPENed for random (R) read and write. Both input from and output to a random file may be performed without closing and reopening the file. You also see an additional number (64 in this example) at the end of the OPEN statement. This number is the fixed length (in bytes) of all of the records in the file. In this example we have chosen to make each record 64 bytes long. Some systems allow you to specify the record length as shown here. On other computers the record length is fixed, and you may not have the option of choosing. Typically, if the record length is fixed by the computer or if you do not specify what you wish it to be, it may be set at either 256 bytes or the length of one granule on your machine.

Writing to a random access file requires that a record first be set into a buffer, which is an image of how the record will appear in the file. Then the

```
Clear space for strings
What are the name and number of the file?
Open the file for random (R) read (GET) or write (PUT)
Define the fields in the buffer for the file
Initialize the record counter (I=0)
Set unused fields to blank dummy variables

┌──── Write records into the file ─────────────────────────┐
│          Increment record number pointer (I)              │
│          Request a record                                 │
│          Set the fields of the record into the fields     │
│                  of the buffer (using LSET and/or RSET)   │
│          PUT the buffer contents into record I of the file│
└───────────────── Repeat unless the record is STOP ────────┘

Close the file
Stop
```

FIGURE 15–1(a). Create a Random Access File—Pseudocode

```
2400 REM *********** CREATE A RANDOM FILE ***********
2405 REM CLEAR SPACE FOR STRINGS, OPEN & FIELD A RANDOM FILE,
2410 REM THEN WRITE THE STRINGS INTO THE FILE
2420 CLEAR 2000
2425 INPUT "WHAT IS THE NAME OF YOUR FILE";NM$
2427 INPUT "BY WHAT NUMBER SHOULD I REFER TO THE FILE";NO
2430 OPEN "R",NO,NM$,64
2440 FIELD NO, 20 AS P$, 20 AS Q$, 8 AS R$, 16 AS DUMMY$
2445 I=0: D$="": LSET DUMMY$=D$
2450 PRINT "GIVE ME STRINGS A$,B$,C$(TERMINATE WITH A$=STOP)"
2452 I = I + 1
2455 INPUT A$, B$, C$
2460 IF A$ = "STOP" GOTO 2490
2465 LSET P$ = A$
2466 LSET Q$ = B$
2467 RSET R$ = C$
2475 PUT NO, I
2479 GOTO 2452
2490 CLOSE NO
2499 END
```

FIGURE 15–1(b). Create a Random Access File—The Program

contents of the buffer are moved to the file using a PUT command. The fields in the buffer, hence the appearance of the records, are defined in this version of BASIC by a FIELD command as shown in line 2440 (Figure 15–1). In our example, each record (and the buffer) will appear as follows:

byte no.	1	20	21	40	41	48	49	64
content	variable P$		variable Q$		R$		DUMMY$	

```
WHAT IS THE NAME OF YOUR FILE? RNDATA
BY WHAT NUMBER SHOULD I REFER TO THE FILE? 1
GIVE ME STRINGS A$,B$,C$(TERMINATE WITH A$=STOP)
? BUZZ, UZRA*BILL, 1968
? NOODLEY, HOLMES*NORRIS, 1975
? SKINNY, WILSON*TOM, 1982
? MISTY, JONES*SALLY, 1980
? LIZ, SMITH*ELIZABETH, 1974
? HIGHPOCKETS, RICH*HOWARD, 1980
? GRUMBLY, SMITH*TED, 1983
? RED, BARTON*FRITZ, 1978
? SNIPPETS, WILKINS*MARY, 1982
? TRUDGEON, FISH*ARNOLD, 1980
? TOPPER, PEARSON*TOM, 1975
? STOP
??
```

FIGURE 15–2(a). Running the Program to Create a Random Access File

```
BUZZ                UZRA*BILL               1968
NOODLEY             HOLMES*NORRIS           1975
SKINNY              WILSON*TOM              1982
MISTY               JONES*SALLY             1980
LIZ                 SMITH*ELIZABETH         1974
HIGHPOCKETS         RICH*HOWARD             1980
GRUMBLY             SMITH*TED               1983
RED                 BARTON*FRITZ            1978
SNIPPETS            WILKINS*MARY            1982
TRUDGEON            FISH*ARNOLD             1980
TOPPER              PEARSON*TOM             1975
EOF
```

FIGURE 15–2(b). The Resulting File

DUMMY$ is a variable which fills space that we don't wish to use at the end of the record. We have entered all blanks into the DUMMY$ field of the buffer by initially setting a variable to a blank (D$=" "). Then, by using the LSET command, we made this variable the leftmost character in the DUMMY$ field, followed automatically by sufficient blanks to fill the field (LSET DUMMY$=D$). The variables A$, B$, and C$ were also moved into the buffer as P$, Q$, and R$, respectively, by the LSET and RSET commands. LSET P$=A$, for example, places A$ into the leftmost bytes of the first field (P$) of the buffer and fills the remainder of the field with blanks. RSET R$=C$ places C$ into the rightmost bytes in the buffer field R$ and fills any unused leading bytes in the field with blanks.

The PUT NO,I command moves the contents of the buffer into the Ith record of logical file number NO. If the record number (I) is not specified, the buffer contents will be moved to the "current" record. The "current" record is record 1 when the file is opened. If no record number is specified, the current record pointer is automatically incremented by 1 each time a PUT command is executed. When the record number (I) is specified in the PUT command, the current record pointer is set to I+1 after the command is executed.

Of course, every file must be CLOSEd after it is used.

READING FROM A RANDOM ACCESS FILE

In the program for recalling records from a random access file (Figure 15–3) the file must again be OPENed and the buffer FIELDed. Remember, when a file is opened for random access (R), you may write (PUT) into the file or read (GET) from the file without having to close and reopen. In order to read from an already existing random file, you should remember with what record lengths the file was created and the field format in which the records were written. If you choose to read in a different format from that in which you wrote, you may get results which are difficult to decipher.

Two valuable functions are available in most languages for finding the number of the last record in the file and for determining the value of the "current" record pointer. We have used one of these in the program as it is commonly written in BASIC. In line 2528 (N = LOF(NO)) we found the file's largest record number at LOF(NO), where NO is the logical file number. The other function is generally used in BASIC in a form similar to I = LOC(NO), which would set I equal to the number of the latest record which has been read.

```
Clear space for strings
What are the name and number of the file?
What is the record length (in bytes) of records in the file?
Open the file for random (R) read (GET) or write (PUT)
Define the fields in the buffer for the file
Find the number of the last record in the file (N=LOF)
Set counter (CT) to N

┌──────GET and print the records in reverse order──────┐
│          GET the record at location of counter (CT)   │
│          Print the counter and the fields of the buffer│
│          Decrement the counter                        │
└──────────────────Repeat until counter < 1─────────────┘

Close the file
Stop
```

FIGURE 15–3(a). Recall Records from a Random Access File—Pseudocode

```
2500 REM *********** RECALL A RANDOM FILE ***********
2505 REM CLEAR SPACE FOR STRINGS, OPEN THE RANDOM FILE,
2507 REM FIELD THE BUFFER, READ DATA (IN REVERSE ORDER)
2510 CLEAR 2000
2512 INPUT "WHAT IS THE NAME OF YOUR FILE";NM$
2514 INPUT "BY WHAT NUMBER SHOULD I REFER TO THE FILE";NO
2520 INPUT "WHAT IS THE (FIXED) RECORD LENGTH (BYTES)";RL
2525 OPEN "R", NO, NM$, RL
2527 FIELD NO, 20 AS A$, 20 AS B$, 8 AS C$, 16 AS DUMMY$
2528 N = LOF(NO)
2530 FOR I = 1 TO N
2532      CT = N-I+1
2534      GET NO, CT
2536      PRINT "RECORD";CT;":";A$;B$;C$
2539 NEXT I
2540 CLOSE NO
2549 END
```

FIGURE 15–3(b). Recall Records from a Random Access File—The Program

In order to read a record from the file, the entire record must be moved into the buffer. Then the variables can be used as their names appear in the latest FIELD command. The instruction to move record number I from file NO to the buffer is GET NO,I. If the record number (I) is not specified, the next record (following the latest which was read) will be accessed.

In our example we have chosen to read and print the records in reverse order from the way they were written just to show that the records can be accessed individually or in any order we choose. Figure 15–4 is a sample run of the program. Compare this with the file itself, which is shown in Figure 15–2b.

```
WHAT IS THE NAME OF YOUR FILE? RNDATA
BY WHAT NUMBER SHOULD I REFER TO THE FILE? 1
WHAT IS THE (FIXED) RECORD LENGTH (BYTES)? 64
RECORD 11 :TOPPER               PEARSON*TOM          1975
RECORD 10 :TRUDGEON             FISH*ARNOLD          1980
RECORD 9 :SNIPPETS             WILKINS*MARY         1982
RECORD 8 :RED                  BARTON*FRITZ         1978
RECORD 7 :GRUMBLY              SMITH*TED            1983
RECORD 6 :HIGHPOCKETS          RICH*HOWARD          1980
RECORD 5 :LIZ                  SMITH*ELIZABETH      1974
RECORD 4 :MISTY                JONES*SALLY          1980
RECORD 3 :SKINNY               WILSON*TOM           1982
RECORD 2 :NOODLEY              HOLMES*NORRIS        1975
RECORD 1 :BUZZ                 UZRA*BILL            1968
```

FIGURE 15–4. Running the Program to Recall Records from a Random Access File

SEARCHING

Linear Search (Sequential Files)

In order to make the linear search more meaningful, the program from Chapter 14 to create a sequential file (Figure 14–1) was used to create the file PHONESEQ shown in Figure 15–5, which contains last and first names and telephone numbers of 50 fictitious persons. The program in Figure 15–6 searches such a sequential file, one record at a time from beginning to end, for a specified last and first name. If the name is found, the phone number is printed. Figure 15–7 shows the result of running the program to perform such a search.

Two concepts are important in the linear search program of Figure 15–6. First, note that (in line 2770) a check is made to determine whether the end of file (EOF) has been reached *before* reading (Input) the next record. This is critical, because a program will terminate with an error message if one tries to read the end of file.

Line 2777 of the program adds sufficient blanks to the ends of the search names, L$ and F$, to ensure that they have the same number of characters which were read from the file as A$ and B$ respectively. This is accomplished for L$, for example, by first adding (concatenating) 20 blanks (as defined by variable BL$ in line 2752) to the end of L$ (L$ + BL$). Then the number of characters in A$ (the length of A$) is found by the BASIC function LEN(A$). Finally, the leftmost LEN(A$) characters of L$ + 20 blanks are assigned to variable L$ by the LEFT$(variable, no. of characters) command, 2777 L$ = LEFT$(L$ + BL$, LEN(A$)). If the strings L$ and A$ are not the same length, many versions of BASIC will not recognize them to be equivalent. Note that the search file, PHONESEQ, Figure 15–5, has not been sorted. For a linear search the order of records is unimportant.

Linear Search (Random Access Files)

In order to illustrate a linear search of a random access file, we need to have such a file. The program in Figure 15–8 is a housekeeping program to copy the contents of a sequential file into a random file. The program was used to copy the sequential data file PHONESEQ to the random file, PHONRAND, shown in Figure 15–9.

You should observe in the copy program (Figure 15–8) that two files were opened, the sequential file for Input (Read), and the random file into which we will write. Three fields (A$, B$, C$) are read from each record of the sequential file and stored as the three fields P$, Q$, and R$ in the random

```
WEAVER      ,  JANE      ,  731-1150
MAYS        ,  JAMES     ,  782-7644
TRIMBLE     ,  ALAN      ,  393-8318
BUTTE       ,  ALICE     ,  782-8760
FISHER      ,  RICHARD   ,  451-9993
HOWE        ,  KAREN     ,  394-1445
POULTER     ,  VERNON    ,  544-1454
WILEY       ,  STEPHEN   ,  773-7178
HANSON      ,  RALPH     ,  829-3317
ANDRUS      ,  JOHN      ,  825-9081
GWYNN       ,  KEITH     ,  544-9876
MORITZ      ,  WILLIAM   ,  829-6662
CUMMINGS    ,  ROLAND    ,  479-3797
NELSON      ,  THERESA   ,  479-0135
TRIP        ,  GEORGE    ,  773-0502
DEXTER      ,  SAM       ,  773-7744
DIAZ        ,  HECTOR    ,  393-6523
ABBOTT      ,  DUANE     ,  451-5943
BLAKE       ,  PETER     ,  776-5911
MURPHY      ,  DOROTHEA  ,  776-0301
TIBBETS     ,  GLEN      ,  392-3217
JENSEN      ,  WAYNE     ,  544-5871
BROWN       ,  COLISTA   ,  451-7878
GROSS       ,  GREG      ,  546-0011
BELT        ,  RAYMOND   ,  546-4567
COOK        ,  LAMAR     ,  773-1666
DENNIS      ,  FLOYD     ,  392-9052
HAMMER      ,  LORIN     ,  393-6154
PIERCE      ,  EDWIN     ,  394-4386
MURPHY      ,  JOSEPH    ,  399-1749
ZUNDELL     ,  WILFORD   ,  825-0431
YOUNG       ,  KARL      ,  825-9834
PETTY       ,  STEVE     ,  773-0719
GREEN       ,  ALLEN     ,  782-7355
KAISER      ,  DEAN      ,  782-1330
BUTLER      ,  PARLEY    ,  394-0914
ADAMS       ,  DON       ,  776-7777
SHERMAN     ,  RANDY     ,  773-0476
WILSON      ,  RFRTHA    ,  825-2176
SIMON       ,  MORRIS    ,  621-2574
KAISER      ,  ELMER     ,  479-9582
BROWN       ,  DALE      ,  731-1234
DEXTER      ,  VERNE     ,  731-8066
DEAN        ,  LIONEL    ,  394-8193
FULLER      ,  LAUREL    ,  546-6653
JUDD        ,  KAY       ,  731-4103
MEYER       ,  DWAYNE    ,  825-1558
NELSON      ,  HENRY     ,  393-4204
STEEL       ,  ORSON     ,  731-0125
GIBBS       ,  ELSIE     ,  479-4698
EOF
```

FIGURE 15–5. A Sequential Phone List File, PHONESEQ

```
Clear string space
Initialize a variable BL$ to 20 blanks
What are the name and number of the search file?
What are the last and first names for which to search?
Open the file for Input

        Read a record from the file
        Compare with the search names (adjusted with appropriate blanks)
              Repeat until search name is found or until end of file

If the search name has been found, print the record.
       Otherwise indicate that the name is not in the file.
Close the file
Stop
```

FIGURE 15–6(a). Perform a Linear Search on a Sequential File—Pseudocode

```
2750 REM *********** LINEAR SEARCH (SEQUENTIAL) ***********
2752 CLEAR 2000: BL$="                    "
2755 INPUT "WHAT IS THE NAME OF THE (SEQUENTIAL) SEARCH FILE";NM$
2757 INPUT "BY WHAT NUMBER SHOULD I REFER TO THE FILE";NO
2760 INPUT "WHAT IS THE LAST NAME FOR WHICH TO SEARCH";L$
2762 INPUT "WHAT IS THE FIRST NAME";F$
2765 OPEN "I",NO,NM$
2770 IF NOT(EOF(NO)) GOTO 2775
2772      PRINT L$;",";F$;" WAS NOT FOUND IN THE FILE."
2774      GOTO 2795
2775 INPUT #NO,A$,B$,C$
2777 L$=LEFT$(L$+BL$,LEN(A$)): F$=LEFT$(F$+BL$,LEN(B$))
2782 IF A$<>L$ OR B$<>F$ GOTO 2770
2785      PRINT "THE PHONE NUMBER OF ";L$;",";F$;" IS ";C$
2795 CLOSE NO
2799 END
```

FIGURE 15–6(b). Perform a Linear Search on a Sequential File—The Program

```
WHAT IS THE NAME OF THE (SEQUENTIAL) SEARCH FILE? PHONESEQ
BY WHAT NUMBER SHOULD I REFER TO THE FILE? 1
WHAT IS THE LAST NAME FOR WHICH TO SEARCH? NELSON
WHAT IS THE FIRST NAME? HENRY
THE PHONE NUMBER OF NELSON              ,HENRY               IS 393-4204
```

```
WHAT IS THE NAME OF THE (SEQUENTIAL) SEARCH FILE? PHONESEQ
BY WHAT NUMBER SHOULD I REFER TO THE FILE? 1
WHAT IS THE LAST NAME FOR WHICH TO SEARCH? BELT
WHAT IS THE FIRST NAME? SAM
BELT             ,SAM                 WAS NOT FOUND IN THE FILE.
```

FIGURE 15–7. Running the Program to Perform a Linear Search on a Sequential File

```
Clear string space
Initialize record counter (I=0)
What is the name of the sequential source file?
What is the name of the random destination file?
Open the source file for Input (read)
Open and Field the destination file.

   ┌── Increment record counter ─────────────────┐
   │   Read (Input) a record from the source file │
   │   Write (PUT) the record into the destination file
   └──────────────── Repeat until end of source file ┘

Close the files
Stop
```

FIGURE 15–8(a). Copy from a Sequential File to a Random Access File—Pseudocode

```
2800 REM *********** MOVE SEQUENTIAL TO RANDOM ***********
2802 CLEAR 2000: I=0
2805 INPUT "WHAT IS THE NAME OF THE SEQUENTIAL SOURCE FILE";N1$
2810 INPUT "WHAT IS THE NAME OF THE RANDOM DESTINATION FILE";N2$
2815 OPEN "I",1,N1$
2817 OPEN "R",2,N2$,48
2820 FIELD 2, 18 AS P$, 18 AS Q$, 12 AS R$
2825 IF EOF(1) GOTO 2845
2830      I=I+1
2832      INPUT #1,A$,B$,C$
2835      LSET P$=A$: LSET Q$=B$: LSET R$=C$
2837      PUT #2,I
2839      GOTO 2825
2845 CLOSE 1,2
2849 END
```

FIGURE 15–8(b). Copy from a Sequential File to a Random Access File—The Program

```
WHAT IS THE NAME OF THE SEQUENTIAL SOURCE FILE? PHONESEQ
WHAT IS THE NAME OF THE RANDOM DESTINATION FILE? PHONRAND
```

FIGURE 15–8(c). Running the Program to Copy from a Sequential File to a Random Access File

```
WEAVER          JANE          731-1150
MAYS            JAMES         782-7644
TRIMBLE         ALAN          393-8318
BUTTE           ALICE         782-8760
FISHER          RICHARD       451-9993
HOWE            KAREN         394-1445
POULTER         VERNON        544-1454
WILEY           STEPHEN       773-7178
HANSON          RALPH         829-3317
ANDRUS          JOHN          825-9081
GWYNN           KEITH         544-9876
MORITZ          WILLIAM       829-6662
CUMMINGS        ROLAND        479-3797
NELSON          THERESA       479-0135
TRIP            GEORGE        773-0502
DEXTER          SAM           773-7744
DIAZ            HECTOR        393-6523
ABBOTT          DUANE         451-5943
BLAKE           PETER         776-5911
MURPHY          DOROTHEA      776-0301
TIBBETS         GLEN          392-3217
JENSEN          WAYNE         544-5871
BROWN           COLISTA       451-7878
GROSS           GREG          546-0011
BELT            RAYMOND       546-4567
COOK            LAMAR         773-1666
DENNIS          FLOYD         392-9052
HAMMER          LORIN         393-6154
PIERCE          EDWIN         394-4386
MURPHY          JOSEPH        399-1749
ZUNDELL         WILFORD       825-0431
YOUNG           KARL          825-9834
PETTY           STEVE         773-0719
GREEN           ALLEN         782-7355
KAISER          DEAN          782-1330
BUTLER          PARLEY        394-0914
ADAMS           DON           776-7777
SHERMAN         RANDY         773-0476
WILSON          BERTHA        825-2176
SIMON           MORRIS        621-2574
KAISER          ELMER         479-9582
BROWN           DALE          731-1234
DEXTER          VERNE         731-8066
DEAN            LIONEL        394-8193
```

FIGURE 15–9. A Random Access Phone List File, PHONRAND

```
FULLER          LAUREL          546-6653
JUDD            KAY             731-4103
MEYER           DWAYNE          825-1558
NELSON          HENRY           393-4204
STEEL           ORSON           731-0125
GIBBS           ELSIE           479-4698
EOF
```

FIGURE 15–9. Continued

file. In this case, the random file record length was chosen, rather arbitrarily, to be 48 bytes and fielded with 18 bytes for P$, 18 bytes for Q$, and 12 bytes for R$.

We now have an unsorted random access file, PHONRAND, on which we can perform a linear search. The search program is shown in Figure 15–10, with sample runs in Figure 15–11. There are no significant differences between the linear search of a random access file (the program in Figure 15–10) and the linear search of a sequential file (the program in Figure 15–6). Of course, the file is opened for Random access rather than sequential Input, and we GET the data records rather than using the sequential INPUT command. Rather than check for end of file, we chose in this program to determine how many records are in the file, using the LOF function.

Binary Search

Two conditions are important in performing a binary search. First, the file has to be sorted in order by search key; and second, we need to be able

```
Clear string space
Initialize record counter (I=0)
Initialize a variable BL$ to 20 blanks
What are the name and number of the search file?
What are the last and first names for which to search?
Open and Field the file

 ----------------------------------------------------------------
|        Increment the record counter (I)
|        Read (GET) record I from the file
|        Compare with the search names (adjusted with appropriate blanks)
 -------------Repeat until search name is found or last record (LOF) is read-

If the search name has been found, print the record.
        Otherwise indicate that the name is not in the file.
Close the file
Stop
```

FIGURE 15–10(a). Perform a Linear Search on a Random Access File—Pseudocode

```
2700 REM *********** LINEAR SEARCH (RANDOM FILE) ***********
2702 CLEAR 2000: I=0: BL$="                                "
2705 INPUT "WHAT IS THE NAME OF THE (RANDOM) SEARCH FILE";NM$
2707 INPUT "BY WHAT NUMBER SHOULD I REFER TO THE FILE";NO
2710 INPUT "WHAT IS THE LAST NAME FOR WHICH TO SEARCH";L$
2712 INPUT "WHAT IS THE FIRST NAME";F$
2715 OPEN "R",NO,NM$,48
2717 FIELD NO, 18 AS P$, 18 AS Q$, 12 AS R$
2720 I=I+1
2722 IF I<=LOF(NO) GOTO 2728
2724      PRINT L$;",";F$;" WAS NOT FOUND IN THE FILE."
2726      GOTO 2745
2728 GET NO,I
2730 L$=LEFT$(L$+BL$,LEN(P$)): F$=LEFT$(F$+BL$,LEN(Q$))
2732 IF P$<>L$ OR F$<>Q$ GOTO 2720
2735      PRINT "THE PHONE NUMBER OF ";L$;",";F$;" IS ";R$
2745 CLOSE NO
2749 END
```

FIGURE 15–10(b). Perform a Linear Search on a Random Access File—The Program

to read each record without having to read the entire file. Thus, a binary search requires a sorted random access file.

The program in Figure 15–12 performs a quick sort on a random file. It was used to sort the random phone list, PHONRAND, and to produce the sorted phone list, RNDATSRT, shown in Figure 15–13. The file from which the fields are read is random rather than sequential. Also, the entire record is maintained, and a new subroutine (lines 2400–2499) has been added to our previous quick sort program in order to write the sorted records into a new file. In addition, the nonessential PRINT statement and printing subroutines have been removed in the interest of speed. Otherwise, this sort program is the same as that for sequential files in Chapter 14, Figure 14–13.

```
WHAT IS THE NAME OF THE (RANDOM) SEARCH FILE? PHONRAND
BY WHAT NUMBER SHOULD I REFER TO THE FILE? 1
WHAT IS THE LAST NAME FOR WHICH TO SEARCH? BROWN
WHAT IS THE FIRST NAME? COLISTA
THE PHONE NUMBER OF BROWN             ,COLISTA          IS 451-7878
```

```
WHAT IS THE NAME OF THE (RANDOM) SEARCH FILE? PHONRAND
BY WHAT NUMBER SHOULD I REFER TO THE FILE? 1
WHAT IS THE LAST NAME FOR WHICH TO SEARCH? BROWN
WHAT IS THE FIRST NAME? DALE
THE PHONE NUMBER OF BROWN             ,DALE             IS 731-1234
```

FIGURE 15–11. Running the Program to Perform a Linear Search on Random Access File, PHONRAND

```
Clear and dimension string and stack space
Read the data (See Figure 15-3)
Print the list of data
Set LO and HI pointers to ends of list
Set I and J pointers to ends of list
Perform the quick sort and print the final list (See Figure 14-13)
Write the new file (See Figure 15-1)
Stop
```

FIGURE 15–12(a). Perform a Quick Sort on a Random Access File—Pseudocode

```
800 REM *********** QUICK SORT (RANDOM FILE) ***********
802 REM CLEAR STRING SPACE, DIMENSION STACK (ST) AND VARIABLES
805 CLEAR 6000
807 DIM ST(20,2), A$(60), B$(60), C$(60)
810 REM RECALL LIST OF ELEMENTS (A$)
812 GOSUB 1100
820 REM PRINT THE LIST OF ELEMENTS
822 I=0: J=0: LO=1: HI=N
824 PRINT: PRINT "THE ORIGINAL LIST IS"
826 GOSUB 1400
830 REM INITIALIZE I AND J POINTERS
832 I=1: J=N: LO=1: HI=J
840 REM PERFORM THE QUICK SORT
841 PRINT: PRINT "PLEASE BE PATIENT. I'M SORTING": PRINT
842 GOSUB 1900
843 REM WRITE THE NEW FILE
844 GOSUB 2400
845 REM END OF PROGRAM
849 GOTO 9999


1100 REM *********** RECALL THE ELEMENTS ***********
1147 INPUT "WHAT IS THE NAME OF YOUR FILE";NM$
1148 INPUT "BY WHAT NUMBER SHOULD I REFER TO THE FILE";NO
1160 OPEN "R",NO,NM$,48
1165 FIELD NO, 18 AS P$, 18 AS Q$, 12 AS R$
1170      N=LOF(NO)
1180      FOR I=1 TO N
1190           GET NO,I
1195           A$(I)=P$: B$(I)=Q$: C$(I)=R$
1200      NEXT I
1240 CLOSE NO
1249 RETURN


1400 REM *********** PRINT THE LIST ***********
1420 FOR CT=LO TO HI
1430      PRINT A$(CT); B$(CT); C$(CT);
1440 NEXT CT
1445 PRINT
1449 RETURN
```

FIGURE 15–12(b). Perform a Quick Sort on a Random Access File—The Program

```
1900 REM *********** PERFORM THE QUICK SORT ***********
1902 REM INITIALIZE STACK POINTER (STACK INITIALLY EMPTY)
1905 SP=0
1910 REM INITIALIZE LIMITS
1925 REM SET J-FLAG TO DECREMENT J (JF=1)
1927 JF=1
1930 REM COMPARE, IF A$(I)>A$(J) EXCHANGE & RESET J-FLAG
1932 IF A$(I)<A$(J) GOTO 1940
1934      IF A$(I)=A$(J) AND B$(I)<=B$(J) GOTO 1940
1935            T1$=A$(I): T2$=B$(I): T3$=C$(I)
1936            A$(I)=A$(J): B$(I)=B$(J): C$(I)=C$(J)
1937            A$(J)=T1$: B$(J)=T2$: C$(J)=T3$
1938      JF = (-1)*JF
1940 IF JF=1 THEN J=J-1 ELSE I=I+1
1950 IF J>I GOTO 1930
1960 IF JF=1 THEN J=J+1 ELSE I=I-1
2000 REM PUSH LO AND I
2004      P=LO: Q=I: GOSUB 1600
2010 REM SORT LIST FROM J TO HI UNLESS J=HI
2012 IF J>=HI GOTO 2020
2014      LO=J: I=J: J=HI
2016      GOTO 1925
2020 REM POP NEXT LOWER LIST LIMITS FROM THE STACK
2022 GOSUB 1650
2024 REM STOP WHEN HI = LO = 1
2026 IF LO=1 AND HI=1 GOTO 2040
2030      I=LO: J=HI
2032 REM IF I<>J SORT FROM I TO J, OTHERWISE POP FROM STACK
2034 IF I=J GOTO 2020
2036      GOTO 1925
2040 REM PRINT THE FINAL LIST AND END SORTING
2041 PRINT
2042 PRINT "THE FINAL SORTED LIST LOOKS LIKE"
2043 LO=1: HI=N: I=0: J=0
2045 GOSUB 1400
2049 RETURN

1600 REM *********** PUSH P AND Q ONTO THE STACK ***********
1605 SP=SP+1
1620 ST(SP,1)=P: ST(SP,2)=Q
1649 RETURN

1650 REM *********** POP LO AND HI FROM THE STACK ***********
1680 LO=ST(SP,1): HI=ST(SP,2)
1682 SP=SP-1
1699 RETURN

2400 REM *********** WRITE THE SORTED RANDOM FILE **********
2425 INPUT "WHAT SHOULD BE THE NAME OF THE SORTED FILE";NM$
2427 INPUT "BY WHAT NUMBER SHOULD I REFER TO THE FILE";NO
2430 OPEN "R",NO,NM$,48
```

FIGURE 15–12(b). Continued

```
2440 FIELD NO, 18 AS P$, 18 AS Q$, 12 AS R$
2452 FOR I=1 TO N
2455     LSET P$=A$(I): LSET Q$=B$(I): LSET R$=C$(I)
2460     PUT NO,I
2465 NEXT I
2490 CLOSE NO
2499 RETURN


9999 END
```

FIGURE 15–12(b). Continued

ABBOTT	DUANE	451-5943
ADAMS	DON	776-7777
ANDRUS	JOHN	825-9081
BELT	RAYMOND	546-4567
BLAKE	PETER	776-5911
BROWN	COLISTA	451-7878
BROWN	DALE	731-1234
BUTLER	PARLEY	394-0914
BUTTE	ALICE	782-8760
COOK	LAMAR	773-1666
CUMMINGS	ROLAND	479-3797
DEAN	LIONEL	394-8193
DENNIS	FLOYD	392-9052
DEXTER	SAM	773-7744
DEXTER	VERNE	731-8066
DIAZ	HECTOR	393-6523
FISHER	RICHARD	451-9993
FULLER	LAUREL	546-6653
GIBBS	ELSIE	479-4698
GREEN	ALLEN	782-7355
GROSS	GREG	546-0011
GWYNN	KEITH	544-9876
HAMMER	LORIN	393-6154
HANSON	RALPH	829-3317
HOWE	KAREN	394-1445
JENSEN	WAYNE	544-5871
JUDD	KAY	731-4103
KAISER	DEAN	782-1330
KAISER	ELMER	479-9582
MAYS	JAMES	782-7644
MEYER	DWAYNE	825-1558
MORITZ	WILLIAM	829-6662

FIGURE 15–13. The Sorted Phone List, RNDATSRT, Produced by the Random File Quick Sort Program

```
MURPHY          DOROTHEA        776-0301
MURPHY          JOSEPH          399-1749
NELSON          HENRY           393-4204
NELSON          THERESA         479-0135
PETTY           STEVE           773-0719
PIERCE          EDWIN           394-4386
POULTER         VERNON          544-1454
SHERMAN         RANDY           773-0476
SIMON           MORRIS          621-2574
STEEL           ORSON           731-0125
TIBBETS         GLEN            392-3217
TRIMBLE         ALAN            393-8318
TRIP            GEORGE          773-0502
WEAVER          JANE            731-1150
WILEY           STEPHEN         773-7178
WILSON          BERTHA          825-2176
YOUNG           KARL            825-9834
ZUNDELL         WILFORD         825-0431
EOF
```

FIGURE 15–13. Continued

```
Clear string space
Initialize a variable BL$ to 20 blanks
What are the name and number of the file to be searched?
Open and Field the file
What are the last and first names for which to search?
Read the first record and adjust the length of search names to match record
Initialize LO and HI to ends of file
Set the first record number (RN) to the middle of the file
Initialize the flag (FL=0) which (when >1) will indicate that the search names
      are not in the file

 ----- Search the records ---------------------------------------------------
|     GET record RN                                                          |
|     If this matches search names, print the record                         |
|           and exit Search the records routine                              |
|     Otherwise, set the record number (RN) to middle of appropriate         |
|           interval. If at end of the interval, make certain the end        |
|           of the interval is examined (RN=RN+1 or RN=RN-1 and FL=FL+1).    |
 ------------------ Repeat until search name is found or until adjacent -----
                    record are read twice (indicating names not found)

If the names were not found, print the message that they are not in the file
Close the file
Stop
```

FIGURE 15–14(a). Perform a Binary Search—Pseudocode

```
2600 REM *********** BINARY SEARCH ***********
2605 CLEAR 2000: BL$="                               "
2610 INPUT "WHAT IS THE NAME OF THE (RANDOM) SEARCH FILE";NM$
2612 INPUT "BY WHAT NUMBER SHOULD I REFER TO THE FILE";NO
2615 OPEN "R",NO,NM$,48
2617 FIELD NO, 18 AS P$, 18 AS Q$, 12 AS R$
2620 INPUT "WHAT IS THE LAST NAME FOR WHICH TO SEARCH";L$
2622 INPUT "WHAT IS THE FIRST NAME";F$
2625 GET NO,1
2627 L$=LEFT$(L$+BL$,LEN(P$)): F$=LEFT$(F$+BL$,LEN(Q$))
2630 LO=1: HI=LOF(NO)
2632 RN = INT((LO+HI)/2): FL=0
2635 IF ABS(HI-LO)<=1 AND FL>1 GOTO 2680
2640 GET NO,RN
2642 PRINT "THE RECORD JUST FOUND IS NO.";RN;" ";P$;Q$;R$
2645 IF P$<L$ GOTO 2660
2646   IF P$>L$ GOTO 2670
2647      IF Q$<F$ GOTO 2660
2648         IF Q$>F$ GOTO 2670
2650            PRINT:PRINT "THE PHONE NUMBER OF ";L$;",";F$;" IS ";R$
2652            GOTO 2690
2660 LO=RN
2662 RN = INT((RN+HI)/2)
2664 IF RN<>LO GOTO 2668
2665   RN=RN+1: FL=FL+1
2668 GOTO 2635
2670 HI=RN
2672 RN = INT((LO+RN)/2)
2674 IF RN<>HI GOTO 2678
2675   RN=RN-1: FL=FL+1
2678 GOTO 2635
2680 PRINT:PRINT L$;",";F$;" WAS NOT FOUND IN THE FILE"
2690 CLOSE NO
2699 END
```

FIGURE 15–14(b). Perform a Binary Search—The Program

Now that we have a sorted random access file, we are ready to perform a binary search. The program in Figure 15–14 performs that search. It is applied in Figure 15–15 to the sorted phone list. A few lines of the program require some explanation. In lines 2625–2627, the first record of the file is read (GET) simply to obtain the length (LEN) of the name fields so that the search names can be adjusted (L$ = LEFT$(L$ + BL$,LEN(P$))) with blanks to match the lengths of the fields in the file.

At line 2630, the limits of the file are defined (LO = 1, HI = LOF). The first record number (RN) is set at the middle of the list (RN = ((HI + LO)/2)) in line 2632. A flag (FL) is also set in this line, which is used to determine (in line 2635) when adjacent records have been read twice, indicating that the

```
WHAT IS THE NAME OF THE (RANDOM) SEARCH FILE? RNDATSRT
BY WHAT NUMBER SHOULD I REFER TO THE FILE? 1
WHAT IS THE LAST NAME FOR WHICH TO SEARCH? POULTER
WHAT IS THE FIRST NAME? VERNON
THE RECORD JUST FOUND IS NO. 25  HOWE           KAREN       394-1445

THE RECORD JUST FOUND IS NO. 37  PETTY          STEVE       773-0719

THE RECORD JUST FOUND IS NO. 43  TIBBETS        GLEN        392-3217

THE RECORD JUST FOUND IS NO. 40  SHERMAN        RANDY       773-0476

THE RECORD JUST FOUND IS NO. 38  PIERCE         EDWIN       394-4386

THE RECORD JUST FOUND IS NO. 39  POULTER        VERNON      544-1454


THE PHONE NUMBER OF POULTER          ,VERNON          IS 544-1454




WHAT IS THE NAME OF THE (RANDOM) SEARCH FILE? RNDATSRT
BY WHAT NUMBER SHOULD I REFER TO THE FILE? 1
WHAT IS THE LAST NAME FOR WHICH TO SEARCH? MATHER
WHAT IS THE FIRST NAME? BILL
THE RECORD JUST FOUND IS NO. 25  HOWE           KAREN       394-1445

THE RECORD JUST FOUND IS NO. 37  PETTY          STEVE       773-0719

THE RECORD JUST FOUND IS NO. 31  MEYER          DWAYNE      825-1558

THE RECORD JUST FOUND IS NO. 28  KAISER         DEAN        782-1330

THE RECORD JUST FOUND IS NO. 29  KAISER         ELMER       479-9582

THE RECORD JUST FOUND IS NO. 30  MAYS           JAMES       782-7644

THE RECORD JUST FOUND IS NO. 29  KAISER         ELMER       479-9582

THE RECORD JUST FOUND IS NO. 30  MAYS           JAMES       782-7644

THE RECORD JUST FOUND IS NO. 29  KAISER         ELMER       479-9582

MATHER          ,BILL            WAS NOT FOUND IN THE FILE
```

FIGURE 15–15. Running the Program to Perform a Binary Search

search name has not been found in the file. Lines 2660–2662 and 2670–2672 reset the record number (RN) to the middle of the next appropriate interval.

HASHING

The Hashed File

To illustrate hash coding, we will apply a hash function to the data stored in the sequential phone list file, PHONESEQ (Figure 15–5), store the records in a random access file, HASHOUT (Figure 15–17), and then find records in that file by converting the name key back to the storage address.

Figure 15–16 is a program which performs the hashing and creates the random file. The last and first names are read (Input) one at a time from the sequential file. Then the hash function is applied by the subroutine in lines 2850 through 2899. The hash method used in this example examines the search names to find two consecutive blanks, which we assume to indicate the end of the name. This is done for the last name L$, for example, by using the function MID$(L$,I,2), which picks two characters from the middle of L$, beginning with the Ith position; e. g., in L$ = BROWN, MID$(L$,3,2) is the two characters OW. The names are truncated to length, LE, which includes all of the characters up to but not including trailing blanks (L$ = LEFT$(L$,LE)). Then the characters are separated one by one, using MID$(L$,I,1) for I = 1 to LE. At this point, the position of each character in the alphabet is found (ASC(character) − 64 = ASCII for the character minus 64 = position in the alphabet, since ASCII for "A" is 65). The positions of the characters in the alphabet are added to a sum (SU). Finally, the quotient/remainder method is used to convert SU to an ADdress. With 80% packing, 50 records require (50/0.8 = 62.5) 63 record spaces. The next smaller prime number, 61, is used. SU is divided by 61, and the remainder plus 6 is the ADdress. Note that the addresses used are in the range 6 through 66, rather than 1 to 61, because records 1 through 5 are used as a convenient place to record the instructions for the hashing which is done by lines 2570 through 2599 of the program.

The progressive overflow method is used (in lines 2950 to 2999) to store the records. The file was filled at first with blanks (lines 2900 to 2949). When a record is to be stored at an address AD, the contents of that address are examined. If that location contains blanks, then the record is written (PUT) there. Otherwise, the record counter is incremented, and successive locations are examined until an empty location is found at which the record can be stored. Note that location 6 logically follows location 66 in this file.

```
Clear string space

┌──────Open files and record the hash code────────────────────────
│       What is the name of the input file?
│       What is the name of the destination, hashed file?
│       Open both files
│       Write (PUT) the description of the hash code in the first 5 records
│              of the destination file
└─────────────────────────────────────────────────────────────────

Print "Please Be Patient..."
Field the output file to receive the records

┌────── Fill the output file with blanks ─────────────────────────
│       Initialize BL$ to 20 blanks
│       Put BL$ into all three fields for records 6 through 66
└─────────────────────────────────────────────────────────────────

┌──────Read, Hash, and Store the records──────────────────────────
│       Read (Input) a record from the sequential input file
│       ┌──────Convert name to address (apply hash function)───────
│       │       Initialize B2$ to 2 blanks
│       │
│       │   ┌──────────────────────────────────────────────────
│       │   │   Examine name 2 characters at a time until 2 blanks
│       │   │          are found.
│       │   │   Remove trailing blanks from the name
│       │   │   Convert each character in the name to
│       │   │          its position in the alphabet
│       │   │   Add position to SUm
│       │   └──────────── Repeat for Last and First Names ──────
│       │
│       │       Divide SUm by 61 (number of record spaces allowed)
│       │       Add 6 to remainder to obtain address between 6 and 66
│       │       Print names, SUm of letter positions, ADdress
│       └──────────────────────────────────────────────────────────
│   ┌──────────Store record in hashed file────────────────────────
│   │           I=ADdress
│   │   ┌──────────GET record I───────────────────────────────────
│   │   │           If record I is not empty, increment I (reset to
│   │   │                  6 when 66 is exceeded)
│   │   └──────────────────── Repeat until first empty record at or
│   │                         after ADdress is found
│   │
│   │           PUT the record in I
│   └─────────────────────────────────────────────────────────────
└────────────────────── Repeat until End Of input File is encountered

Close the files
Stop
```

FIGURE 15–16(a). Create a Hashed File—Pseudocode

```
750 REM *********** MAKE HASH ***********
755 CLEAR 2000
760 REM OPEN FILES & RECORD HASH CODE
765 GOSUB 2550
770 REM READ, CONVERT, & STORE
772 PRINT: PRINT "PLEASE BE PATIENT."
773 PRINT "I'M INITIALIZING THE OUTPUT FILE.": PRINT
775 GOSUB 3000
799 GOTO 9999


2550 REM *********** OPEN FILES & RECORD HASH CODE ***********
2555 INPUT "WHAT IS THE NAME OF (SEQUENTIAL) INPUT FILE";N1$
2560 INPUT "WHAT IS THE NAME OF OUTPUT (HASHED) FILE";N2$
2565 OPEN "I",1,N1$
2570 OPEN "R",2,N2$,48
2572 FIELD 2, 48 AS M$
2580 A$="HASH CODE: SUM PLACE VALUES OF ALL LETTERS"
2581 LSET M$=A$: PUT #2,1
2583 A$="EG.A=1,B=2...Z=26, IN 1ST AND LAST NAMES. IGNORE"
2584 LSET M$=A$: PUT #2,2
2586 A$="ALL OTHER CHARACTERS. DIVIDE BY 61, ADD 6 TO"
2587 LSET M$=A$: PUT #2,3
2589 A$="REMAINDER. PLACE IN NEXT AVAILABLE LOCATION."
2590 LSET M$=A$: PUT #2,4
2592 A$ = "AD = INT((SU/61-INT(SU/61))*61 + 0.1) + 6"
2593 LSET M$=A$: PUT #2,5
2599 RETURN


3000 REM *********** READ, CONVERT, & STORE ***********
3005 FIELD 2, 18 AS A$, 18 AS B$, 12 AS C$
3007 REM FILL FILE WITH BLANK RECORDS
3009 GOSUB 2900
3010 PRINT: PRINT "NAME","SUM OF LETTERS","ADDRESS": PRINT
3015 IF EOF(1) GOTO 3045
3017 INPUT #1,L$,F$,PH$
3020 REM CONVERT AND PRINT
3025 GOSUB 2850
3030 REM STORE IN NEW FILE
3035 GOSUB 2950
3040 GOTO 3015
3045 CLOSE 1, 2
3049 RETURN

2900 REM ********** FILL FILE WITH BLANK RECORDS ***********
2905 BL$="                  "
2910 LSET A$=BL$: LSET B$=BL$: LSET C$=BL$
2920 FOR I=6 TO 66
2925       PUT #2,I
2930 NEXT I
2949 RETURN
```

FIGURE 15–16(b). Create a Hashed File—The Program

```
2850 REM *********** CONVERT NAME TO ADDRESS ***********
2855 B2$="  ": I=0
2860 I=I+1
2862 T$=MID$(L$,I,2)
2864 IF T$<>B2$ GOTO 2860
2865 LE=I-1: L$=LEFT$(L$,LE)
2867 SU=0
2870 FOR I=1 TO LE
2872      SU = SU + ASC(MID$(L$,I,1)) - 64
2874 NEXT I
2875 I=0
2880 I=I+1
2882 T$=MID$(F$,I,2)
2884 IF T$<>B2$ GOTO 2880
2885 LE=I-1: F$=LEFT$(F$,LE)
2887 FOR I=1 TO LE
2889      SU = SU + ASC(MID$(F$,I,1)) - 64
2890 NEXT I
2892 AD = INT((SU/61-INT(SU/61))*61 + 0.1) + 6
2895 PRINT L$;",";F$,SU,AD
2899 RETURN



2950 REM *********** STORE IN NEW FILE ***********
2952 I=AD-1
2955 I=I+1
2960 IF I>66 THEN I=6
2965 GET #2,I
2970 IF LEFT$(A$,10)<>LEFT$(BL$,10) GOTO 2955
2972 LSET A$=L$: LSET B$=F$: LSET C$=PH$
2975 PUT #2,I
2999 RETURN



9999 END
```

FIGURE 15–16(b). Continued

```
WHAT IS THE NAME OF (SEQUENTIAL) INPUT FILE? PHONESEQ
WHAT IS THE NAME OF OUTPUT (HASHED) FILE? HASHOUT

PLEASE BE PATIENT.
I'M INITIALIZING THE OUTPUT FILE.
```

FIGURE 15–17(a). Running the Program to Create a Hashed File

NAME	SUM OF LETTERS	ADDRESS
WEAVER,JANE	104	49
MAYS,JAMES	106	51
TRIMBLE,ALAN	107	52
BUTTE,ALICE	98	43
FISHER,RICHARD	126	10
HOWE,KAREN	100	45
POULTER,VERNON	195	18
WILEY,STEPHEN	161	45
HANSON,RALPH	126	10
ANDRUS,JOHN	124	8
GWYNN,KEITH	136	20
MORITZ,WILLIAM	180	64
CUMMINGS,ROLAND	163	47
NELSON,THERESA	155	39
TRIP,GEORGE	120	65
DEXTER,SAM	109	54
DIAZ,HECTOR	109	54
ABBOTT,DUANE	105	50
BLAKE,PETER	95	40
MURPHY,DOROTHEA	187	10
TIBBETS,GLEN	115	60
JENSEN,WAYNE	135	19
BROWN,COLISTA	151	35
GROSS,GREG	115	60
BELT,RAYMOND	129	13
COOK,LAMAR	89	34
DENNIS,FLOYD	127	11
HAMMER,LORIN	126	10
PIERCE,EDWIN	111	56
MURPHY,JOSEPH	174	58
ZUNDELL,WILFORD	181	65
YOUNG,KARL	124	8
PETTY,STEVE	157	41
GREEN,ALLEN	93	38
KAISER,DEAN	87	32
BUTLER,PARLEY	155	39
ADAMS,DON	71	16
SHERMAN,RANDY	140	24
WILSON,BERTHA	146	30
SIMON,MORRIS	162	46
KAISER,ELMER	116	61
BROWN,DALE	94	39
DEXTER,VERNE	140	24
DEAN,LIONEL	91	36
FULLER,LAUREL	143	27
JUDD,KAY	76	21
MEYER,DWAYNE	138	22
NELSON,HENRY	149	33
STEEL,ORSON	142	26
GIBBS,ELSIE	89	34

FIGURE 15–17(a). Continued

1	HASH CODE: SUM PLACE VALUES OF ALL LETTERS		
2	EG.A=1,B=2...Z=26, IN 1ST AND LAST NAMES. IGNORE		
3	ALL OTHER CHARACTERS. DIVIDE BY 61, ADD 6 TO		
4	REMAINDER. PLACE IN NEXT AVAILABLE LOCATION.		
5	AD = INT((SU/61-INT(SU/61))*61 + 0.1) + 6		
6			
7			
8	ANDRUS	JOHN	825-9081
9	YOUNG	KARL	825-9834
10	FISHER	RICHARD	451-9993
11	HANSON	RALPH	829-3317
12	MURPHY	DOROTHEA	776-0301
13	BELT	RAYMOND	546-4567
14	DENNIS	FLOYD	392-9052
15	HAMMER	LORIN	393-6154
16	ADAMS	DON	776-7777
17			
18	POULTER	VERNON	544-1454
19	JENSEN	WAYNE	544-5871
20	GWYNN	KEITH	544-9876
21	JUDD	KAY	731-4103
22	MEYER	DWAYNE	825-1558
23			
24	SHERMAN	RANDY	773-0476
25	DEXTER	VERNE	731-8066
26	STEEL	ORSON	731-0125
27	FULLER	LAUREL	546-6653
28			
29			
30	WILSON	BERTHA	825-2176
31			
32	KAISER	DEAN	782-1330
33	NELSON	HENRY	393-4204
34	COOK	LAMAR	773-1666
35	BROWN	COLISTA	451-7878
36	DEAN	LIONEL	394-8193
37	GIBBS	ELSIE	479-4698
38	GREEN	ALLEN	782-7355
39	NELSON	THERESA	479-0135
40	BLAKE	PETER	776-5911
41	PETTY	STEVE	773-0719
42	BUTLER	PARLEY	394-0914
43	BUTTE	ALICE	782-8760
44	BROWN	DALE	731-1234
45	HOWE	KAREN	394-1445
46	WILEY	STEPHEN	773-7178
47	CUMMINGS	ROLAND	479-3797
48	SIMON	MORRIS	621-2574
49	WEAVER	JANE	731-1150
50	ABBOTT	DUANE	451-5943
51	MAYS	JAMES	782-7644
52	TRIMBLE	ALAN	393-8318

FIGURE 15–17(b). The Resulting Hashed Phone List, File, HASHOUT

```
53
54          DEXTER          SAM            773-7744
55          DIAZ            HECTOR         393-6523
56          PIERCE          EDWIN          394-4386
57
58          MURPHY          JOSEPH         399-1749
59
60          TIBBETS         GLEN           392-3217
61          GROSS           GREG           546-0011
62          KAISER          ELMER          479-9582
63
64          MORITZ          WILLIAM        829-6662
65          TRIP            GEORGE         773-0502
66          ZUNDELL         WILFORD        825-0431
```

FIGURE 15–17(b). Continued

Figure 15–17 is a sample run of the hashing program, illustrating the keys (last and first names), the SUm of the letters, and the storage ADdress calculated for each record. Also shown in that figure is the final file HASHOUT. Notice that we have somewhat more than 20 percent synonyms with this method. You may wish to rewrite the program so that it uses a "better" hash function for this data set.

The search program in Figure 15–18 asks for a last and first name key and performs the same hash coding as was applied (in Figure 15–16) to calculate the ADdress at which a record is stored. Again, the search for a record is done using progressive overflow. If a record is not found at the address to which its key converts, successive locations are searched until the record is found or until the entire file has been examined. You may wish to put a smaller limit (in line 3132) on the number of consecutive records to be searched before the program tells you the record cannot be found.

Example searches, using the program of Figure 15–18, are shown in Figure 15–19.

A Scatter Table

One purpose of a scatter table is to index a sorted random file so that the file can be read in sequential order by keys while maintaining the capability of using hashing for locating any record immediately. The scatter table will appear similar to a hashed file of the same data except that the table will contain the key of the record and the address of the data in the sorted file.

Figure 15–20 is a program to create a scatter table. It is almost like the program to create a hashed file (Figure 15–16). One difference is that the input

```
Clear string space
Initialize BL$ to 20 blanks
What is the name of the file to search?
Open the file

        Read the hash code from the file
                Field the buffer
                GET and print the first 5 records

        What are the last and first names for which to search?
        Pad the names on the right with blanks (so that exactly the
                same algorithm can be used as in the program which created the file)

        Find the name
                Define the 3 fields of the buffer
                Convert the name to address (See Figure 15-16)
                Initialize count (CT=0)
                Set record number (I) to ADdress of name

                Read (GET) record I
                        Adjust length of names to match fields of record
                        If record I contains the search names, print the record
                                Otherwise increment I (reset to 6 if > 66)
                                        Repeat if Counter < length of file
                                        until name is found

                If the search name was not found, indicate with a message
                                        Repeat if another name is desired

Close files
Stop
```

FIGURE 15–18(a). Apply Hashing to Find a Record—Pseudocode

```
550 REM *********** FIND HASH ***********
552 CLEAR 2000: BL$="                    "
555 INPUT "WHAT IS THE NAME OF THE (RANDOM) FILE";NM$
557 OPEN "R",1,NM$,48
560 REM READ HASH CODE
562 GOSUB 3050
565 PRINT
567 INPUT "FOR WHAT LAST AND FIRST NAMES TO SEARCH";L$,F$
568 L$=L$+BL$: F$=F$+BL$
570 REM FIND THE NAME
572 GOSUB 3100
580 PRINT
582 INPUT "WOULD YOU LIKE TO SEARCH FOR ANOTHER NAME";Y$
584 IF LEFT$(Y$,1)="Y" GOTO 565
599 GOTO 9999
```

FIGURE 15–18(b). Apply Hashing to Find a Record—The Program

```
3050 REM *********** READ HASH CODE FROM FILE ***********
3055 PRINT "HERE IS HOW THE FIELD WAS HASHED"
3060 FIELD #1,48 AS A$
3065 FOR I=1 TO 5
3070     GET #1,I
3075     PRINT A$
3080 NEXT I
3085 PRINT
3099 RETURN


3100 REM *********** FIND THE NAME ***********
3105 FIELD 1, 18 AS A$, 18 AS B$, 12 AS C$
3110 REM CONVERT TO ADDRESS
3112 GOSUB 2850
3114 CT=0: I=AD-1
3115 CT=CT+1 : I=I+1
3118 IF I>66 THEN I=6
3120 GET #1,I
3122 PRINT "RECORD";I;"  ";A$;B$;C$
3125 L$=LEFT$(L$+BL$,LEN(A$)): F$=LEFT$(F$+BL$,LEN(B$))
3130 IF L$=A$ AND F$=B$ GOTO 3140
3132     IF CT<=66 GOTO 3115
3134         PRINT: PRINT L$;",";F$;" IS NOT IN THE FILE."
3136         GOTO 3149
3140 PRINT: PRINT "THE PHONE NUMBER OF ";L$;F$;" IS ";C$
3149 RETURN

2850 REM *********** CONVERT NAME TO NUMBER ***********
2855 B2$="  ": I=Ø
2860 I=I+1
2862 T$=MID$(L$,I,2)
2864 IF T$<>B2$ GOTO 2860
2865 LE=I-1: L$=LEFT$(L$,LE)
2867 SU=Ø
2870 FOR I=1 TO LE
2872     SU = SU + ASC(MID$(L$,I,1)) - 64
2874 NEXT I
2875 I=Ø
2880 I=I+1
2882 T$=MID$(F$,I,2)
2884 IF T$<>B2$ GOTO 2880
2885 LE=I-1: F$=LEFT$(F$,LE)
2887 FOR I=1 TO LE
2889     SU = SU + ASC(MID$(F$,I,1)) - 64
2890 NEXT I
2892 AD = INT((SU/61-INT(SU/61))*61 + Ø.1) + 6
2895 PRINT L$;",";F$,SU,AD
2899 RETURN

9999 END
```

FIGURE 15–18(b). Continued

```
WHAT IS THE NAME OF THE (RANDOM) FILE? HASHOUT
HERE IS HOW THE FIELD WAS HASHED
HASH CODE: SUM PLACE VALUES OF ALL LETTERS
EG.A=1,B=2...Z=26, IN 1ST AND LAST NAMES. IGNORE
ALL OTHER CHARACTERS. DIVIDE BY 61, ADD 6 TO
REMAINDER. PLACE IN NEXT AVAILABLE LOCATION.
AD = INT((SU/61-INT(SU/61))*61 + 0.1) + 6


FOR WHAT LAST AND FIRST NAMES TO SEARCH? BUTTE, ALICE
BUTTE,ALICE       98                43
RECORD 43   BUTTE              ALICE               782-8760

THE PHONE NUMBER OF BUTTE              ALICE                IS 782-8760

WOULD YOU LIKE TO SEARCH FOR ANOTHER NAME? NO
```

FIGURE 15–19. Running the Program to Find a Record by Hashing

```
Clear string space and dimension

┌──────Open files and record the hash code──────────────────
│       What is the name of the sorted random input file?
│       The scatter table file will be called SCATTER
│       Open both files
│       Write the hash code into the first 5 records of SCATTER
└───────────────────────────────────────────────────────────

Print "Please be patient..."

┌──────Read, convert, and store─────────────────────────────
│       Fill the scatter table with blanks
│       Convert record no. J to string J1$ (see Figure 14-17)
│       GET record J from the sorted file
│       Convert name key to an address AD (see Figure 15-16)
│
│       ┌──────Store name key and record number J1$ in scatter table
│       │       If record AD is empty, store
│       │       Otherwise increment record number
│       └──────────────Repeat until an empty location is found
│
└──────────────────────────── Repeat for all records in the
                              sorted input file

┌──────Print the scatter table──────────────────────────────
│       Read and print the first 5 records, hash code
│       Read and print records 6 through 66 from scatter table
└───────────────────────────────────────────────────────────

Close files
Stop
```

FIGURE 15–20(a). Create a Scatter Table—Pseudocode

```
500 REM *********** MAKE SCATTER TABLE ***********
505 CLEAR 2000: DIM D(10)
510 REM OPEN FILES & RECORD HASH CODE
515 GOSUB 2550
520 REM READ, CONVERT, & STORE IN SCATTER TABLE
522 PRINT: PRINT "PLEASE BE PATIENT."
523 PRINT "I'M CREATING THE SCATTER TABLE": PRINT
525 GOSUB 3000
599 GOTO 9999



2550 REM *********** OPEN FILES & RECORD HASH CODE ***********
2555 INPUT "WHAT IS THE NAME OF SORTED RANDOM INPUT FILE";N1$
2560 PRINT "THE SCATTER TABLE FILE WILL BE CALLED SCATTER"
2565 OPEN "R",1,N1$,48
2570 OPEN "R",2,"SCATTER",48
2572 FIELD 2, 48 AS M$
2574 FIELD 1, 18 AS A1$, 18 AS B1$, 12 AS C1$
2580 A$="SCATTER CODE: SUM VALUES OF ALL LETTERS"
2581 LSET M$=A$: PUT #2,1
2583 A$="EG.A=1,B=2...Z=26, IN 1ST AND LAST NAMES. IGNORE"
2584 LSET M$=A$: PUT #2,2
2586 A$="ALL OTHER CHARACTERS. DIVIDE BY 61, ADD 6 TO"
2587 LSET M$=A$: PUT #2,3
2589 A$="REMAINDER. PLACE IN NEXT AVAILABLE LOCATION."
2590 LSET M$=A$: PUT #2,4
2592 A$ = "AD = INT((SU/61-INT(SU/61))*61 + 0.1) + 6"
2593 LSET M$=A$: PUT #2,5
2599 RETURN



3000 REM *********** READ, CONVERT, & STORE ***********
3005 FIELD 2, 18 AS A$, 18 AS B$, 12 AS C$
3007 REM FILL SCATTER TABLE WITH BLANK RECORDS
3009 GOSUB 2900
3015 FOR J=1 TO LOF(1)
3016      REM CONVERT J TO STRING J1$
3017      GOSUB 850
3019      GET #1,J
3020      L$=A1$+BL$: F$=B1$+BL$: R$=J1$: PH$=C1$
3023      REM CONVERT AND PRINT
3025      GOSUB 2850
3030      REM STORE IN NEW FILE
3035      GOSUB 2950
3040 NEXT J
3042 REM PRINT THE SCATTER TABLE
3043 GOSUB 3150
3045 CLOSE 1, 2
3049 RETURN
```

FIGURE 15–20(b). Create a Scatter Table—The Program

```
2900 REM ********** FILL FILE WITH BLANK RECORDS ***********
2905 BL$="                              "
2910 LSET A$=BL$: LSET B$=BL$: LSET C$=BL$
2920 FOR I=6 TO 66
2925       PUT #2,I
2930 NEXT I
2949 RETURN
```

```
850 REM *********** CHANGE J TO STRING J1$ ***********
855 NU=J
860 REM INITIALIZE STRING TO EMPTY
862 J1$="": K=0
865 K=K+1
870 REM D IS THE RIGHTMOST DIGIT OF NU
872 D(K)=INT((NU/10-INT(NU/10))*10+0.1)
874 REM CHANGE NU TO WHAT IS LEFT AFTER A DIGIT IS REMOVED
875 NU=INT(NU/10)
879 IF NOT(NU < 1) GOTO 865
880 REM CONCATENATE THE STRINGS FOR THE DIGITS
882 FOR L=1 TO K
884     CT=K-L+1
886     J1$=J1$ + CHR$(D(CT) + 48)
888 NEXT L
899 RETURN
```

```
2850 REM *********** CONVERT NAME TO ADDRESS ***********
2855 B2$="  ": S=0
2860 S=S+1
2862 T$=MID$(L$,S,2)
2864 IF T$<>B2$ GOTO 2860
2865 LE=S-1: L$=LEFT$(L$,LE)
2867 SU=0
2870 FOR S=1 TO LE
2872     SU = SU + ASC(MID$(L$,S,1)) - 64
2874 NEXT S
2875 S=0
2880 S=S+1
2882 T$=MID$(F$,S,2)
2884 IF T$<>B2$ GOTO 2880
2885 LE=S-1: F$=LEFT$(F$,LE)
2887 FOR S=1 TO LE
2889     SU = SU + ASC(MID$(F$,S,1)) - 64
2890 NEXT S
2892 AD = INT((SU/61-INT(SU/61))*61 + 0.1) + 6
2899 RETURN
```

FIGURE 15–20(b). Continued

```
2950 REM *********** STORE IN SCATTER TABLE ***********
2952 I=AD-1
2955 I=I+1
2960 IF I>66 THEN I=6
2965 GET #2,I
2970 IF LEFT$(A$,10)<>LEFT$(BL$,10) GOTO 2955
2972 LSET A$=L$: LSET B$=F$: LSET C$=R$
2975 PUT #2,I
2999 RETURN


3150 REM *********** PRINT THE SCATTER TABLE ***********
3155 PRINT:PRINT "SCATTER TABLE"
3156 PRINT "-------------"
3160 FIELD #2, 48 AS M$
3162 FOR J=1 TO 5
3164      GET #2,J
3166      PRINT M$
3168 NEXT J
3170 PRINT:PRINT "TABLE REC. NO. ";" KEY ",," FILE ADDRESS "
3175 FIELD #2, 18 AS A$, 18 AS B$, 12 AS C$
3176      GET #2,J
3177 FOR J=6 TO 66
3179      GET #2,J
3182      PRINT J,A$;",";B$;C$
3184 NEXT J
3199 RETURN


9999 END
```

FIGURE 15–20(b). Continued

file to the program in Figure 15–20 is a sorted random data file. In addition, once a name key has been converted to an address, the key and record number in the data file are stored at that address in the scatter table. Progressive overflow is used again in this program to place the key and the address at the first available location in the scatter table. Two subroutines have been added, one beginning at 850 (the same as Figure 14–17) to convert an integer record number J to a string J1$, so that it can be stored as a string in the scatter table. The other new subroutine, beginning at line 3150, prints the scatter table for purposes of illustration.

Figure 15–21 is a sample run, creating and showing a scatter table for the sorted random phone list file RNDATSRT.

```
WHAT IS THE NAME OF SORTED RANDOM INPUT FILE? RNDATSRT
THE SCATTER TABLE FILE WILL BE CALLED SCATTER

PLEASE BE PATIENT.
I'M CREATING THE SCATTER TABLE


SCATTER TABLE
-------------
SCATTER CODE: SUM VALUES OF ALL LETTERS
EG.A=1,B=2...Z=26, IN 1ST AND LAST NAMES. IGNORE
ALL OTHER CHARACTERS. DIVIDE BY 61, ADD 6 TO
REMAINDER. PLACE IN NEXT AVAILABLE LOCATION.
AD = INT((SU/61-INT(SU/61))*61 + 0.1) + 6

TABLE REC. NO.   KEY                                     FILE ADDRESS
 6                                  ,
 7                                  ,
 8               ANDRUS             ,JOHN                  3
 9               YOUNG              ,KARL                  49
 10              FISHER             ,RICHARD               17
 11              DENNIS             ,FLOYD                 13
 12              HAMMER             ,LORIN                 23
 13              BELT               ,RAYMOND               4
 14              HANSON             ,RALPH                 24
 15              MURPHY             ,DOROTHEA              33
 16              ADAMS              ,DON                   2
 17                                 ,
 18              POULTER            ,VERNON                39
 19              JENSEN             ,WAYNE                 26
 20              GWYNN              ,KEITH                 22
 21              JUDD               ,KAY                   27
 22              MEYER              ,DWAYNE                31
 23                                 ,
 24              DEXTER             ,VERNE                 15
 25              SHERMAN            ,RANDY                 40
 26              STEEL              ,ORSON                 42
 27              FULLER             ,LAUREL                18
 28                                 ,
 29                                 ,
 30              WILSON             ,BERTHA                48
 31                                 ,
 32              KAISER             ,DEAN                  28
 33              NELSON             ,HENRY                 35
 34              COOK               ,LAMAR                 10
 35              BROWN              ,COLISTA               6
 36              DEAN               ,LIONEL                12
 37              GIBBS              ,ELSIE                 19
 38              GREEN              ,ALLEN                 20
 39              BROWN              ,DALE                  7
 40              BLAKE              ,PETER                 5
```

FIGURE 15–21. Running the Program to Create a Scatter Table

```
41     BUTLER      ,PARLEY     8
42     NELSON      ,THERESA    36
43     BUTTE       ,ALICE      9
44     PETTY       ,STEVE      37
45     HOWE        ,KAREN      25
46     SIMON       ,MORRIS     41
47     CUMMINGS    ,ROLAND     11
48     WILEY       ,STEPHEN    47
49     WEAVER      ,JANE       46
50     ABBOTT      ,DUANE      1
51     MAYS        ,JAMES      30
52     TRIMBLE     ,ALAN       44
53                 ,
54     DEXTER      ,SAM        14
55     DIAZ        ,HECTOR     16
56     PIERCE      ,EDWIN      38
57                 ,
58     MURPHY      ,JOSEPH     34
59                 ,
60     GROSS       ,GREG       21
61     KAISER      ,ELMER      29
62     TIBBETS     ,GLEN       43
63                 ,
64     MORITZ      ,WILLIAM    32
65     TRIP        ,GEORGE     45
66     ZUNDELL     ,WILFORD    50
```

FIGURE 15–21. Continued

In Figure 15–22 is a program to use the scatter table. The sorted random data file and the scatter table file are both opened at the beginning of this program. Then the user is given a choice of listing the data file sequentially or of finding one individual record.

Reading the data file in sequential order is simply a matter of GETting and printing all of the records from the first to LOF. Finding an individual record is done in the same manner as in Figure 15–18. The search key is converted to an ADdress, which is now a scatter table record number. The record is read (GET) from the scatter table and examined to determine whether it matches the search key. Progressive overflow is used to search succeeding records, if necessary, until the search key is found or until the record is found nowhere in the table. Once the search key is found in the scatter table, the location of the record in the sorted file is read from the scatter table record, and the data is retrieved from the sorted file.

Figure 15–23 illustrates use of the scatter table file SCATTER to find records in the sorted phone list file RNDATSRT.

```
Clear string space
Set BL$ to 20 blanks
What is the name of the sorted random file?
What is the name of the scatter table file?
Open and Field both files

------- Menu ---------------------------------------------------------
|
|    --------- Read the sorted file sequentially ---------------
|    |         Read a record                                    |
|    |         Print the record                                 |
|    ---------------Repeat for all records in sorted file-------
|
|              Set flag to return to menu (FL=-1) and return to Menu
|
|    --------- Find one individual record ---------------------------
|    |         What are the last and first names for which to search?
|    |         Convert search name to ADdress (see Figure 15-16)
|    |         ------Find the record in the scatter table----------
|    |         |     GET record at ADdress                        |
|    |         |     If record contains search name               |
|    |         |     ------GET record from sorted file---------   |
|    |         |     |     RN=address field from scatter table record
|    |         |     |     GET record RN from sorted file     |   |
|    |         |     |     Print the record                   |   |
|    |         |     ------------------------------------------   |
|    |         |                                                  |
|    |         |     Otherwise increment the record number        |
|    |         ------------Repeat until record is found or until entire---
|    |                     scatter table has been searched
|    |
|    |         If record was not found, indicate with a message
|    -----------------------------------------------------------------
|              Set flag to return to menu (FL=-1) and return to Menu
|
|    --------- Exit and stop ---------------------
|    |               Set Flag to exit (FL=1)     |
|    ---------------------------------------------
|
------------------------------ Return to Menu while FL = -1 ----------

Close files
Stop
```

FIGURE 15–22(a). A Scatter Table—Pseudocode

SUBPROGRAMS BY NUMBER

A list of all of the subprograms used in Chapters 14 and 15 is provided in Table 15–1. These are listed by line number, title, and the programs in which they are used. You may find these subprograms useful as guidelines in creating some of your own file handling methods.

```
400 REM *********** READ SCATTER TABLE ***********
405 CLEAR 2000: BL$="                              "
407 REM OPEN AND FIELD THE FILES
409 INPUT "WHAT IS THE NAME OF THE SORTED RANDOM FILE";N1$
411 INPUT "WHAT IS THE NAME OF THE SCATTER TABLE FILE";N2$
415 OPEN "R",1,N1$,48
416 OPEN "R",2,N2$,48
418 FIELD 1, 18 AS A1$, 18 AS B1$, 12 AS C1$
419 FIELD 2, 18 AS A2$, 18 AS B2$, 12 AS C2$
425 REM CHOOSE SEQUENTIAL READ OR FIND ONE RECORD
427 PRINT: PRINT "WOULD YOU LIKE TO (CHOOSE THE NUMBER)"
429 PRINT "      1. LIST THE FILE SEQUENTIALLY ?"
430 PRINT "      2. FIND ONE INDIVIDUAL RECORD ?"
431 PRINT "      3. EXIT AND STOP ?"
432 INPUT "WHAT IS YOUR CHOICE";CH
433 PRINT
435 ON CH GOSUB 2500,3200,450
440 IF FL>0 GOTO 490
445 GOTO 425


2500 REM *********** READ THE FILE SEQUENTIALLY ***********
2528 N=LOF(1)
2530 FOR I=1 TO N
2534      GET #1,I
2536      PRINT A1$;B1$;C1$
2539 NEXT I
2540 FL=-1
2549 RETURN


3200 REM *********** FIND A RECORD FROM SCATTER TABLE ***********
3205 INPUT "FOR WHAT LAST AND FIRST NAMES TO SEARCH";L$,F$
3207 L$=L$+BL$: F$=F$+BL$
3209 REM CONVERT TO ADDRESS
3210 GOSUB 2850
3212 REM FIND THE RECORD
3214 CT=0: I=AD-1
3215 CT=CT+1: I=I+1
3218 IF I>66 THEN I=6
3220 GET #2,I
3222 PRINT "SCATTER TABLE ENTRY";I;" ";A2$;B2$;C2$
3225 L$=LEFT$(L$+BL$,LEN(A2$)): F$=LEFT$(F$+BL$,LEN(B2$))
3230 IF L$=A2$ AND F$=B2$ GOTO 3240
3232      IF CT<=66 GOTO 3215
3234           PRINT:PRINT L$;",";F$;" IS NOT LISTED IN THE SCATTER TABLE
3236      GOTO 3290
3240 RN = VAL(C2$)
3245 GET #1,RN
3250 PRINT "RECORD NO.";RN;"IN THE FILE CONTAINS"
3254 PRINT A1$;B1$;C1$: PRINT
3290 FL=-1
3299 RETURN
```

FIGURE 15–22(b). Read a Scatter Table—The Program

```
2850 REM *********** CONVERT NAME TO ADDRESS ***********
2855 BS$="  ": S=0
2860 S=S+1
2862 T$=MID$(L$,S,2)
2864 IF T$<>BS$ GOTO 2860
2865 LE=S-1: L$=LEFT$(L$,LE)
2867 SU=0
2870 FOR S=1 TO LE
2872     SU = SU + ASC(MID$(L$,S,1)) - 64
2874 NEXT S
2875 S=0
2880 S=S+1
2882 T$=MID$(F$,S,2)
2884 IF T$<>BS$ GOTO 2880
2885 LE=S-1: F$=LEFT$(F$,LE)
2887 FOR S=1 TO LE
2889     SU = SU + ASC(MID$(F$,S,1)) - 64
2890 NEXT S
2892 AD = INT((SU/61-INT(SU/61))*61 + 0.1) + 6
2899 RETURN


450 REM SET EXIT FLAG
455 FL=1
459 RETURN
490 CLOSE 1,2
499 GOTO 9999


9999 END
```

FIGURE 15–22(b). Continued

```
WHAT IS THE NAME OF THE SORTED RANDOM FILE? RNDATSRT
WHAT IS THE NAME OF THE SCATTER TABLE FILE? SCATTER

WOULD YOU LIKE TO (CHOOSE THE NUMBER)
     1. LIST THE FILE SEQUENTIALLY ?
     2. FIND ONE INDIVIDUAL RECORD ?
     3. EXIT AND STOP ?
WHAT IS YOUR CHOICE? 2

FOR WHAT LAST AND FIRST NAMES TO SEARCH? DIAZ, HECTOR
SCATTER TABLE ENTRY 54  DEXTER            SAM                14
SCATTER TABLE ENTRY 55  DIAZ              HECTOR             16
RECORD NO. 16 IN THE FILE CONTAINS
DIAZ               HECTOR           393-6523
```

FIGURE 15–23. Running the Program to Read a Scatter Table

```
WOULD YOU LIKE TO (CHOOSE THE NUMBER)
     1. LIST THE FILE SEQUENTIALLY ?
     2. FIND ONE INDIVIDUAL RECORD ?
     3. EXIT AND STOP ?
WHAT IS YOUR CHOICE? 2

FOR WHAT LAST AND FIRST NAMES TO SEARCH? WEAVER, JANE
SCATTER TABLE ENTRY 49  WEAVER          JANE              46
RECORD NO. 46 IN THE FILE CONTAINS
WEAVER          JANE            731-1150


WOULD YOU LIKE TO (CHOOSE THE NUMBER)
     1. LIST THE FILE SEQUENTIALLY ?
     2. FIND ONE INDIVIDUAL RECORD ?
     3. EXIT AND STOP ?
WHAT IS YOUR CHOICE? 1

ABBOTT          DUANE           451-5943
ADAMS           DON             776-7777
ANDRUS          JOHN            825-9081
BELT            RAYMOND         546-4567
BLAKE           PETER           776-5911
BROWN           COLISTA         451-7878
BROWN           DALE            731-1234
BUTLER          PARLEY          394-0914
BUTTE           ALICE           782-8760
COOK            LAMAR           773-1666
CUMMINGS        ROLAND          479-3797
DEAN            LIONEL          394-8193
DENNIS          FLOYD           392-9052
DEXTER          SAM             773-7744
DEXTER          VERNE           731-8066
DIAZ            HECTOR          393-6523
FISHER          RICHARD         451-9993
FULLER          LAUREL          546-6653
GIBBS           ELSIE           479-4698
GREEN           ALLEN           782-7355
GROSS           GREG            546-0011
GWYNN           KEITH           544-9876
HAMMER          LORIN           393-6154
HANSON          RALPH           829-3317
HOWE            KAREN           394-1445
JENSEN          WAYNE           544-5871
JUDD            KAY             731-4103
KAISER          DEAN            782-1330
KAISER          ELMER           479-9582
MAYS            JAMES           782-7644
MEYER           DWAYNE          825-1558
MORITZ          WILLIAM         829-6662
MURPHY          DOROTHEA        776-0301
MURPHY          JOSEPH          399-1749
```

FIGURE 15–23. Continued

```
NELSON          HENRY           393-4204
NELSON          THERESA         479-0135
PETTY           STEVE           773-0719
PIERCE          EDWIN           394-4386
POULTER         VERNON          544-1454
SHERMAN         RANDY           773-0476
SIMON           MORRIS          621-2574
STEEL           ORSON           731-0125
TIBBETS         GLEN            392-3217
TRIMBLE         ALAN            393-8318
TRIP            GEORGE          773-0502
WEAVER          JANE            731-1150
WILEY           STEPHEN         773-7178
WILSON          BERTHA          825-2176
YOUNG           KARL            825-9834
ZUNDELL         WILFORD         825-0431

WOULD YOU LIKE TO (CHOOSE THE NUMBER)
     1. LIST THE FILE SEQUENTIALLY ?
     2. FIND ONE INDIVIDUAL RECORD ?
     3. EXIT AND STOP ?
WHAT IS YOUR CHOICE? 3
```

FIGURE 15–23. Continued

TABLE 15–1. Subprograms Used in Chapters 14 and 15.

Line Nos.	*Description of Procedure*	*Used in Figures*
100–199	Bubble, Selection Sort Control	14–5,7
400–499	Read Scatter Table	15–22
500–549	Make a Scatter Table	15–20
550–599	Find a Hashed Record	15–18
600–699	Circular Queue Control	14–18
700–749	List Linker Control	14–15
750–799	Create a Hashed File	15–16
800–849	Quick Sort Control	14–13, 15–12
850–899	Convert an Integer to String	14–17, 15–20
900–999	Stack Handler, Stack Arithmetic Control	14–9,11
1000–1099	Create or Rewrite Sequential File	14–1,15
1100–1249	Recall Sequential File	14–3,5,7,13,15, 15–12

TABLE 15–1. Continued

Line Nos.	*Description of Procedure*	*Used in Figures*
1250–1299	Print a Stack	14–9,11,13
1300–1399	Perform Bubble Sort, Link a List	14–5,15
1400–1449	Print an Array	14–5,7,13, 15–12
1450–1499	Print a Queue	14–18
1500–1599	Perform Selection Sort	14–7
1600–1649	PUSH	14–9,11,13,15, 15–12
1650–1699	POP	14–9,11,13, 15–12
1700–1799	Stack Arithmetic Menu	14–11
1800–1899	Stack Arithmetic Operations	14–11
1900–1999	Quick Sort, Single Pass	14–13, 15–12
2000–2049	Quick Sort, Logic	14–13, 15–12
2100–2149	Read and Print in Linked Order	14–15
2200–2249	Find Smaller Array Elements	14–15
2300–2349	Add to a Queue	14–18
2350–2399	Remove from a Queue	14–18
2400–2499	Create a Random File	15–1,12
2500–2549	Recall from a Random File	15–3,22
2550–2599	Open Files and Record Hash Code	15–16,20
2600–2699	Binary Search	15 14
2700–2749	Linear Search (Random File)	15–10
2750–2799	Linear Search (Sequential File)	15–6
2800–2849	Copy Sequential to Random File	15–8
2850–2899	Convert a Name to an Address (Hash)	15–16,18,20,22
2900–2949	Fill a Random File with Blank Records	15–16,20
2950–2999	Store Hash Order Data in Random File	15–16,20
3000–3049	Read, Convert, Store (Perform Hashing)	15–16,20
3050–3099	Read a Hash Code from a File	15–18
3100–3149	Find a Name by Using a Hash Code	15–18
3150–3199	Print a Scatter Table	15–20
3200–3299	Find a Record from a Scatter Table	15–22
9999	END	All

QUESTIONS

1. Modify the programs of Figures 15–1 and 15–3 as necessary to create and read the file shown in Figure 15–2 on *your* computer.
2. Write a sort program which could handle a random file so large that only half (or less) of the file could fit into memory at one time. Read the first part of the file, perform a quick sort, and rewrite. Read the next part, quick sort, and rewrite. Then merge the two sorted parts.
3. Write a program to insert the records

```
FARMER     ELMER      546-1043
PRIDE      MARK       392-6914
```

   into the appropriate position in the sorted phone list RNDATSRT, Figure 15–13. Then delete

```
COOK       LAMAR      773-1666
WILEY      STEPHEN    773-7178
```

   Also change the spelling of STEEL, ORSON to STEELE, ORSEN and the phone number of KAISER, DEAN to 776-4105.
4. Rewrite the stack handler program of Figure 14–9 to put the stack into a random access file rather than into an array.
5. Rewrite the list linker program of Figure 14–15 so that the file linked is a random file with only a few records read into memory at one time. Also, place the stack in a random file rather than in an array.
6. Make the following changes to the hashed phone list file:

```
Add
           BAER, HILDA       392-9987
           KOCOR, ALMA       781-6622
           LOOSE, STERN      492-1513
Delete
           KAISER, DEAN      782-1330
           HAMMER, LORIN     393-6154
```

7. a. Rewrite the programs of Figures 15–16 and 15–18 to use a different hash algorithm to convert the names of the phone list file to addresses so that fewer than 20 percent synonyms are produced.

   b. Modify the programs so that the records are stored and read in a two-pass, linked load order.

8. In the sorted random phone list file RNDATSRT and in the scatter table SCATTER, add and delete the records indicated in Problem 6.

9. a. Rewrite the programs of Figure 15–20 and 15–22 to use a different hash algorithm to convert the names of the phone list file so that fewer than 20 percent synonyms are produced.

   b. Modify the programs so that records are stored and read in the scatter table in two-pass, linked load order.

10. Write programs to create and access an indexed sequential file.

11. Write a program to handle

    a. a Multilist File   b. an Inverted File.

APPENDIX

ANSWERS TO SELECTED QUESTIONS

CHAPTER 1

3. a. 298 feet c. 833 minutes

11. New file: 1. Apre 2. Ather 3. Brown (changed) 4. Crab
5. Gnu 6. JCN 7. Mort 8. Olson
9. Tarpen 10. Unvar 11. Witch

CHAPTER 2

1. c. D6 hex 214 decimal

3. 4 bytes

5. 1,048,575 decimal FFFFF hex

6. c. 1 1110 0101 binary 1E5 hex

7. a(2). 365 octal b(2). 001 100 001 001 777 decimal
c(2). 760 octal 111 110 000 binary

12. a. 9 bits

CHAPTER 3

2. b. 144 seconds c(4). 117,500 records
6. b. 1311 seconds
8. b. 28,800 bytes per screen
10. 64 tracks
12. c. 268,435 pages
14. d. 260 milliseconds
18. d. 158,175 pages per disk pack
19. b. 36 tapes
21. a. 12,208 stripes

CHAPTER 4

1. b. 7,902,720,000 bytes
7. a. Channel 1 only

CHAPTER 5

6. b. 0.00628 inches
10. c. 79.9%
11. f. 17 cylinders
13. b. 100 logical records per track
15. b. 3150 sectors
17. f. 625 tracks

CHAPTER 6

4. c. static
7. c. partitioned
10. b. BSAM—used for sequentially organized files, BDAM—used for directly organized files

CHAPTER 7

4. a. the tape stops at each gap
7. a. 100 cylinders = 16.7% of the disk pack
9. c. total number of reads = 6 track searches + 7 records on track 19 = 13 reads
10. d. $LOG_2 524 - 1$ = approximately 8 reads

CHAPTER 8

2.

Location	Key	Pointer
100	Start Pointer =	~~101~~ 102
101	~~Akron~~	~~102~~
102	Butte	~~103~~ 108
103	Chino	~~104~~ 105
104	~~Dallas~~	~~105~~

Location	Key	Pointer
105	Fresno	~~106~~ 107
106	Jackson	End
107	Furth	106
108	Cameron	103

6. b. FIRST = 65520 LIMIT = 65535
   c(2). IN = 65529 OUT = 65522

8. Stack at 32,760 Perform A/ [B − (C × D)] where A = 63, B = 45, C = 4, D = 9.
   For example (there are other ways to do it)

Operation	Comment	Stack (Top ←) Location	Content
PUSH 63		32760	63 ←
PUSH 45		32760	63
		32761	45 ←
PUSH 4		32760	63
		32761	45
		32762	4 ←
PUSH 9		32760	63
		32761	45
		32762	4
		32763	9 ←

LOAD	9 in Accumulator	32760 63
		32761 45
		32762 4 ←
MUL	4×9=36 in Acc	32760 63
		32761 45 ←
STORE		32760 63
		32761 45
		32762 36 ←
XCH		32760 63
		32761 36
		32762 45 ←
LOAD	45 in Accumulator	32760 63
		32761 36 ←
SUB	45−36=9 in Acc	32760 63 ←
STORE		32760 63
		32761 9 ←
XCH		32760 9
		32761 63 ←
LOAD	63 in Accumulator	32760 9 ←
DIV	63/9=7 in Acc	Empty
STORE		32760 7 ←
PRN	Print 7	
HALT		

10. 63/[45−(4×9)]

	63 ENTER	45 ENTER	4 ENTER	9	MUL	SUB	DIV
Top→	63	63	63	63	63	63	7
		→45	45	45	45	→ 9	
			→4	4	→36		
				→ 9			

14. b. 19 reads to find the Manager of Distribution
16. c. 1.4 $LOG_2 31$ = approximately 7
17. b. $LOG_4 341$ = approximately 4.2

18. a. $N = M + M^2 + M^3 + \ldots + M^L$

$MN = \quad M^2 + M^3 + \ldots + M^L + M^{L+1}$

$(1 - M)N = M - M^{L+1}$

$N = M(1 - M^L) / (1 - M) = (M^L - 1) \times (M / (M - 1))$

$M^L = 1 + ((M - 1) / M) \times N$

$L = LOG_M(1 + ((M - 1) / M) \times N)$ Q.E.D.

A rigorous analysis can be found in E.H. Sussenguth, "Use of Tree Structures for Processing Files", *Communications of the ACM,* May 1963, Vol. 6, No. 5, pages 272–279. Also see D.E. Knuth, *Sorting and Searching,* Vol. III, Addison-Wesley, Reading, MA, 1973.

CHAPTER 9

3. C3PO R2D2 RX37 2H13

a. branches $36 \times 36 \times 36 \times 36 = 1{,}679{,}616$
empty $= 1{,}679{,}616 - 5{,}000 = 1{,}674{,}616$

b. $N \times M \times D = 5000 \times 4 \times 36 = 720{,}000$
$N = 5000$ elements $M = 4$ characters per key
$D = 36$ different characters

c. bubble or selection sort comparisons

$$\frac{N^2 - N - 2}{2} = \frac{5000^2 - 5000 - 2}{2} = 12{,}497{,}499$$

5. h.41.7 hours j. 20,048 times
8. c(1) $14 \times LOG_2 15$ = approximately 55 comparisons

CHAPTER 10

6. a. Take the middle three digits as the storage address.
8. a. 25,000 spaces
9. c. Track 308 Record 4
13. Absolute address: Cylinder 203, Track 15, Record 17
14. d. 285th track, 4th record
f. Cylinder 113, Track 19, Record 4
16. b. Key $89216 + 33046 = 122262$
If divide by 400, relative address = 263
If divide by 397, relative address = 384

17. b. Key base 13 = 3046, base 10 = 6649
    If divide by 400, relative address = 650; if div. by 997 addr. = 668
20. 3 collisions
23. JOHN KENNEDY, address = 1
    LYNDON JOHNSON, address = 5
25. e. place into the 5th spot in bucket 496
30. b. average reads per record = 1.62
31. d. average reads per record = 1.575
32. e. average reads per record = 1.82

CHAPTER 11

2. Yes.
4. a. No
7. 60 members
14. g. 08163
15. e. (v) 71 1109
17. d. 0608 Wilson 0715
21. a. Prime Data Area

0908	*Wilson*	Werner	White 1008/2	Wicker	Wilson
0909	*Wright*	Wirth 1008/1	Wrmwd 1008/3	Wrnglr 1009/1	Wright
0910	*Zwumbly*	Wylie	Yeates	Young	Zwumbly
	Overflow Area				
1008	Witch 0909/2		Whyte 0908/3	Worth 0909/3	
1009	Wren 0909/4				

23. a. 1. Search master index, find key >= Baker, namely Friar 0605
    2. Search cylinder index block 0605, find key >= Baker, Brown 0702
    3. Search track index block 0702, find key >= Baker, Baker 1008/3
    4. Go to overflow area, block 1008, record 3. Is it Baker? No, Atters 1008/1
    5. Go to block 1008, record 1. Is this Baker? Yes.

25. (strikethroughs indicate logical deletion)

	Prime Data Area				
0717	*Able*	Aal	Aaron	Abar 0255	~~Able~~
0718	*Afton*	Acort 1008/2	~~Acres~~ 1009/2	Acum 1009/1	Adams 1009/3
	Overflow Area				
1008	Asner 0719/2		Acron 0718/3		Atters 0719/4
1009	Adair 0718/4		~~Acrid~~ 1008/2		Afton 0255

CHAPTER 12

5. b(1). If an empty CI is available in the control area, then the control area might appear as follows:

0	220	778			896		1023	
A	AC	Free			A 220	AC 558		
1024	1304	1491	1559	1915	1920			2047
AM	AS	AT	AU	Free	AM280	AS187	AT68	AU356
2048	2234	2318			2944		3071	
AI	AL	Free			AI186	AL84		

7. b. Use a second index (perhaps ultimately dense, one entry per record) to point to records by alternate key, or create multilists or access lists.
11. Ultimately you must create a target list for 1984 and JUL and 02 . . . , which contains pointers 1103 and 1105.
12. b. ADAM, CREN, HENR, JUST, RICH
14. a. Examine Division file to determine that building ET236 contains the divisions D001 and D002. Search the Employees file for those who work in D001 or D002, namely SMITH, WILLS, RICH, WOOD, and BRICK.
15. a. Begin with root and read entire file by a tree search until Species Devil's Shoelace is found, OR search a Species index for Devil's Shoelace. Devil's Shoelace should have a pointer to its parent, Fam-

ily Laminariaceae, which in turn should have a pointer to grandparent, Order Laminariales, which points to great grandparent, Class Phaeophyceae (Brown Algae).

CHAPTER 13

3. The first user ties up all but one of the devices of the type needed by the second user.
5. b. Programs which are too large to fit into useable primary memory maybe divided into pages or segments and moved between memory and the DASD as needed. This program staging is the virtual memory concept.
8. FTC = file control table, resides within the user's program area, contains information about all the files needed by a specific program.
   DUT = device unit table, resides in system storage area, contains information about all the devices on the system, including status, and which volume is loaded on the device.
9. One is the AFT because not every user should have access to every open file.

INDEX